Itsuwaribito ◆空◆

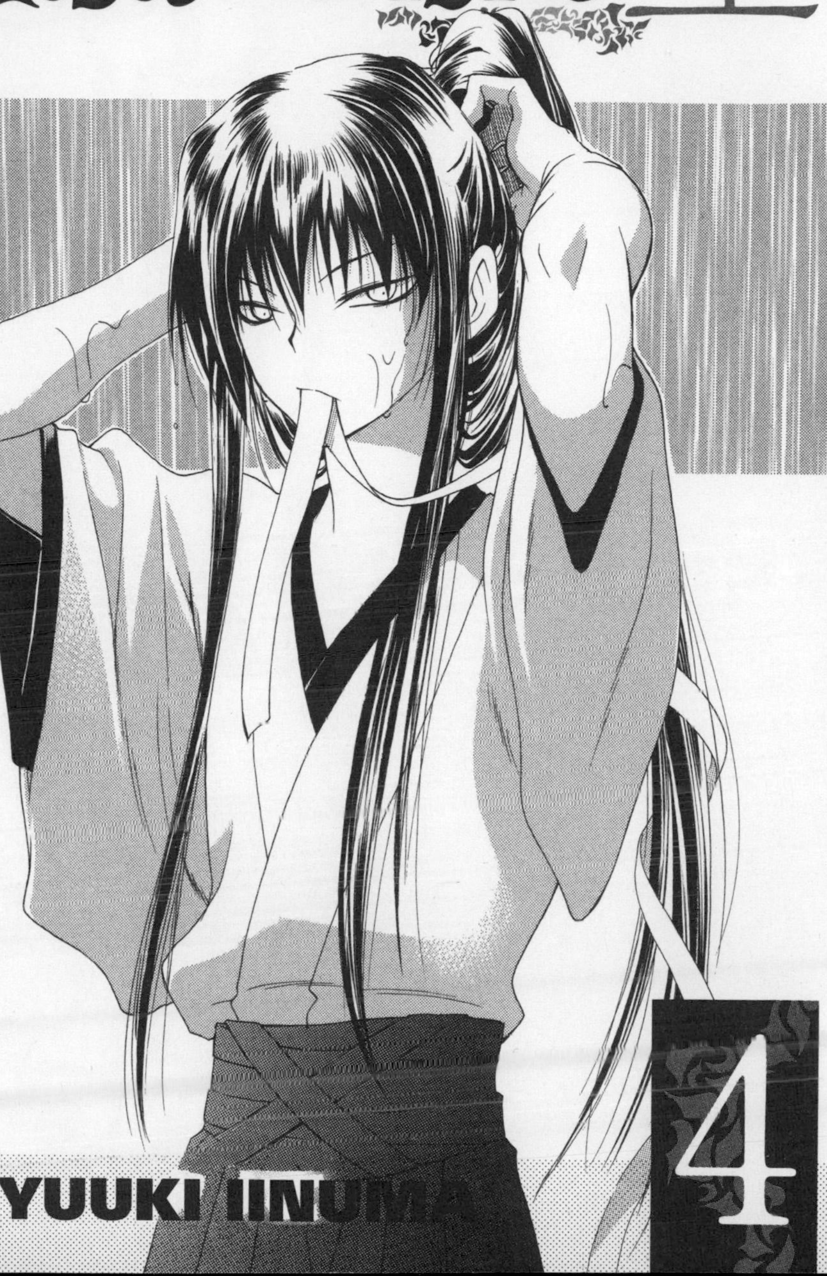

4

YUUKI IINUMA

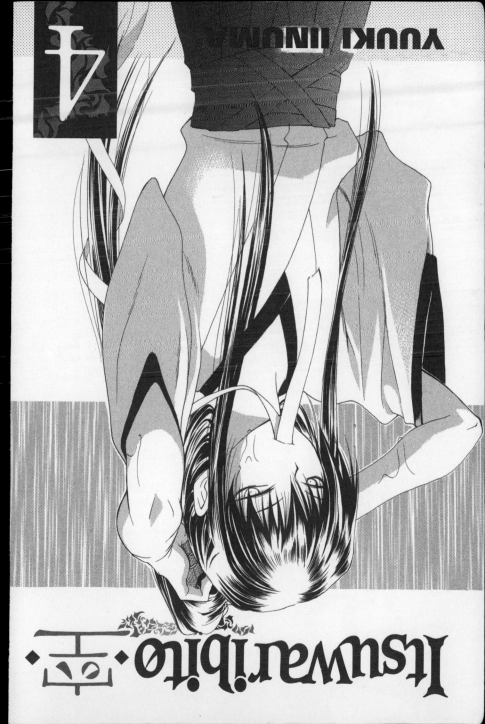

Contents

Chapter 28 Behind the Miracle

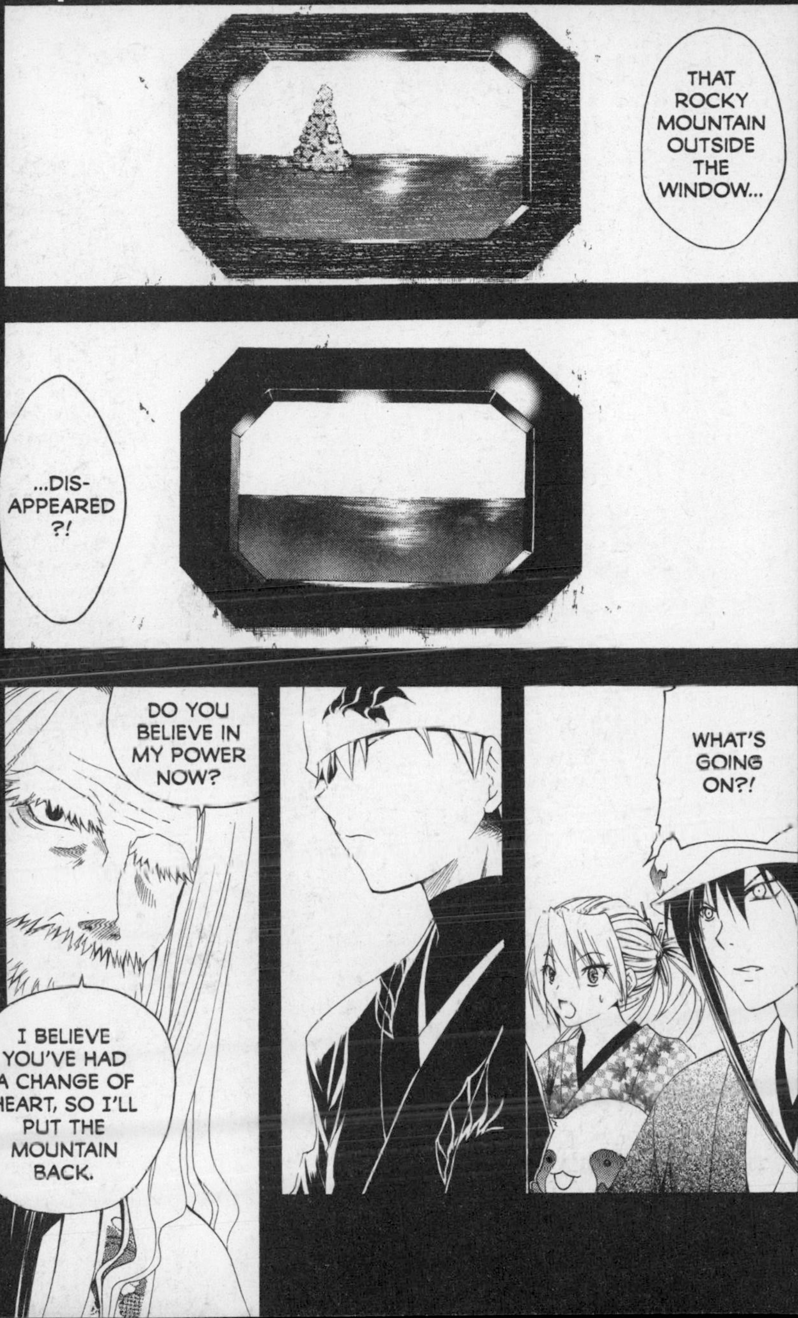
THAT ROCKY MOUNTAIN OUTSIDE THE WINDOW...
...DIS-APPEARED ?!
WHAT'S GOING ON?!
DO YOU BELIEVE IN MY POWER NOW?
I BELIEVE YOU'VE HAD A CHANGE OF HEART, SO I'LL PUT THE MOUNTAIN BACK.

Chapter 28
Behind the Miracle

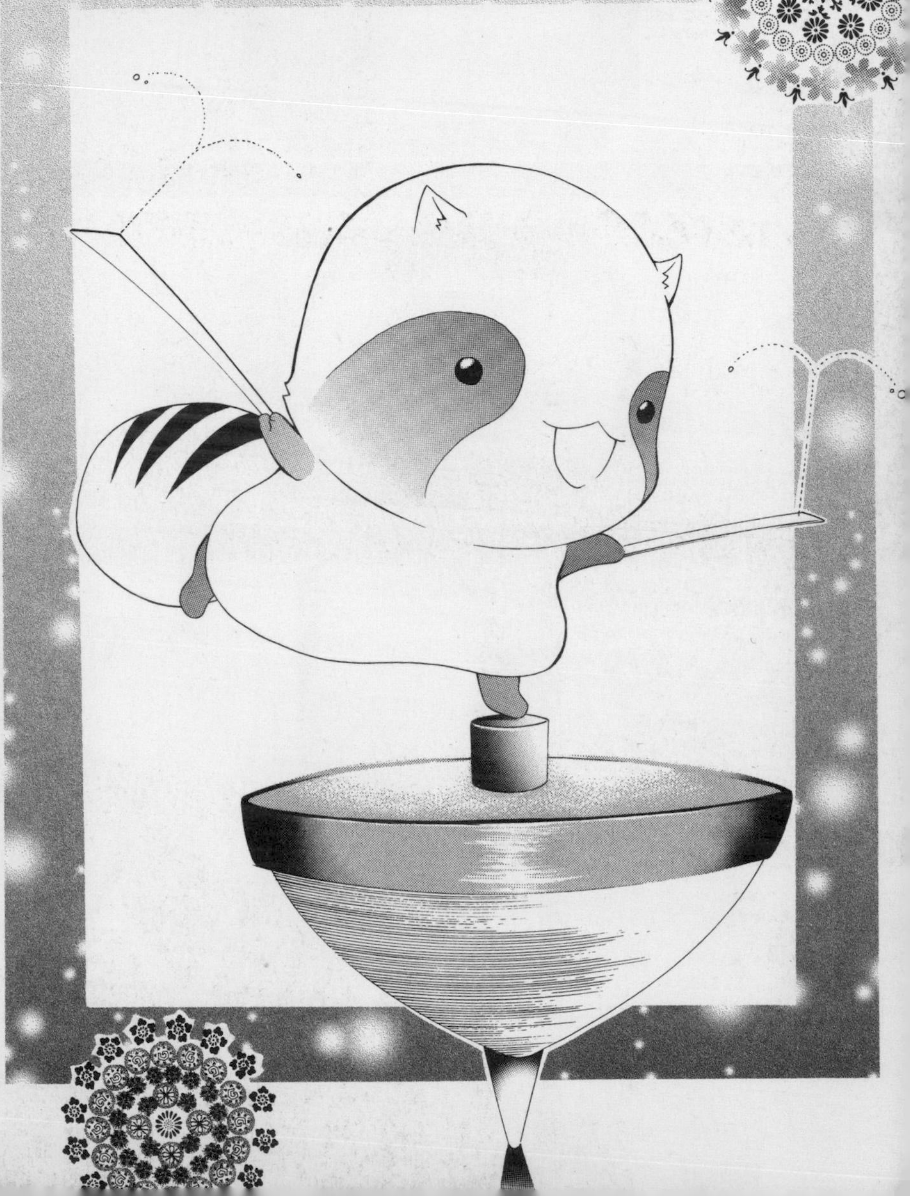

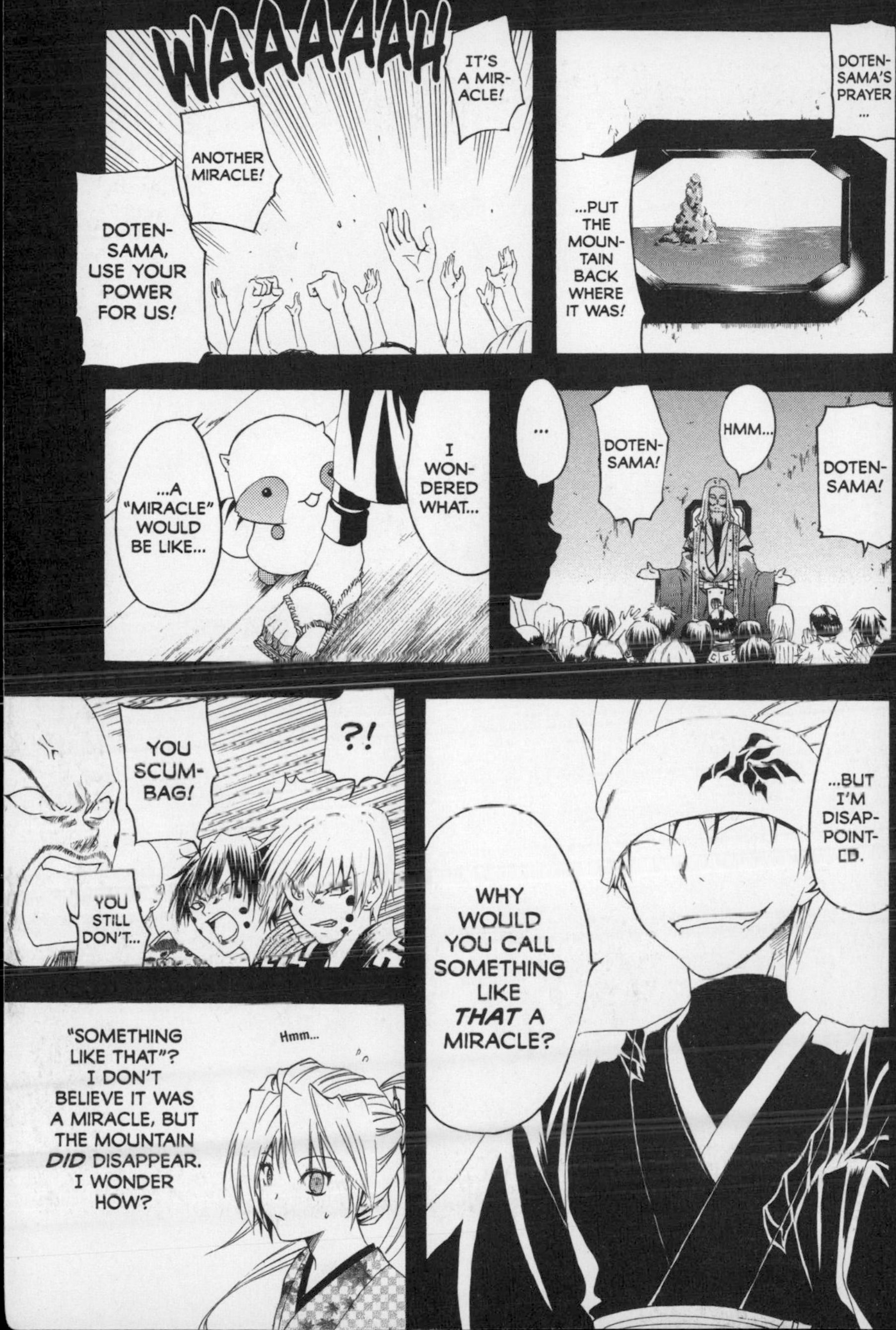
DOTEN-SAMA'S PRAYER ...
...PUT THE MOUNTAIN BACK WHERE IT WAS!
WAAAAAH
IT'S A MIRACLE!
ANOTHER MIRACLE!
DOTEN-SAMA, USE YOUR POWER FOR US!
DOTEN-SAMA!
HMM...
DOTEN-SAMA!
...
I WONDERED WHAT...
...A "MIRACLE" WOULD BE LIKE...
...BUT I'M DISAPPOINTED.
WHY WOULD YOU CALL SOMETHING LIKE *THAT* A MIRACLE?
?!
YOU SCUMBAG!
YOU STILL DON'T...
Hmm...
"SOMETHING LIKE THAT"? I DON'T BELIEVE IT WAS A MIRACLE, BUT THE MOUNTAIN *DID* DISAPPEAR. I WONDER HOW?

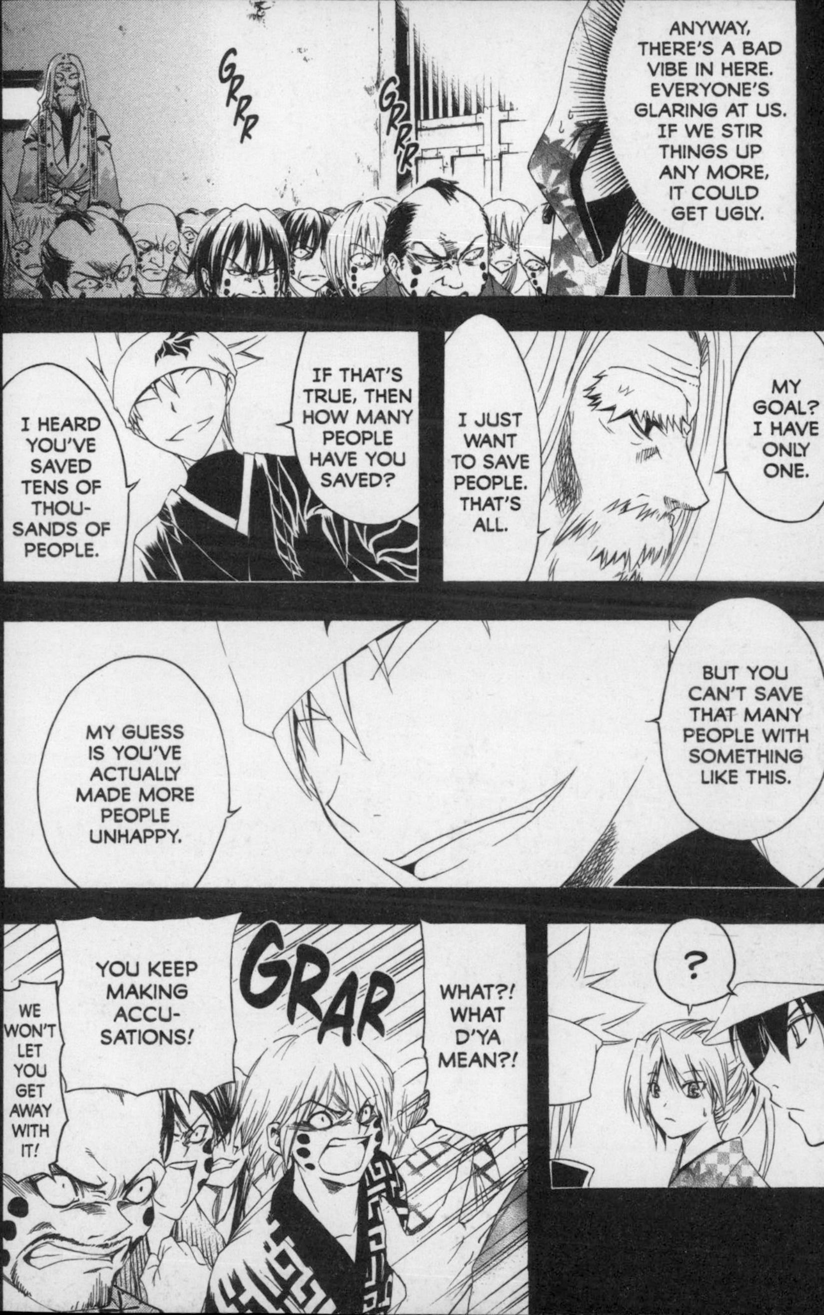
ANYWAY, THERE'S A BAD VIBE IN HERE. EVERYONE'S GLARING AT US. IF WE STIR THINGS UP ANY MORE, IT COULD GET UGLY.
GRRR
GRRR
MY GOAL? I HAVE ONLY ONE.
I JUST WANT TO SAVE PEOPLE. THAT'S ALL.
IF THAT'S TRUE, THEN HOW MANY PEOPLE HAVE YOU SAVED?
I HEARD YOU'VE SAVED TENS OF THOU-SANDS OF PEOPLE.
BUT YOU CAN'T SAVE THAT MANY PEOPLE WITH SOMETHING LIKE THIS.
MY GUESS IS YOU'VE ACTUALLY MADE MORE PEOPLE UNHAPPY.
?
WHAT?! WHAT D'YA MEAN?!
GRAR
YOU KEEP MAKING ACCU-SATIONS!
WE WON'T LET YOU GET AWAY WITH IT!

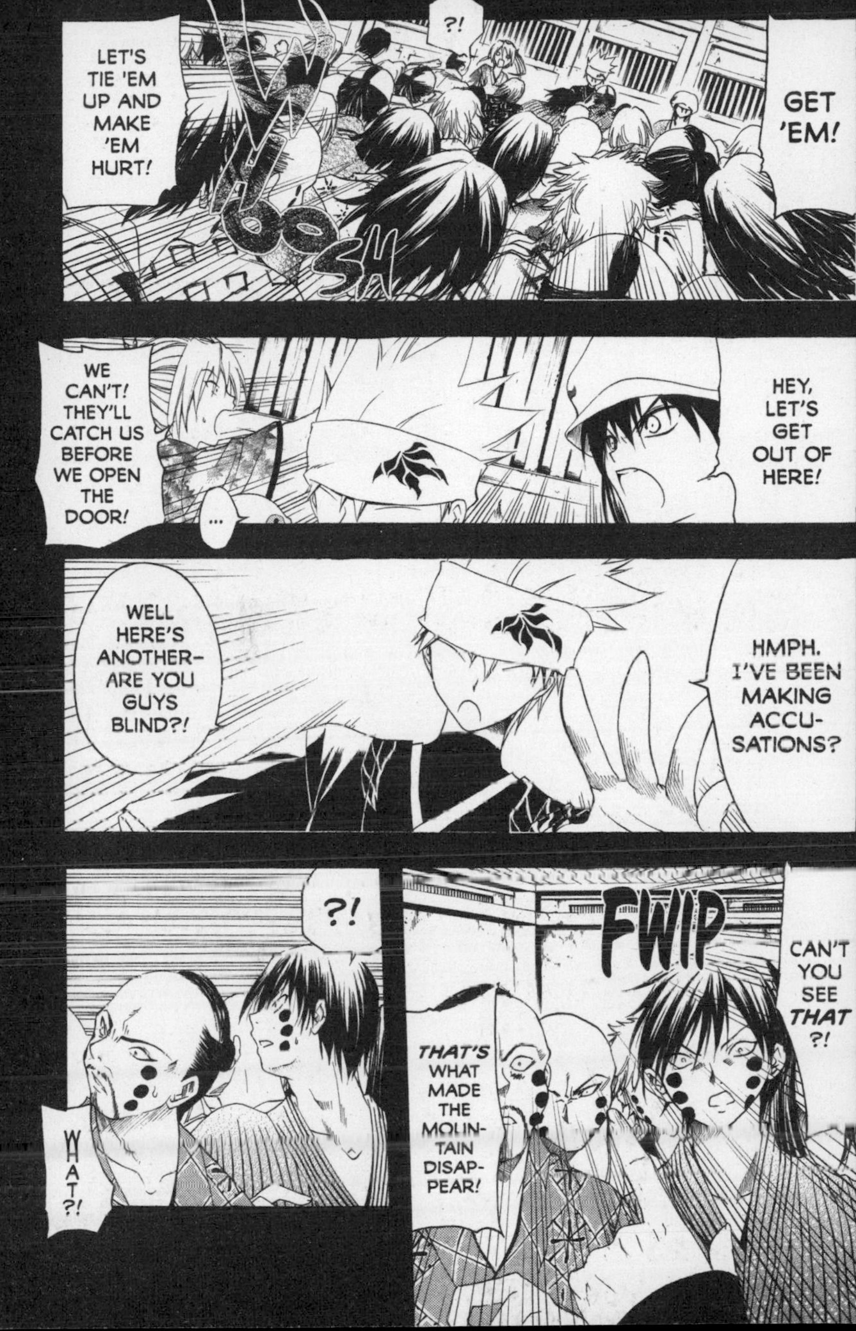
GET 'EM!
?!
LET'S TIE 'EM UP AND MAKE 'EM HURT!
WHOOSH
HEY, LET'S GET OUT OF HERE!
WE CAN'T! THEY'LL CATCH US BEFORE WE OPEN THE DOOR!
...
HMPH. I'VE BEEN MAKING ACCUSATIONS?
WELL HERE'S ANOTHER–ARE YOU GUYS BLIND?!
CAN'T YOU SEE *THAT* ?!
FWIP
THAT'S WHAT MADE THE MOUNTAIN DISAPPEAR!
?!
WHAT?!

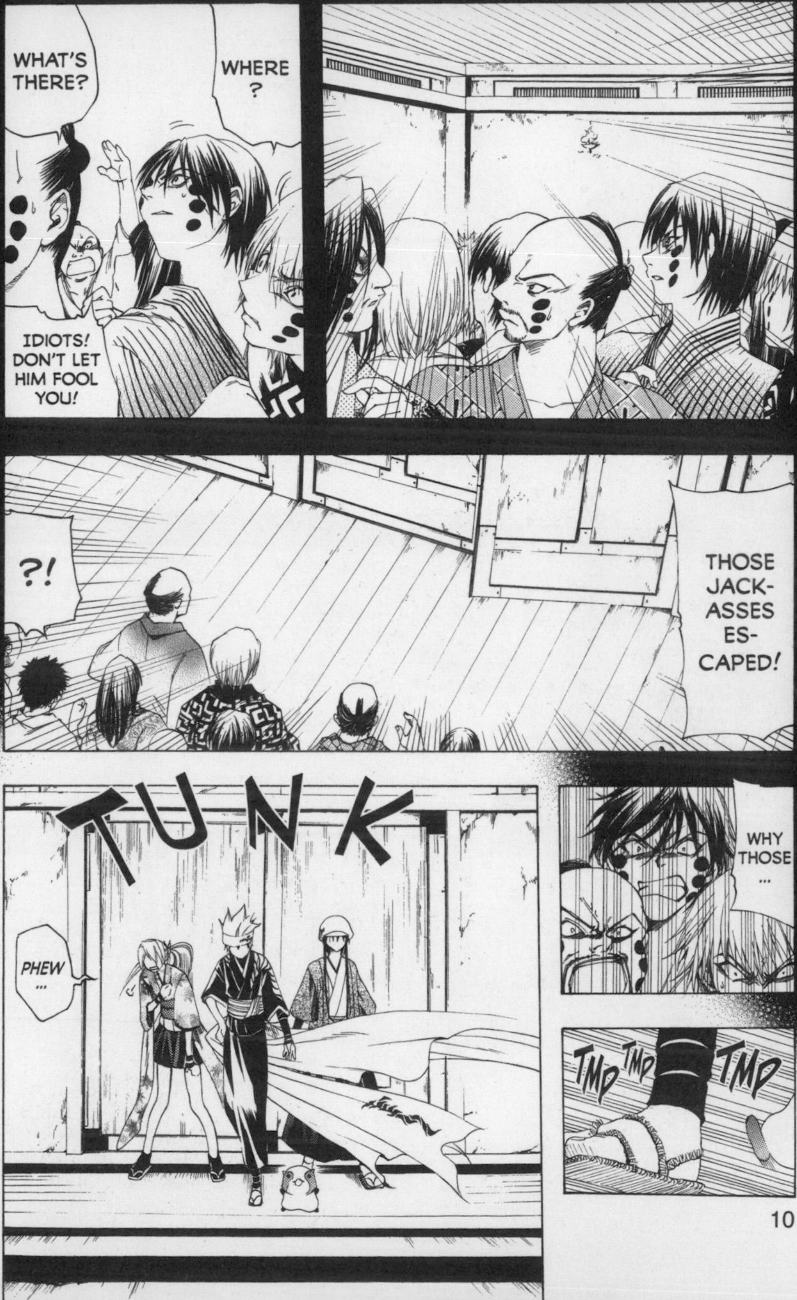
WHERE ?
WHAT'S THERE?
IDIOTS! DON'T LET HIM FOOL YOU!
THOSE JACK-ASSES ES-CAPED!
?!
WHY THOSE ...
TMP TMP TMP
TUNK
PHEW ...

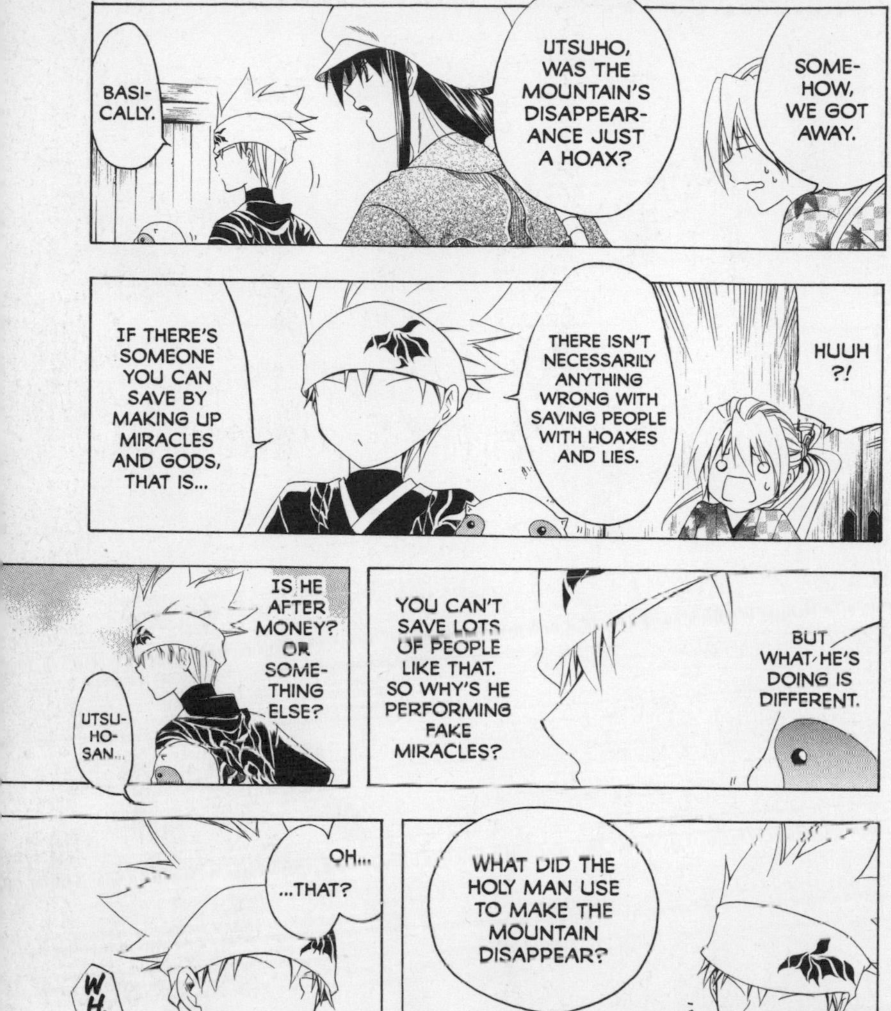
SOME-HOW, WE GOT AWAY.
UTSUHO, WAS THE MOUNTAIN'S DISAPPEAR-ANCE JUST A HOAX?
BASI-CALLY.
HUUH ?!
THERE ISN'T NECESSARILY ANYTHING WRONG WITH SAVING PEOPLE WITH HOAXES AND LIES.
IF THERE'S SOMEONE YOU CAN SAVE BY MAKING UP MIRACLES AND GODS, THAT IS...
BUT WHAT HE'S DOING IS DIFFERENT.
YOU CAN'T SAVE LOTS OF PEOPLE LIKE THAT. SO WHY'S HE PERFORMING FAKE MIRACLES?
IS HE AFTER MONEY? OR SOME-THING ELSE?
UTSU-HO-SAN...
WHAT DID THE HOLY MAN USE TO MAKE THE MOUNTAIN DISAPPEAR?
OH...
...THAT?
WHAM
WHAM

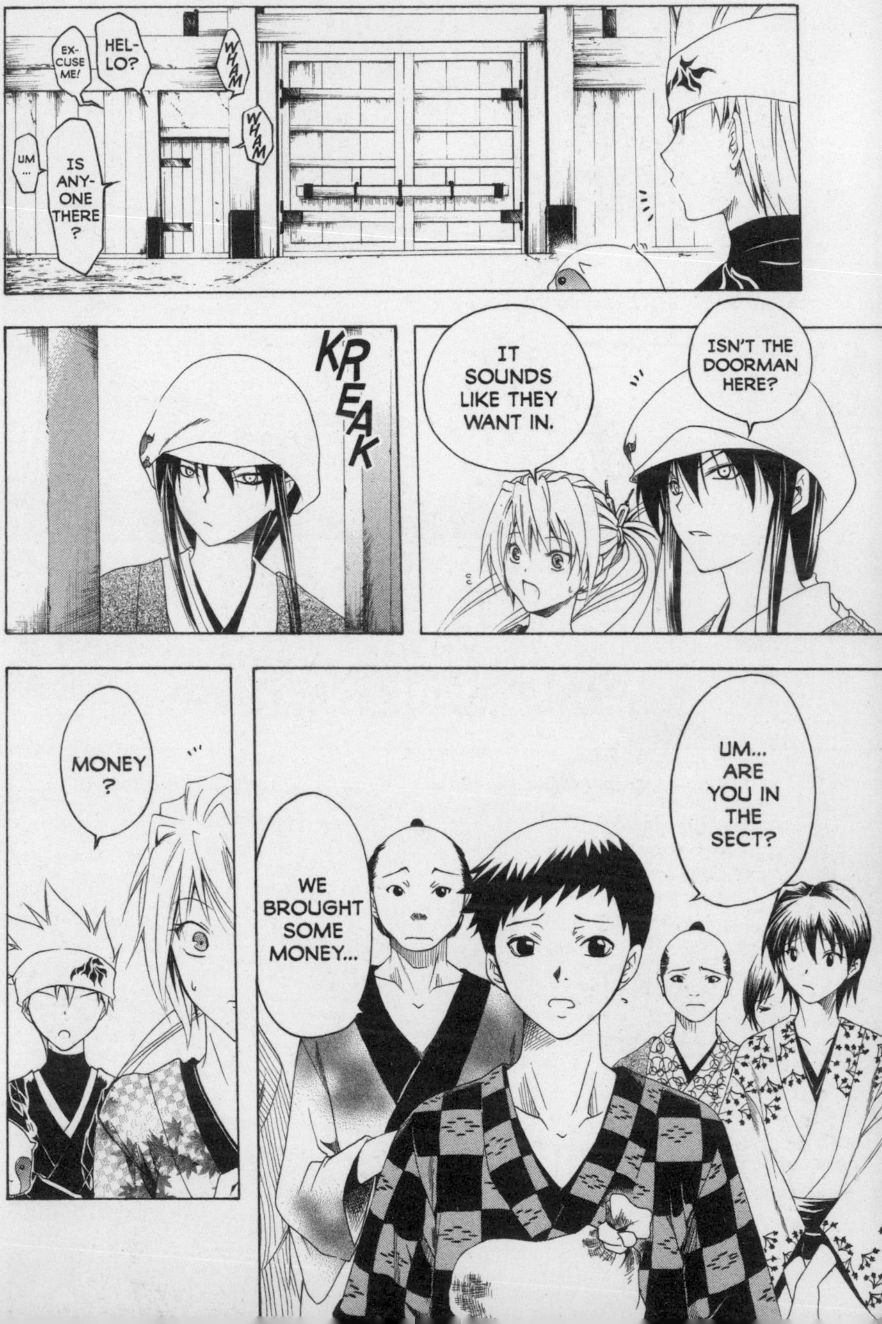
EX-CUSE ME!
HEL-LO?
UM ...
IS ANY-ONE THERE?
WHAM
WHAM
ISN'T THE DOORMAN HERE?
IT SOUNDS LIKE THEY WANT IN.
KREAK
UM... ARE YOU IN THE SECT?
WE BROUGHT SOME MONEY...
MONEY?

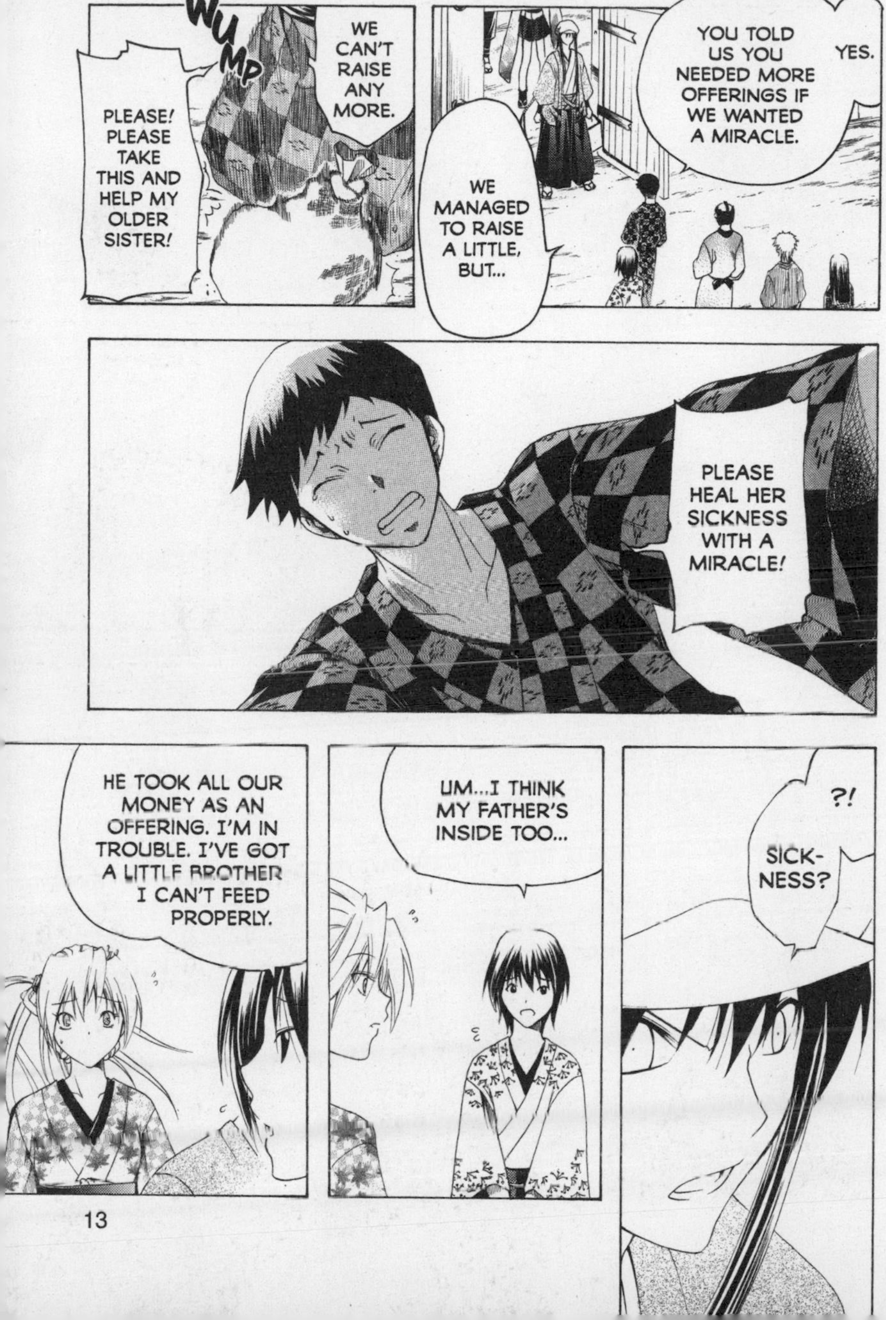
YES.
YOU TOLD US YOU NEEDED MORE OFFERINGS IF WE WANTED A MIRACLE.
WE MANAGED TO RAISE A LITTLE, BUT...
WE CAN'T RAISE ANY MORE.
WUMP
PLEASE! PLEASE TAKE THIS AND HELP MY OLDER SISTER!
PLEASE HEAL HER SICKNESS WITH A MIRACLE!
?!
SICK-NESS?
UM...I THINK MY FATHER'S INSIDE TOO...
HE TOOK ALL OUR MONEY AS AN OFFERING. I'M IN TROUBLE. I'VE GOT A LITTLE BROTHER I CAN'T FEED PROPERLY.

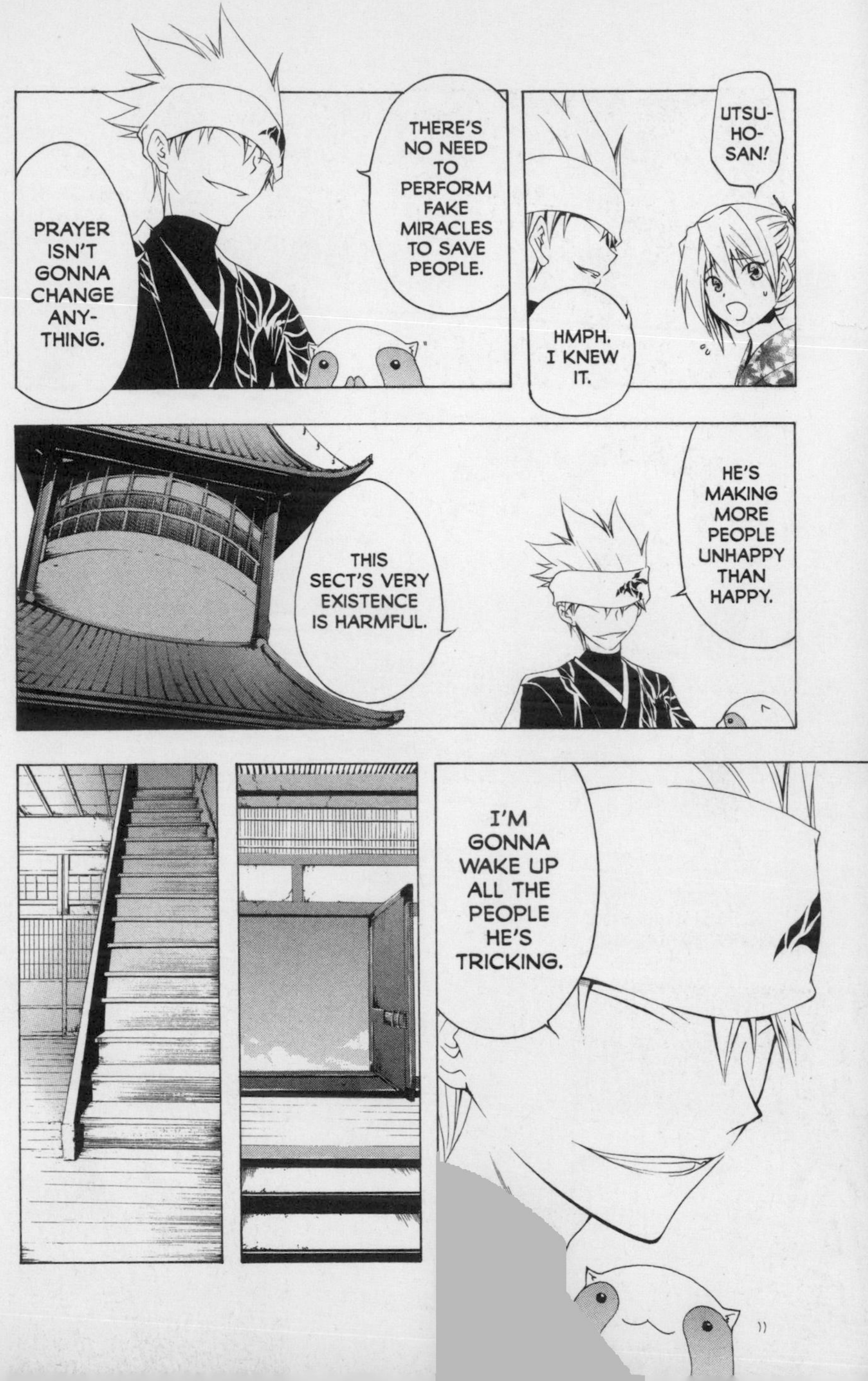
UTSU-HO-SAN!
HMPH. I KNEW IT.
THERE'S NO NEED TO PERFORM FAKE MIRACLES TO SAVE PEOPLE.
PRAYER ISN'T GONNA CHANGE ANY-THING.
HE'S MAKING MORE PEOPLE UNHAPPY THAN HAPPY.
THIS SECT'S VERY EXISTENCE IS HARMFUL.
I'M GONNA WAKE UP ALL THE PEOPLE HE'S TRICKING.

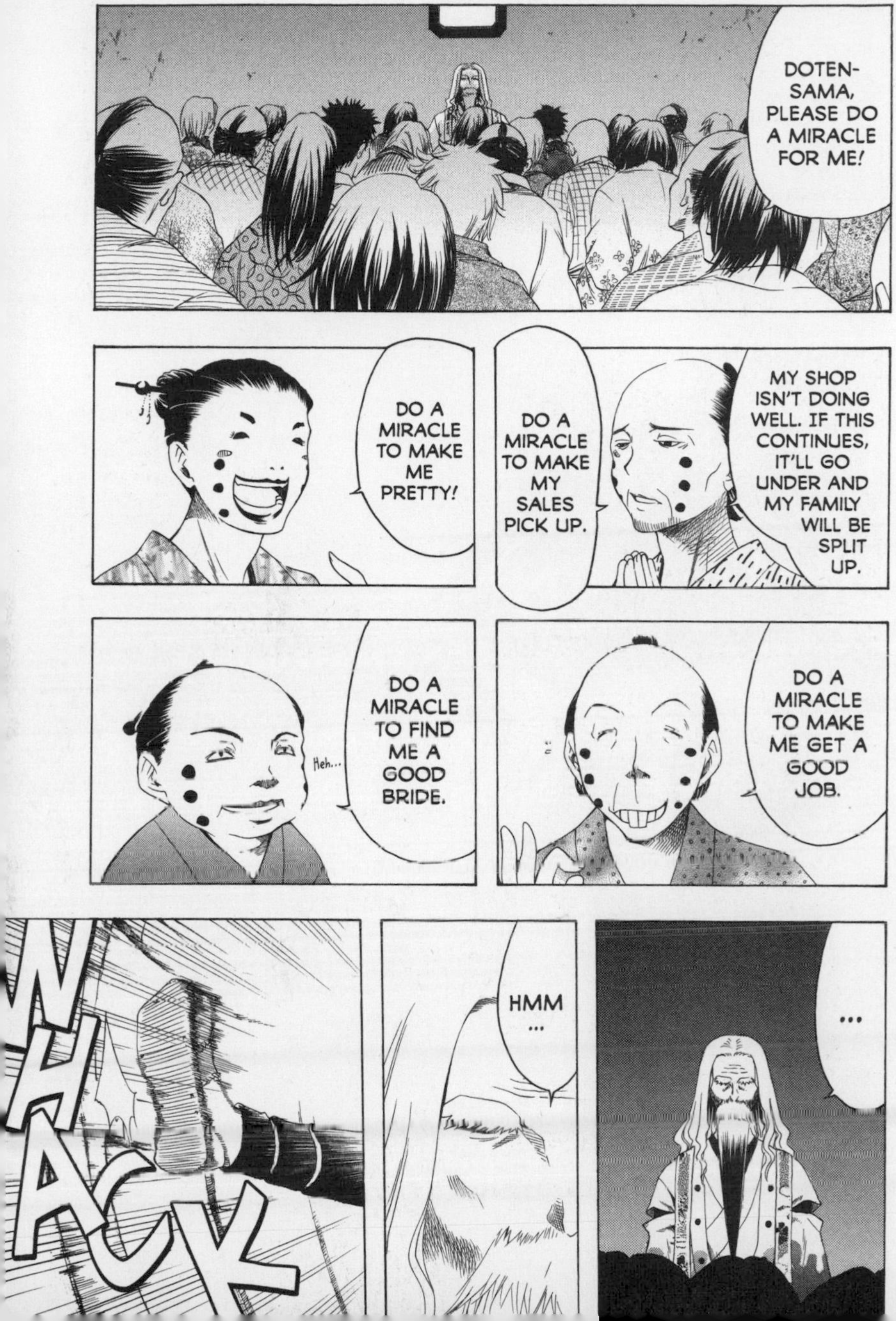
DOTEN-SAMA, PLEASE DO A MIRACLE FOR ME!
MY SHOP ISN'T DOING WELL. IF THIS CONTINUES, IT'LL GO UNDER AND MY FAMILY WILL BE SPLIT UP.
DO A MIRACLE TO MAKE MY SALES PICK UP.
DO A MIRACLE TO MAKE ME PRETTY!
DO A MIRACLE TO MAKE ME GET A GOOD JOB.
Heh...
DO A MIRACLE TO FIND ME A GOOD BRIDE.
...
HMM ...
WHACK

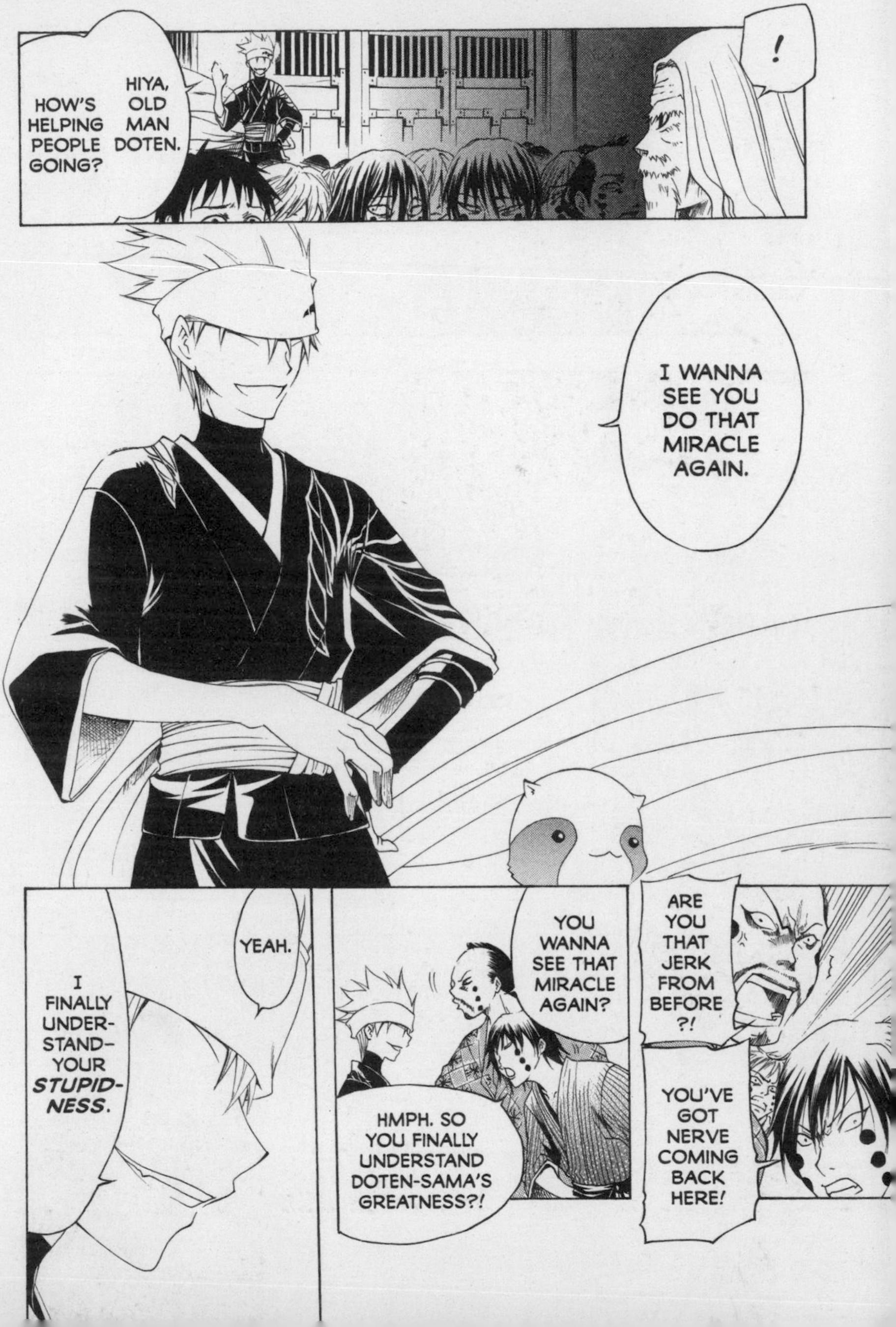
!
HIYA, OLD MAN DOTEN.
HOW'S HELPING PEOPLE GOING?
I WANNA SEE YOU DO THAT MIRACLE AGAIN.
ARE YOU THAT JERK FROM BEFORE ?!
YOU'VE GOT NERVE COMING BACK HERE!
YOU WANNA SEE THAT MIRACLE AGAIN?
HMPH. SO YOU FINALLY UNDERSTAND DOTEN-SAMA'S GREATNESS?!
YEAH.
I FINALLY UNDER-STAND-YOUR ***STUPID-NESS***.

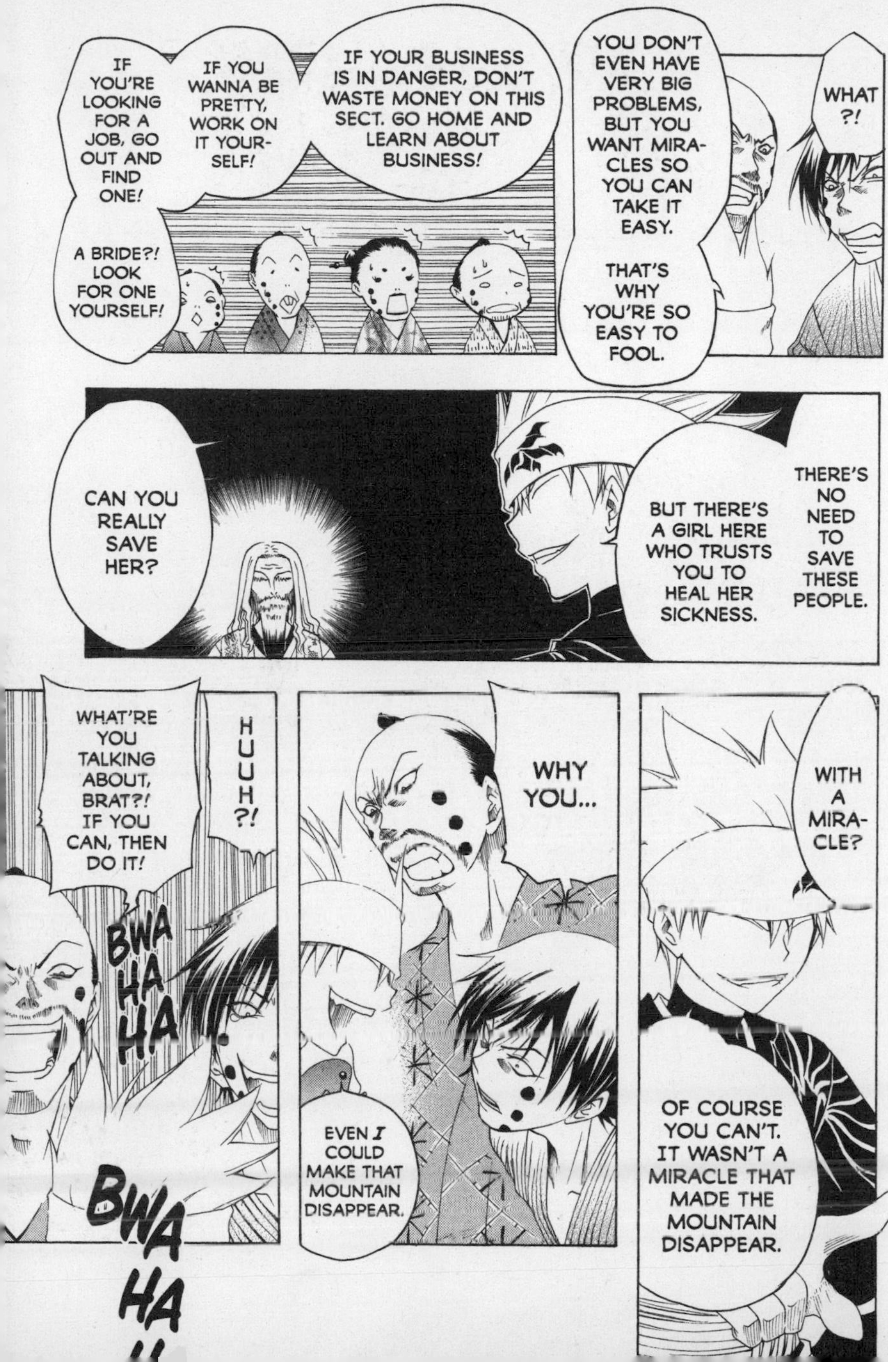
WHAT ?!
YOU DON'T EVEN HAVE VERY BIG PROBLEMS, BUT YOU WANT MIRACLES SO YOU CAN TAKE IT EASY.
THAT'S WHY YOU'RE SO EASY TO FOOL.
IF YOUR BUSINESS IS IN DANGER, DON'T WASTE MONEY ON THIS SECT. GO HOME AND LEARN ABOUT BUSINESS!
IF YOU WANNA BE PRETTY, WORK ON IT YOURSELF!
IF YOU'RE LOOKING FOR A JOB, GO OUT AND FIND ONE!
A BRIDE?! LOOK FOR ONE YOURSELF!
THERE'S NO NEED TO SAVE THESE PEOPLE.
BUT THERE'S A GIRL HERE WHO TRUSTS YOU TO HEAL HER SICKNESS.
CAN YOU REALLY SAVE HER?
WITH A MIRACLE?
OF COURSE YOU CAN'T. IT WASN'T A MIRACLE THAT MADE THE MOUNTAIN DISAPPEAR.
WHY YOU...
EVEN I COULD MAKE THAT MOUNTAIN DISAPPEAR.
HUUH?!
WHAT'RE YOU TALKING ABOUT, BRAT?! IF YOU CAN, THEN DO IT!
BWA HA HA HA
BWA HA HA

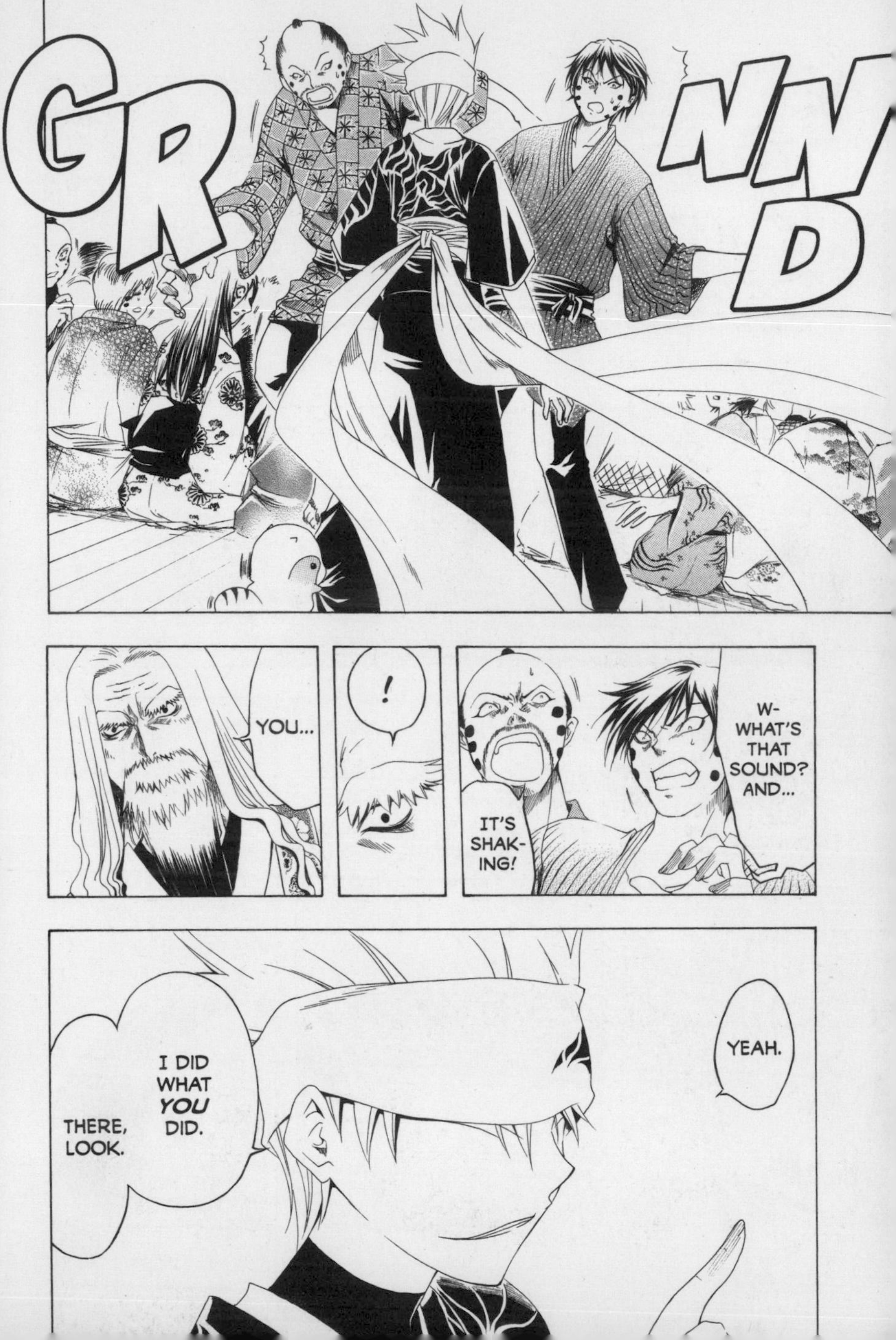
GRNND
W-WHAT'S THAT SOUND? AND...
IT'S SHAKING!
!
YOU...
YEAH.
I DID WHAT *YOU* DID.
THERE, LOOK.

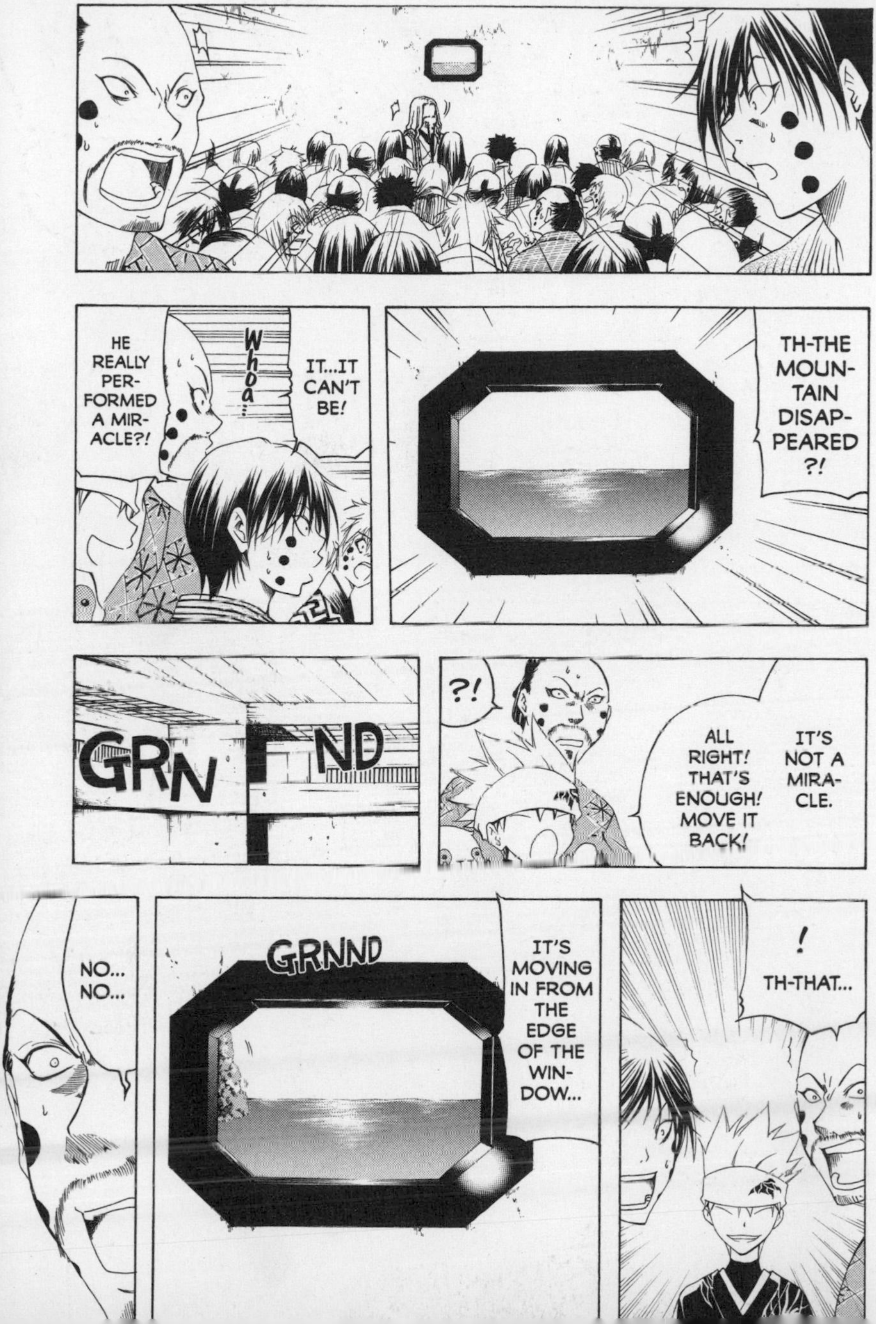
TH-THE MOUNTAIN DISAPPEARED?!
IT...IT CAN'T BE!
Whoa...
HE REALLY PERFORMED A MIRACLE?!
IT'S NOT A MIRACLE.
ALL RIGHT! THAT'S ENOUGH! MOVE IT BACK!
?!
GRN
ND
!
TH-THAT...
IT'S MOVING IN FROM THE EDGE OF THE WINDOW...
GRNND
NO... NO...

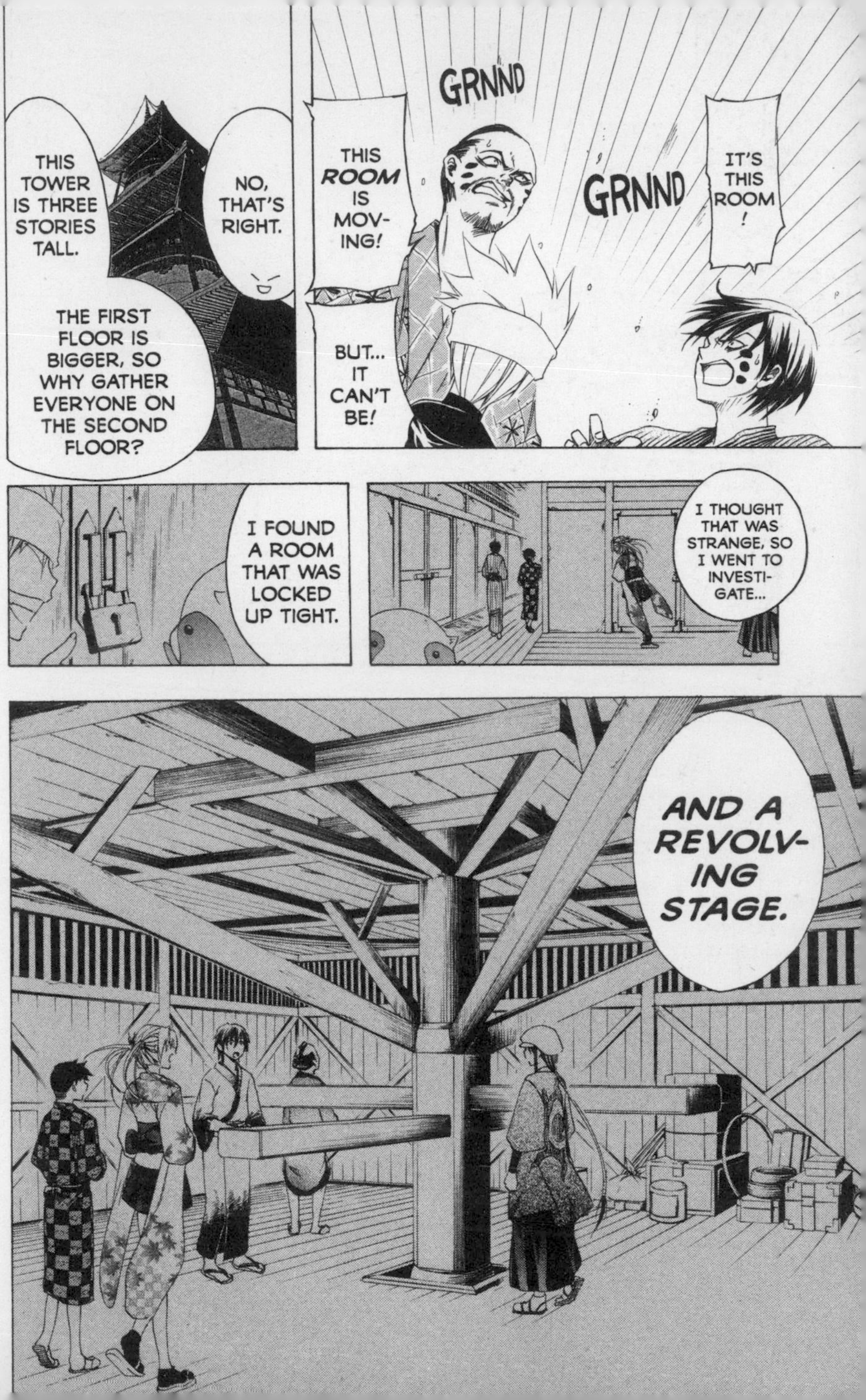
IT'S THIS ROOM!
GRNND
GRNND
THIS *ROOM* IS MOV-ING!
BUT... IT CAN'T BE!
THIS TOWER IS THREE STORIES TALL.
NO, THAT'S RIGHT.
THE FIRST FLOOR IS BIGGER, SO WHY GATHER EVERYONE ON THE SECOND FLOOR?
I THOUGHT THAT WAS STRANGE, SO I WENT TO INVESTI-GATE...
I FOUND A ROOM THAT WAS LOCKED UP TIGHT.
AND A REVOLV-ING STAGE.

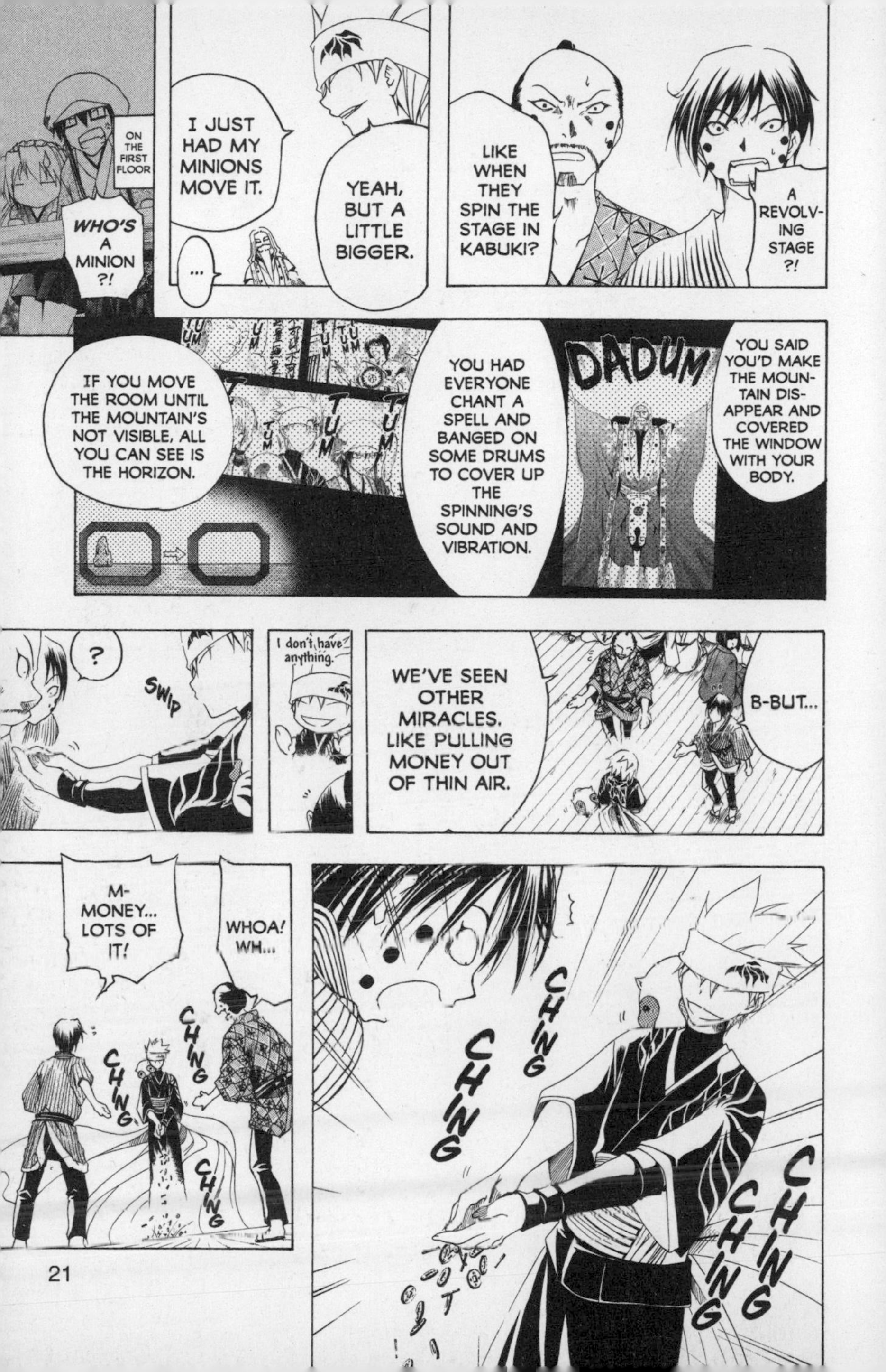
A REVOLVING STAGE ?!
LIKE WHEN THEY SPIN THE STAGE IN KABUKI?
YEAH, BUT A LITTLE BIGGER.
I JUST HAD MY MINIONS MOVE IT.
...
ON THE FIRST FLOOR
WHO'S A MINION ?!
YOU SAID YOU'D MAKE THE MOUNTAIN DISAPPEAR AND COVERED THE WINDOW WITH YOUR BODY.
DADUM
YOU HAD EVERYONE CHANT A SPELL AND BANGED ON SOME DRUMS TO COVER UP THE SPINNING'S SOUND AND VIBRATION.
IF YOU MOVE THE ROOM UNTIL THE MOUNTAIN'S NOT VISIBLE, ALL YOU CAN SEE IS THE HORIZON.
B-BUT...
WE'VE SEEN OTHER MIRACLES. LIKE PULLING MONEY OUT OF THIN AIR.
I don't have anything.
?
SWIP
CHING
CHING
CHING
CHING
WHOA! WH...
M-MONEY... LOTS OF IT!
CHING
CHING
CHING

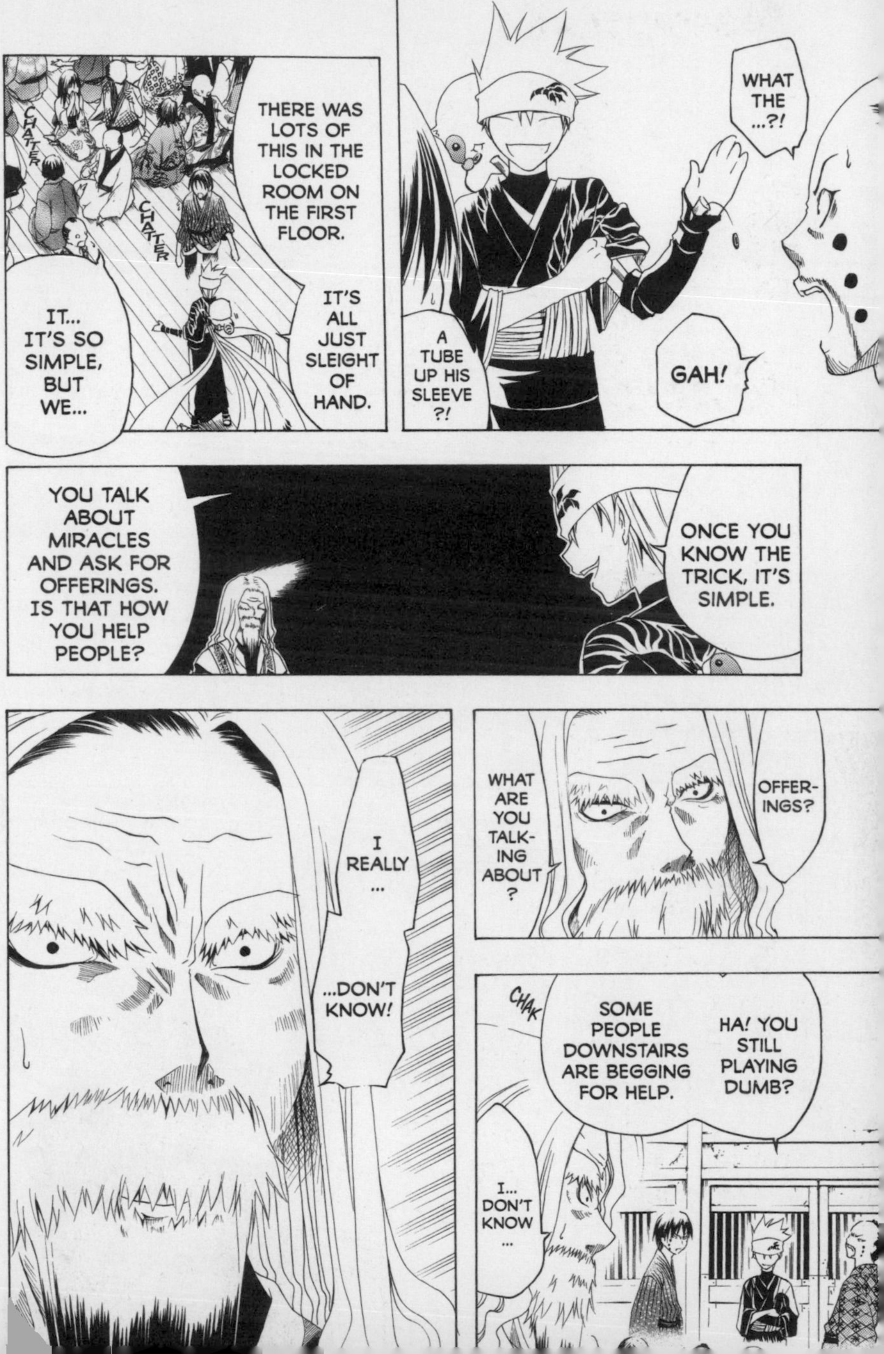
WHAT THE ...?!
GAH!
A TUBE UP HIS SLEEVE ?!
THERE WAS LOTS OF THIS IN THE LOCKED ROOM ON THE FIRST FLOOR.
CHATTER
CHATTER
IT'S ALL JUST SLEIGHT OF HAND.
IT... IT'S SO SIMPLE, BUT WE...
ONCE YOU KNOW THE TRICK, IT'S SIMPLE.
YOU TALK ABOUT MIRACLES AND ASK FOR OFFERINGS. IS THAT HOW YOU HELP PEOPLE?
OFFER-INGS?
WHAT ARE YOU TALK-ING ABOUT ?
HA! YOU STILL PLAYING DUMB?
SOME PEOPLE DOWNSTAIRS ARE BEGGING FOR HELP.
CHAK
I... DON'T KNOW ...
I REALLY ...
...DON'T KNOW!

Chapter 29
Mastermind

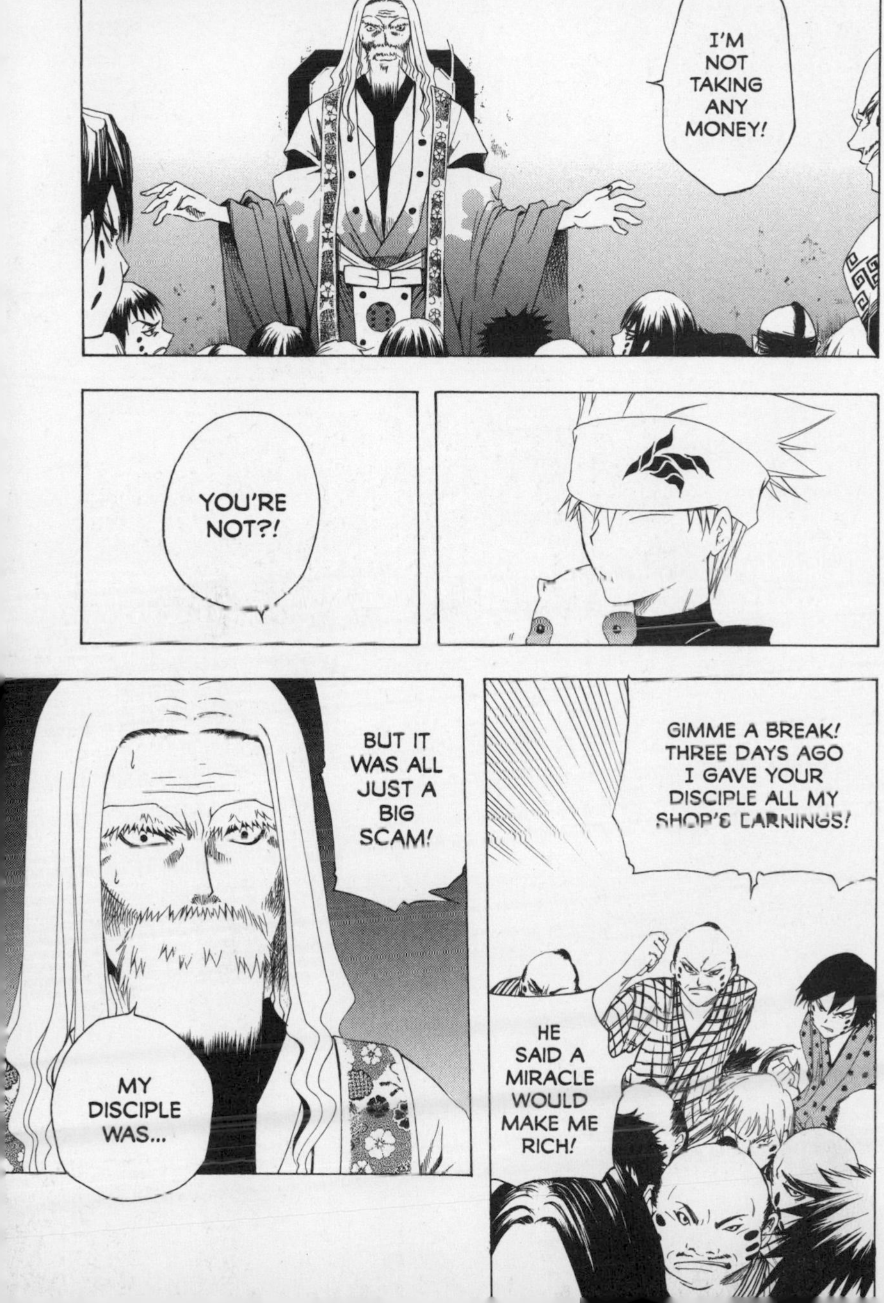

I'M NOT TAKING ANY MONEY!
YOU'RE NOT?!
GIMME A BREAK! THREE DAYS AGO I GAVE YOUR DISCIPLE ALL MY SHOP'S EARNINGS!
HE SAID A MIRACLE WOULD MAKE ME RICH!
BUT IT WAS ALL JUST A BIG SCAM!
MY DISCIPLE WAS...

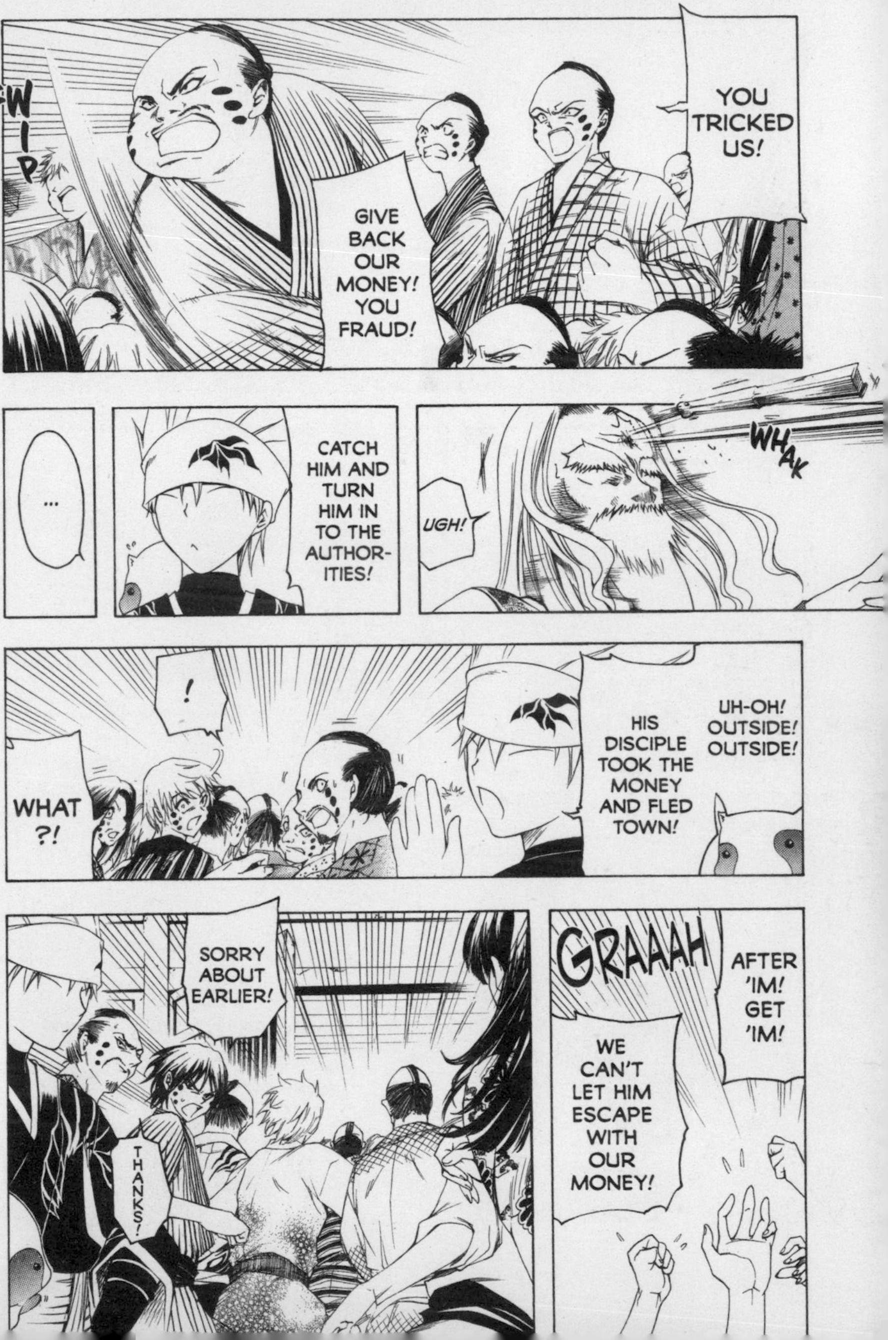
YOU TRICKED US!
FWIP
GIVE BACK OUR MONEY! YOU FRAUD!
WHAK
UGH!
CATCH HIM AND TURN HIM IN TO THE AUTHORITIES!
...
UH-OH! OUTSIDE! OUTSIDE!
HIS DISCIPLE TOOK THE MONEY AND FLED TOWN!
!
WHAT ?!
AFTER 'IM! GET 'IM!
GRAAAH
WE CAN'T LET HIM ESCAPE WITH OUR MONEY!
SORRY ABOUT EARLIER!
THANKS!

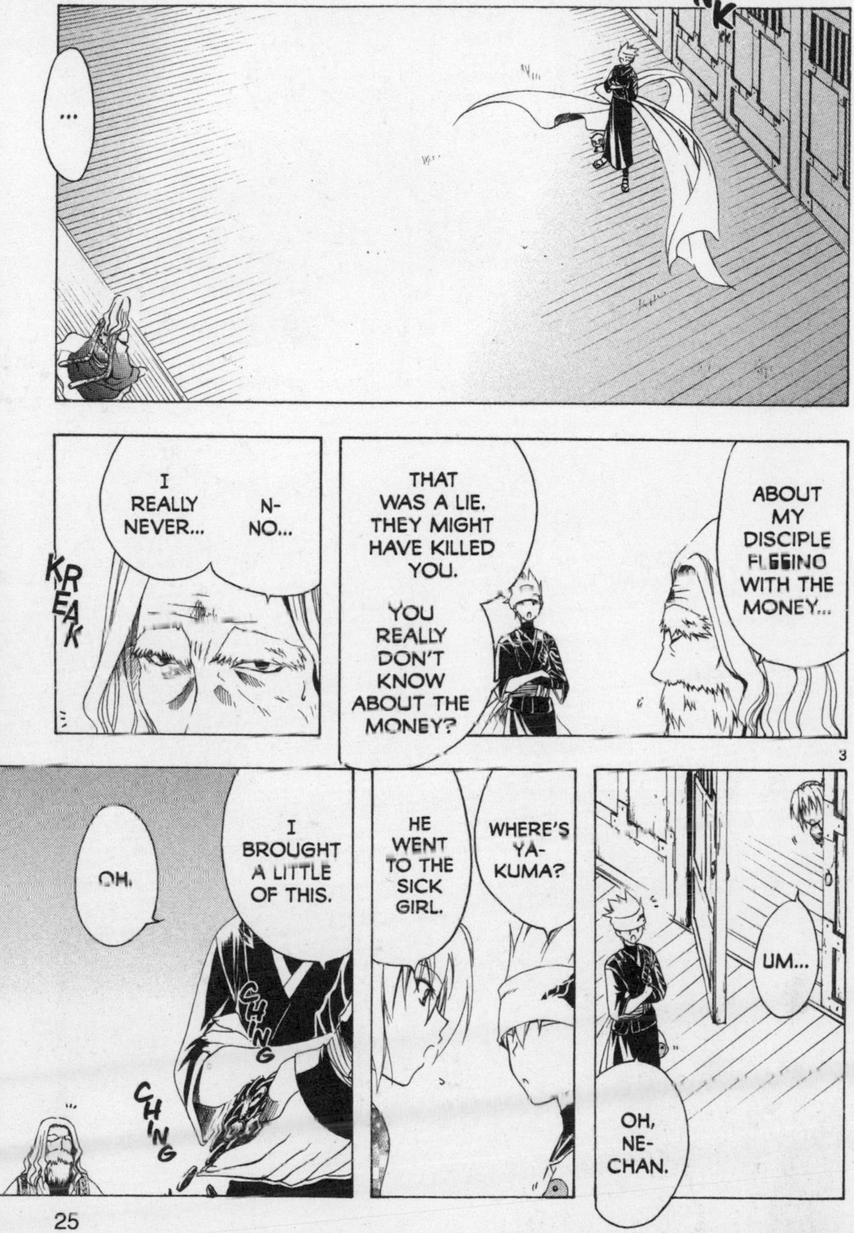
TNK
...
ABOUT MY DISCIPLE FLEEING WITH THE MONEY...
THAT WAS A LIE. THEY MIGHT HAVE KILLED YOU.
YOU REALLY DON'T KNOW ABOUT THE MONEY?
N-NO...
I REALLY NEVER...
KREAK
UM...
OH, NE-CHAN.
WHERE'S YA-KUMA?
HE WENT TO THE SICK GIRL.
I BROUGHT A LITTLE OF THIS.
CHING
CHING
OH.

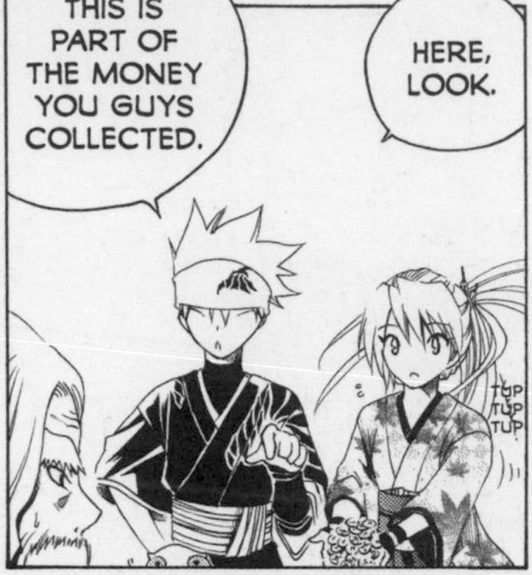
HERE, LOOK.
THIS IS PART OF THE MONEY YOU GUYS COLLECTED.
TUP TUP TUP

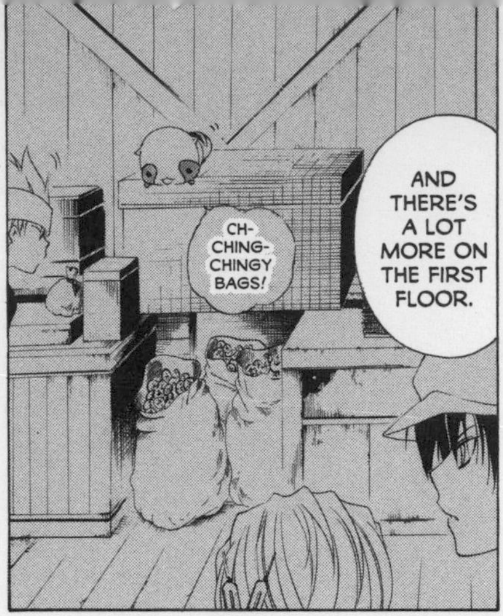
AND THERE'S A LOT MORE ON THE FIRST FLOOR.
CH-CHING-CHINGY BAGS!

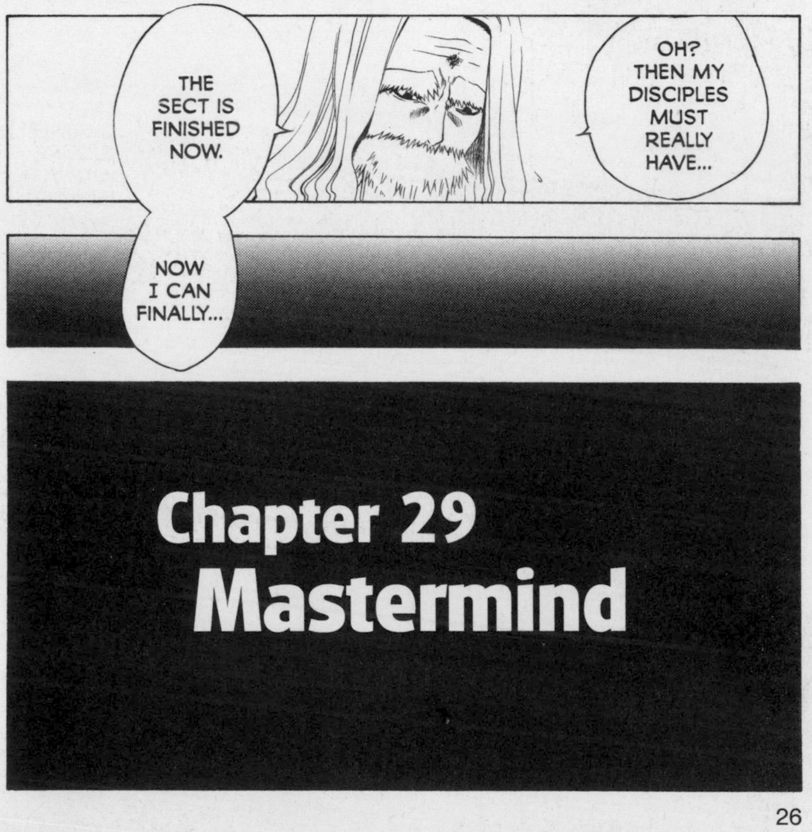
OH? THEN MY DISCIPLES MUST REALLY HAVE...
THE SECT IS FINISHED NOW.
NOW I CAN FINALLY...

Chapter 29
Mastermind

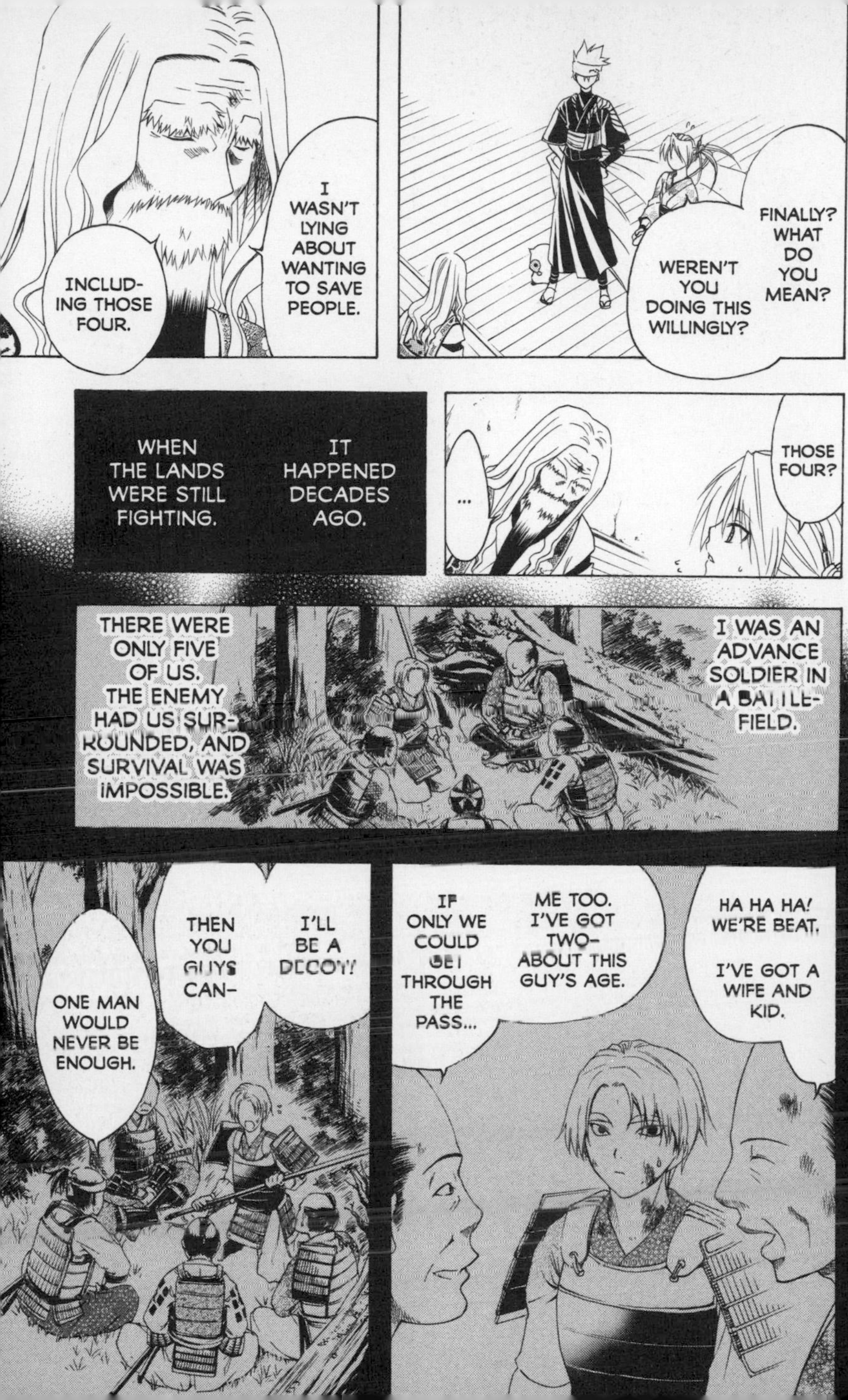
FINALLY? WHAT DO YOU MEAN?
WEREN'T YOU DOING THIS WILLINGLY?
I WASN'T LYING ABOUT WANTING TO SAVE PEOPLE.
INCLUDING THOSE FOUR.
THOSE FOUR?
...
IT HAPPENED DECADES AGO.
WHEN THE LANDS WERE STILL FIGHTING.
I WAS AN ADVANCE SOLDIER IN A BATTLEFIELD.
THERE WERE ONLY FIVE OF US. THE ENEMY HAD US SURROUNDED, AND SURVIVAL WAS IMPOSSIBLE.
HA HA HA! WE'RE BEAT.
I'VE GOT A WIFE AND KID.
ME TOO. I'VE GOT TWO—ABOUT THIS GUY'S AGE.
IF ONLY WE COULD GET THROUGH THE PASS...
I'LL BE A DECOY!
THEN YOU GUYS CAN—
ONE MAN WOULD NEVER BE ENOUGH.

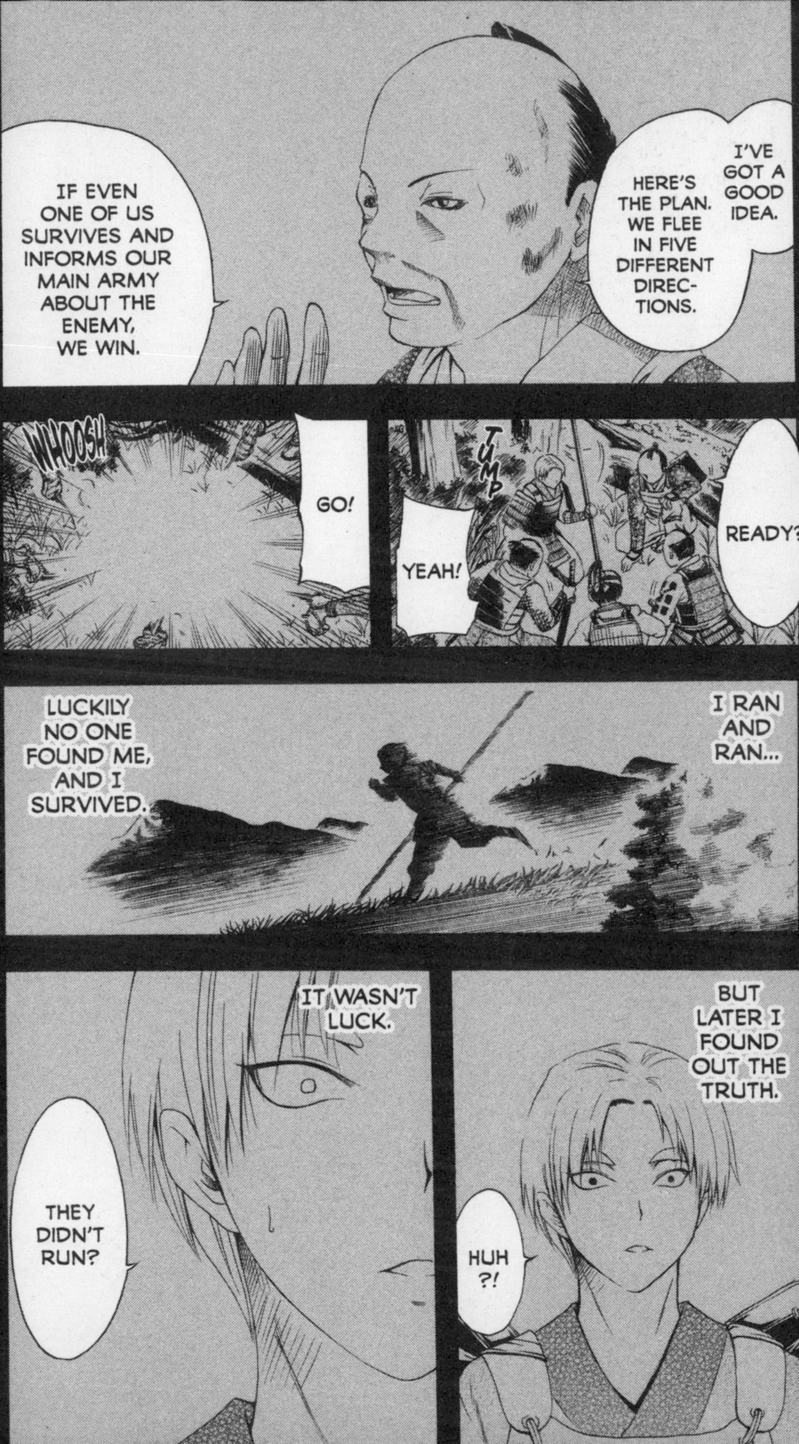
I'VE GOT A GOOD IDEA.
HERE'S THE PLAN. WE FLEE IN FIVE DIFFERENT DIREC-TIONS.
IF EVEN ONE OF US SURVIVES AND INFORMS OUR MAIN ARMY ABOUT THE ENEMY, WE WIN.
READY?
YEAH!
TUMP
GO!
WHOOSH
I RAN AND RAN...
LUCKILY NO ONE FOUND ME, AND I SURVIVED.
BUT LATER I FOUND OUT THE TRUTH.
HUH ?!
IT WASN'T LUCK.
THEY DIDN'T RUN?

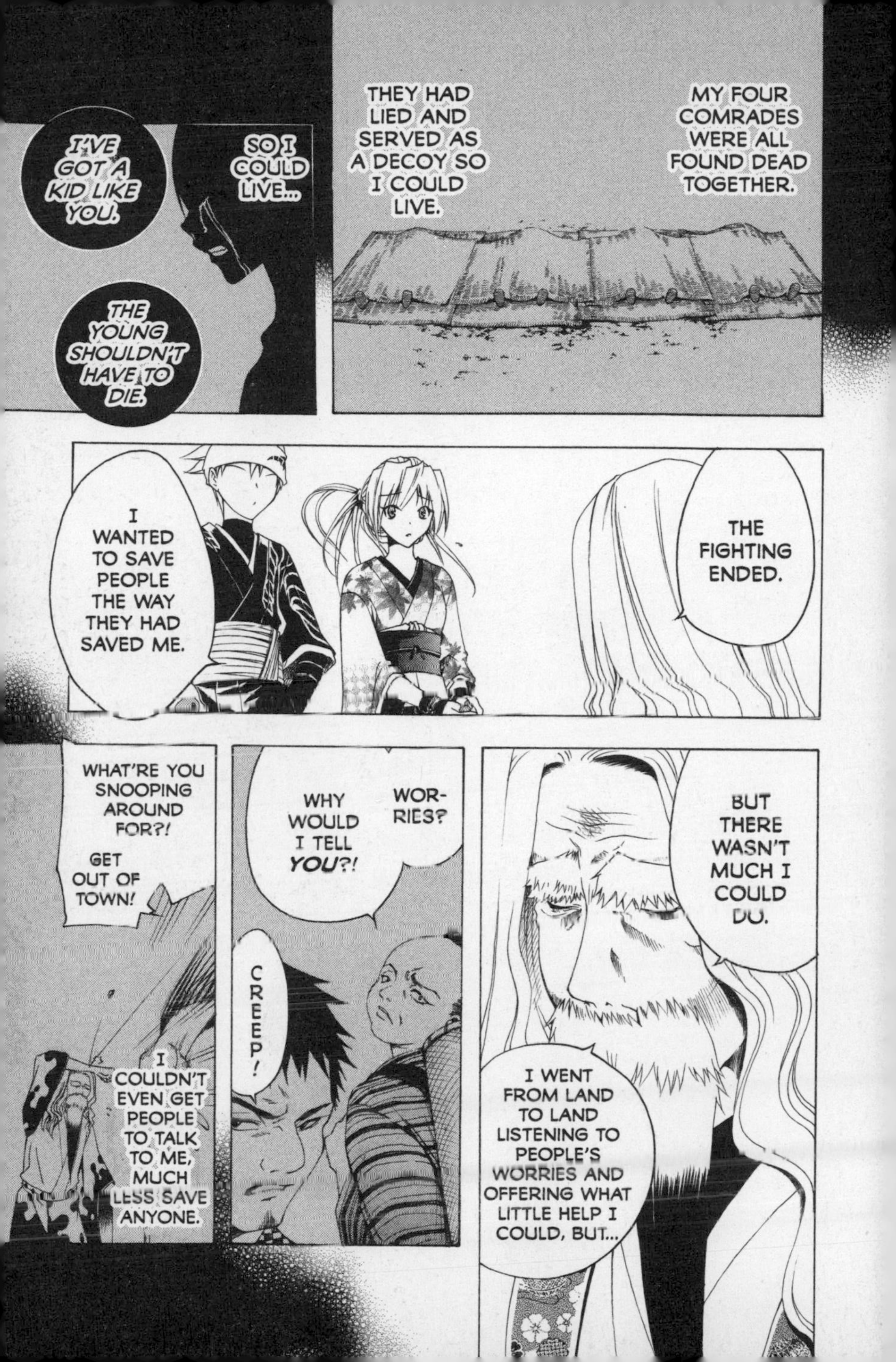
MY FOUR COMRADES WERE ALL FOUND DEAD TOGETHER.
THEY HAD LIED AND SERVED AS A DECOY SO I COULD LIVE.
SO I COULD LIVE...
I'VE GOT A KID LIKE YOU.
THE YOUNG SHOULDN'T HAVE TO DIE.
THE FIGHTING ENDED.
I WANTED TO SAVE PEOPLE THE WAY THEY HAD SAVED ME.
BUT THERE WASN'T MUCH I COULD DO.
I WENT FROM LAND TO LAND LISTENING TO PEOPLE'S WORRIES AND OFFERING WHAT LITTLE HELP I COULD, BUT...
WORRIES? WHY WOULD I TELL YOU?!
CREEP!
WHAT'RE YOU SNOOPING AROUND FOR?!
GET OUT OF TOWN!
I COULDN'T EVEN GET PEOPLE TO TALK TO ME, MUCH LESS SAVE ANYONE.

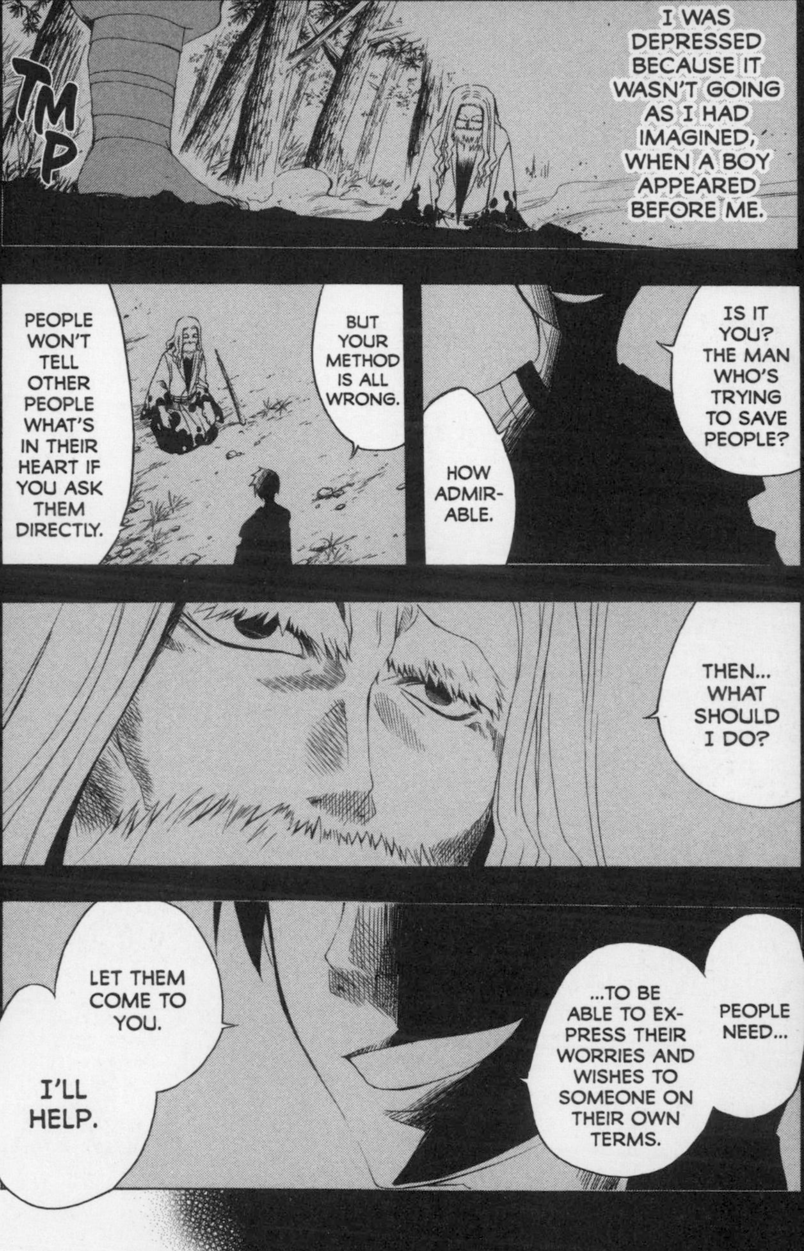
I WAS DEPRESSED BECAUSE IT WASN'T GOING AS I HAD IMAGINED, WHEN A BOY APPEARED BEFORE ME.
TMP
IS IT YOU? THE MAN WHO'S TRYING TO SAVE PEOPLE?
HOW ADMIR-ABLE.
BUT YOUR METHOD IS ALL WRONG.
PEOPLE WON'T TELL OTHER PEOPLE WHAT'S IN THEIR HEART IF YOU ASK THEM DIRECTLY.
THEN... WHAT SHOULD I DO?
PEOPLE NEED...
...TO BE ABLE TO EX-PRESS THEIR WORRIES AND WISHES TO SOMEONE ON THEIR OWN TERMS.
LET THEM COME TO YOU.
I'LL HELP.

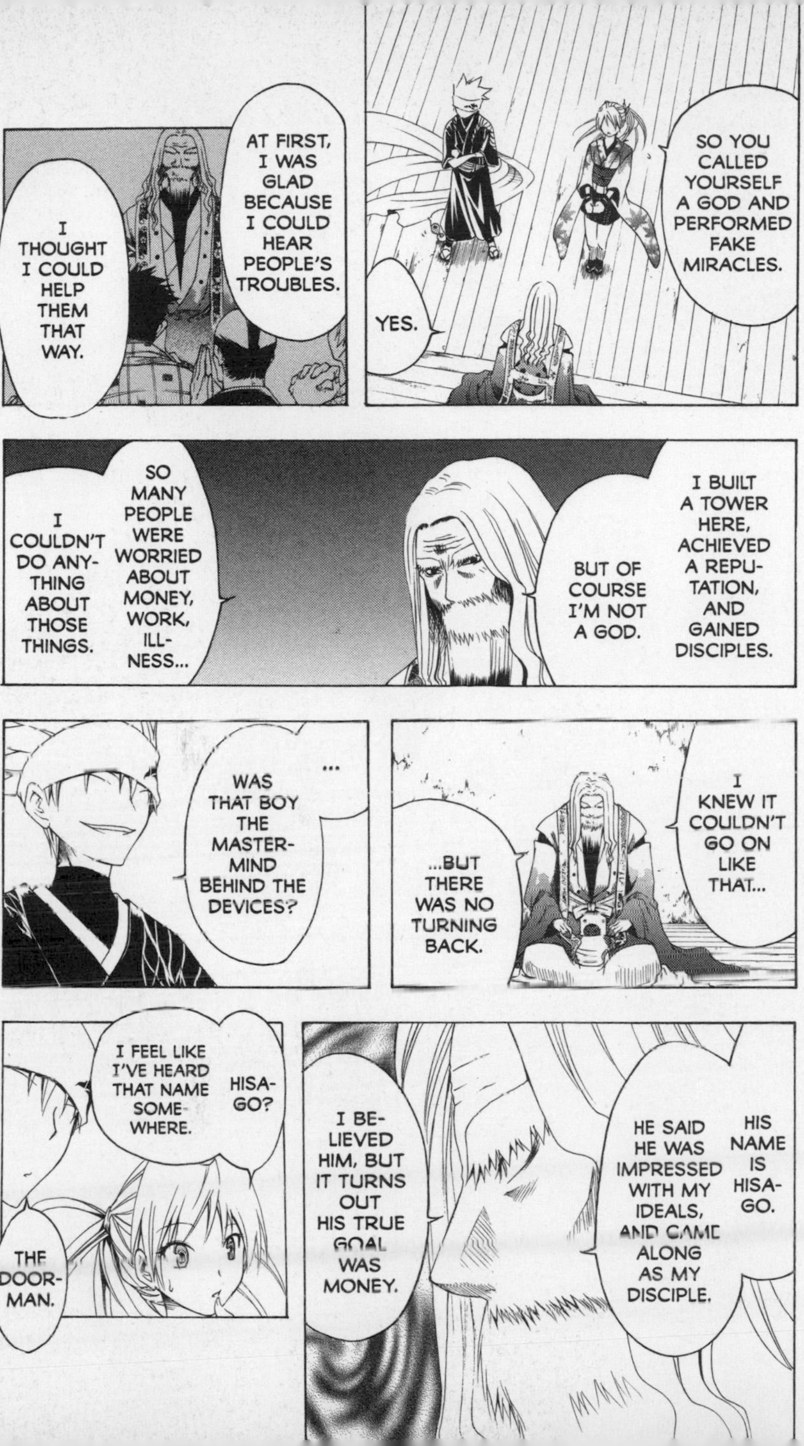
SO YOU CALLED YOURSELF A GOD AND PERFORMED FAKE MIRACLES.
YES.
AT FIRST, I WAS GLAD BECAUSE I COULD HEAR PEOPLE'S TROUBLES.
I THOUGHT I COULD HELP THEM THAT WAY.
I BUILT A TOWER HERE, ACHIEVED A REPUTATION, AND GAINED DISCIPLES.
BUT OF COURSE I'M NOT A GOD.
SO MANY PEOPLE WERE WORRIED ABOUT MONEY, WORK, ILLNESS...
I COULDN'T DO ANYTHING ABOUT THOSE THINGS.
I KNEW IT COULDN'T GO ON LIKE THAT...
...BUT THERE WAS NO TURNING BACK.
...
WAS THAT BOY THE MASTERMIND BEHIND THE DEVICES?
HIS NAME IS HISAGO.
HE SAID HE WAS IMPRESSED WITH MY IDEALS, AND CAME ALONG AS MY DISCIPLE.
I BELIEVED HIM, BUT IT TURNS OUT HIS TRUE GOAL WAS MONEY.
HISAGO?
I FEEL LIKE I'VE HEARD THAT NAME SOMEWHERE.
THE DOORMAN.

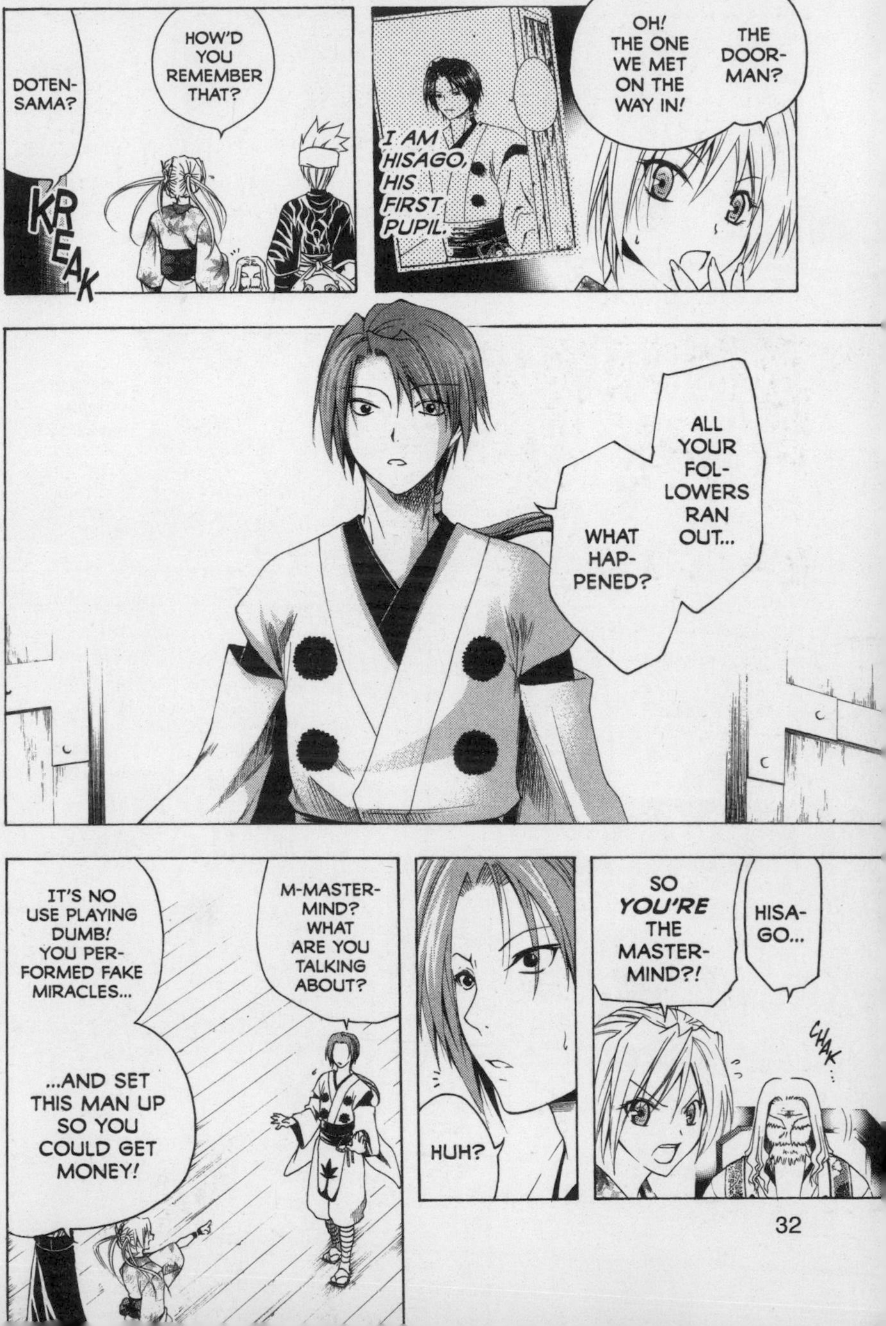
OH! THE ONE WE MET ON THE WAY IN!
THE DOORMAN?
I AM HISAGO, HIS FIRST PUPIL.
HOW'D YOU REMEMBER THAT?
DOTEN-SAMA?
KREAK
ALL YOUR FOLLOWERS RAN OUT...
WHAT HAPPENED?
HISA-GO...
SO YOU'RE THE MASTERMIND?!
CHAK...
HUH?
M-MASTERMIND? WHAT ARE YOU TALKING ABOUT?
IT'S NO USE PLAYING DUMB! YOU PERFORMED FAKE MIRACLES...
...AND SET THIS MAN UP SO YOU COULD GET MONEY!

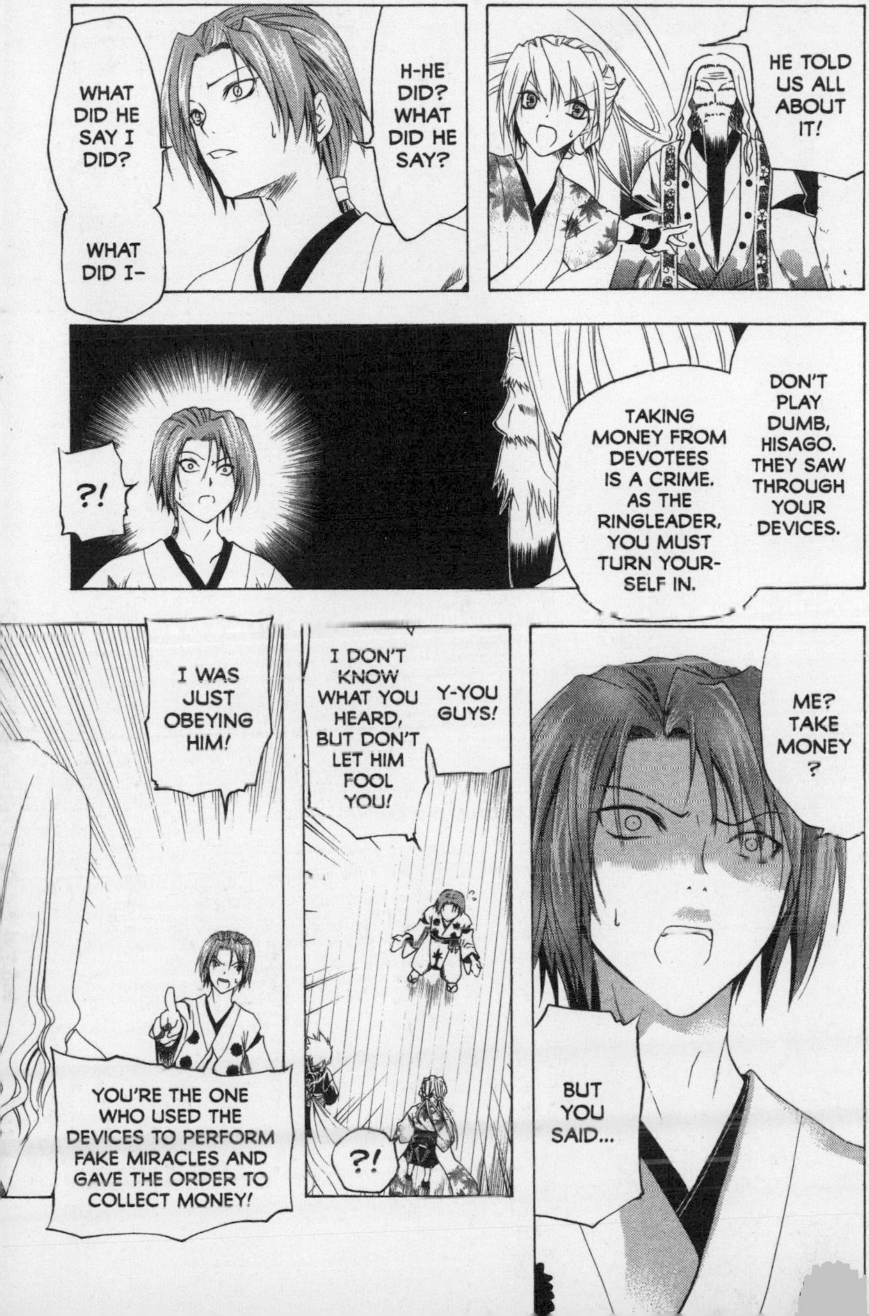
HE TOLD US ALL ABOUT IT!
H-HE DID? WHAT DID HE SAY?
WHAT DID HE SAY I DID?
WHAT DID I–
DON'T PLAY DUMB, HISAGO. THEY SAW THROUGH YOUR DEVICES.
TAKING MONEY FROM DEVOTEES IS A CRIME. AS THE RINGLEADER, YOU MUST TURN YOUR-SELF IN.
?!
ME? TAKE MONEY ?
BUT YOU SAID...
Y-YOU GUYS!
I DON'T KNOW WHAT YOU HEARD, BUT DON'T LET HIM FOOL YOU!
?!
I WAS JUST OBEYING HIM!
YOU'RE THE ONE WHO USED THE DEVICES TO PERFORM FAKE MIRACLES AND GAVE THE ORDER TO COLLECT MONEY!

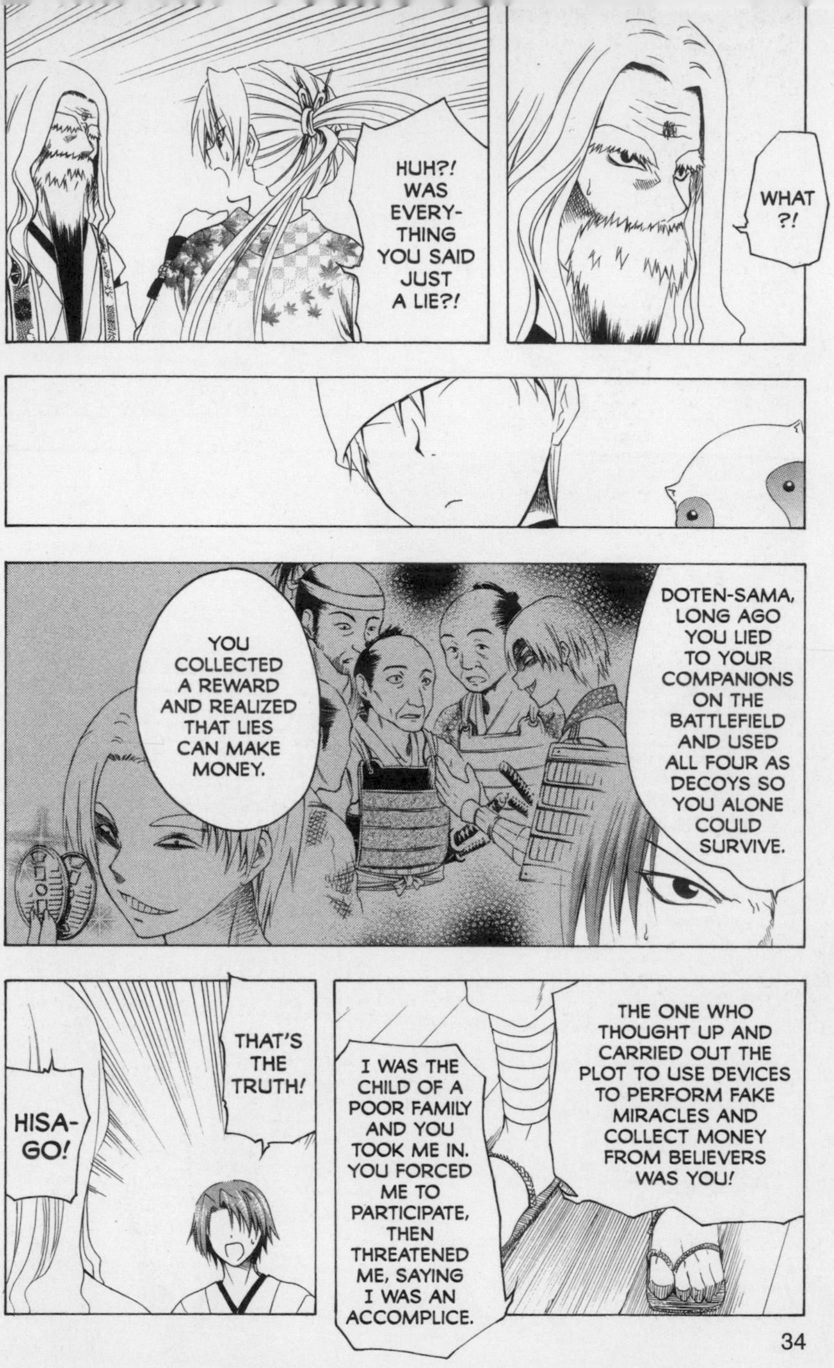
WHAT ?!
HUH?! WAS EVERY-THING YOU SAID JUST A LIE?!
DOTEN-SAMA, LONG AGO YOU LIED TO YOUR COMPANIONS ON THE BATTLEFIELD AND USED ALL FOUR AS DECOYS SO YOU ALONE COULD SURVIVE.
YOU COLLECTED A REWARD AND REALIZED THAT LIES CAN MAKE MONEY.
THE ONE WHO THOUGHT UP AND CARRIED OUT THE PLOT TO USE DEVICES TO PERFORM FAKE MIRACLES AND COLLECT MONEY FROM BELIEVERS WAS YOU!
I WAS THE CHILD OF A POOR FAMILY AND YOU TOOK ME IN. YOU FORCED ME TO PARTICIPATE, THEN THREATENED ME, SAYING I WAS AN ACCOMPLICE.
THAT'S THE TRUTH!
HISA-GO!

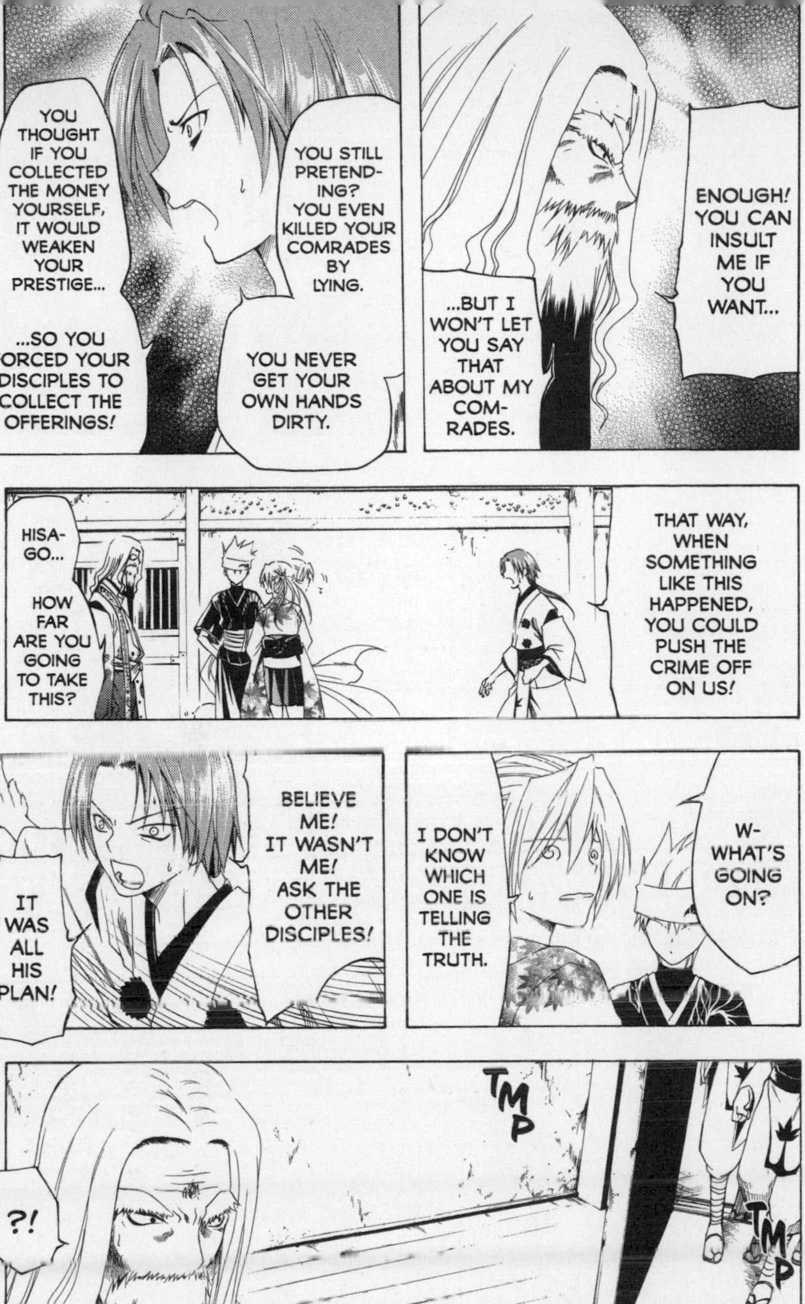

ENOUGH! YOU CAN INSULT ME IF YOU WANT...
...BUT I WON'T LET YOU SAY THAT ABOUT MY COM-RADES.
YOU STILL PRETEND-ING? YOU EVEN KILLED YOUR COMRADES BY LYING.
YOU NEVER GET YOUR OWN HANDS DIRTY.
YOU THOUGHT IF YOU COLLECTED THE MONEY YOURSELF, IT WOULD WEAKEN YOUR PRESTIGE...
...SO YOU FORCED YOUR DISCIPLES TO COLLECT THE OFFERINGS!
THAT WAY, WHEN SOMETHING LIKE THIS HAPPENED, YOU COULD PUSH THE CRIME OFF ON US!
HISA-GO...
HOW FAR ARE YOU GOING TO TAKE THIS?
W-WHAT'S GOING ON?
I DON'T KNOW WHICH ONE IS TELLING THE TRUTH.
BELIEVE ME! IT WASN'T ME! ASK THE OTHER DISCIPLES!
IT WAS ALL HIS PLAN!
TMP
TMP
?!

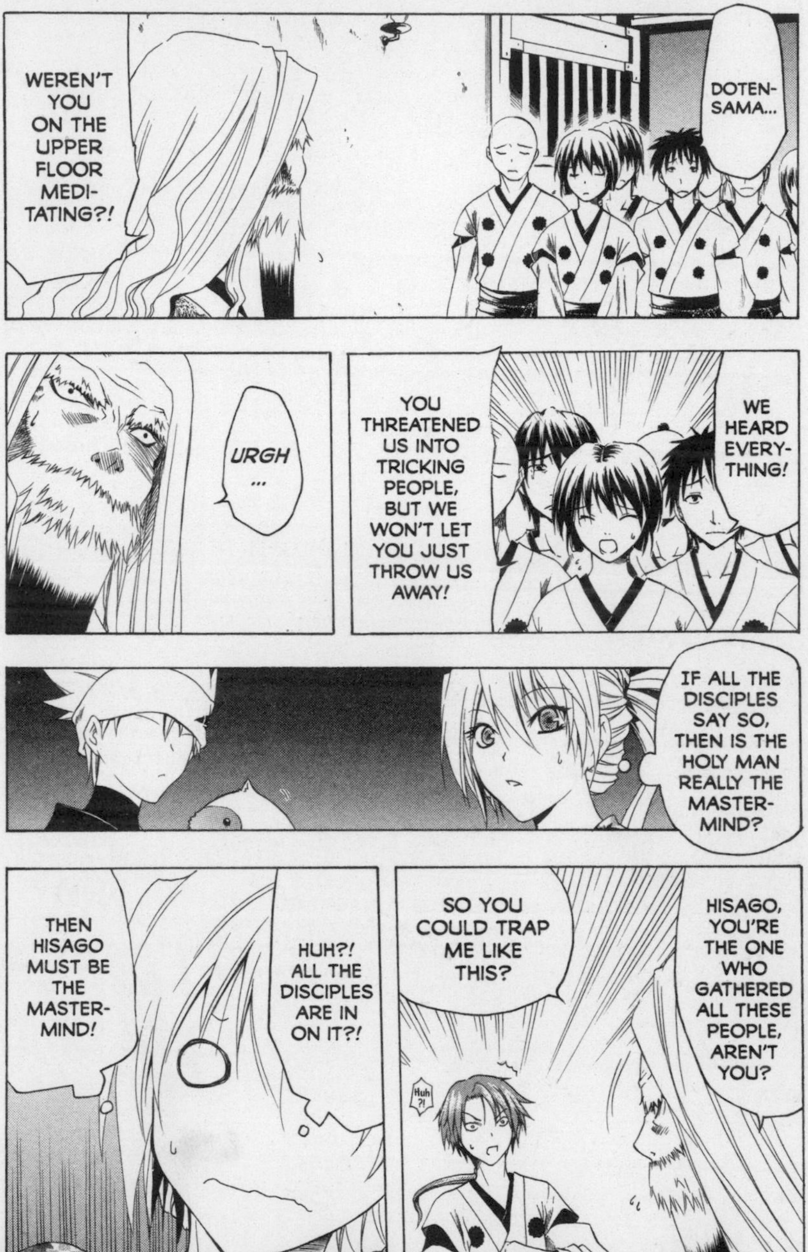
DOTEN-SAMA...
WEREN'T YOU ON THE UPPER FLOOR MEDI-TATING?!
WE HEARD EVERY-THING!
YOU THREATENED US INTO TRICKING PEOPLE, BUT WE WON'T LET YOU JUST THROW US AWAY!
URGH ...
IF ALL THE DISCIPLES SAY SO, THEN IS THE HOLY MAN REALLY THE MASTER-MIND?
HISAGO, YOU'RE THE ONE WHO GATHERED ALL THESE PEOPLE, AREN'T YOU?
SO YOU COULD TRAP ME LIKE THIS?
Huh ?!
HUH?! ALL THE DISCIPLES ARE IN ON IT?!
THEN HISAGO MUST BE THE MASTER-MIND!

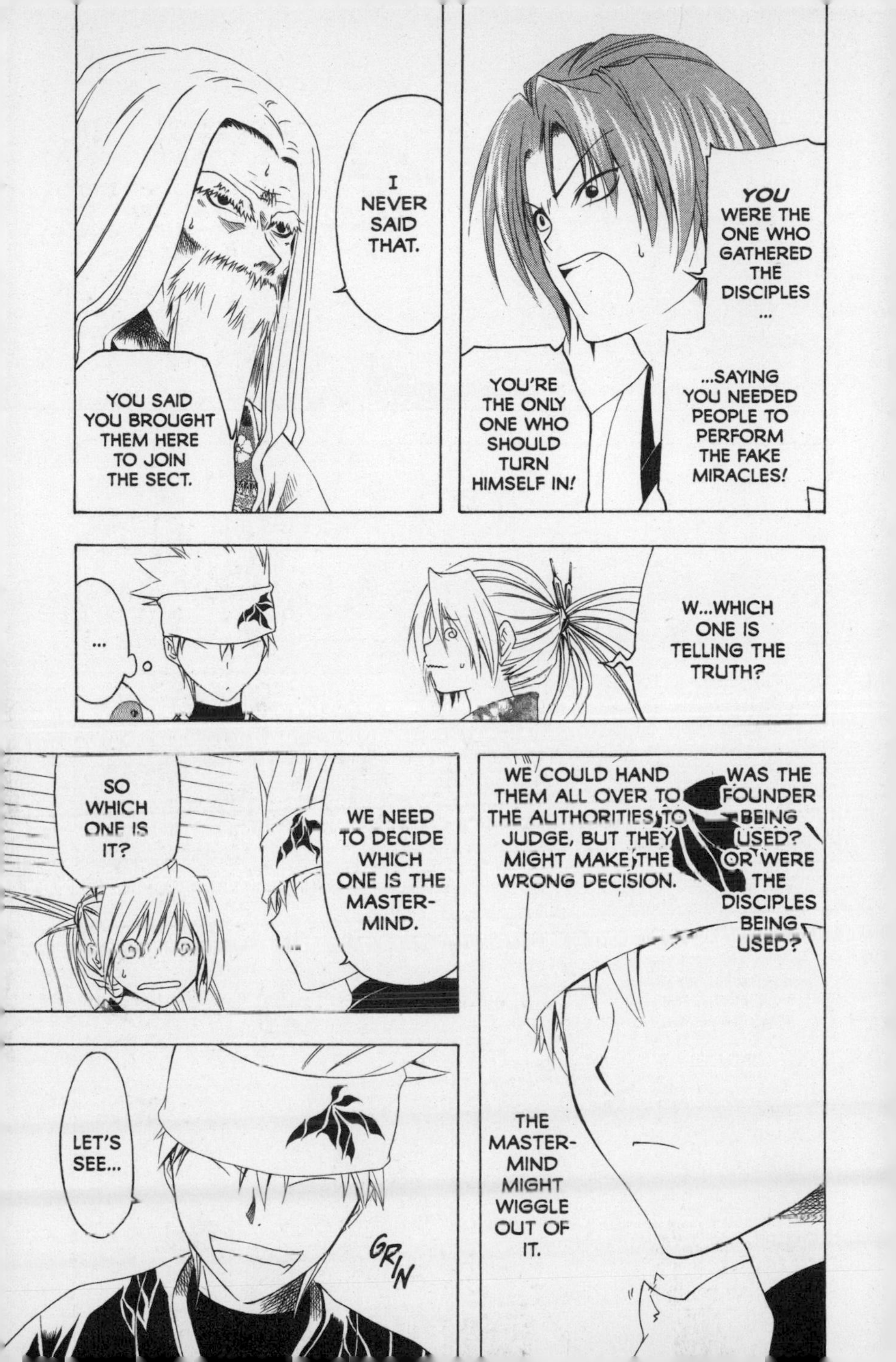
YOU WERE THE ONE WHO GATHERED THE DISCIPLES ...
...SAYING YOU NEEDED PEOPLE TO PERFORM THE FAKE MIRACLES!
YOU'RE THE ONLY ONE WHO SHOULD TURN HIMSELF IN!
I NEVER SAID THAT.
YOU SAID YOU BROUGHT THEM HERE TO JOIN THE SECT.
W...WHICH ONE IS TELLING THE TRUTH?
...
WAS THE FOUNDER BEING USED? OR WERE THE DISCIPLES BEING USED?
WE COULD HAND THEM ALL OVER TO THE AUTHORITIES TO JUDGE, BUT THEY MIGHT MAKE THE WRONG DECISION.
THE MASTER-MIND MIGHT WIGGLE OUT OF IT.
WE NEED TO DECIDE WHICH ONE IS THE MASTER-MIND.
SO WHICH ONE IS IT?
LET'S SEE...
GRIN

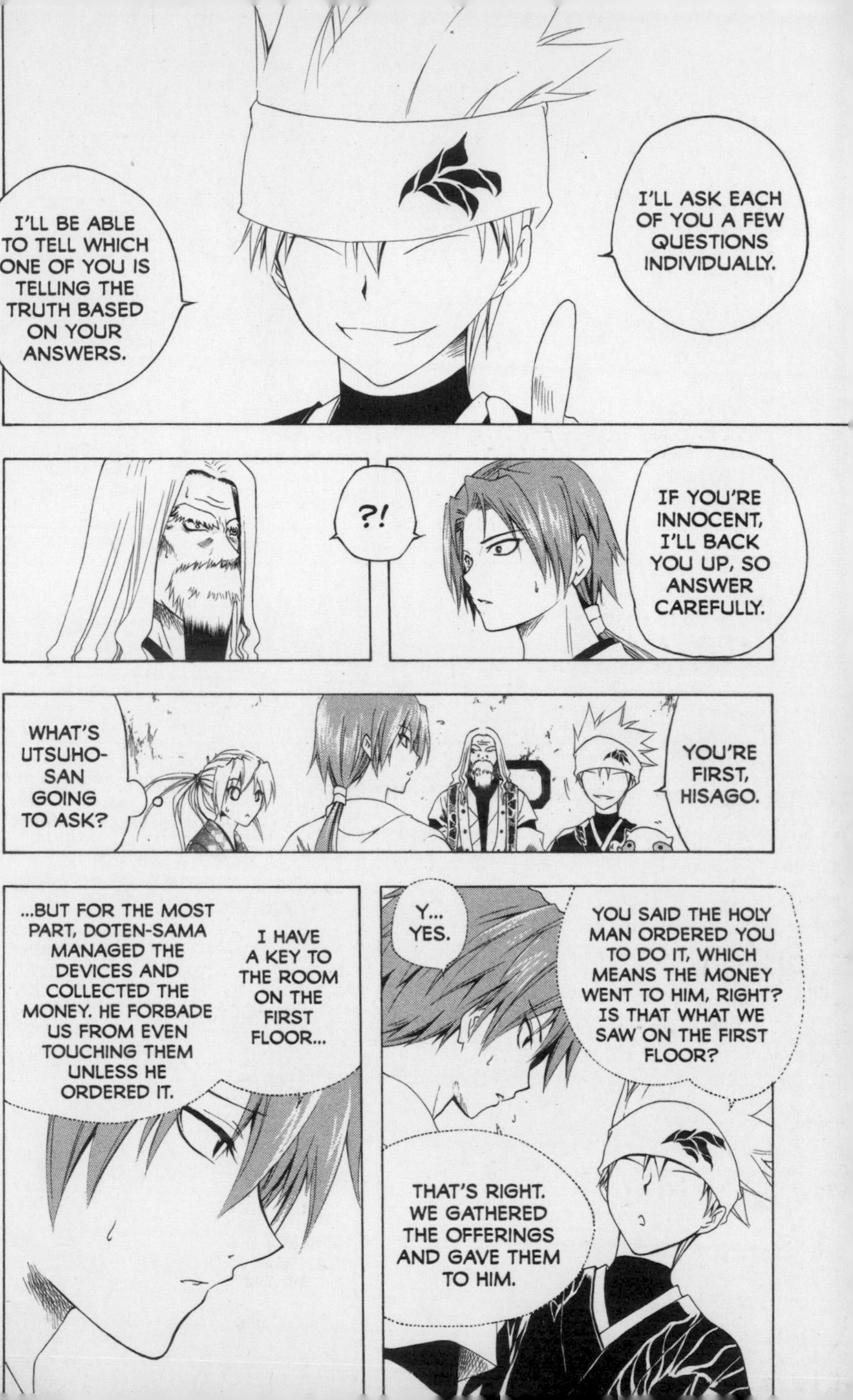
I'LL ASK EACH OF YOU A FEW QUESTIONS INDIVIDUALLY.
I'LL BE ABLE TO TELL WHICH ONE OF YOU IS TELLING THE TRUTH BASED ON YOUR ANSWERS.
IF YOU'RE INNOCENT, I'LL BACK YOU UP, SO ANSWER CAREFULLY.
?!
YOU'RE FIRST, HISAGO.
WHAT'S UTSUHO-SAN GOING TO ASK?
YOU SAID THE HOLY MAN ORDERED YOU TO DO IT, WHICH MEANS THE MONEY WENT TO HIM, RIGHT? IS THAT WHAT WE SAW ON THE FIRST FLOOR?
Y... YES.
THAT'S RIGHT. WE GATHERED THE OFFERINGS AND GAVE THEM TO HIM.
I HAVE A KEY TO THE ROOM ON THE FIRST FLOOR...
...BUT FOR THE MOST PART, DOTEN-SAMA MANAGED THE DEVICES AND COLLECTED THE MONEY. HE FORBADE US FROM EVEN TOUCHING THEM UNLESS HE ORDERED IT.

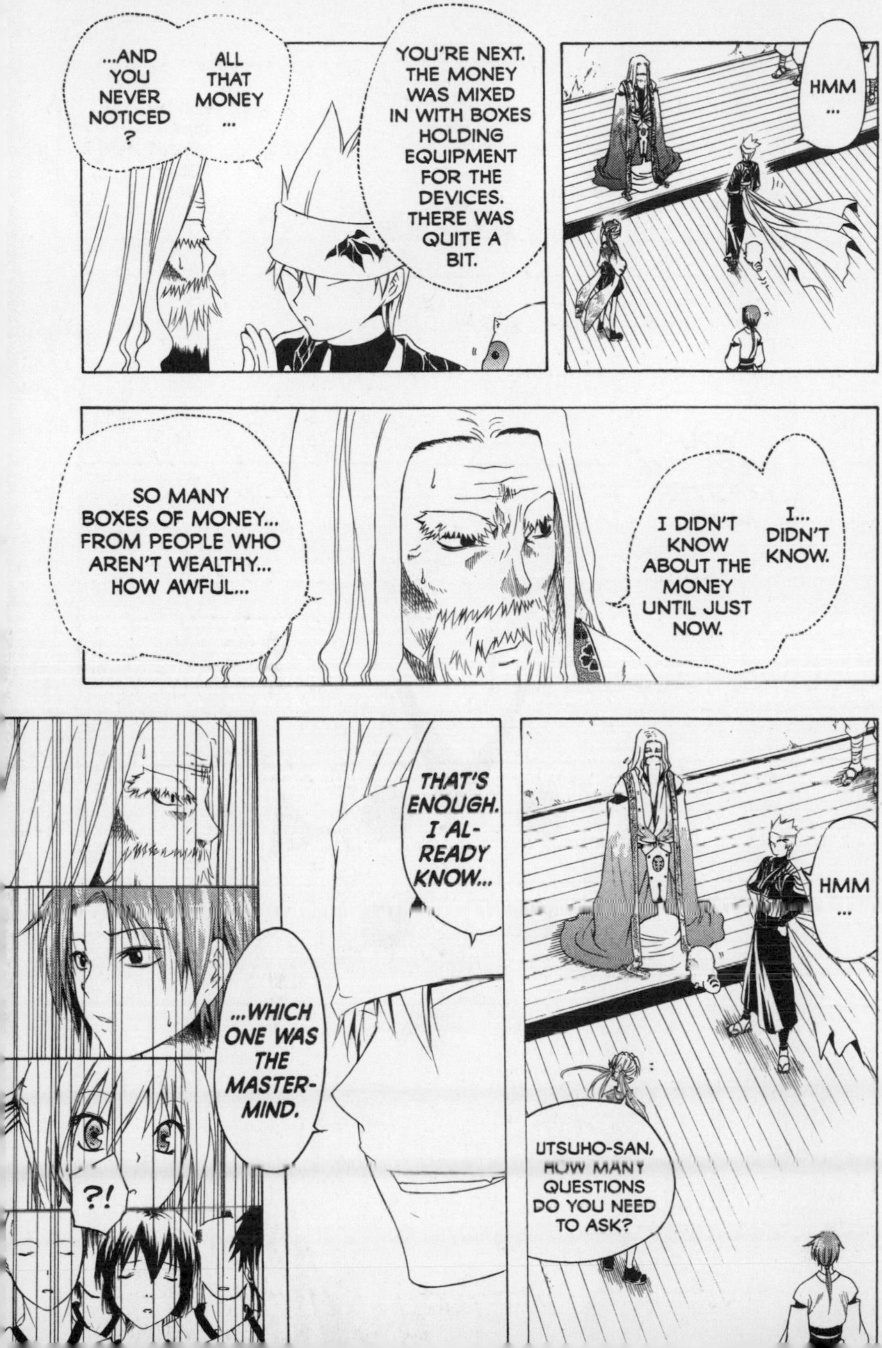
HMM ...
YOU'RE NEXT. THE MONEY WAS MIXED IN WITH BOXES HOLDING EQUIPMENT FOR THE DEVICES. THERE WAS QUITE A BIT.
ALL THAT MONEY ...
...AND YOU NEVER NOTICED ?
I... DIDN'T KNOW.
I DIDN'T KNOW ABOUT THE MONEY UNTIL JUST NOW.
SO MANY BOXES OF MONEY... FROM PEOPLE WHO AREN'T WEALTHY... HOW AWFUL...
HMM ...
UTSUHO-SAN, HOW MANY QUESTIONS DO YOU NEED TO ASK?
THAT'S ENOUGH. I AL-READY KNOW...
...WHICH ONE WAS THE MASTER-MIND.
?!

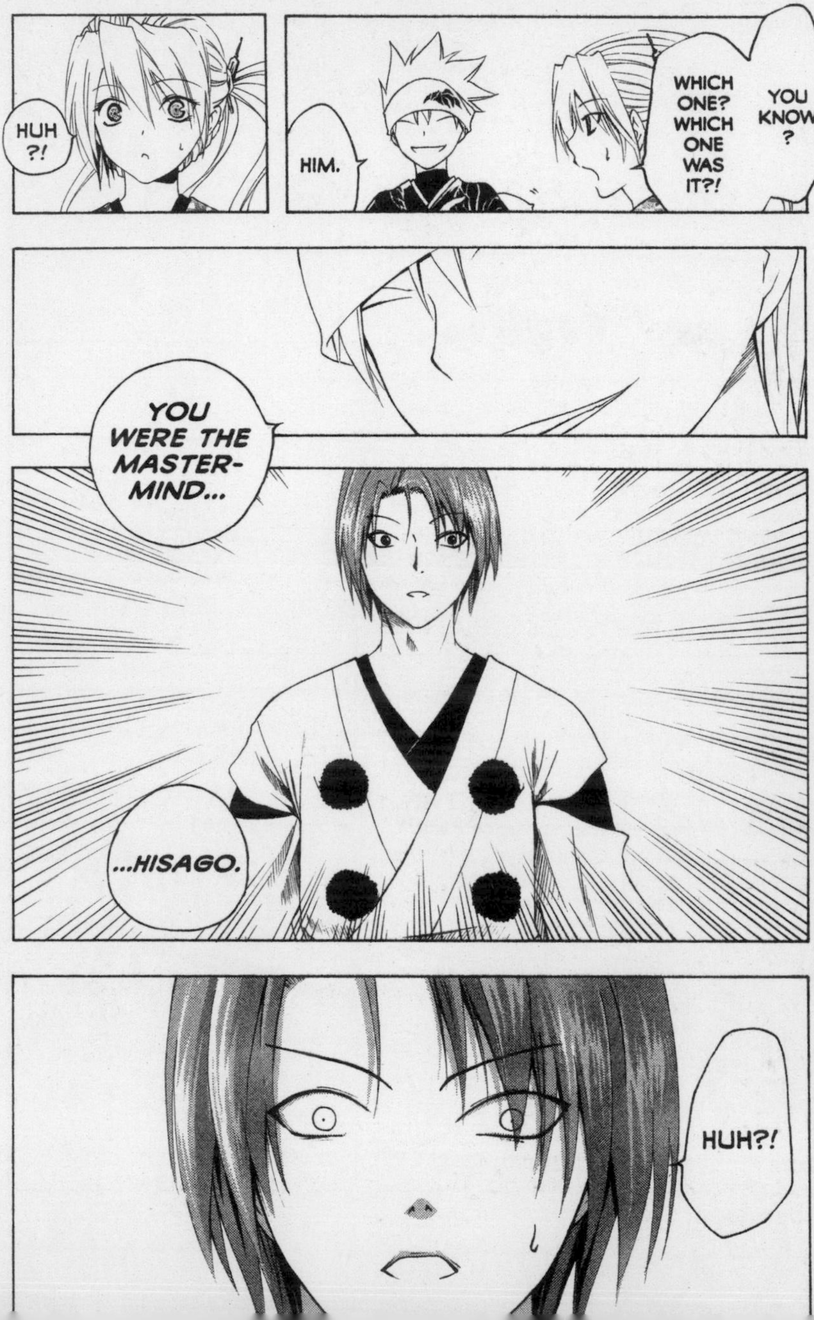
YOU KNOW?
WHICH ONE? WHICH ONE WAS IT?!
HIM.
HUH?!
YOU WERE THE MASTER-MIND...
...HISAGO.
HUH?!

Chapter 30 The Mistake

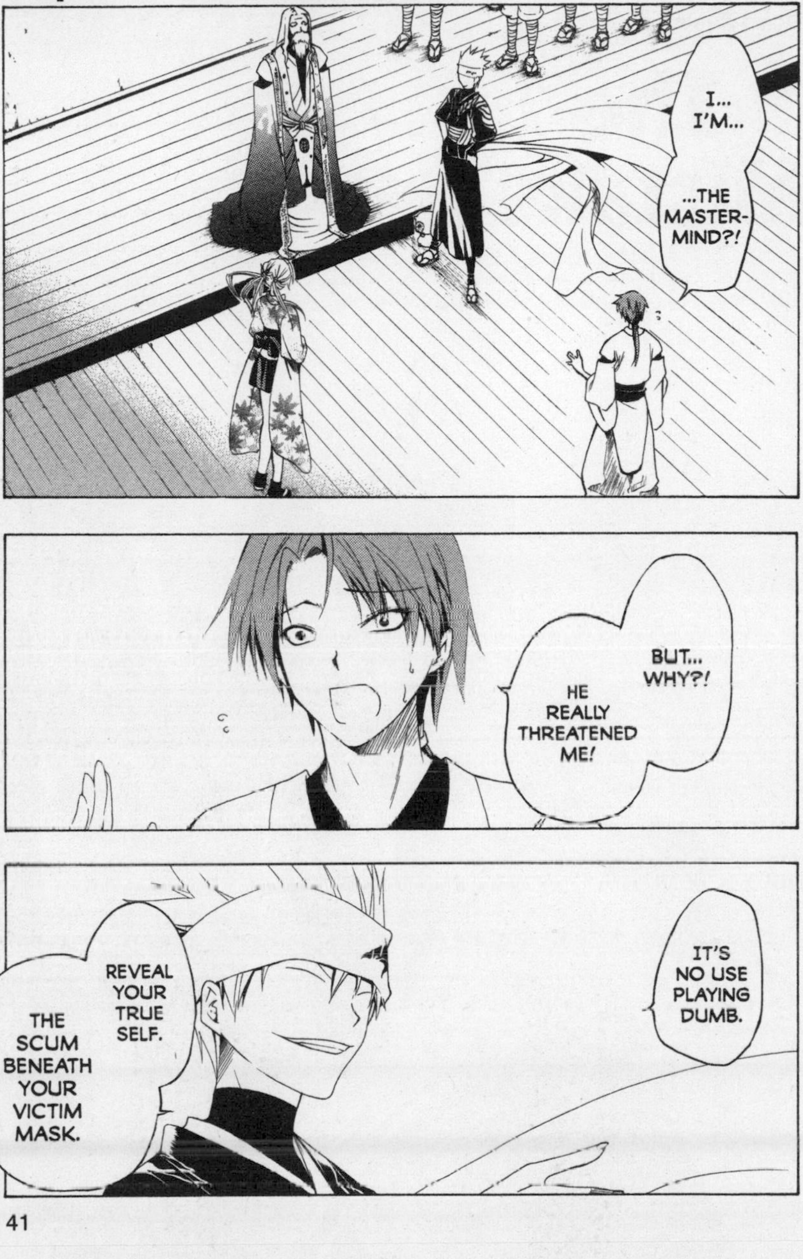
I... I'M...
...THE MASTER-MIND?!
BUT... WHY?!
HE REALLY THREATENED ME!
IT'S NO USE PLAYING DUMB.
REVEAL YOUR TRUE SELF.
THE SCUM BENEATH YOUR VICTIM MASK.

Chapter 30
The Mistake

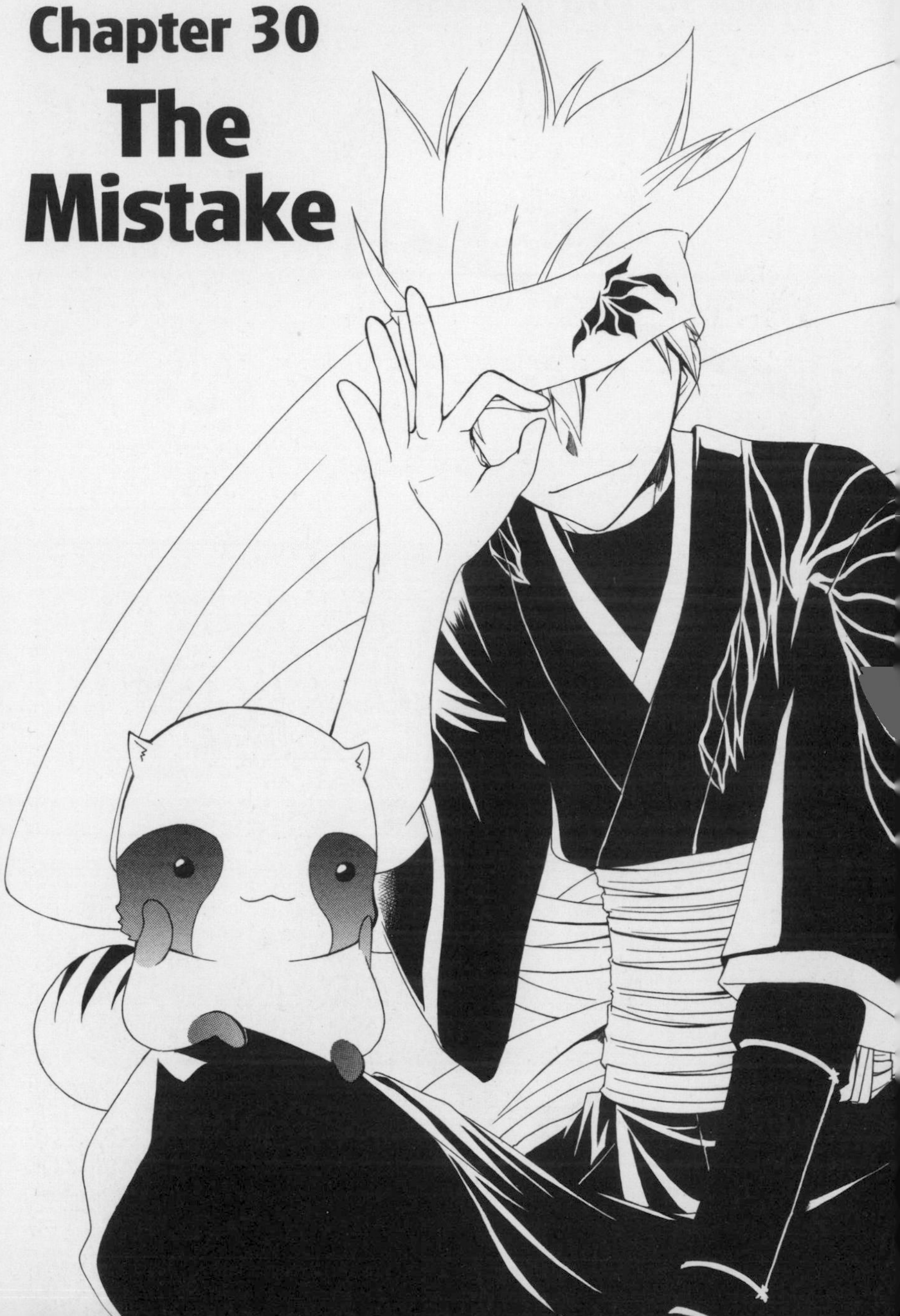

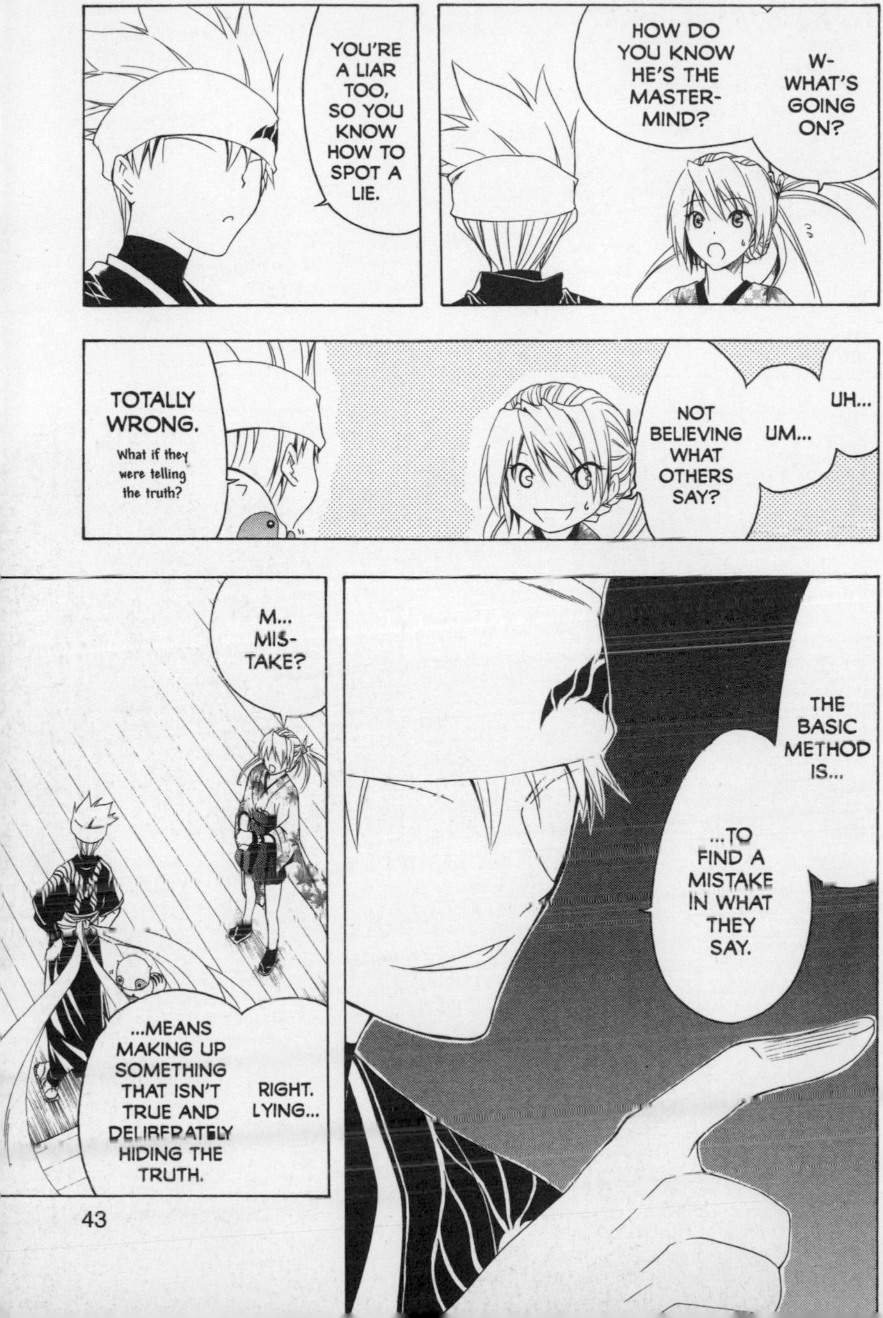
W-
WHAT'S
GOING
ON?
HOW DO
YOU KNOW
HE'S THE
MASTER-
MIND?
YOU'RE
A LIAR
TOO,
SO YOU
KNOW
HOW TO
SPOT A
LIE.
UH...
UM...
NOT
BELIEVING
WHAT
OTHERS
SAY?
TOTALLY
WRONG.
What if they
were telling
the truth?
THE
BASIC
METHOD
IS...
...TO
FIND A
MISTAKE
IN WHAT
THEY
SAY.
M...
MIS-
TAKE?
RIGHT.
LYING...
...MEANS
MAKING UP
SOMETHING
THAT ISN'T
TRUE AND
DELIBERATELY
HIDING THE
TRUTH.

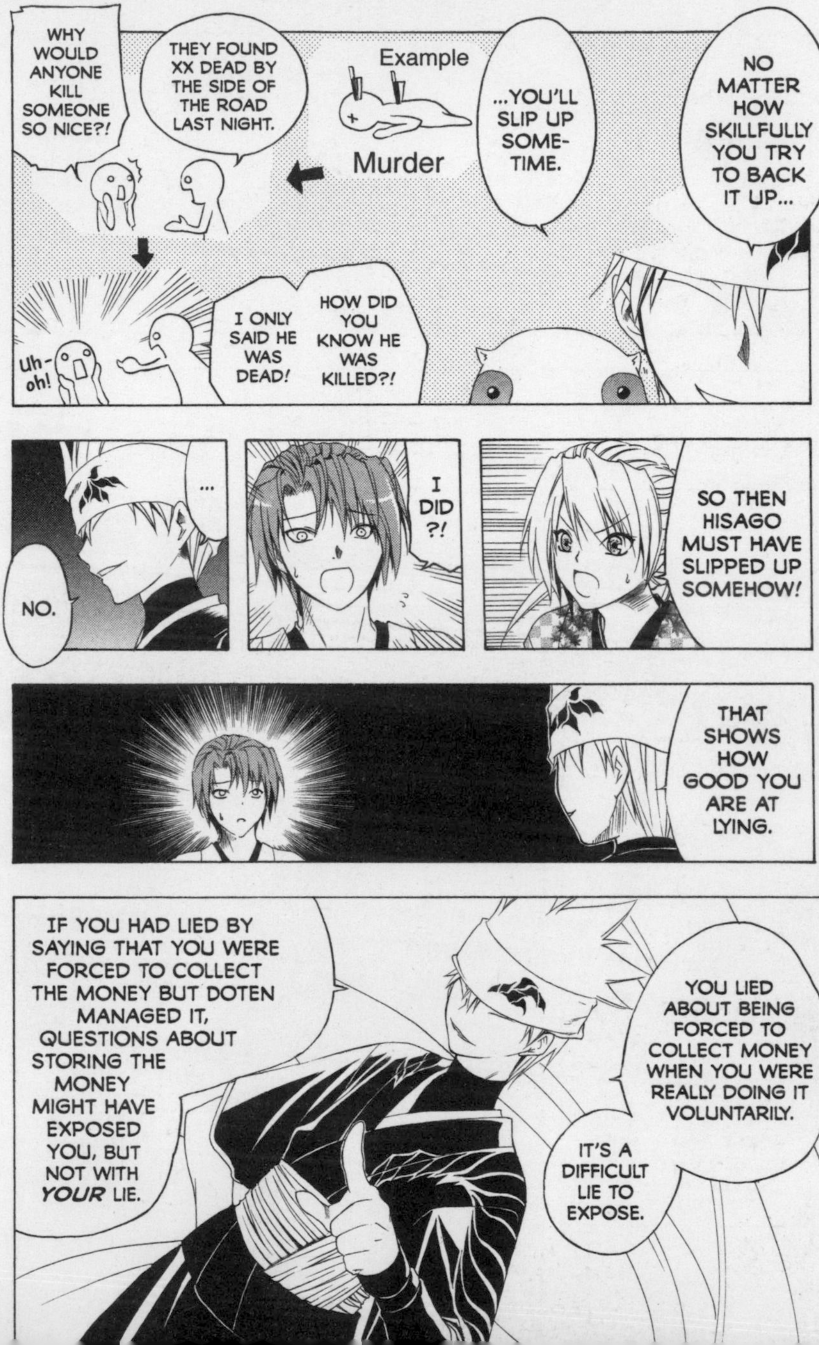
NO MATTER HOW SKILLFULLY YOU TRY TO BACK IT UP...
...YOU'LL SLIP UP SOME-TIME.
Example
Murder
THEY FOUND XX DEAD BY THE SIDE OF THE ROAD LAST NIGHT.
WHY WOULD ANYONE KILL SOMEONE SO NICE?!
HOW DID YOU KNOW HE WAS KILLED?!
I ONLY SAID HE WAS DEAD!
Uh-oh!
SO THEN HISAGO MUST HAVE SLIPPED UP SOMEHOW!
I DID ?!
...
NO.
THAT SHOWS HOW GOOD YOU ARE AT LYING.
YOU LIED ABOUT BEING FORCED TO COLLECT MONEY WHEN YOU WERE REALLY DOING IT VOLUNTARILY.
IT'S A DIFFICULT LIE TO EXPOSE.
IF YOU HAD LIED BY SAYING THAT YOU WERE FORCED TO COLLECT THE MONEY BUT DOTEN MANAGED IT, QUESTIONS ABOUT STORING THE MONEY MIGHT HAVE EXPOSED YOU, BUT NOT WITH ***YOUR*** LIE.

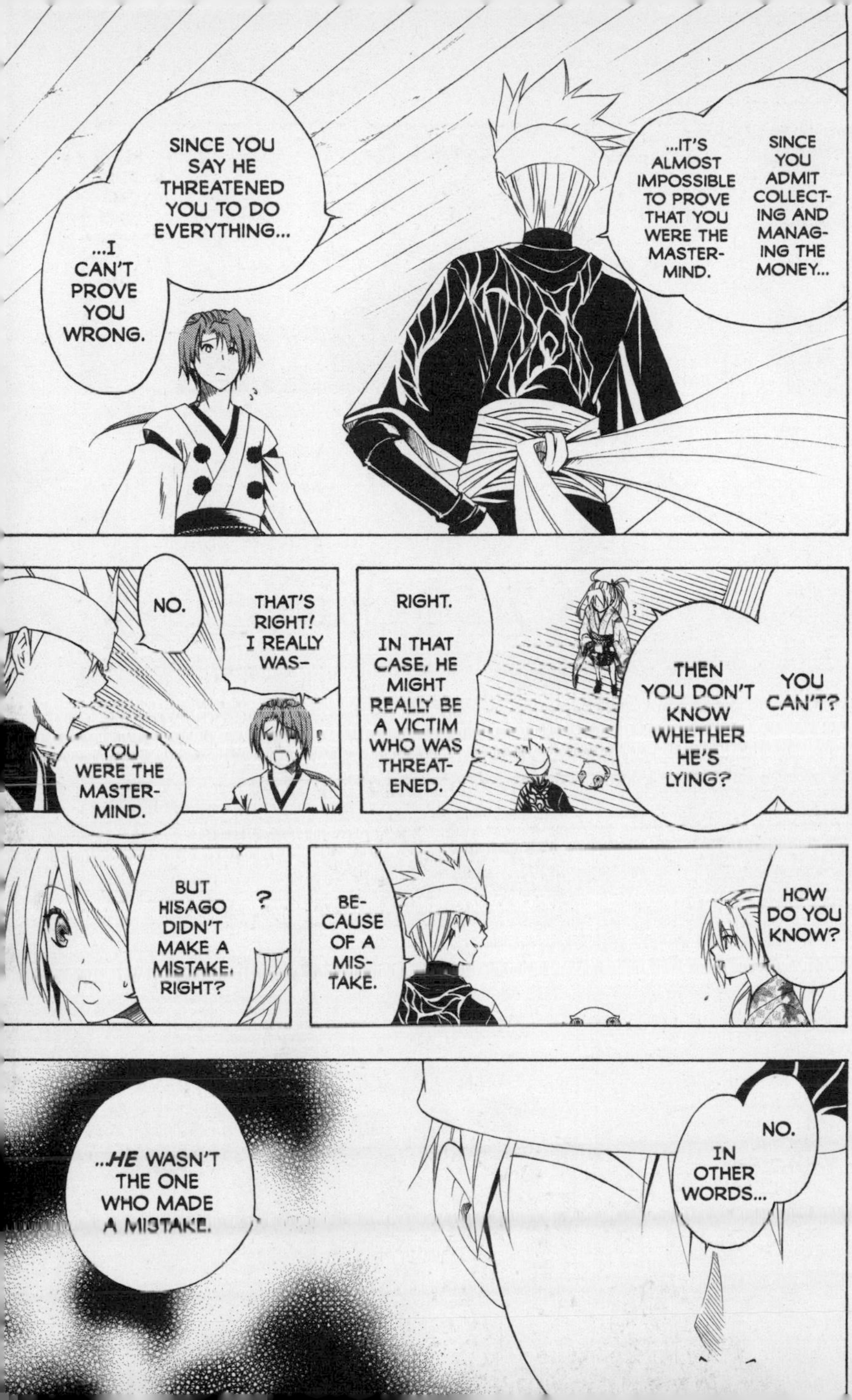
SINCE YOU ADMIT COLLECTING AND MANAGING THE MONEY...
...IT'S ALMOST IMPOSSIBLE TO PROVE THAT YOU WERE THE MASTERMIND.
SINCE YOU SAY HE THREATENED YOU TO DO EVERYTHING...
...I CAN'T PROVE YOU WRONG.
YOU CAN'T?
THEN YOU DON'T KNOW WHETHER HE'S LYING?
RIGHT.
IN THAT CASE, HE MIGHT REALLY BE A VICTIM WHO WAS THREATENED.
NO.
THAT'S RIGHT! I REALLY WAS-
YOU WERE THE MASTERMIND.
HOW DO YOU KNOW?
BECAUSE OF A MISTAKE.
?
BUT HISAGO DIDN'T MAKE A MISTAKE, RIGHT?
NO.
IN OTHER WORDS...
...HE WASN'T THE ONE WHO MADE A MISTAKE.

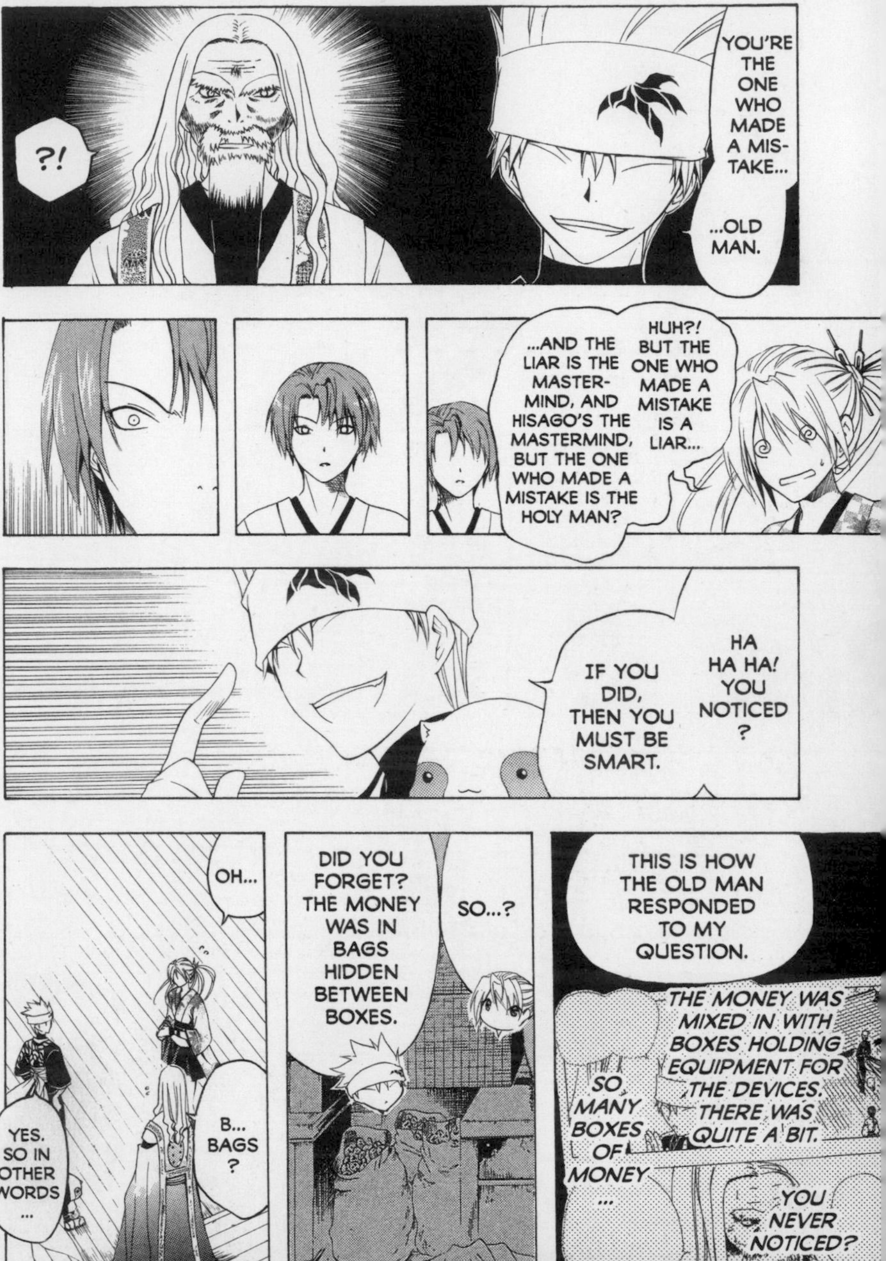
YOU'RE THE ONE WHO MADE A MISTAKE...
...OLD MAN.
?!
HUH?! BUT THE ONE WHO MADE A MISTAKE IS A LIAR...
...AND THE LIAR IS THE MASTERMIND, AND HISAGO'S THE MASTERMIND, BUT THE ONE WHO MADE A MISTAKE IS THE HOLY MAN?
HA HA HA! YOU NOTICED?
IF YOU DID, THEN YOU MUST BE SMART.
THIS IS HOW THE OLD MAN RESPONDED TO MY QUESTION.
THE MONEY WAS MIXED IN WITH BOXES HOLDING EQUIPMENT FOR THE DEVICES. THERE WAS QUITE A BIT.
SO MANY BOXES OF MONEY ...
YOU NEVER NOTICED?
DID YOU FORGET? THE MONEY WAS IN BAGS HIDDEN BETWEEN BOXES.
SO...?
OH...
B... BAGS ?
YES. SO IN OTHER WORDS ...

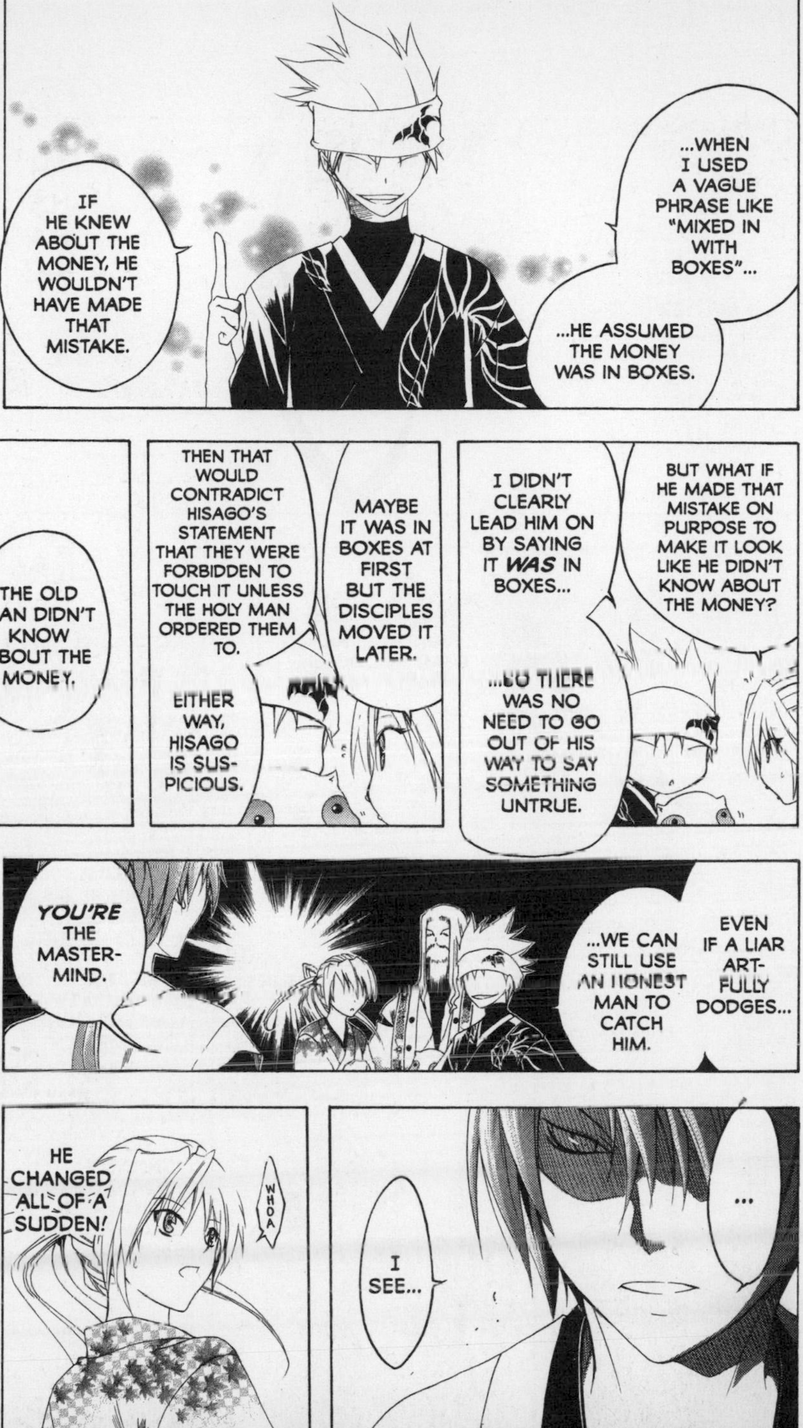
...WHEN I USED A VAGUE PHRASE LIKE "MIXED IN WITH BOXES"...
...HE ASSUMED THE MONEY WAS IN BOXES.
IF HE KNEW ABOUT THE MONEY, HE WOULDN'T HAVE MADE THAT MISTAKE.
BUT WHAT IF HE MADE THAT MISTAKE ON PURPOSE TO MAKE IT LOOK LIKE HE DIDN'T KNOW ABOUT THE MONEY?
I DIDN'T CLEARLY LEAD HIM ON BY SAYING IT *WAS* IN BOXES...
...SO THERE WAS NO NEED TO GO OUT OF HIS WAY TO SAY SOMETHING UNTRUE.
MAYBE IT WAS IN BOXES AT FIRST BUT THE DISCIPLES MOVED IT LATER.
THEN THAT WOULD CONTRADICT HISAGO'S STATEMENT THAT THEY WERE FORBIDDEN TO TOUCH IT UNLESS THE HOLY MAN ORDERED THEM TO.
EITHER WAY, HISAGO IS SUSPICIOUS.
THE OLD MAN DIDN'T KNOW ABOUT THE MONEY.
EVEN IF A LIAR ARTFULLY DODGES...
...WE CAN STILL USE AN HONEST MAN TO CATCH HIM.
YOU'RE THE MASTERMIND.
...
I SEE...
WHOA
HE CHANGED ALL OF A SUDDEN!

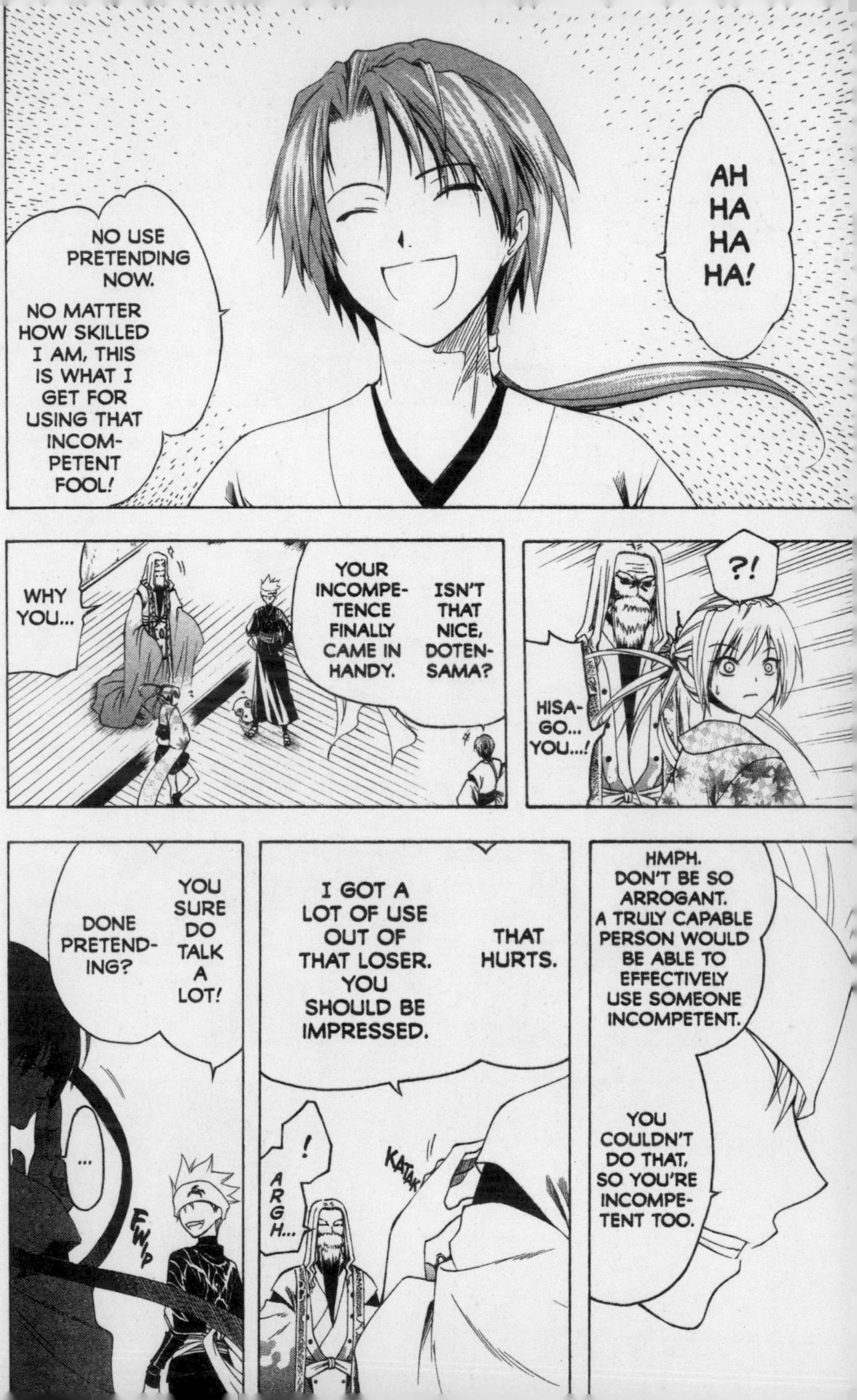
AH HA HA HA!
NO USE PRETENDING NOW.
NO MATTER HOW SKILLED I AM, THIS IS WHAT I GET FOR USING THAT INCOMPETENT FOOL!
?!
HISAGO... YOU...!
ISN'T THAT NICE, DOTEN-SAMA?
YOUR INCOMPETENCE FINALLY CAME IN HANDY.
WHY YOU...
HMPH. DON'T BE SO ARROGANT. A TRULY CAPABLE PERSON WOULD BE ABLE TO EFFECTIVELY USE SOMEONE INCOMPETENT.
YOU COULDN'T DO THAT, SO YOU'RE INCOMPETENT TOO.
THAT HURTS.
I GOT A LOT OF USE OUT OF THAT LOSER. YOU SHOULD BE IMPRESSED.
KATAK
!
ARGH...
YOU SURE DO TALK A LOT!
DONE PRETENDING?
...
FWIP

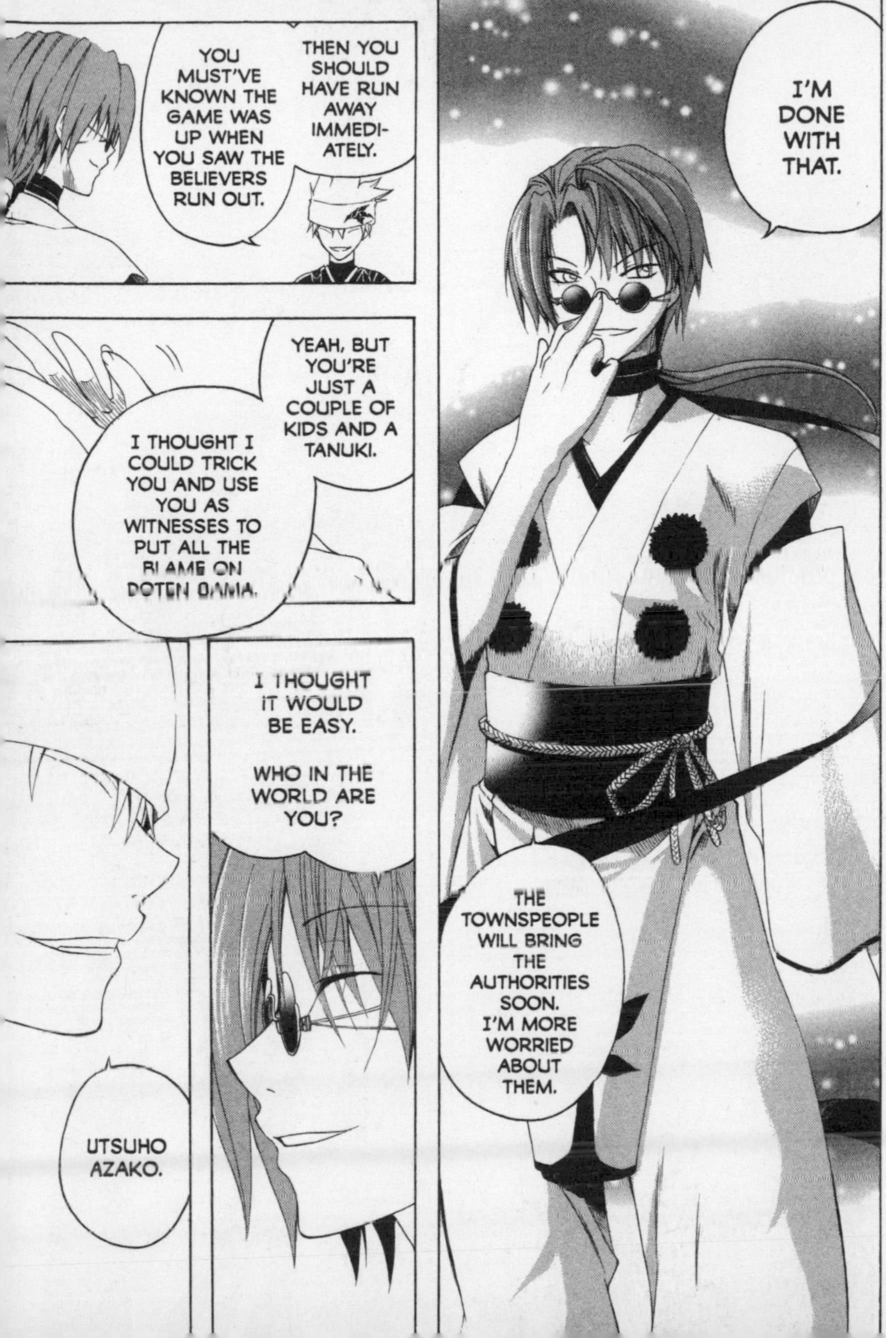
I'M DONE WITH THAT.
THE TOWNSPEOPLE WILL BRING THE AUTHORITIES SOON. I'M MORE WORRIED ABOUT THEM.
YOU MUST'VE KNOWN THE GAME WAS UP WHEN YOU SAW THE BELIEVERS RUN OUT.
THEN YOU SHOULD HAVE RUN AWAY IMMEDI-ATELY.
YEAH, BUT YOU'RE JUST A COUPLE OF KIDS AND A TANUKI.
I THOUGHT I COULD TRICK YOU AND USE YOU AS WITNESSES TO PUT ALL THE BLAME ON DOTEN DAMA.
I THOUGHT IT WOULD BE EASY.
WHO IN THE WORLD ARE YOU?
UTSUHO AZAKO.

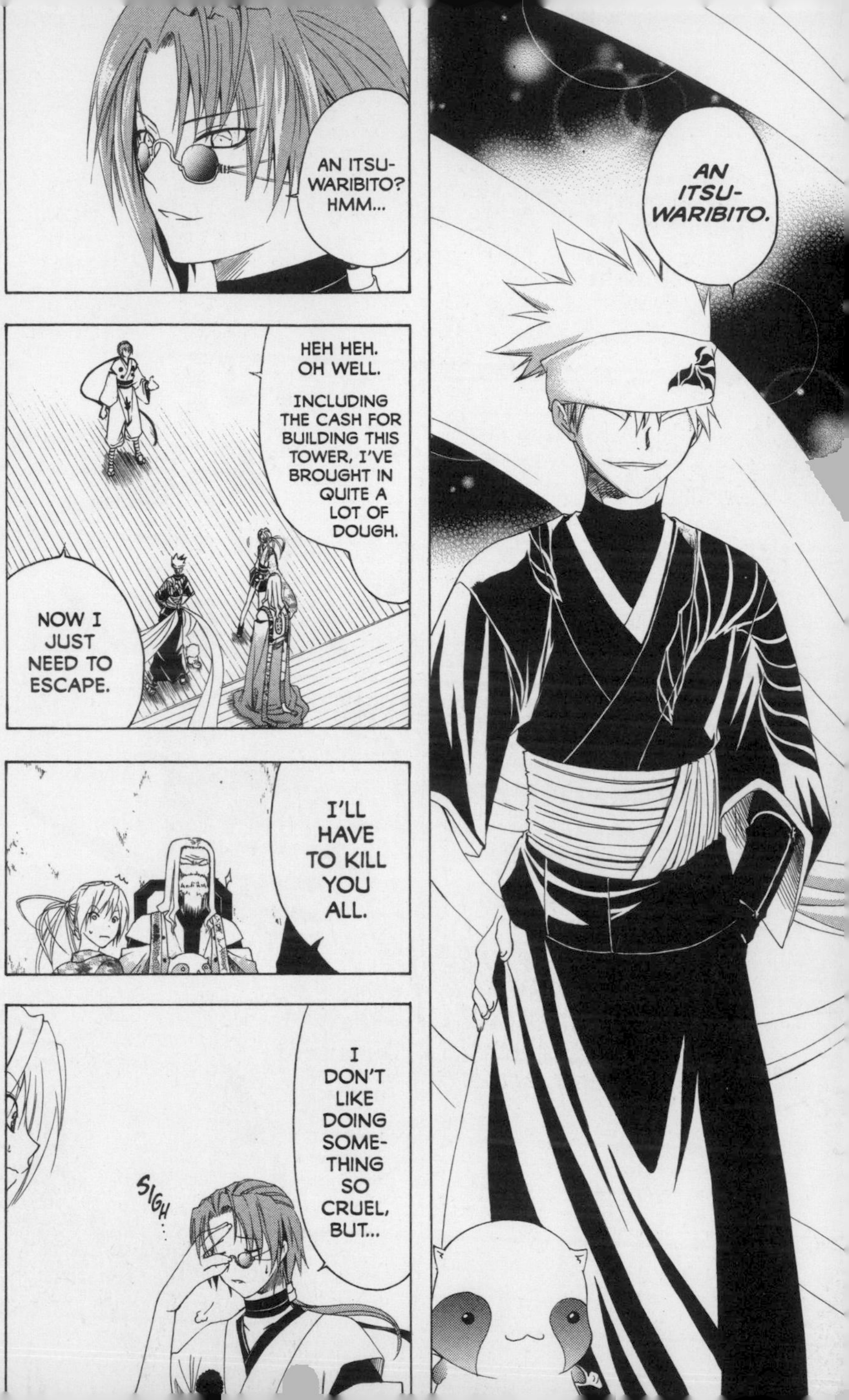
AN ITSU-WARIBITO.
AN ITSU-WARIBITO? HMM...
HEH HEH. OH WELL.
INCLUDING THE CASH FOR BUILDING THIS TOWER, I'VE BROUGHT IN QUITE A LOT OF DOUGH.
NOW I JUST NEED TO ESCAPE.
I'LL HAVE TO KILL YOU ALL.
I DON'T LIKE DOING SOME-THING SO CRUEL, BUT...
SIGH...

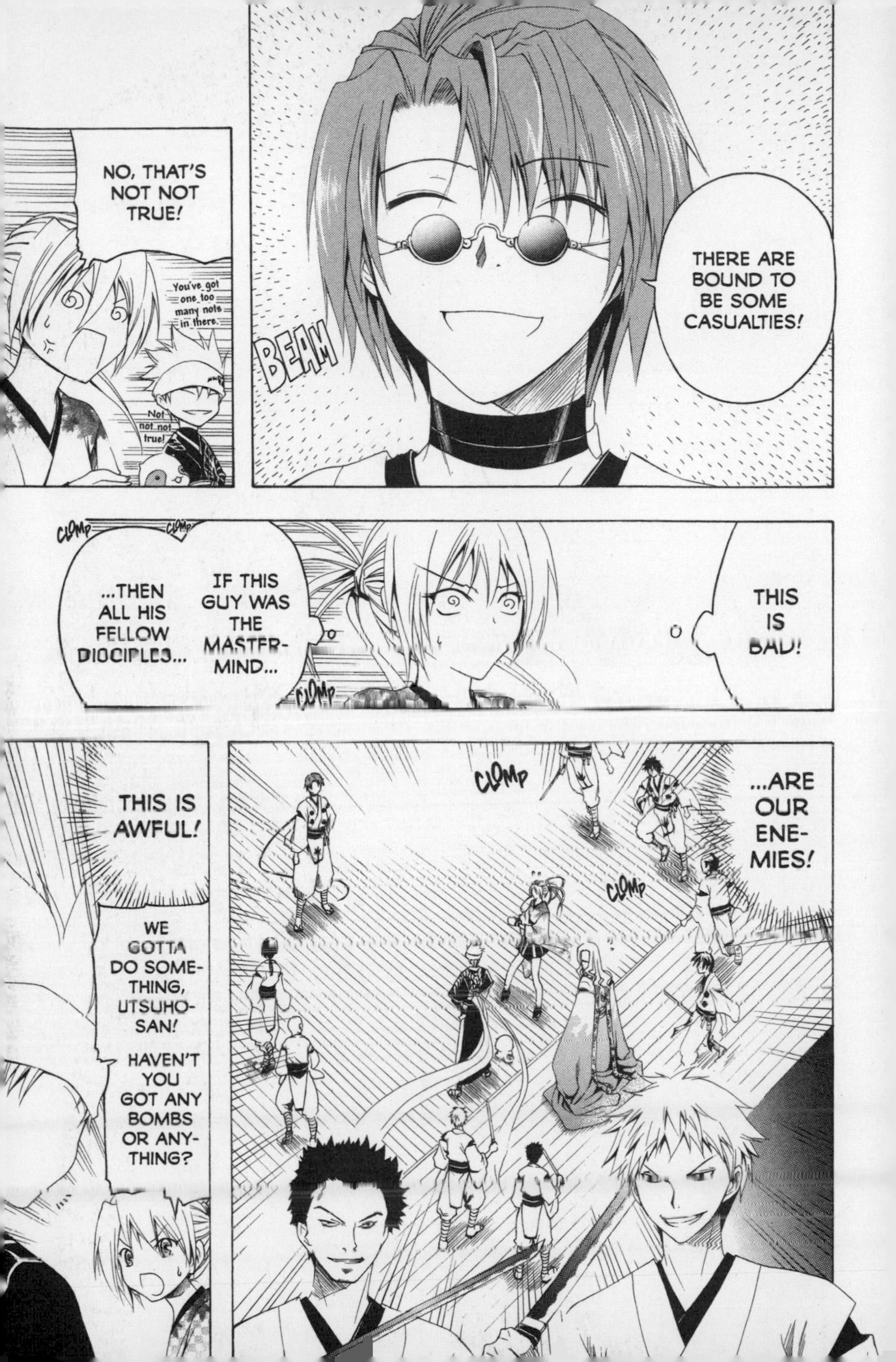
BEAM
THERE ARE BOUND TO BE SOME CASUALTIES!
NO, THAT'S NOT NOT TRUE!
You've got one too many nots in there.
Not not not true!
THIS IS BAD!
IF THIS GUY WAS THE MASTER-MIND...
...THEN ALL HIS FELLOW DISCIPLES...
CLOMP
CLOMP
CLOMP
...ARE OUR ENE-MIES!
CLOMP
CLOMP
THIS IS AWFUL!
WE GOTTA DO SOME-THING, UTSUHO-SAN!
HAVEN'T YOU GOT ANY BOMBS OR ANY-THING?

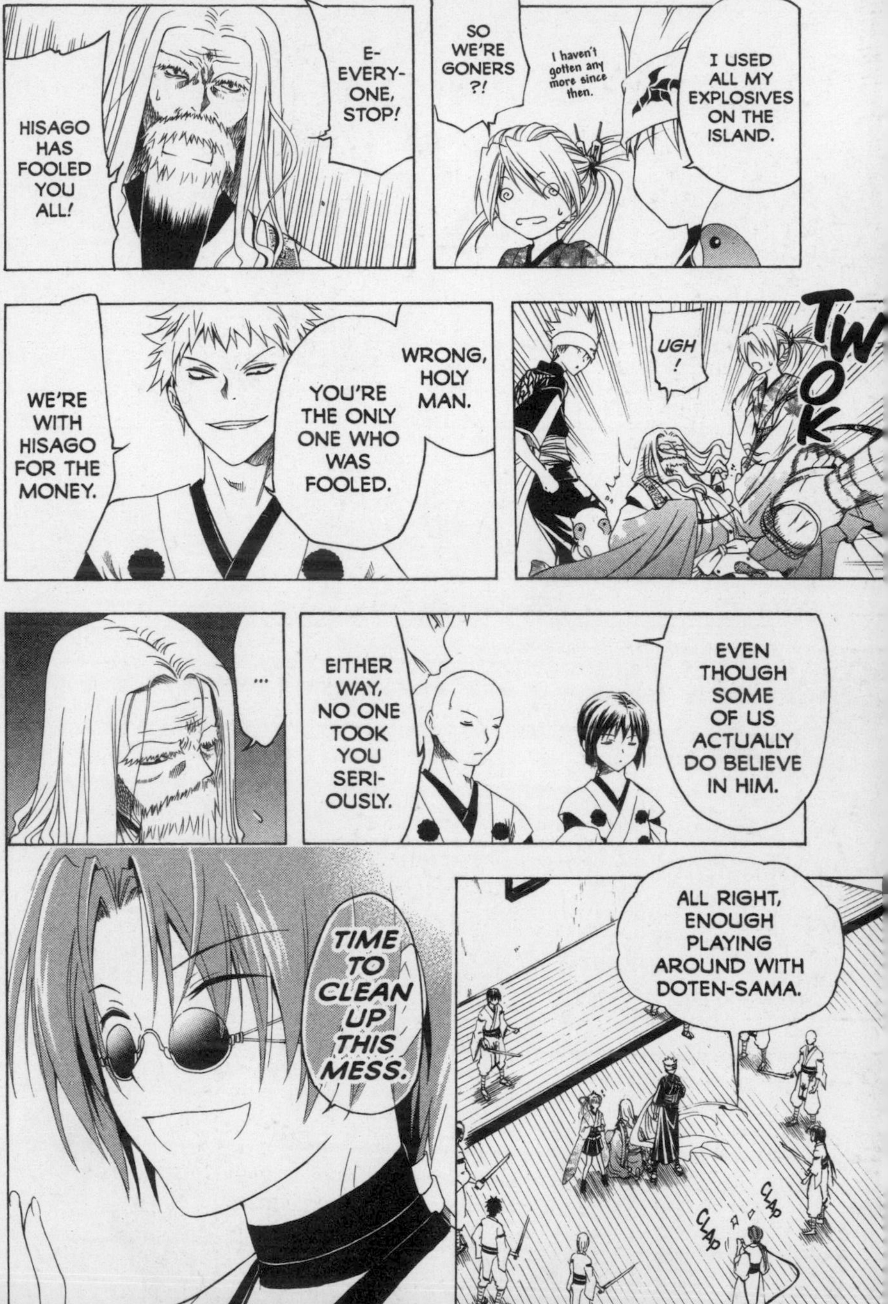
I USED ALL MY EXPLOSIVES ON THE ISLAND.
I haven't gotten any more since then.
SO WE'RE GONERS?!
E- EVERY-ONE, STOP!
HISAGO HAS FOOLED YOU ALL!
TWOK
UGH!
WRONG, HOLY MAN.
YOU'RE THE ONLY ONE WHO WAS FOOLED.
WE'RE WITH HISAGO FOR THE MONEY.
EVEN THOUGH SOME OF US ACTUALLY DO BELIEVE IN HIM.
EITHER WAY, NO ONE TOOK YOU SERI-OUSLY.
...
ALL RIGHT, ENOUGH PLAYING AROUND WITH DOTEN-SAMA.
CLAP
CLAP
TIME TO CLEAN UP THIS MESS.

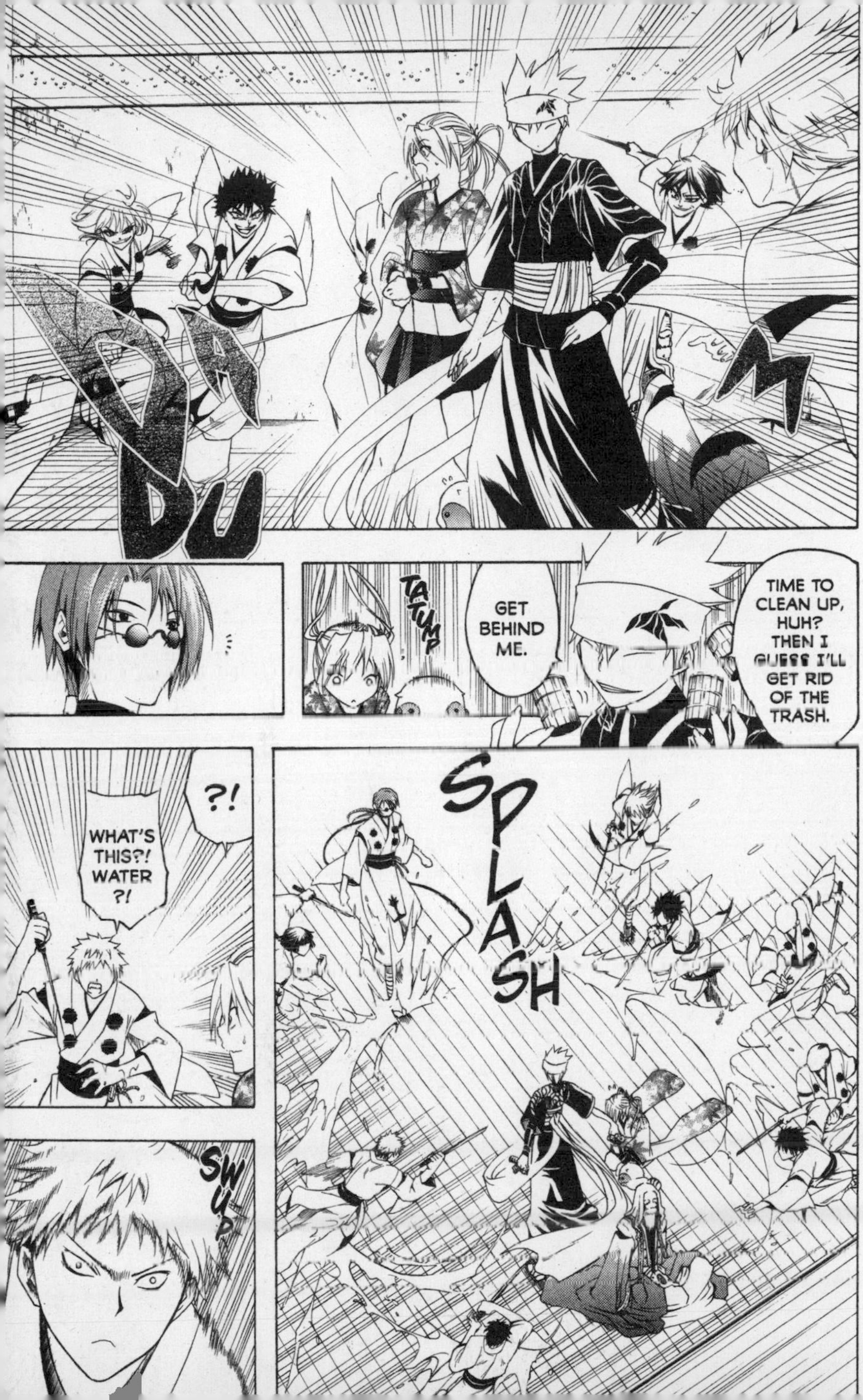
M
DA
DU
TIME TO CLEAN UP, HUH? THEN I GUESS I'LL GET RID OF THE TRASH.
GET BEHIND ME.
TATUMP
SPLASH
?!
WHAT'S THIS?! WATER ?!
SWUP

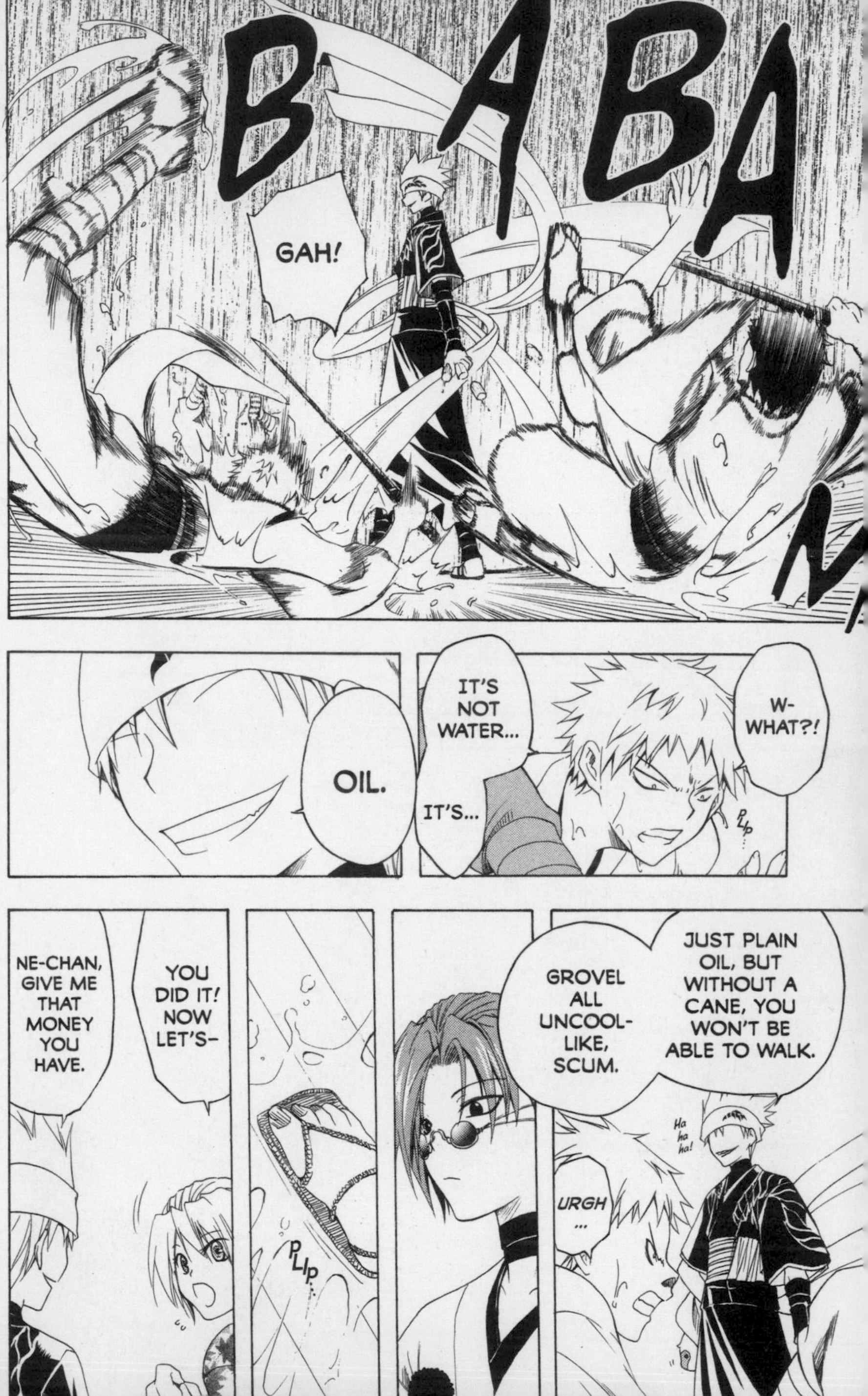
BABAM
GAH!
W-WHAT?!
PLIP...
IT'S NOT WATER...
IT'S...
OIL.
JUST PLAIN OIL, BUT WITHOUT A CANE, YOU WON'T BE ABLE TO WALK.
Ha ha ha!
GROVEL ALL UNCOOL-LIKE, SCUM.
URGH...
PLIP...
YOU DID IT! NOW LET'S-
NE-CHAN, GIVE ME THAT MONEY YOU HAVE.

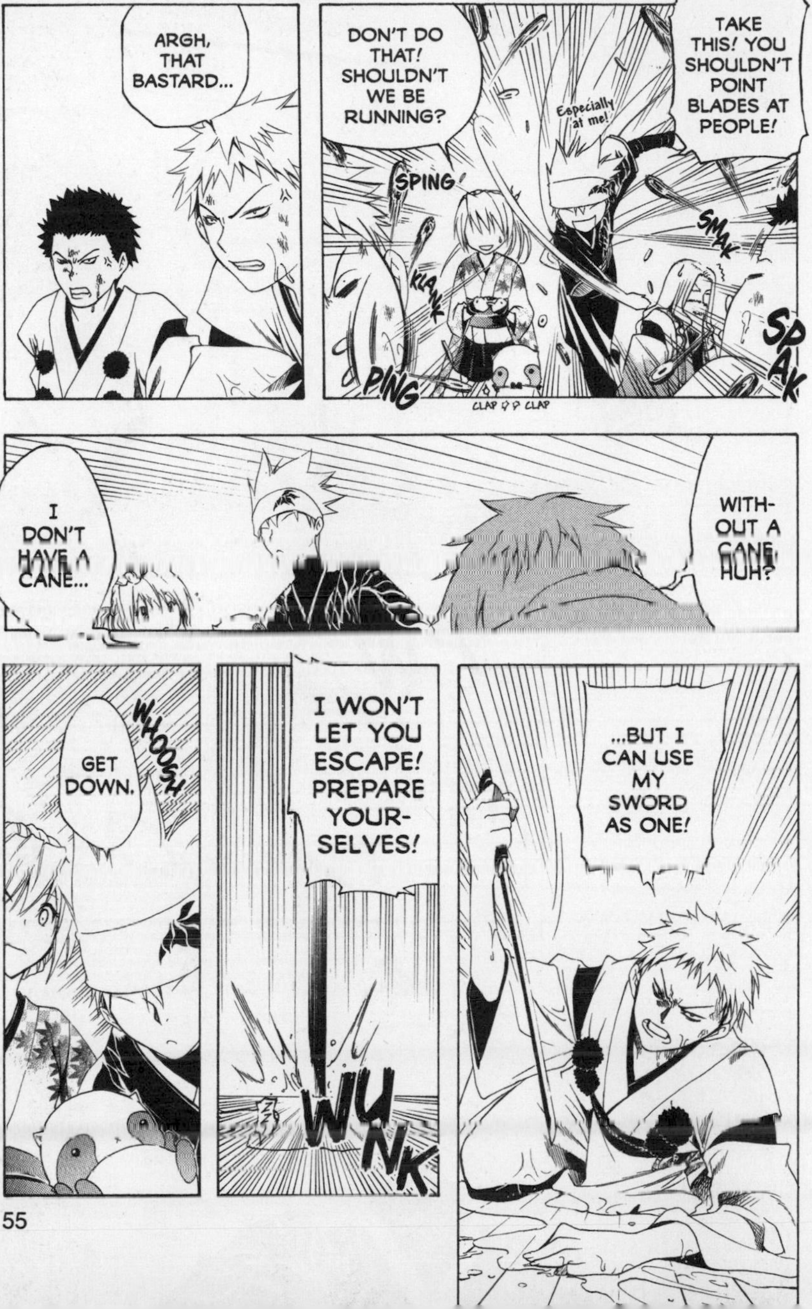
TAKE THIS! YOU SHOULDN'T POINT BLADES AT PEOPLE!
Especially at me!
DON'T DO THAT! SHOULDN'T WE BE RUNNING?
SPING
SMAK
KLANK
SPAK
PING
CLAP CLAP
ARGH, THAT BASTARD...
WITH-OUT A CANE, HUH?
I DON'T HAVE A CANE...
...BUT I CAN USE MY SWORD AS ONE!
I WON'T LET YOU ESCAPE! PREPARE YOUR-SELVES!
WUNK
WHOOSH
GET DOWN.

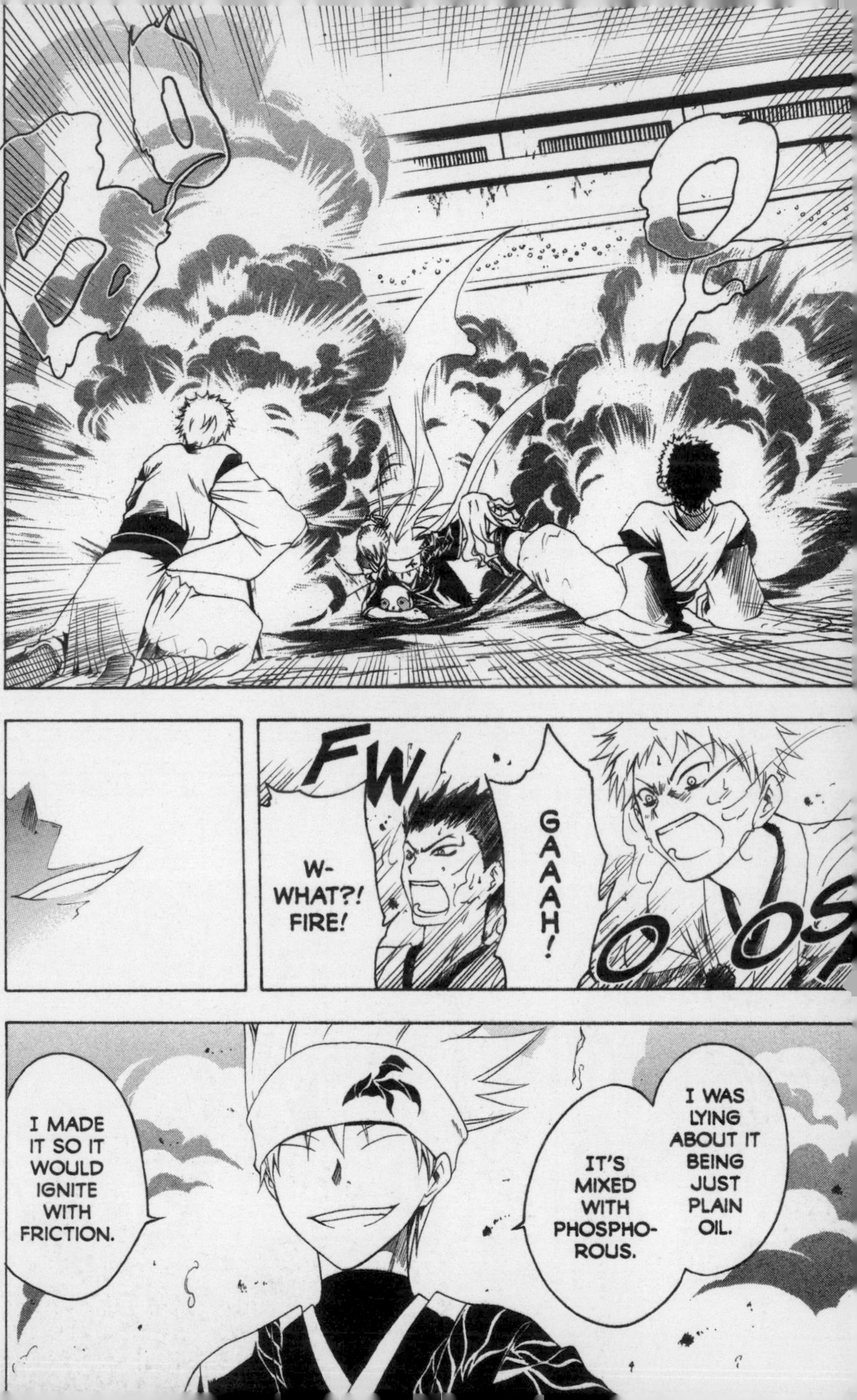
FW
GAAAH!
W- WHAT?! FIRE!
I WAS LYING ABOUT IT BEING JUST PLAIN OIL.
IT'S MIXED WITH PHOSPHO-ROUS.
I MADE IT SO IT WOULD IGNITE WITH FRICTION.

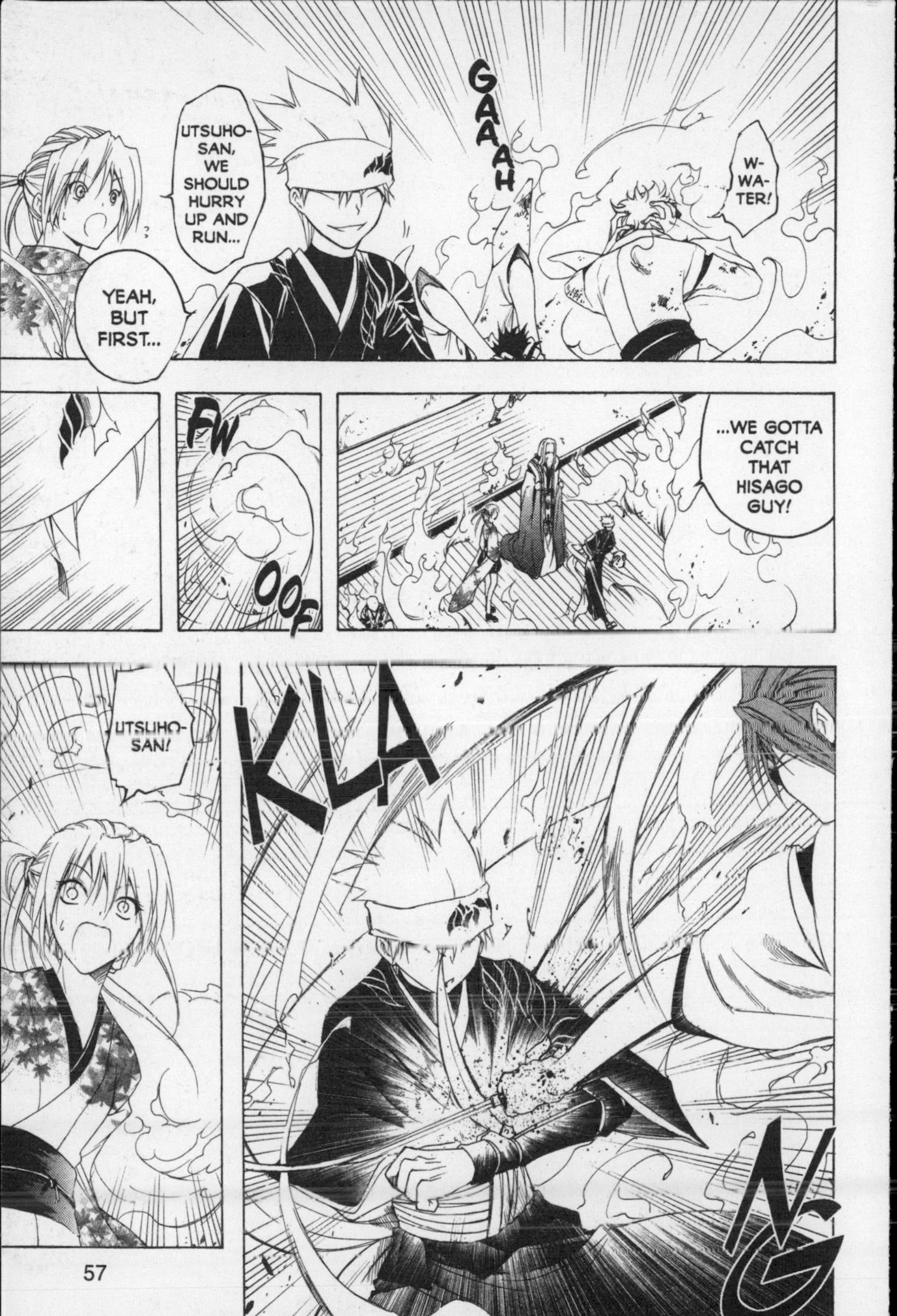
W-WA-TER!
GAAAH
UTSUHO-SAN, WE SHOULD HURRY UP AND RUN...
YEAH, BUT FIRST...
...WE GOTTA CATCH THAT HISAGO GUY!
FW
OOF
KLA
NG
UTSUHO-SAN!

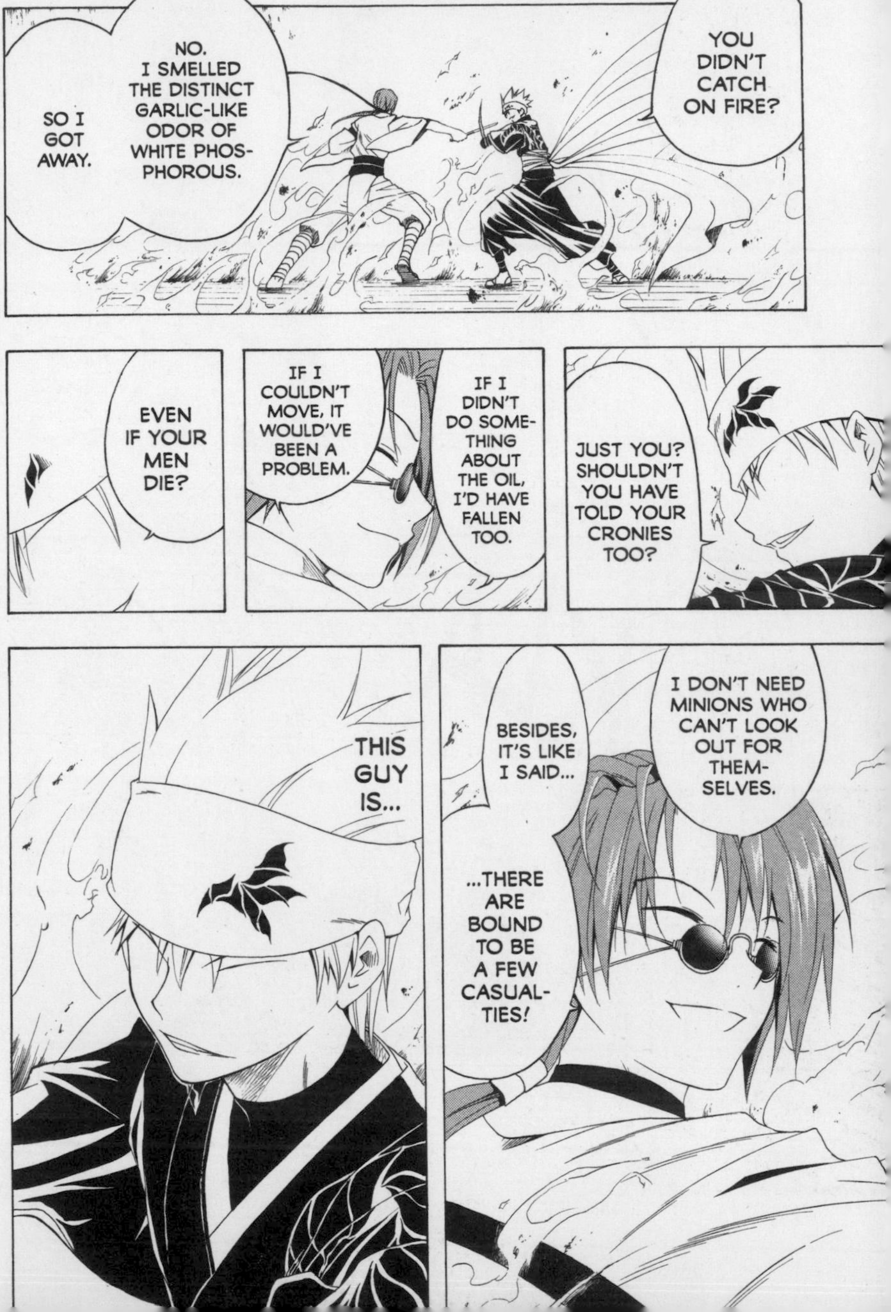
YOU DIDN'T CATCH ON FIRE?
NO. I SMELLED THE DISTINCT GARLIC-LIKE ODOR OF WHITE PHOS-PHOROUS.
SO I GOT AWAY.
JUST YOU? SHOULDN'T YOU HAVE TOLD YOUR CRONIES TOO?
IF I DIDN'T DO SOME-THING ABOUT THE OIL, I'D HAVE FALLEN TOO.
IF I COULDN'T MOVE, IT WOULD'VE BEEN A PROBLEM.
EVEN IF YOUR MEN DIE?
I DON'T NEED MINIONS WHO CAN'T LOOK OUT FOR THEM-SELVES.
BESIDES, IT'S LIKE I SAID...
...THERE ARE BOUND TO BE A FEW CASUAL-TIES!
THIS GUY IS...

Chapter 31 Feint

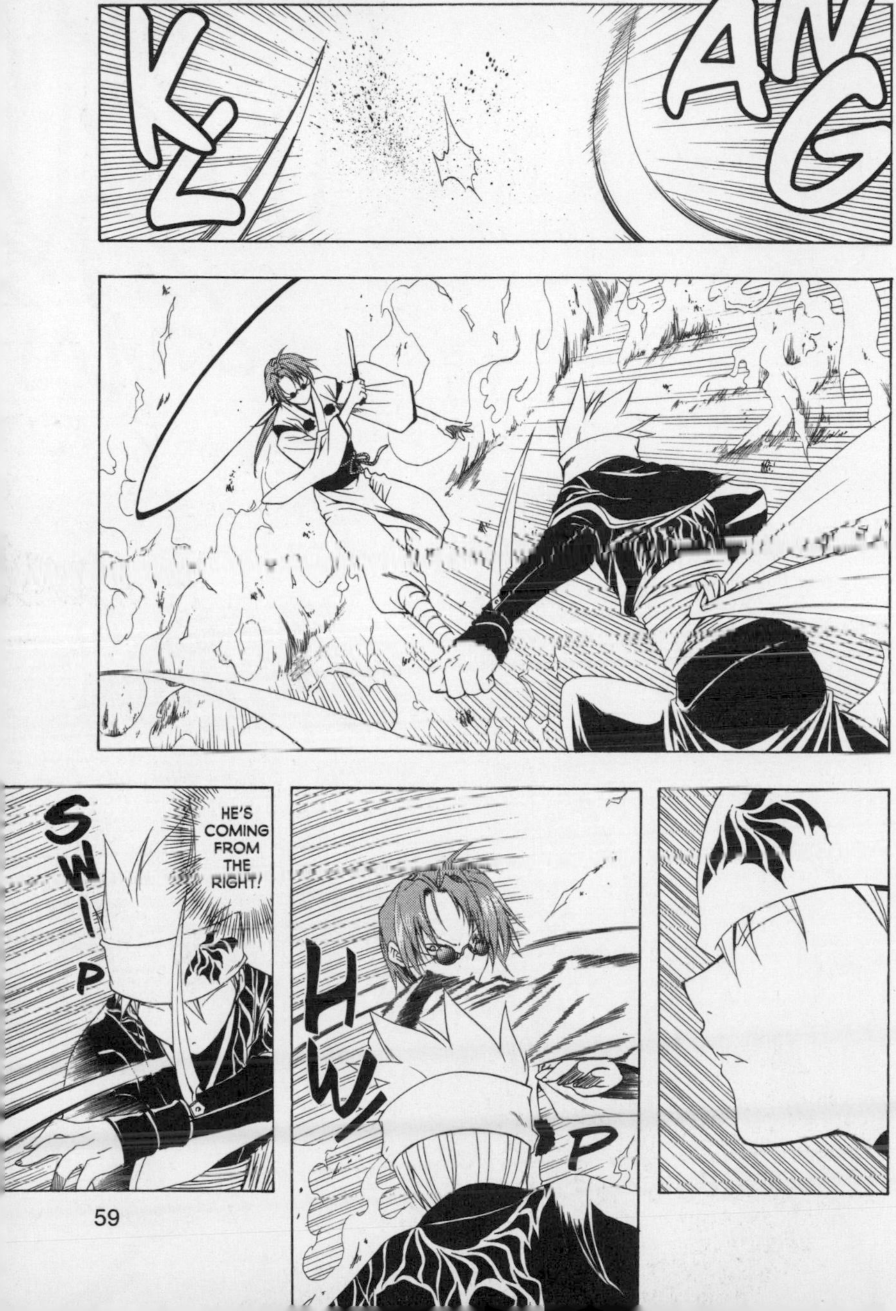
KLANG
HWIP
HE'S COMING FROM THE RIGHT!
SWIP

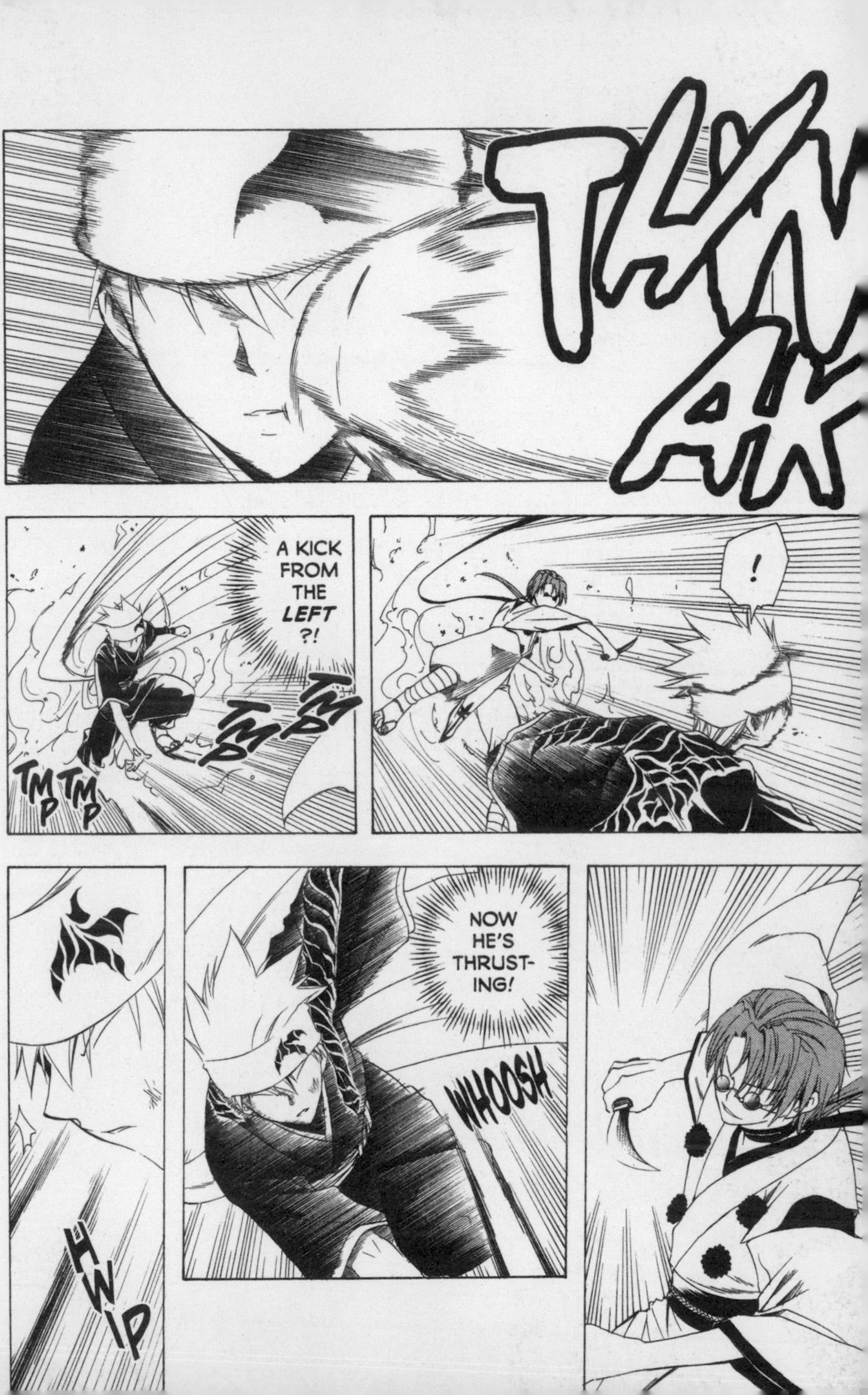
!
A KICK FROM THE LEFT ?!
TMP TMP
TMP TMP
NOW HE'S THRUST-ING!
WHOOSH
HWIP

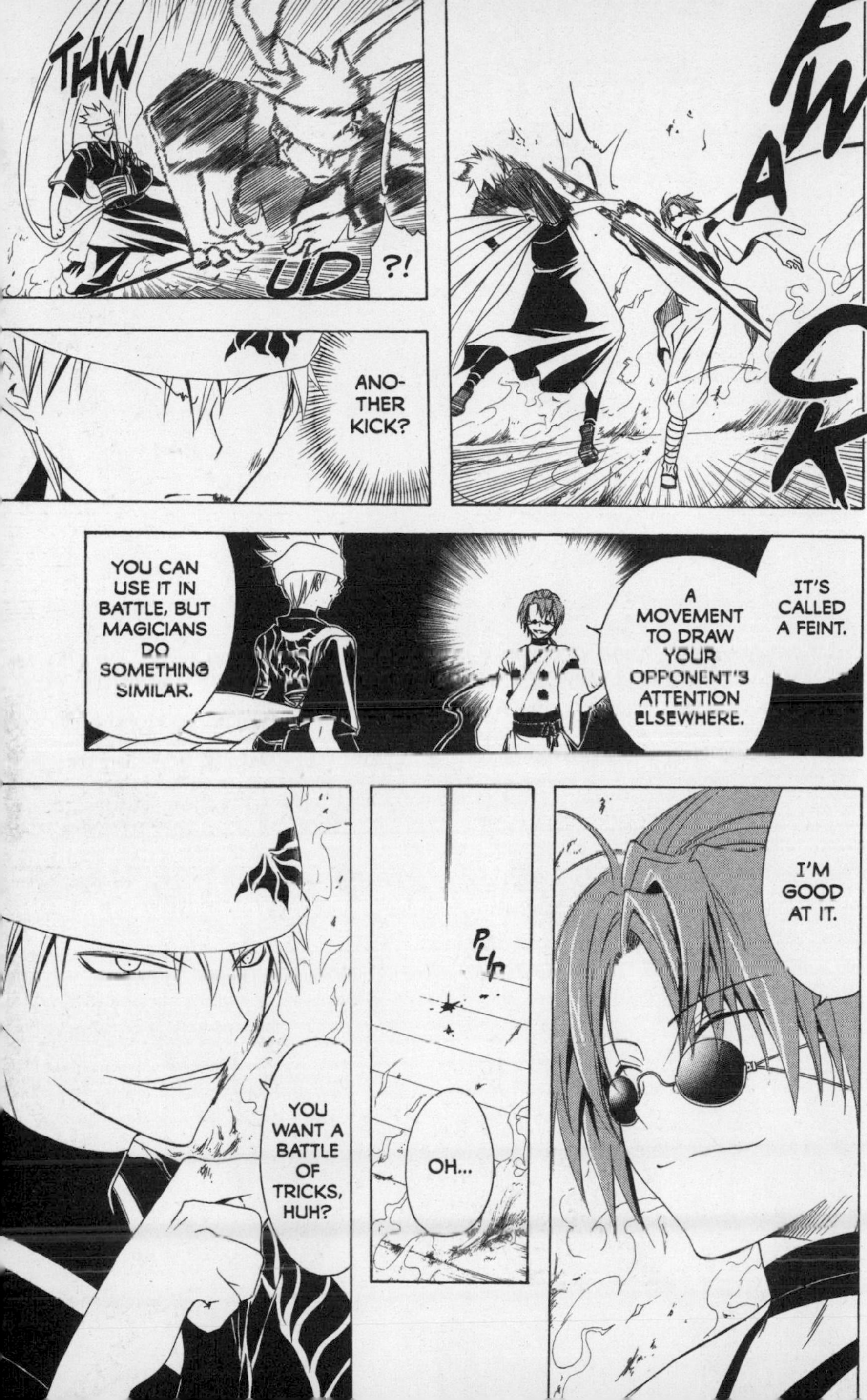
FWACK
THWUD
?!
ANOTHER KICK?
IT'S CALLED A FEINT.
A MOVEMENT TO DRAW YOUR OPPONENT'S ATTENTION ELSEWHERE.
YOU CAN USE IT IN BATTLE, BUT MAGICIANS DO SOMETHING SIMILAR.
I'M GOOD AT IT.
PLIP
OH...
YOU WANT A BATTLE OF TRICKS, HUH?

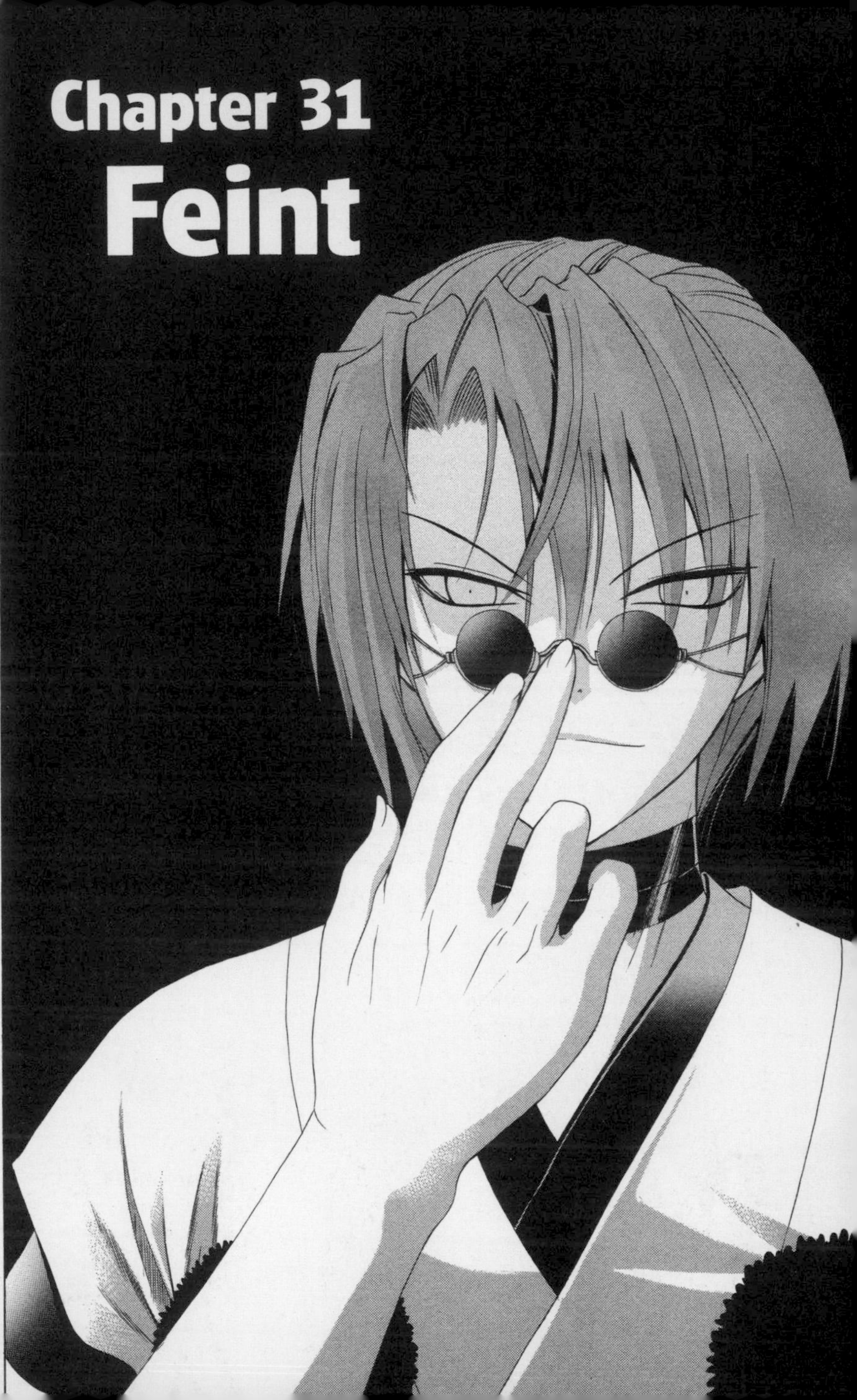
Chapter 31
Feint

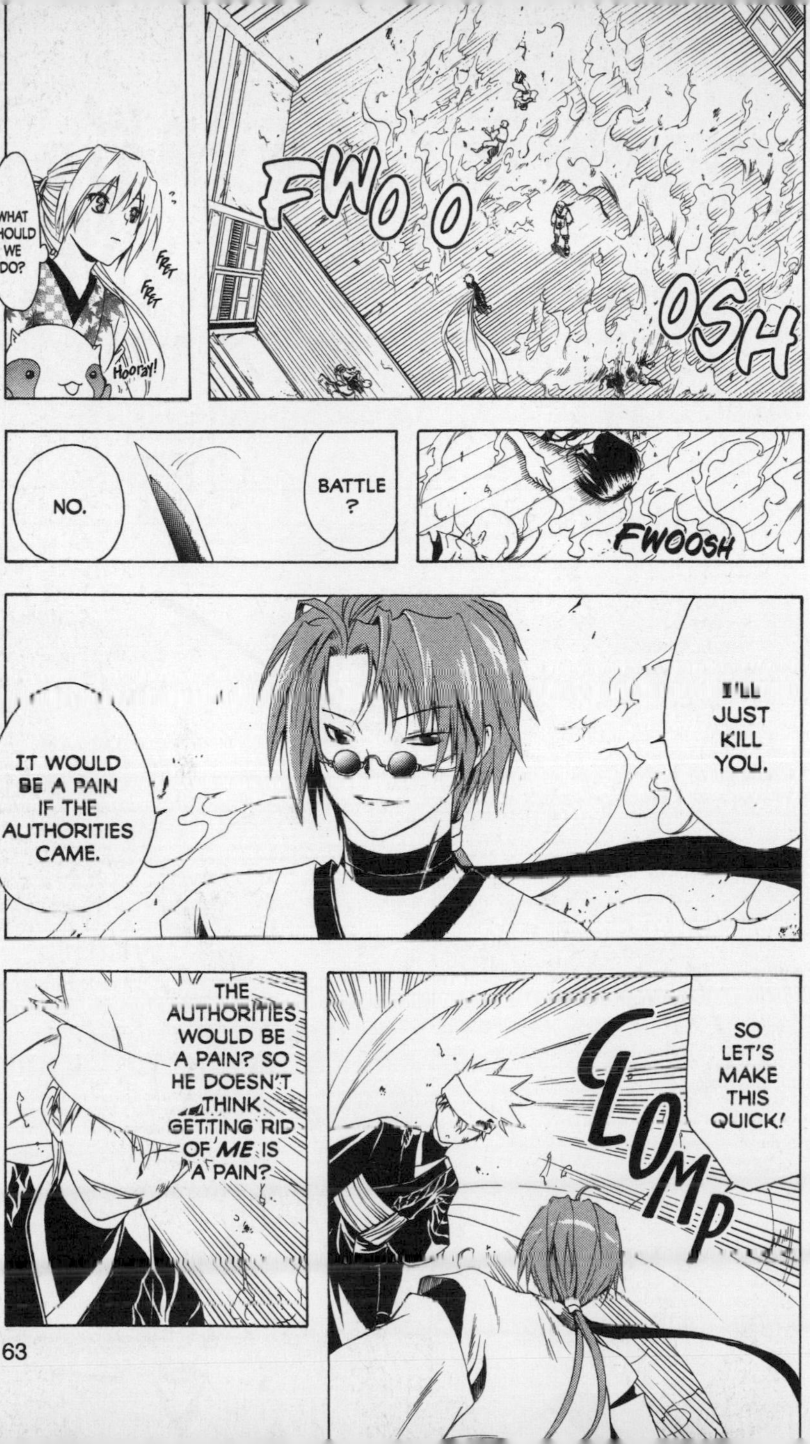
FWOO OSH
WHAT SHOULD WE DO?
FRET FRET
Hooray!
FWOOSH
BATTLE ?
NO.
I'LL JUST KILL YOU.
IT WOULD BE A PAIN IF THE AUTHORITIES CAME.
SO LET'S MAKE THIS QUICK!
CLOMP
THE AUTHORITIES WOULD BE A PAIN? SO HE DOESN'T THINK GETTING RID OF *ME* IS A PAIN?

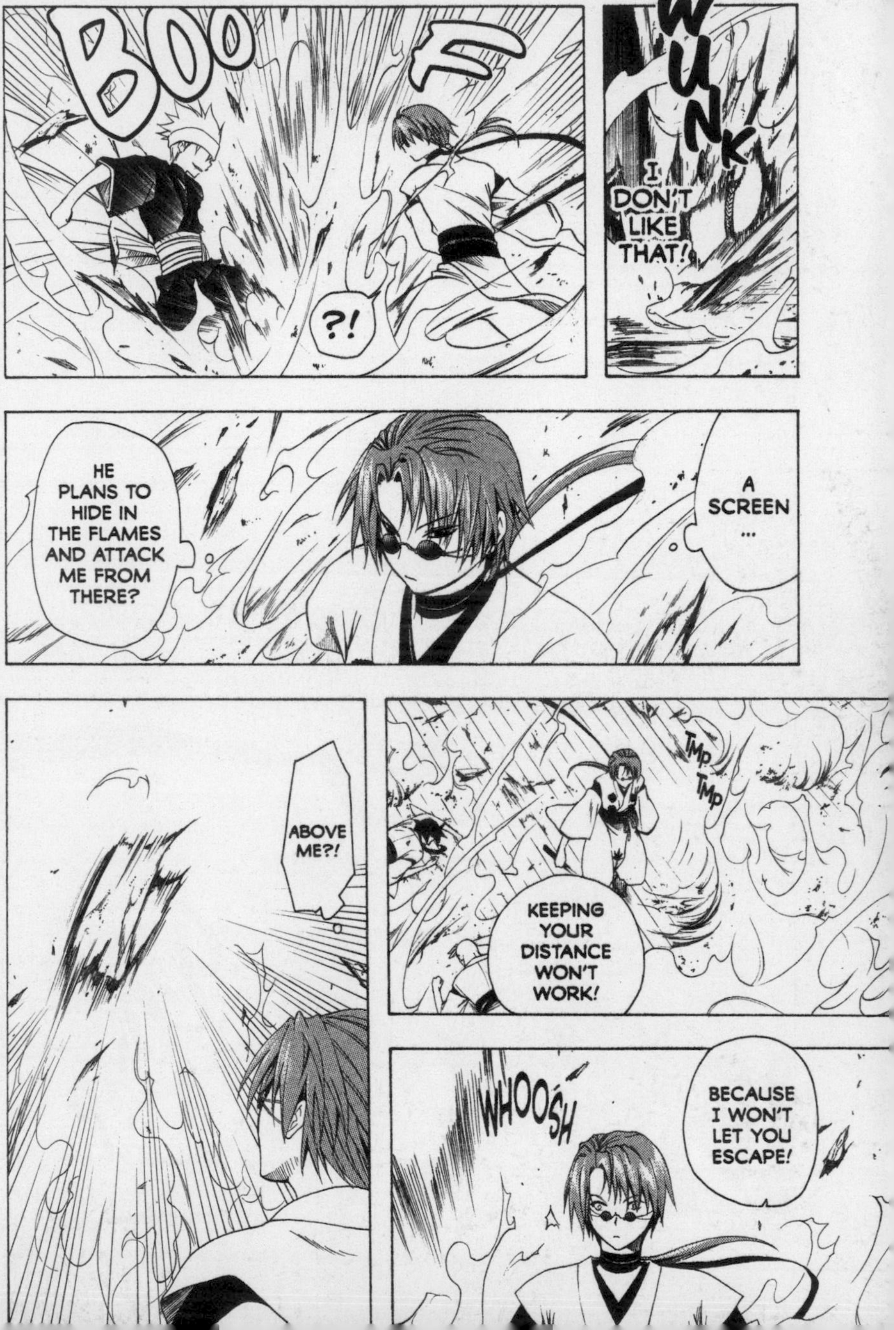
WUNK
I DON'T LIKE THAT!
BOOF
?!
A SCREEN ...
HE PLANS TO HIDE IN THE FLAMES AND ATTACK ME FROM THERE?
TMP TMP
KEEPING YOUR DISTANCE WON'T WORK!
WHOOSH
BECAUSE I WON'T LET YOU ESCAPE!
ABOVE ME?!

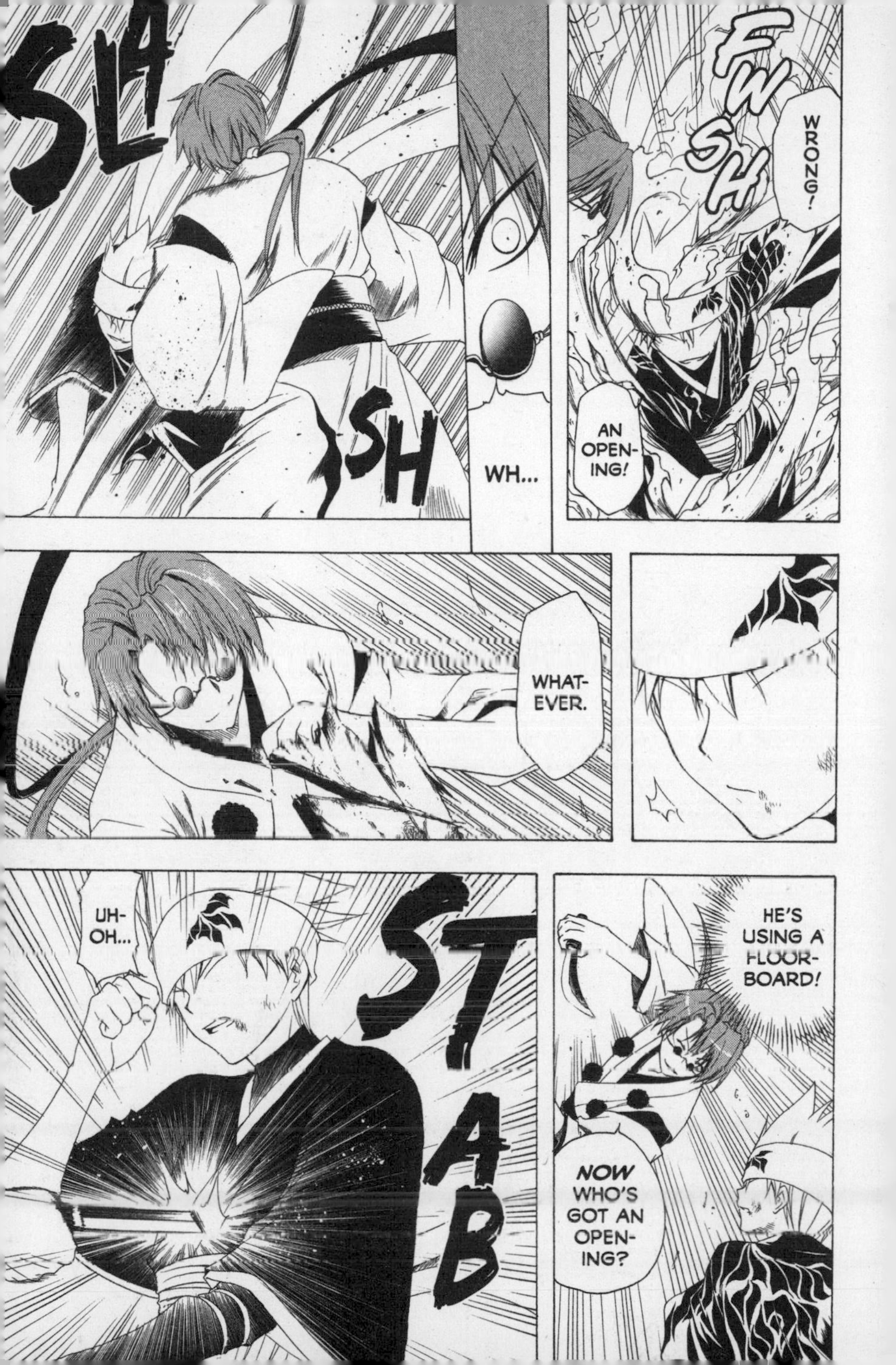
FWSH
WRONG!
AN OPENING!
WH...
SLASH
WHATEVER.
HE'S USING A FLOORBOARD!
NOW WHO'S GOT AN OPENING?
STAB
UH-OH...

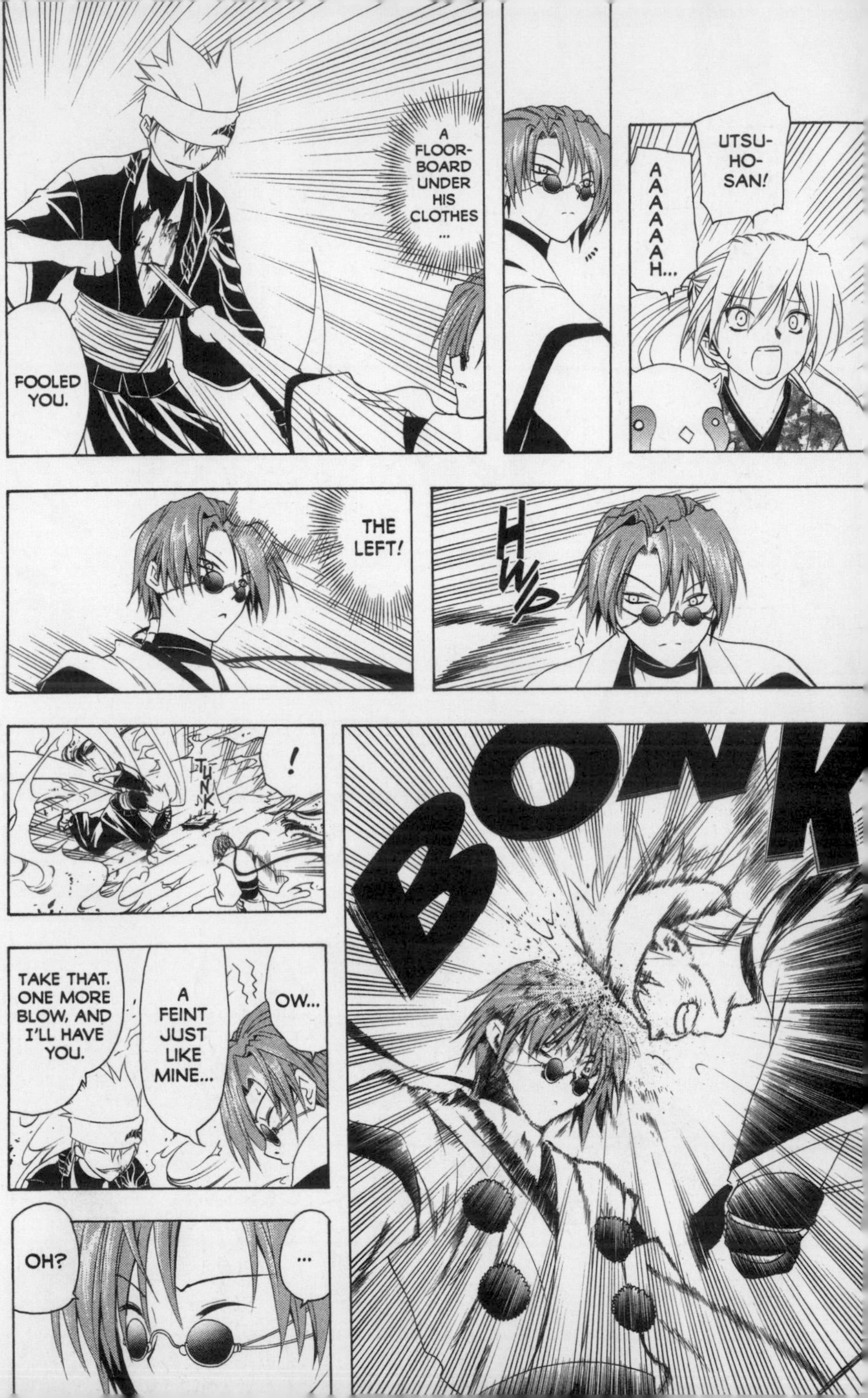
UTSU-HO-SAN!
AAAAAAH...
...
A FLOOR-BOARD UNDER HIS CLOTHES ...
FOOLED YOU.
HWIP
THE LEFT!
BONK
!
TUNK
OW...
A FEINT JUST LIKE MINE...
TAKE THAT. ONE MORE BLOW, AND I'LL HAVE YOU.
...
OH?

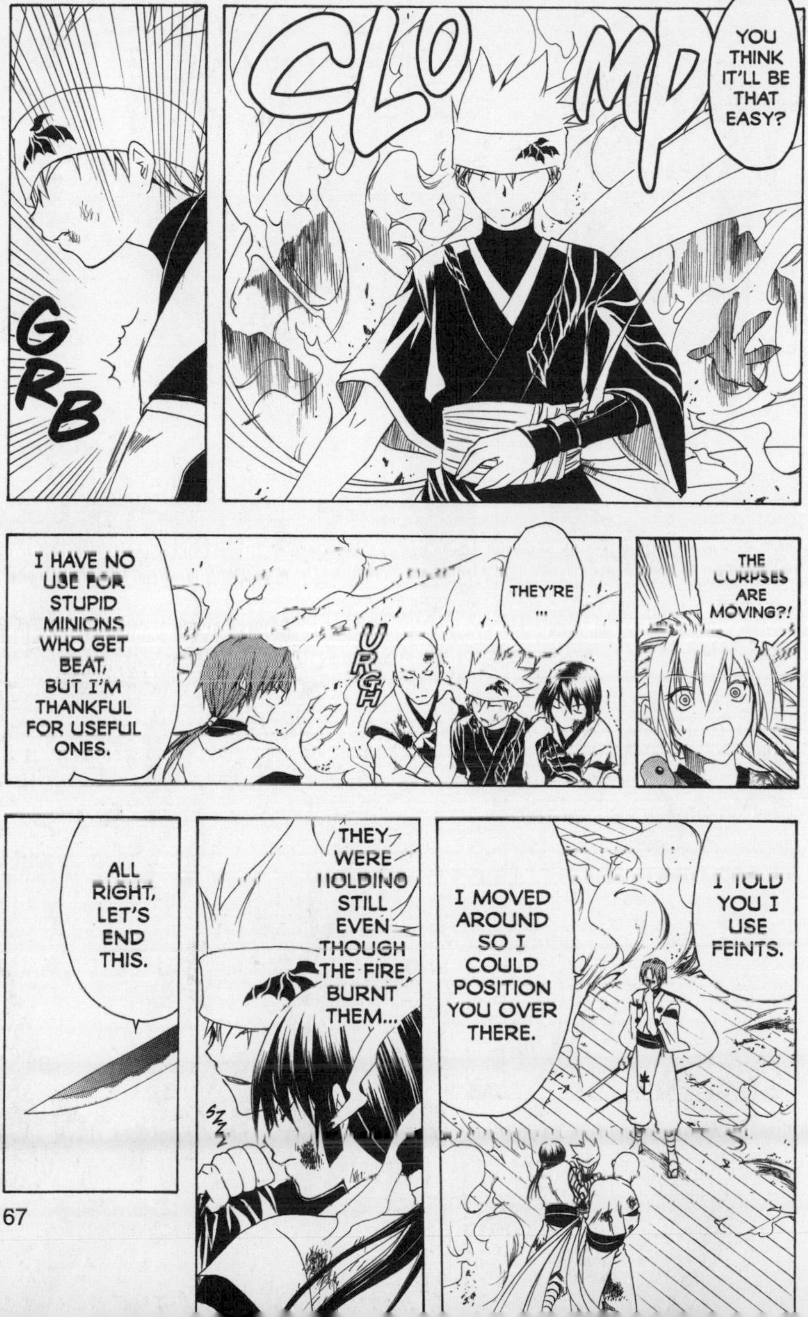
YOU THINK IT'LL BE THAT EASY?
CLOMP
GRB
THE CORPSES ARE MOVING?!
THEY'RE ...
URGH
I HAVE NO USE FOR STUPID MINIONS WHO GET BEAT, BUT I'M THANKFUL FOR USEFUL ONES.
I TOLD YOU I USE FEINTS.
I MOVED AROUND SO I COULD POSITION YOU OVER THERE.
THEY WERE HOLDING STILL EVEN THOUGH THE FIRE BURNT THEM...
SZZZ
ALL RIGHT, LET'S END THIS.

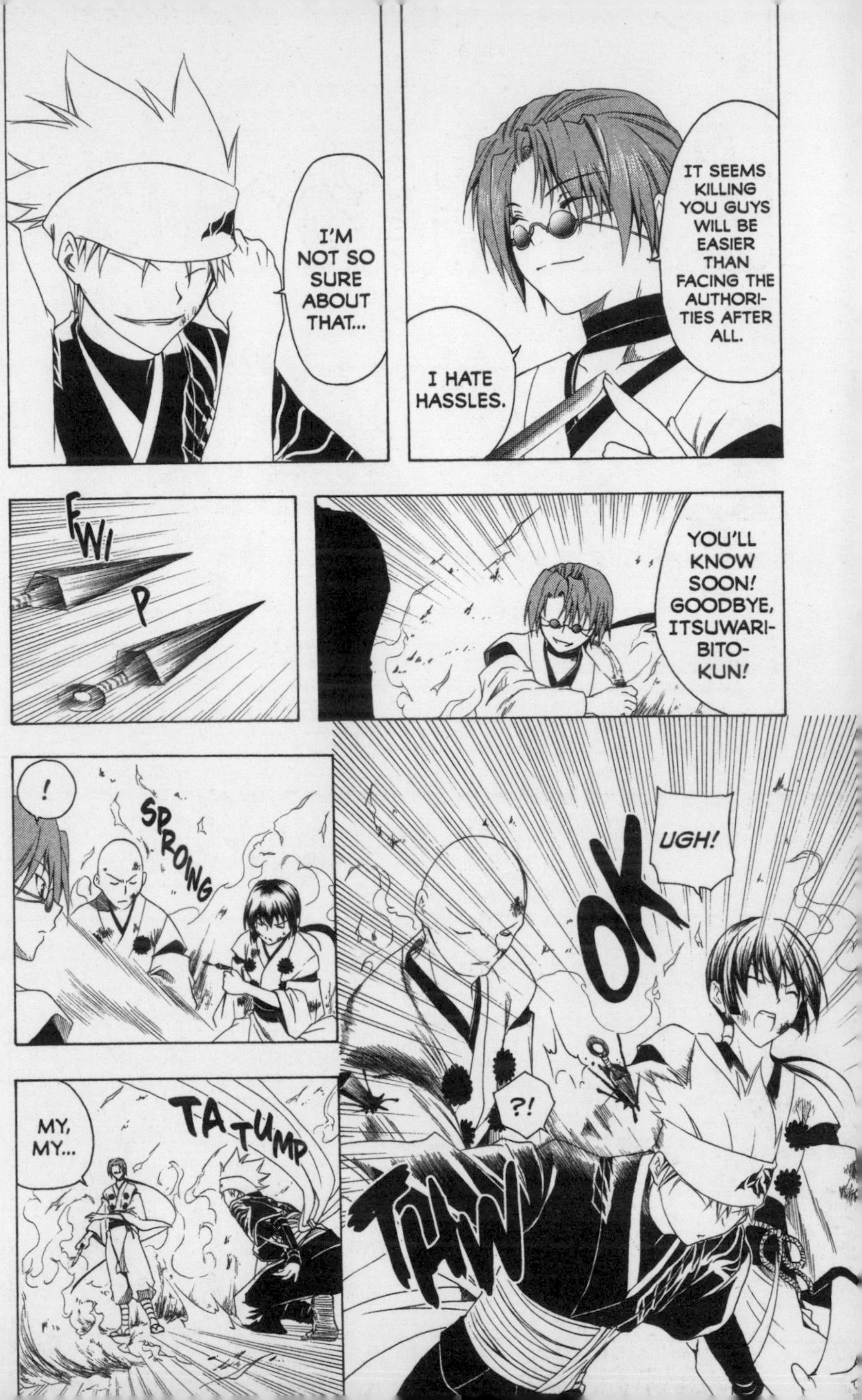
IT SEEMS KILLING YOU GUYS WILL BE EASIER THAN FACING THE AUTHORITIES AFTER ALL.
I HATE HASSLES.
I'M NOT SO SURE ABOUT THAT...
YOU'LL KNOW SOON! GOODBYE, ITSUWARIBITO-KUN!
FWIP
UGH!
THWOK
?!
!
SPROING
MY, MY...
TATUMP

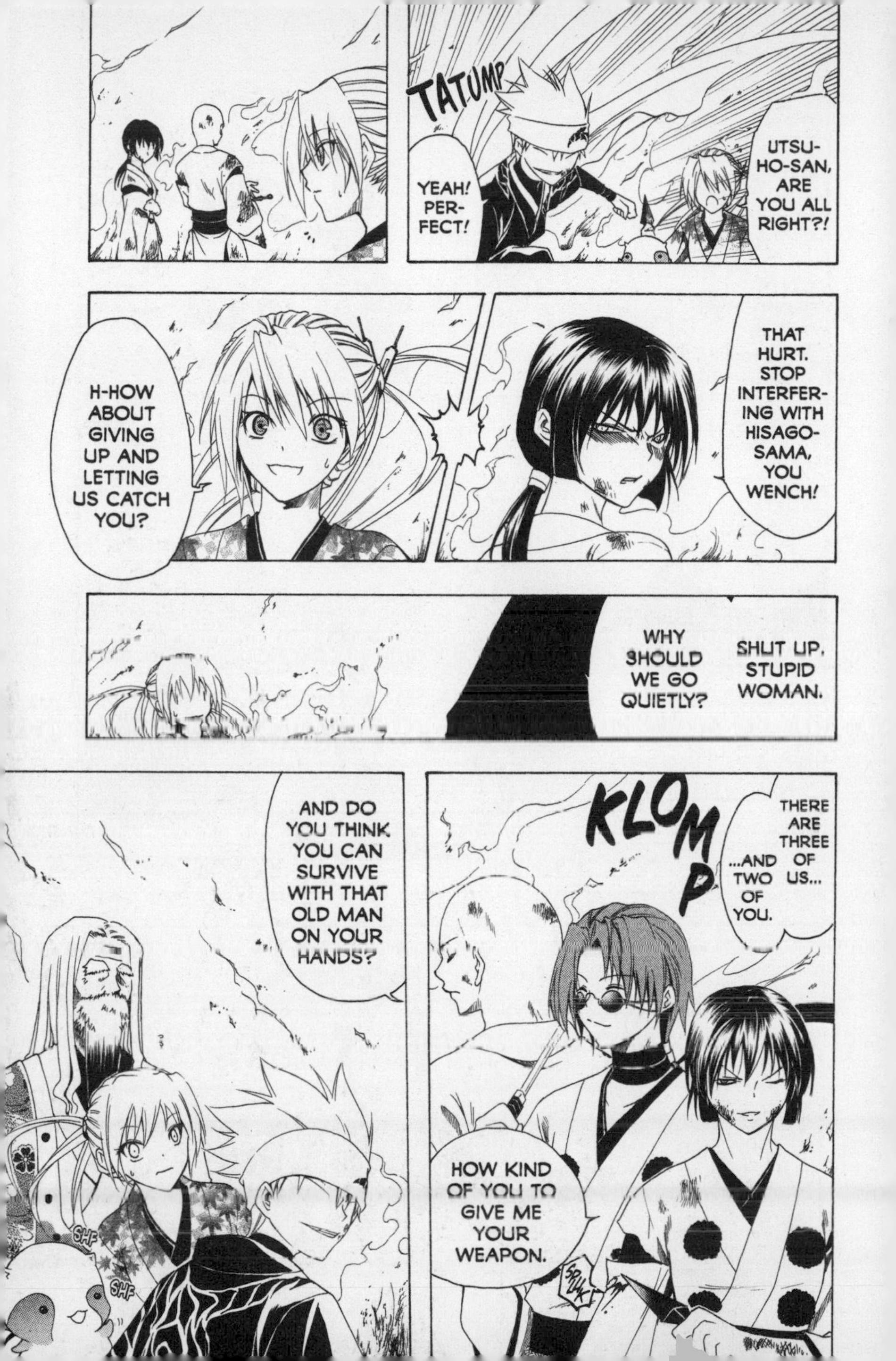
UTSU-HO-SAN, ARE YOU ALL RIGHT?!
TATUMP
YEAH! PER-FECT!
THAT HURT. STOP INTERFERING WITH HISAGO-SAMA, YOU WENCH!
H-HOW ABOUT GIVING UP AND LETTING US CATCH YOU?
SHUT UP, STUPID WOMAN.
WHY SHOULD WE GO QUIETLY?
THERE ARE THREE OF US...
...AND TWO OF YOU.
KLOMP
HOW KIND OF YOU TO GIVE ME YOUR WEAPON.
SPLUK
AND DO YOU THINK YOU CAN SURVIVE WITH THAT OLD MAN ON YOUR HANDS?
SHF
SHF

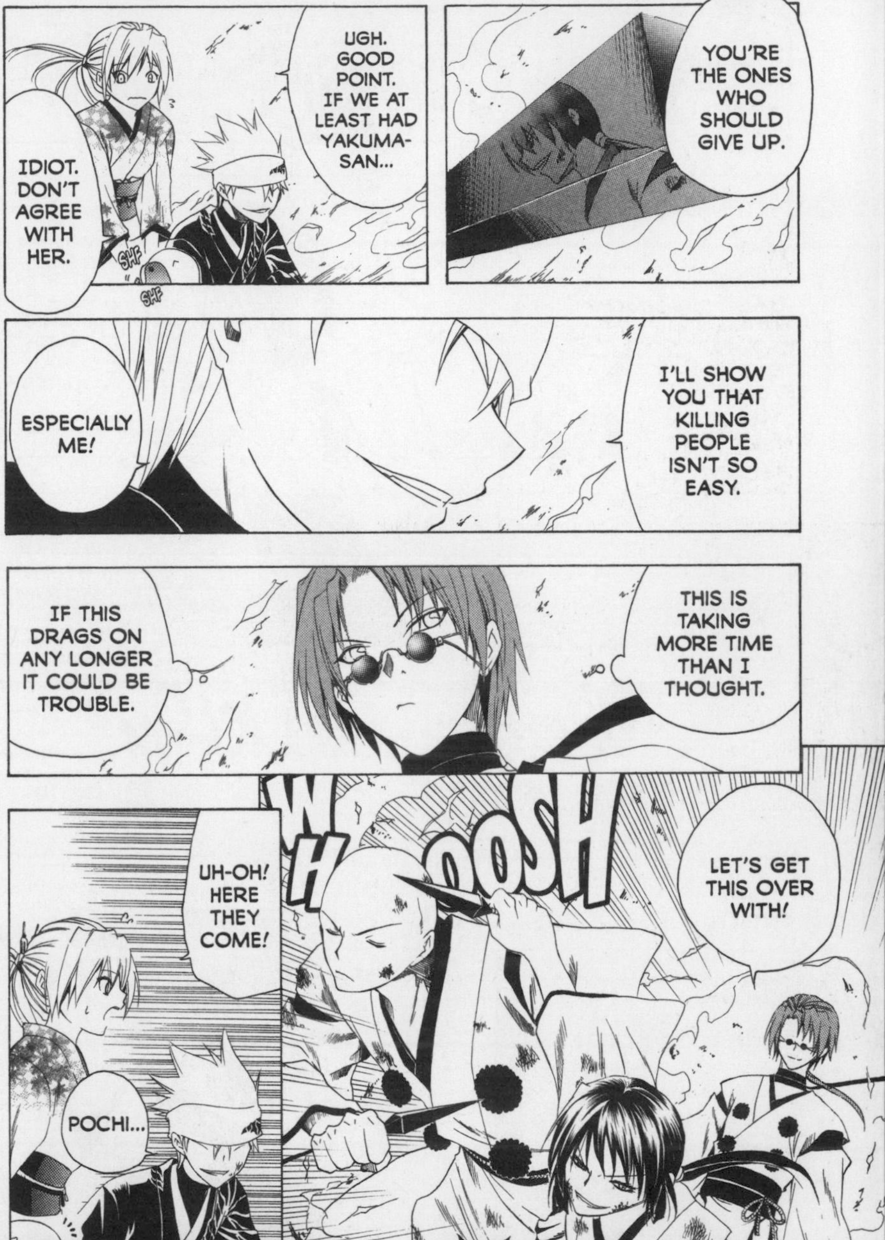
YOU'RE THE ONES WHO SHOULD GIVE UP.
UGH. GOOD POINT. IF WE AT LEAST HAD YAKUMA-SAN...
IDIOT. DON'T AGREE WITH HER.
SHF
SHF
I'LL SHOW YOU THAT KILLING PEOPLE ISN'T SO EASY.
ESPECIALLY ME!
THIS IS TAKING MORE TIME THAN I THOUGHT.
IF THIS DRAGS ON ANY LONGER IT COULD BE TROUBLE.
LET'S GET THIS OVER WITH!
WHOOSH
UH-OH! HERE THEY COME!
POCHI...

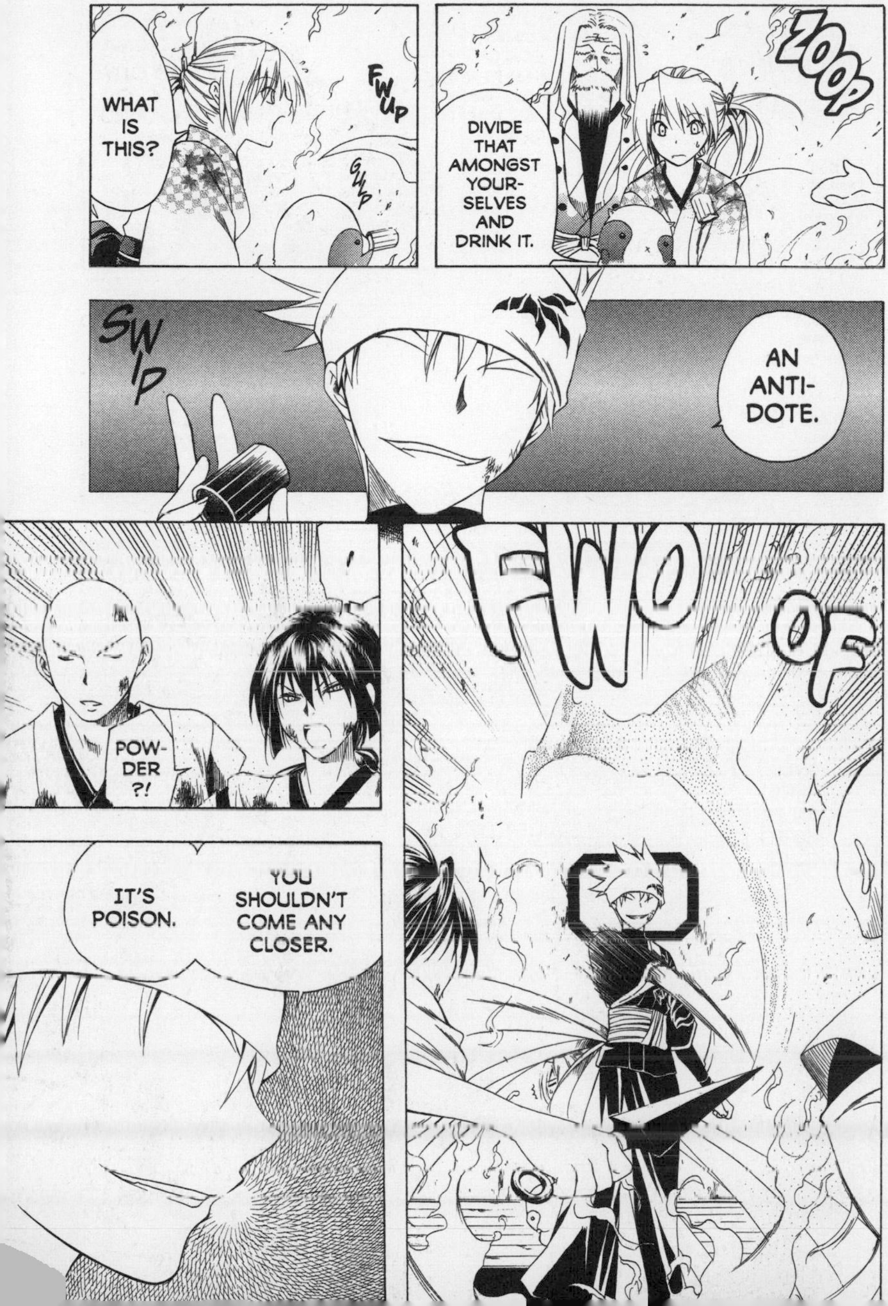
ZOOP
DIVIDE THAT AMONGST YOUR-SELVES AND DRINK IT.
WHAT IS THIS?
FWUP
GULP
AN ANTI-DOTE.
SWIP
FWOOF
POW-DER ?!
YOU SHOULDN'T COME ANY CLOSER.
IT'S POISON.

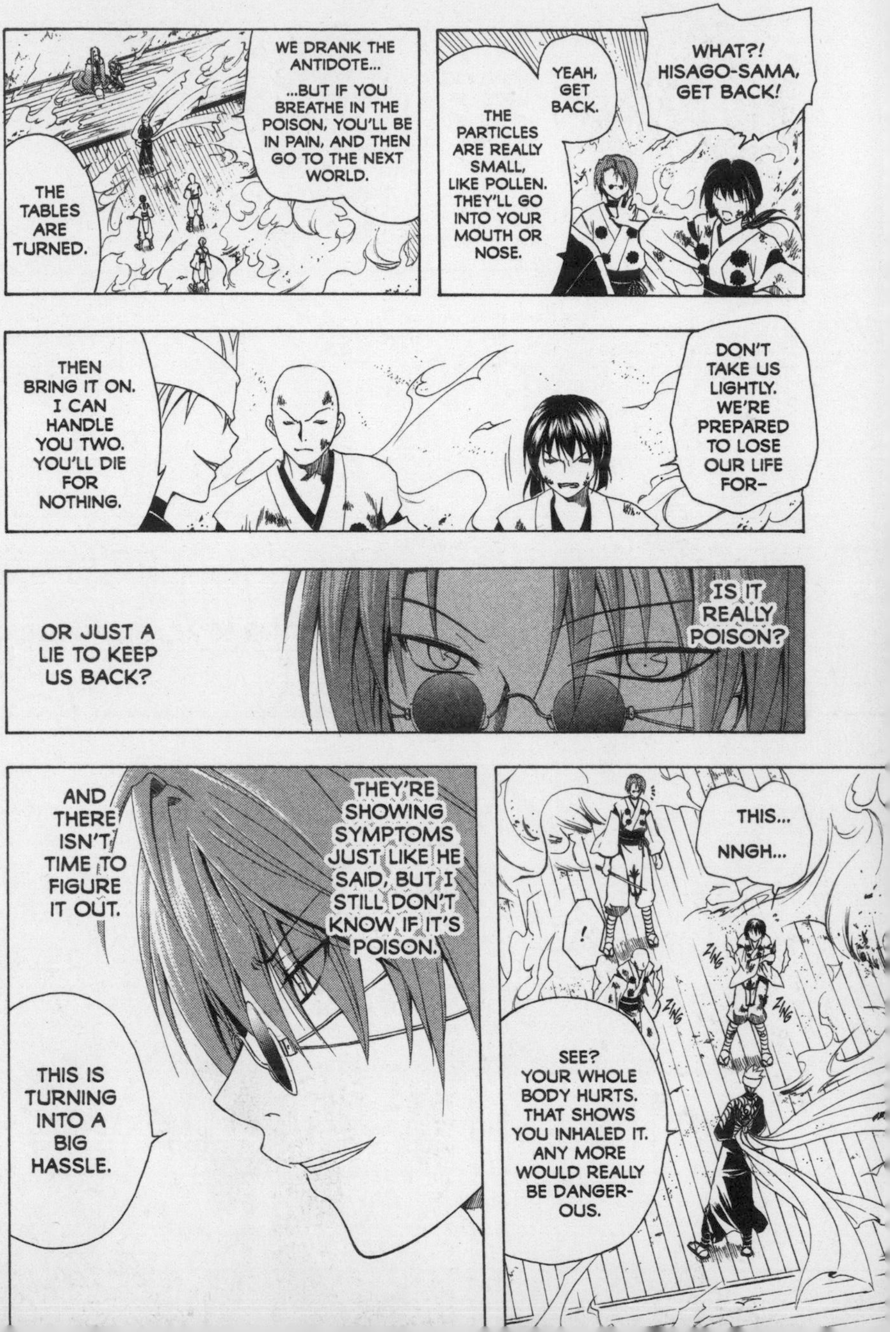
WHAT?! HISAGO-SAMA, GET BACK!
YEAH, GET BACK.
THE PARTICLES ARE REALLY SMALL, LIKE POLLEN. THEY'LL GO INTO YOUR MOUTH OR NOSE.
WE DRANK THE ANTIDOTE...
...BUT IF YOU BREATHE IN THE POISON, YOU'LL BE IN PAIN, AND THEN GO TO THE NEXT WORLD.
THE TABLES ARE TURNED.
DON'T TAKE US LIGHTLY. WE'RE PREPARED TO LOSE OUR LIFE FOR–
THEN BRING IT ON. I CAN HANDLE YOU TWO. YOU'LL DIE FOR NOTHING.
IS IT REALLY POISON?
OR JUST A LIE TO KEEP US BACK?
THIS...
NNGH...
!
ZING
ZING
ZING
SEE? YOUR WHOLE BODY HURTS. THAT SHOWS YOU INHALED IT. ANY MORE WOULD REALLY BE DANGER-OUS.
THEY'RE SHOWING SYMPTOMS JUST LIKE HE SAID, BUT I STILL DON'T KNOW IF IT'S POISON.
AND THERE ISN'T TIME TO FIGURE IT OUT.
THIS IS TURNING INTO A BIG HASSLE.

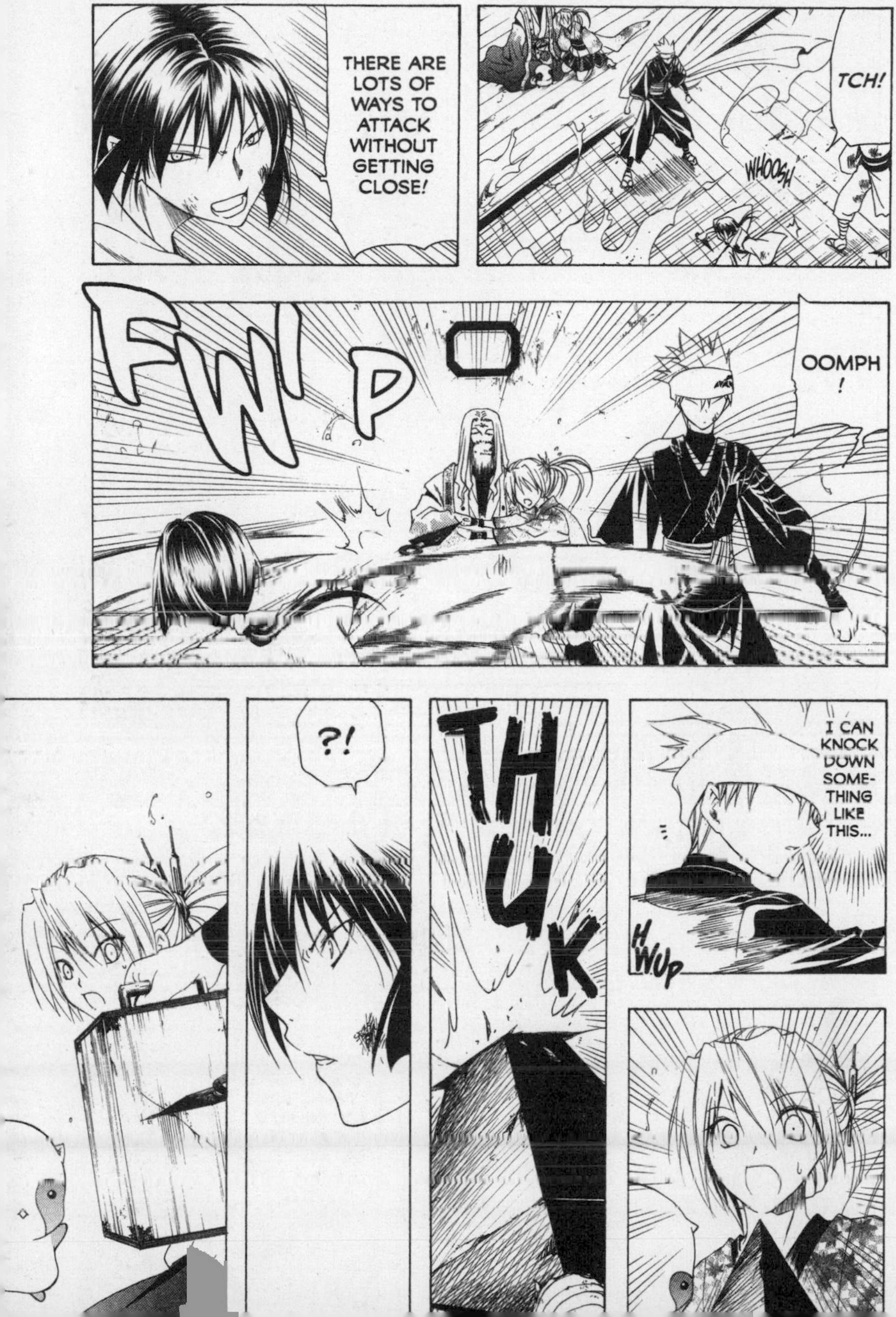
TCH!
WHOOSH
THERE ARE LOTS OF WAYS TO ATTACK WITHOUT GETTING CLOSE!
OOMPH!
FWIP
I CAN KNOCK DOWN SOME-THING LIKE THIS...
HWUP
THUK
?!

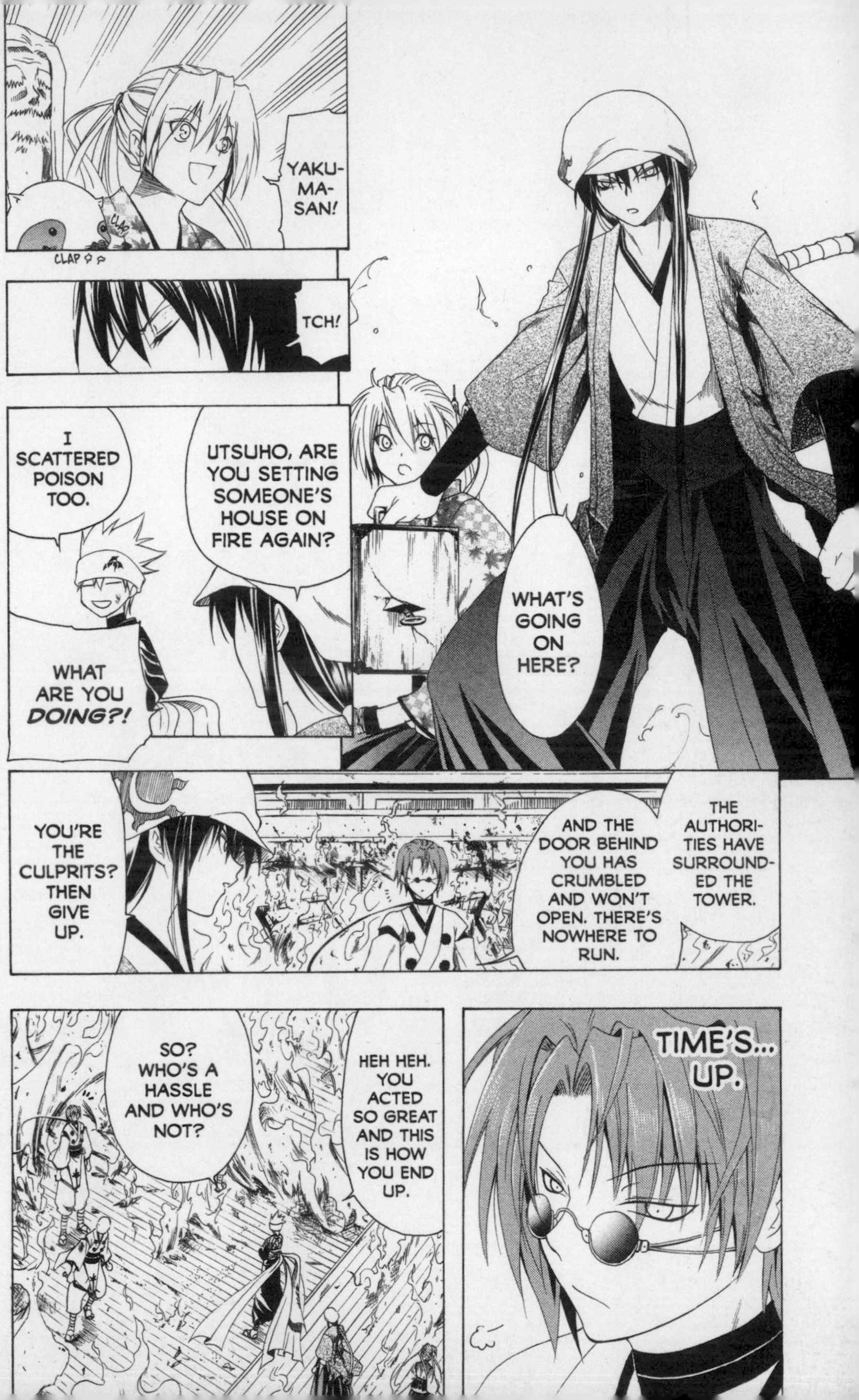
WHAT'S GOING ON HERE?
YAKU-MA-SAN!
CLAP
TCH!
UTSUHO, ARE YOU SETTING SOMEONE'S HOUSE ON FIRE AGAIN?
I SCATTERED POISON TOO.
WHAT ARE YOU DOING?!
THE AUTHORI-TIES HAVE SURROUND-ED THE TOWER.
AND THE DOOR BEHIND YOU HAS CRUMBLED AND WON'T OPEN. THERE'S NOWHERE TO RUN.
YOU'RE THE CULPRITS? THEN GIVE UP.
TIME'S... UP.
HEH HEH. YOU ACTED SO GREAT AND THIS IS HOW YOU END UP.
SO? WHO'S A HASSLE AND WHO'S NOT?

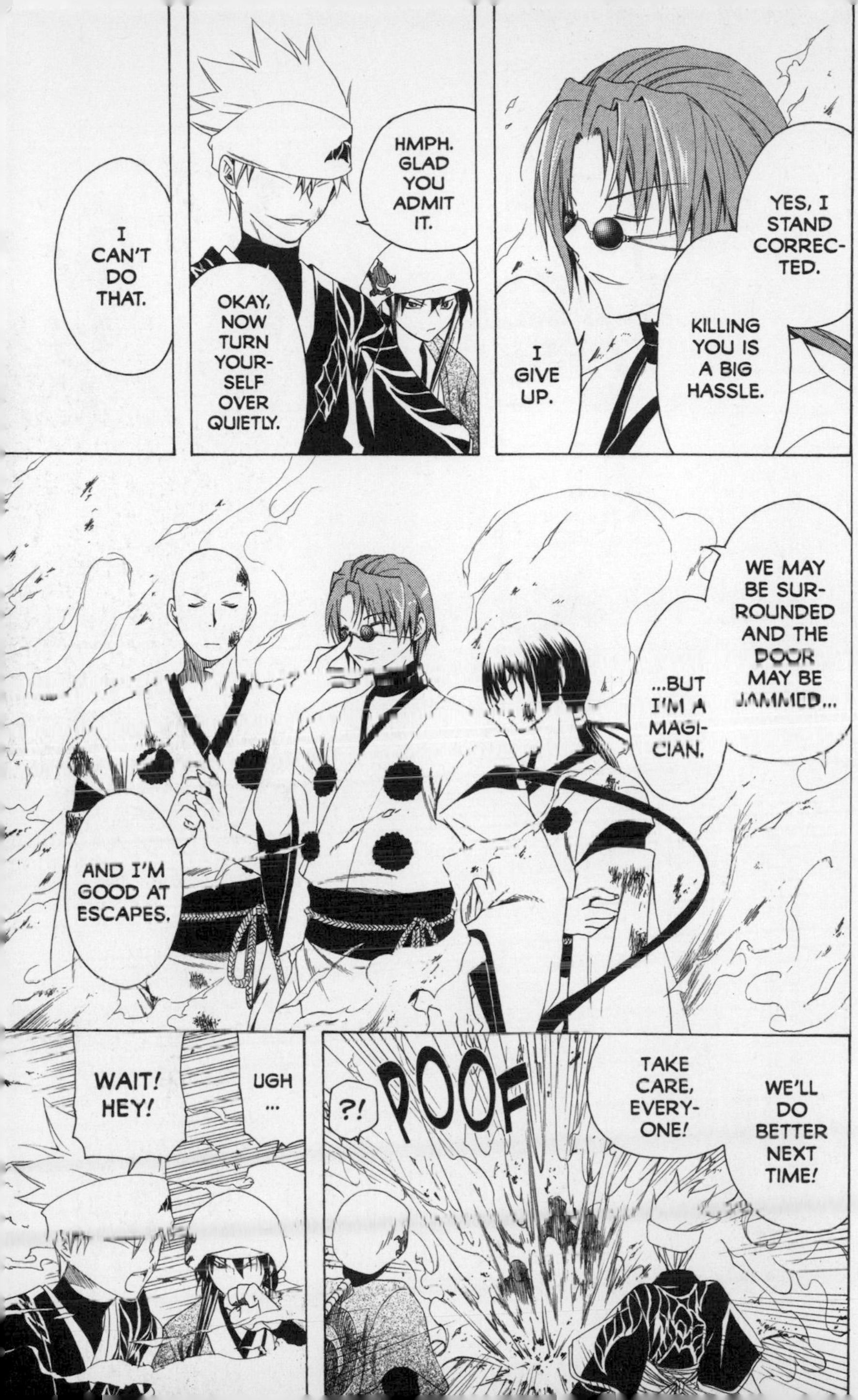
YES, I STAND CORRECTED.
KILLING YOU IS A BIG HASSLE.
I GIVE UP.
HMPH. GLAD YOU ADMIT IT.
OKAY, NOW TURN YOURSELF OVER QUIETLY.
I CAN'T DO THAT.
WE MAY BE SURROUNDED AND THE DOOR MAY BE JAMMED...
...BUT I'M A MAGICIAN.
AND I'M GOOD AT ESCAPES.
TAKE CARE, EVERYONE!
WE'LL DO BETTER NEXT TIME!
POOF
?!
UGH ...
WAIT! HEY!

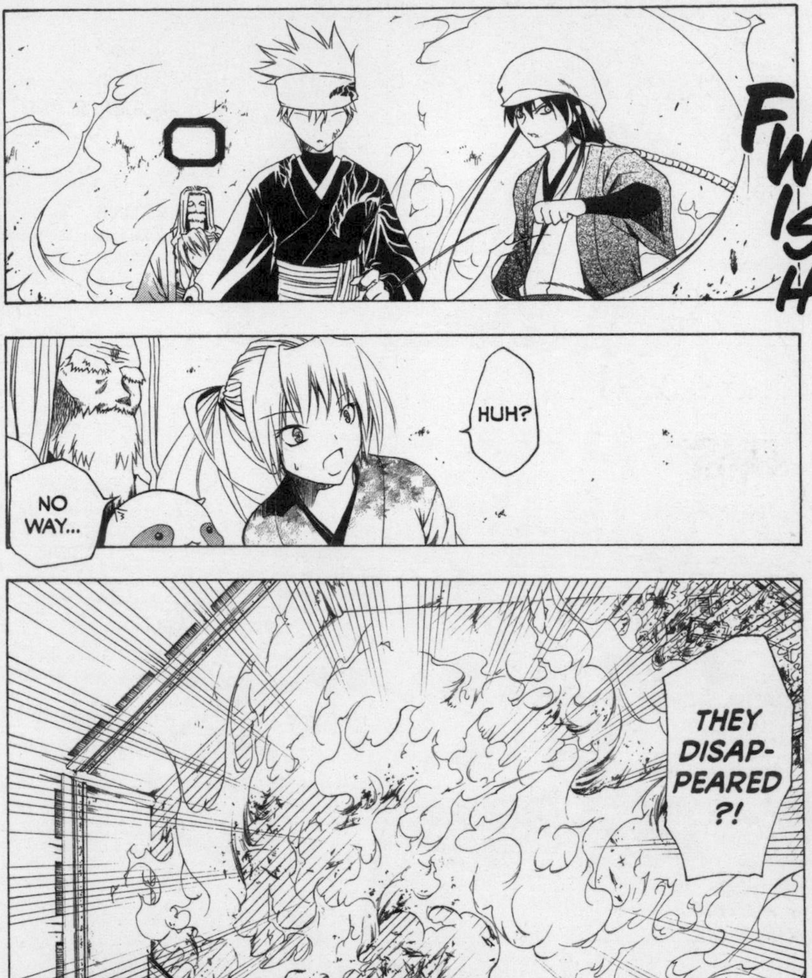
FWISH
HUH?
NO WAY...
THEY DISAP-PEARED ?!

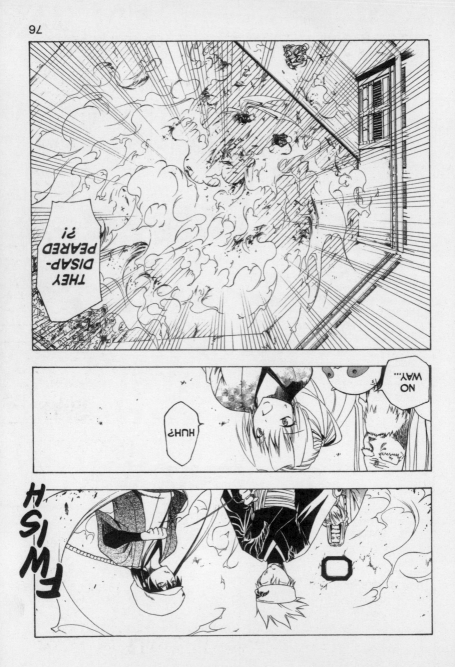

Chapter 32 Lies and Magic

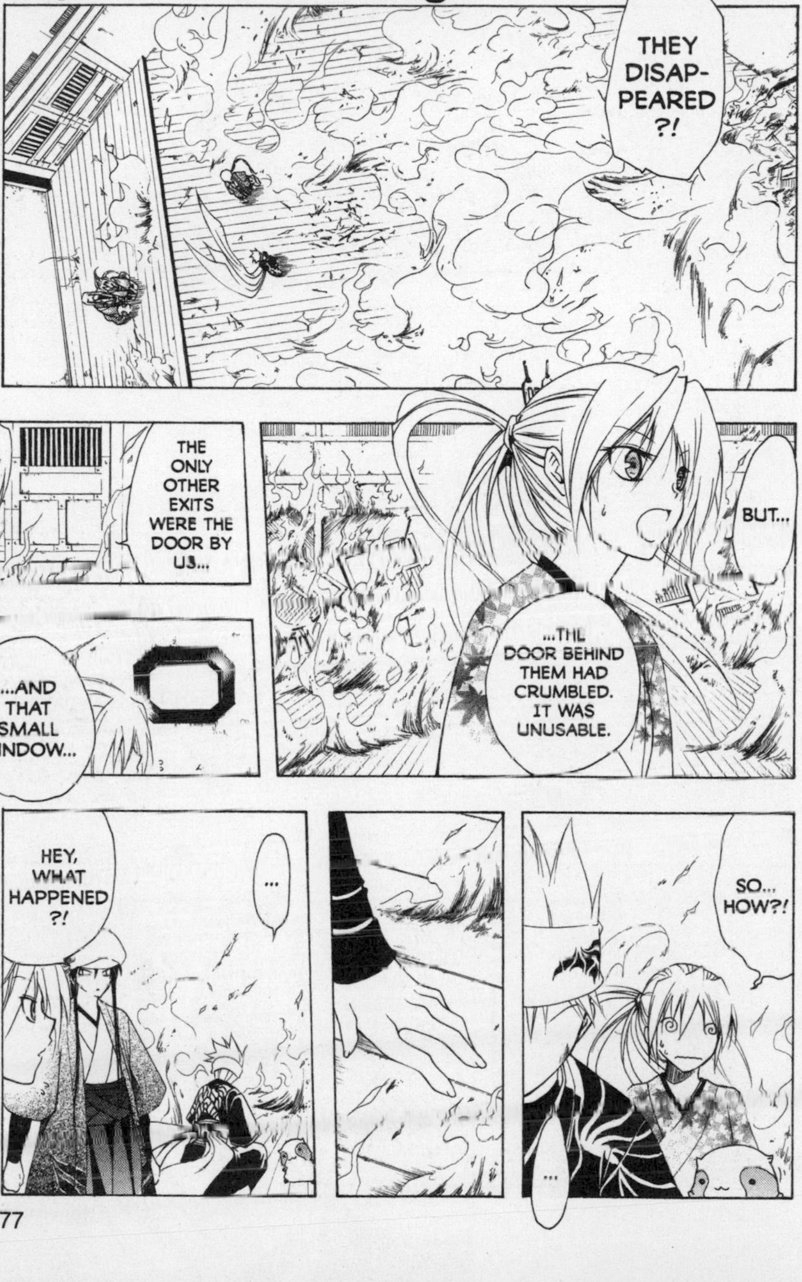

THEY DISAP-PEARED ?!
BUT...
...THL DOOR BEHIND THEM HAD CRUMBLED. IT WAS UNUSABLE.
THE ONLY OTHER EXITS WERE THE DOOR BY US...
...AND THAT SMALL WINDOW...
SO... HOW?!
...
...
HEY, WHAT HAPPENED ?!

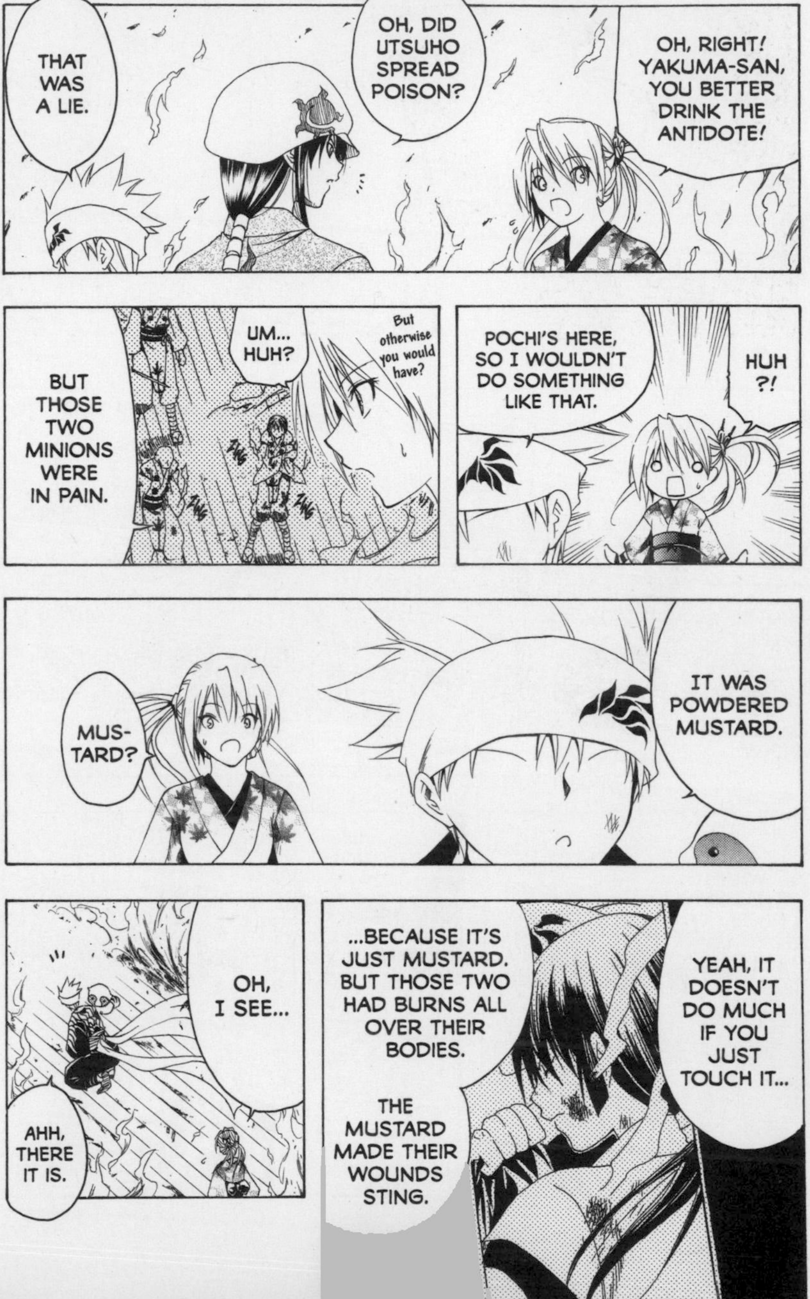
OH, RIGHT! YAKUMA-SAN, YOU BETTER DRINK THE ANTIDOTE!
OH, DID UTSUHO SPREAD POISON?
THAT WAS A LIE.
HUH ?!
POCHI'S HERE, SO I WOULDN'T DO SOMETHING LIKE THAT.
But otherwise you would have?
UM... HUH?
BUT THOSE TWO MINIONS WERE IN PAIN.
IT WAS POWDERED MUSTARD.
MUS-TARD?
YEAH, IT DOESN'T DO MUCH IF YOU JUST TOUCH IT...
...BECAUSE IT'S JUST MUSTARD. BUT THOSE TWO HAD BURNS ALL OVER THEIR BODIES.
THE MUSTARD MADE THEIR WOUNDS STING.
OH, I SEE...
AHH, THERE IT IS.

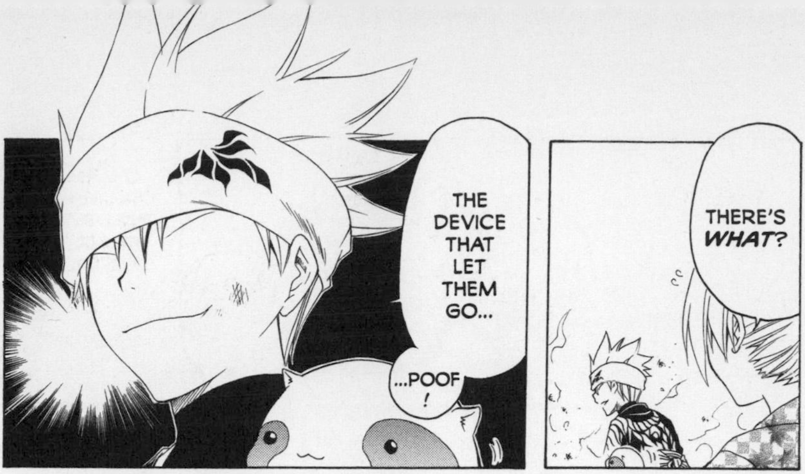
THERE'S *WHAT*?
THE DEVICE THAT LET THEM GO...
...POOF!

Chapter 32
Lies and Magic

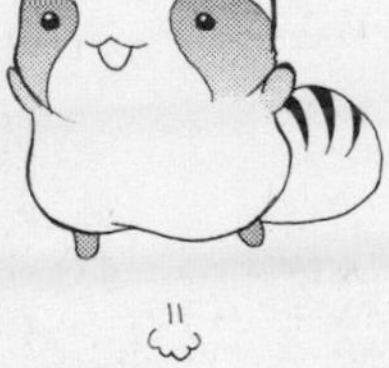

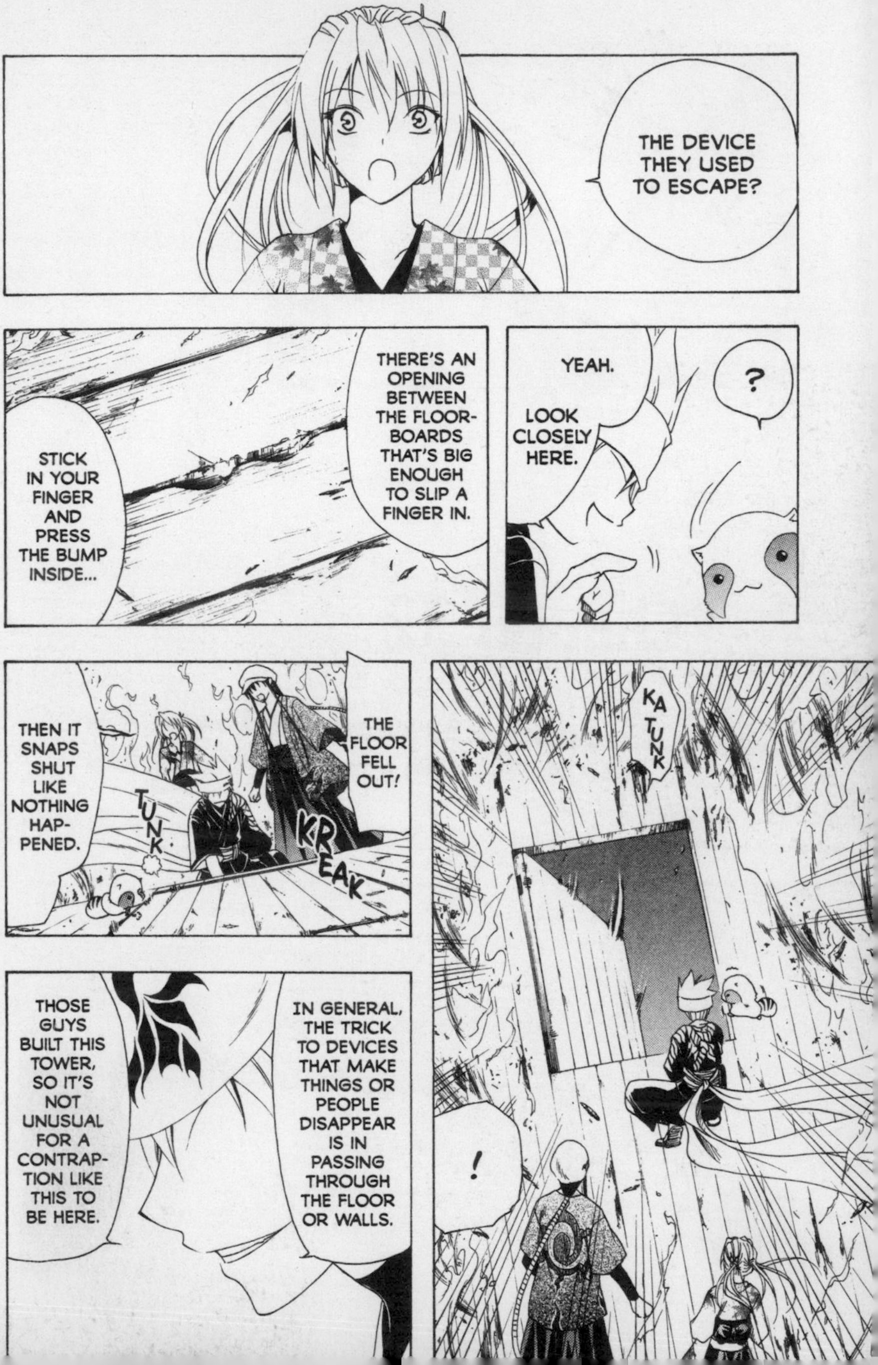
THE DEVICE THEY USED TO ESCAPE?
?
YEAH.
LOOK CLOSELY HERE.
THERE'S AN OPENING BETWEEN THE FLOOR-BOARDS THAT'S BIG ENOUGH TO SLIP A FINGER IN.
STICK IN YOUR FINGER AND PRESS THE BUMP INSIDE...
KA TUNK
!
THE FLOOR FELL OUT!
KREAK
TUNK
THEN IT SNAPS SHUT LIKE NOTHING HAP-PENED.
IN GENERAL, THE TRICK TO DEVICES THAT MAKE THINGS OR PEOPLE DISAPPEAR IS IN PASSING THROUGH THE FLOOR OR WALLS.
THOSE GUYS BUILT THIS TOWER, SO IT'S NOT UNUSUAL FOR A CONTRAPTION LIKE THIS TO BE HERE.

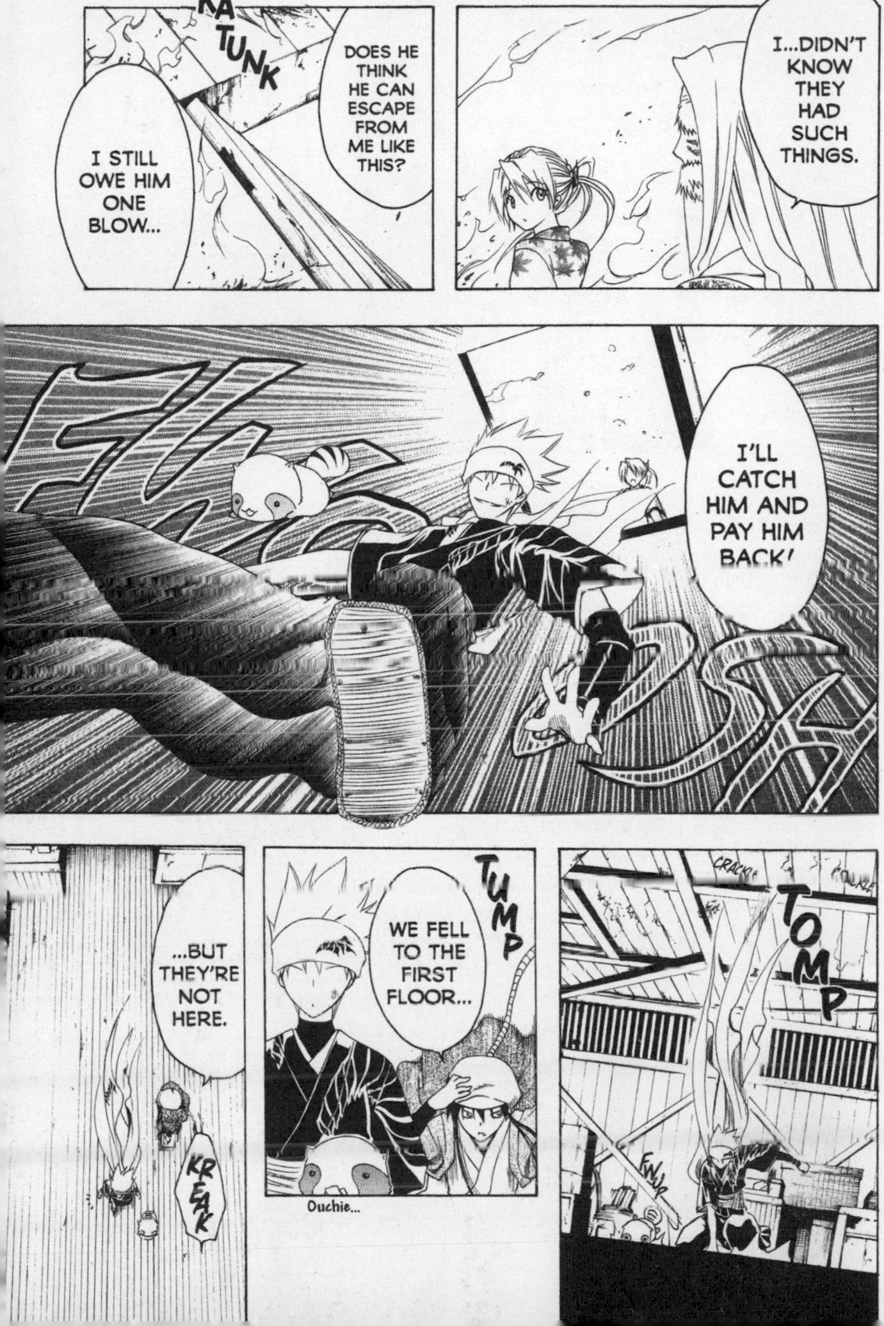
I...DIDN'T KNOW THEY HAD SUCH THINGS.
DOES HE THINK HE CAN ESCAPE FROM ME LIKE THIS?
KATUNK
I STILL OWE HIM ONE BLOW...
I'LL CATCH HIM AND PAY HIM BACK!
TOMP
CRACKLE
WE FELL TO THE FIRST FLOOR...
TUMP
Ouchie...
...BUT THEY'RE NOT HERE.
KREAK

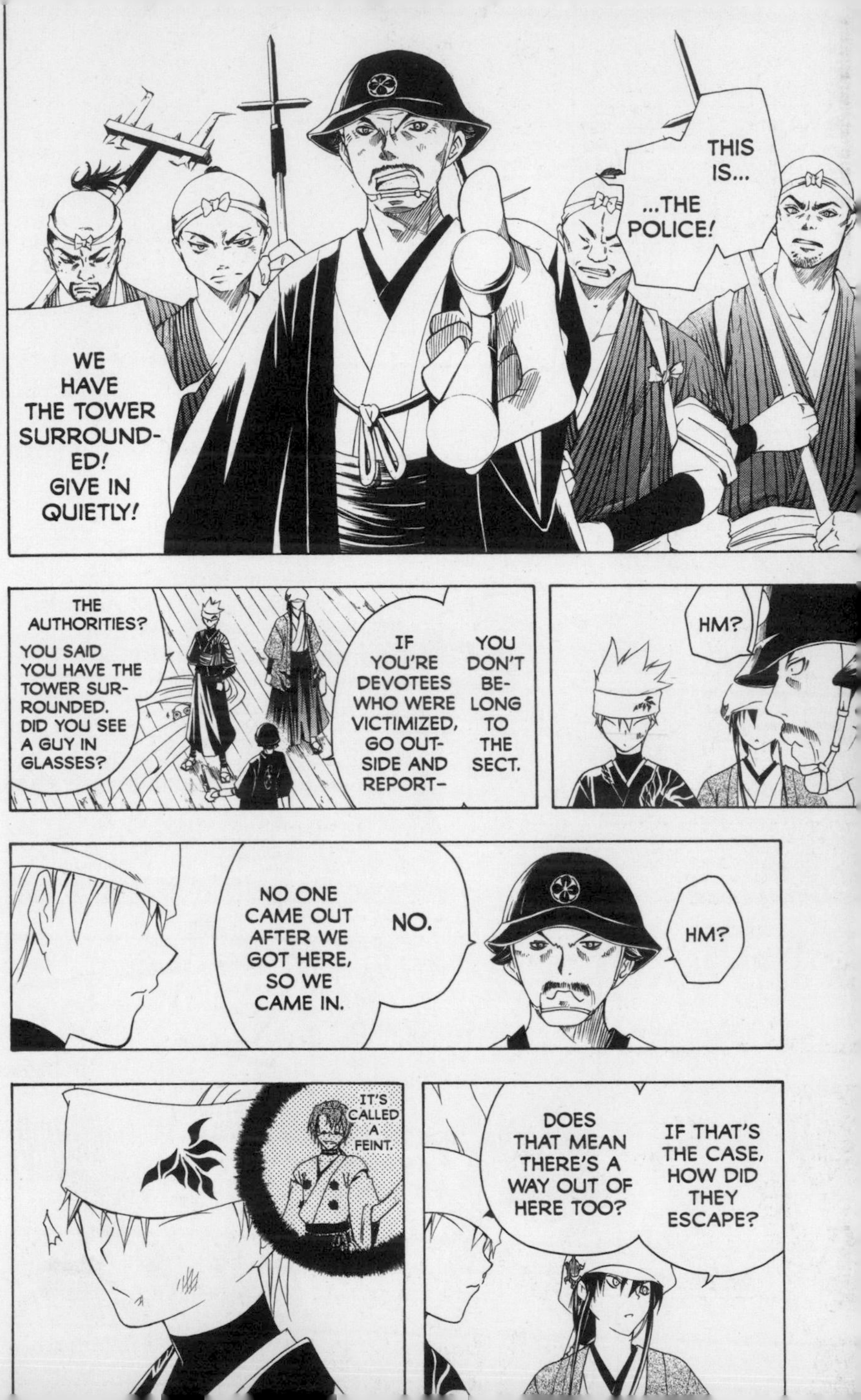
THIS IS... ...THE POLICE!
WE HAVE THE TOWER SURROUND-ED! GIVE IN QUIETLY!
HM?
YOU DON'T BE-LONG TO THE SECT.
IF YOU'RE DEVOTEES WHO WERE VICTIMIZED, GO OUT-SIDE AND REPORT-
THE AUTHORITIES?
YOU SAID YOU HAVE THE TOWER SUR-ROUNDED. DID YOU SEE A GUY IN GLASSES?
HM?
NO.
NO ONE CAME OUT AFTER WE GOT HERE, SO WE CAME IN.
IF THAT'S THE CASE, HOW DID THEY ESCAPE?
DOES THAT MEAN THERE'S A WAY OUT OF HERE TOO?
IT'S CALLED A FEINT.

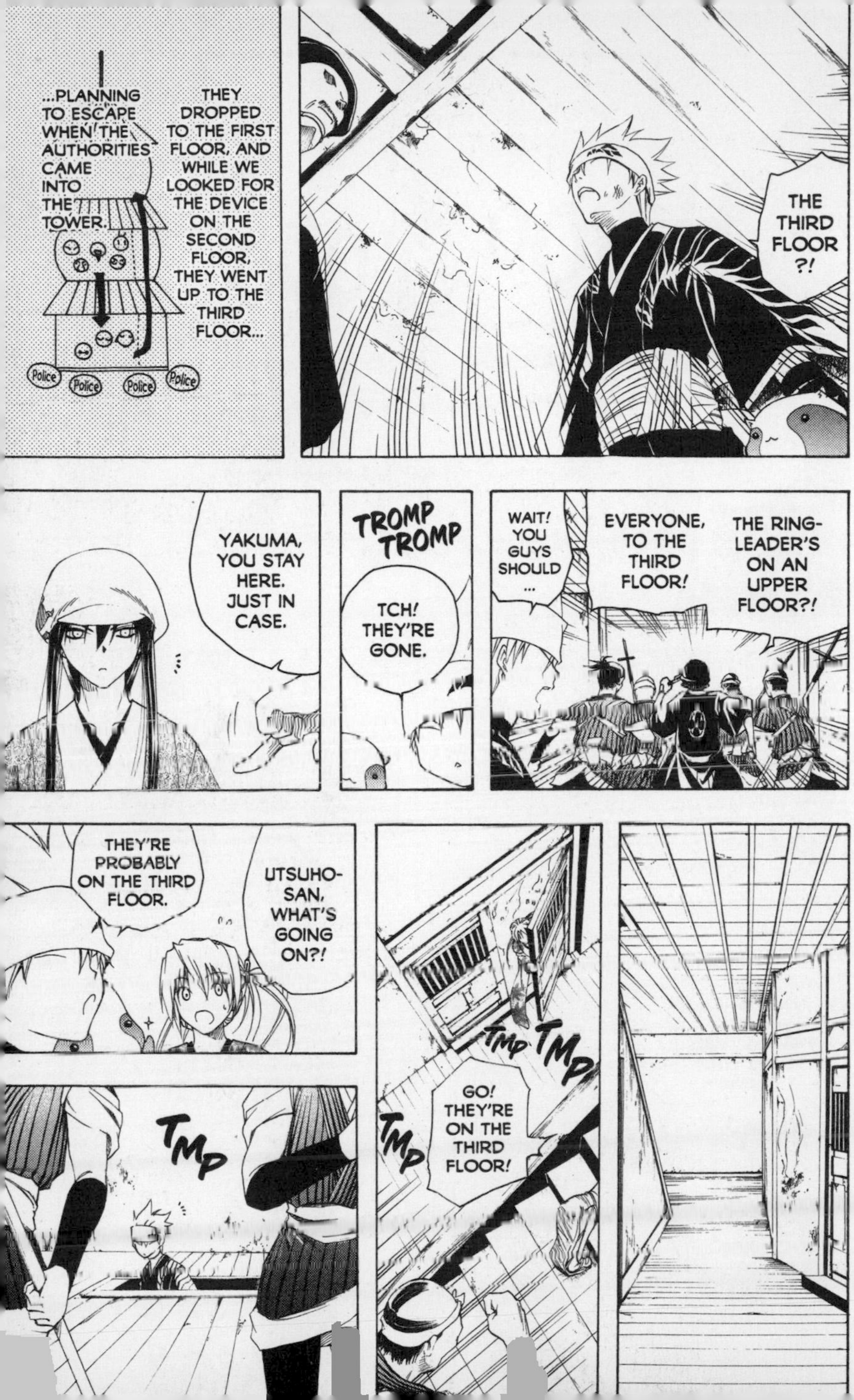
THE THIRD FLOOR ?!
THEY DROPPED TO THE FIRST FLOOR, AND WHILE WE LOOKED FOR THE DEVICE ON THE SECOND FLOOR, THEY WENT UP TO THE THIRD FLOOR...
...PLANNING TO ESCAPE WHEN THE AUTHORITIES CAME INTO THE TOWER.
Police
Police
Police
Police
THE RING-LEADER'S ON AN UPPER FLOOR?!
EVERYONE, TO THE THIRD FLOOR!
WAIT! YOU GUYS SHOULD ...
TROMP TROMP
TCH! THEY'RE GONE.
YAKUMA, YOU STAY HERE. JUST IN CASE.
TMP TMP
GO! THEY'RE ON THE THIRD FLOOR!
TMP
THEY'RE PROBABLY ON THE THIRD FLOOR.
UTSUHO-SAN, WHAT'S GOING ON?!
TMP

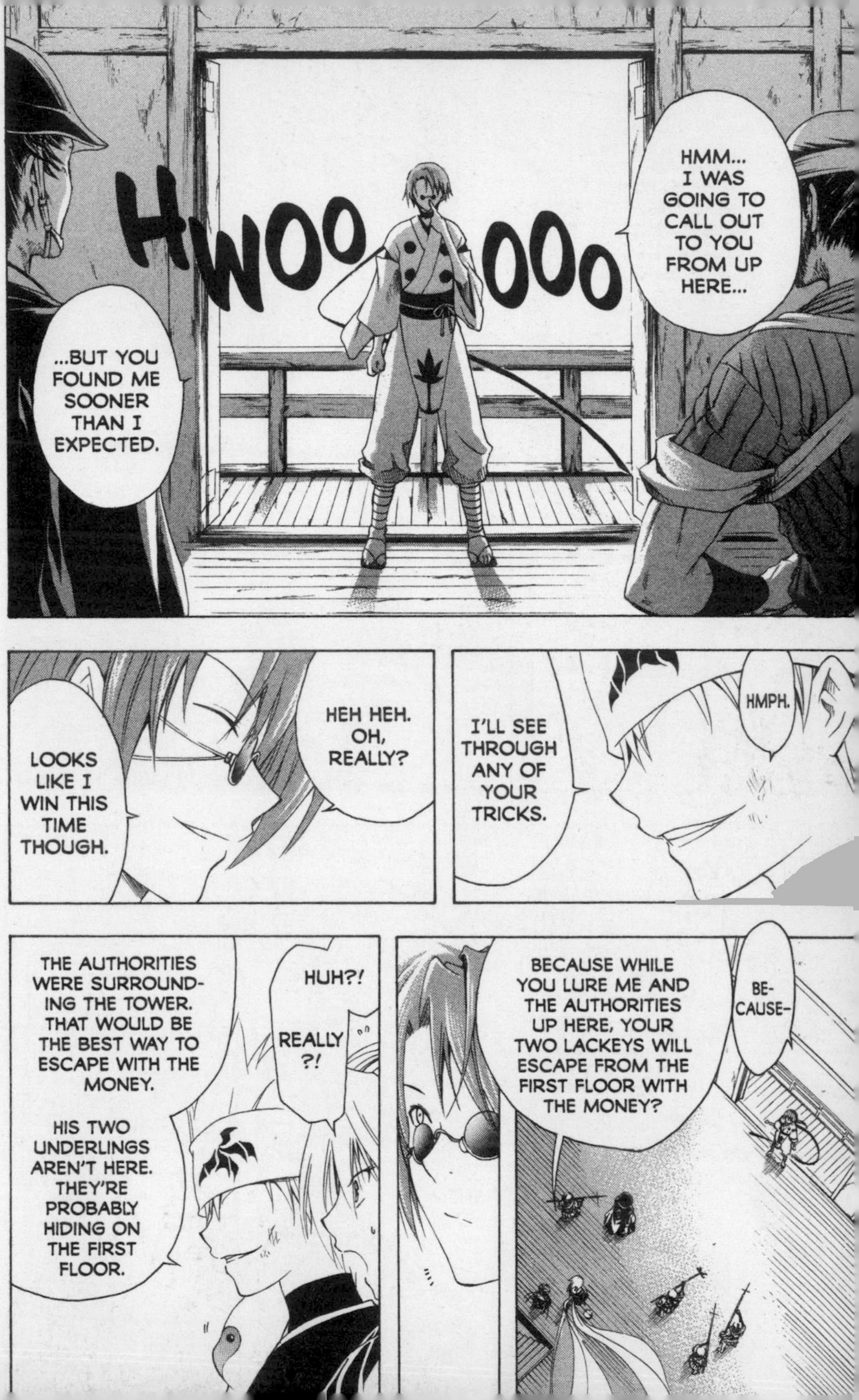
HMM... I WAS GOING TO CALL OUT TO YOU FROM UP HERE...
HWOOOOO
...BUT YOU FOUND ME SOONER THAN I EXPECTED.
HMPH.
I'LL SEE THROUGH ANY OF YOUR TRICKS.
HEH HEH. OH, REALLY?
LOOKS LIKE I WIN THIS TIME THOUGH.
BE- CAUSE-
BECAUSE WHILE YOU LURE ME AND THE AUTHORITIES UP HERE, YOUR TWO LACKEYS WILL ESCAPE FROM THE FIRST FLOOR WITH THE MONEY?
HUH?!
REALLY ?!
THE AUTHORITIES WERE SURROUND- ING THE TOWER. THAT WOULD BE THE BEST WAY TO ESCAPE WITH THE MONEY.
HIS TWO UNDERLINGS AREN'T HERE. THEY'RE PROBABLY HIDING ON THE FIRST FLOOR.

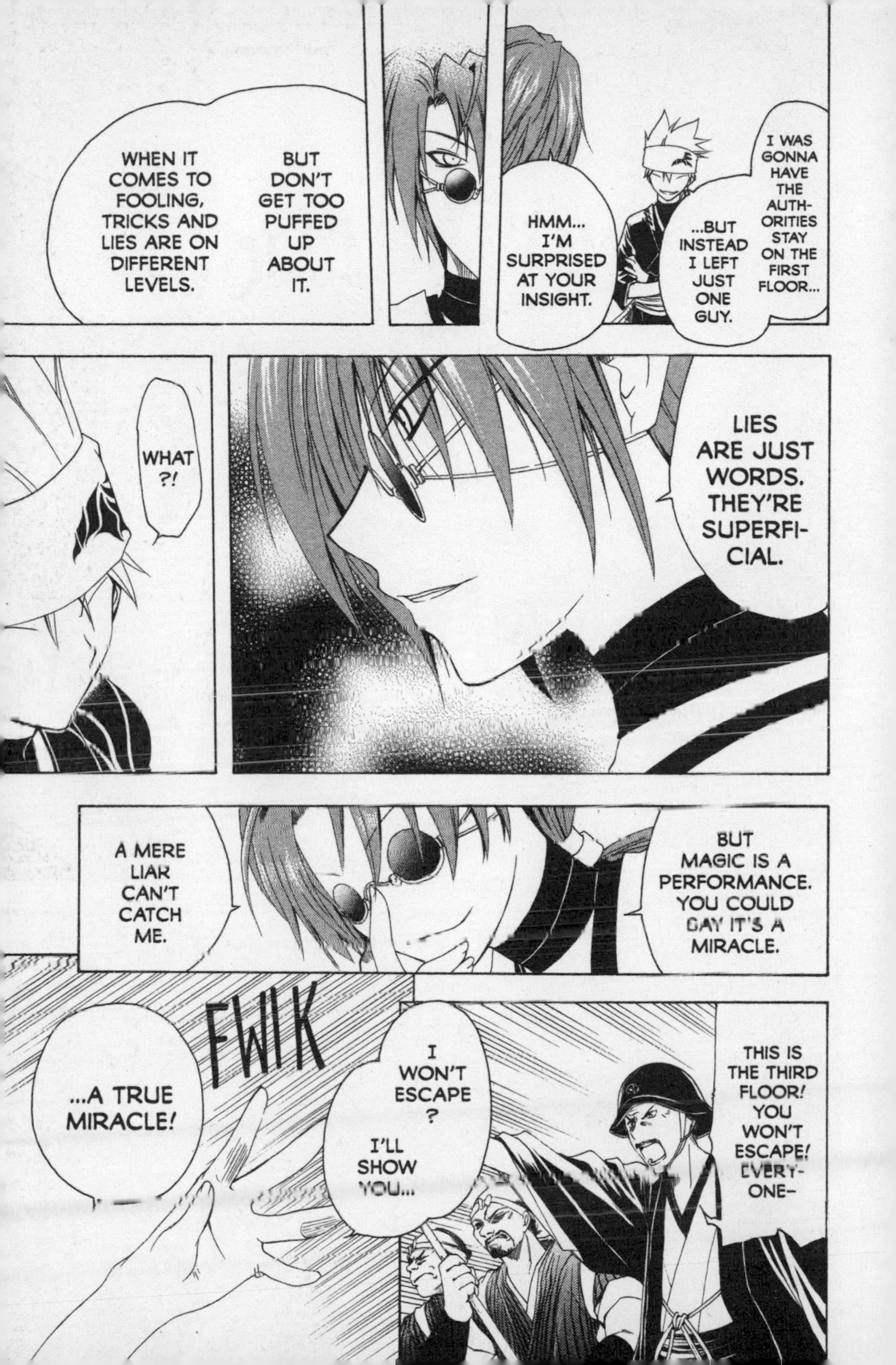
I WAS GONNA HAVE THE AUTHORITIES STAY ON THE FIRST FLOOR...
...BUT INSTEAD I LEFT JUST ONE GUY.
HMM... I'M SURPRISED AT YOUR INSIGHT.
BUT DON'T GET TOO PUFFED UP ABOUT IT.
WHEN IT COMES TO FOOLING, TRICKS AND LIES ARE ON DIFFERENT LEVELS.
LIES ARE JUST WORDS. THEY'RE SUPERFICIAL.
WHAT?!
BUT MAGIC IS A PERFORMANCE. YOU COULD SAY IT'S A MIRACLE.
A MERE LIAR CAN'T CATCH ME.
THIS IS THE THIRD FLOOR! YOU WON'T ESCAPE! EVERY-ONE–
I WON'T ESCAPE?
I'LL SHOW YOU...
FWIK
...A TRUE MIRACLE!

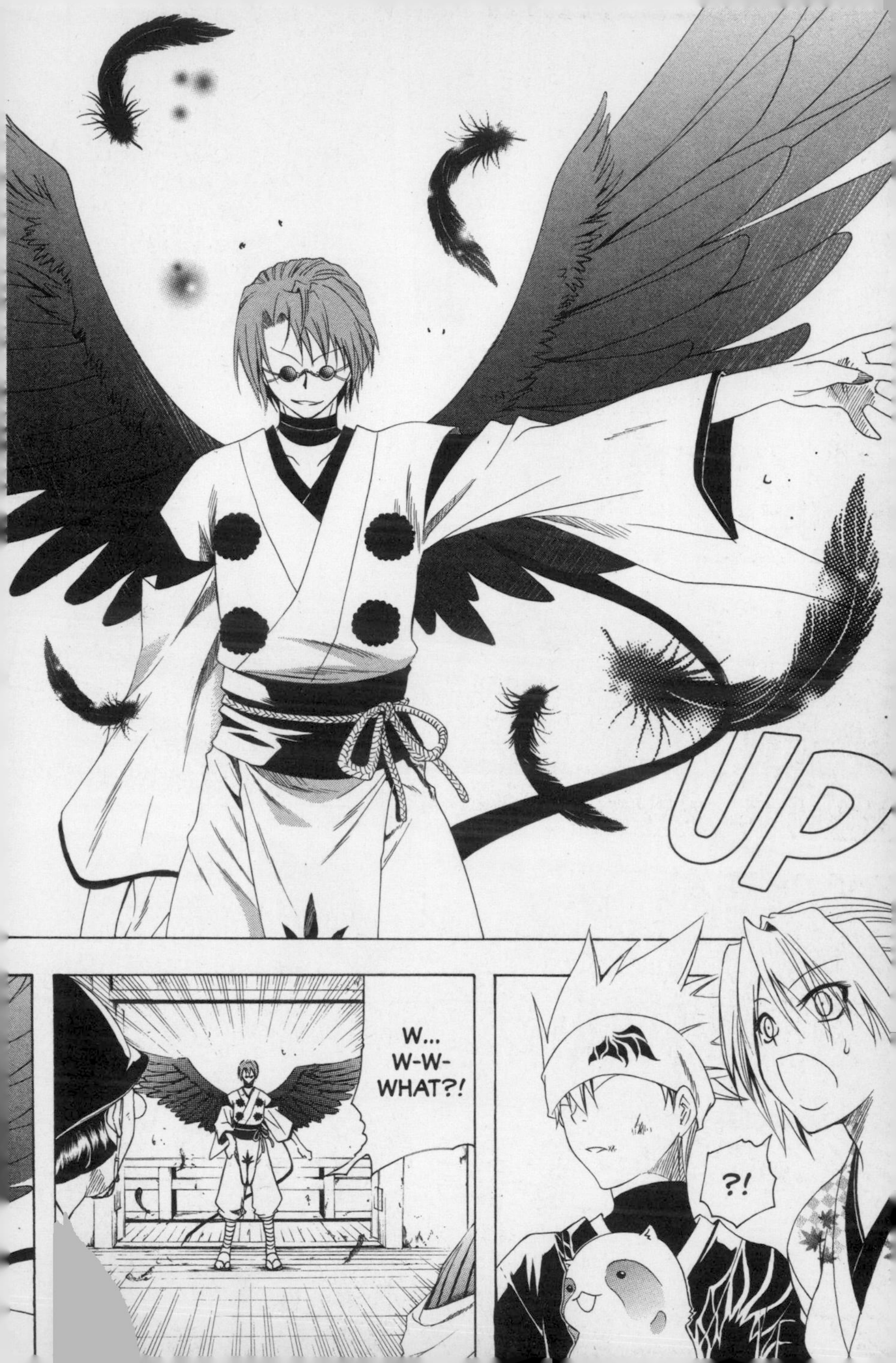
UP
?!
W...
W-W-
WHAT?!

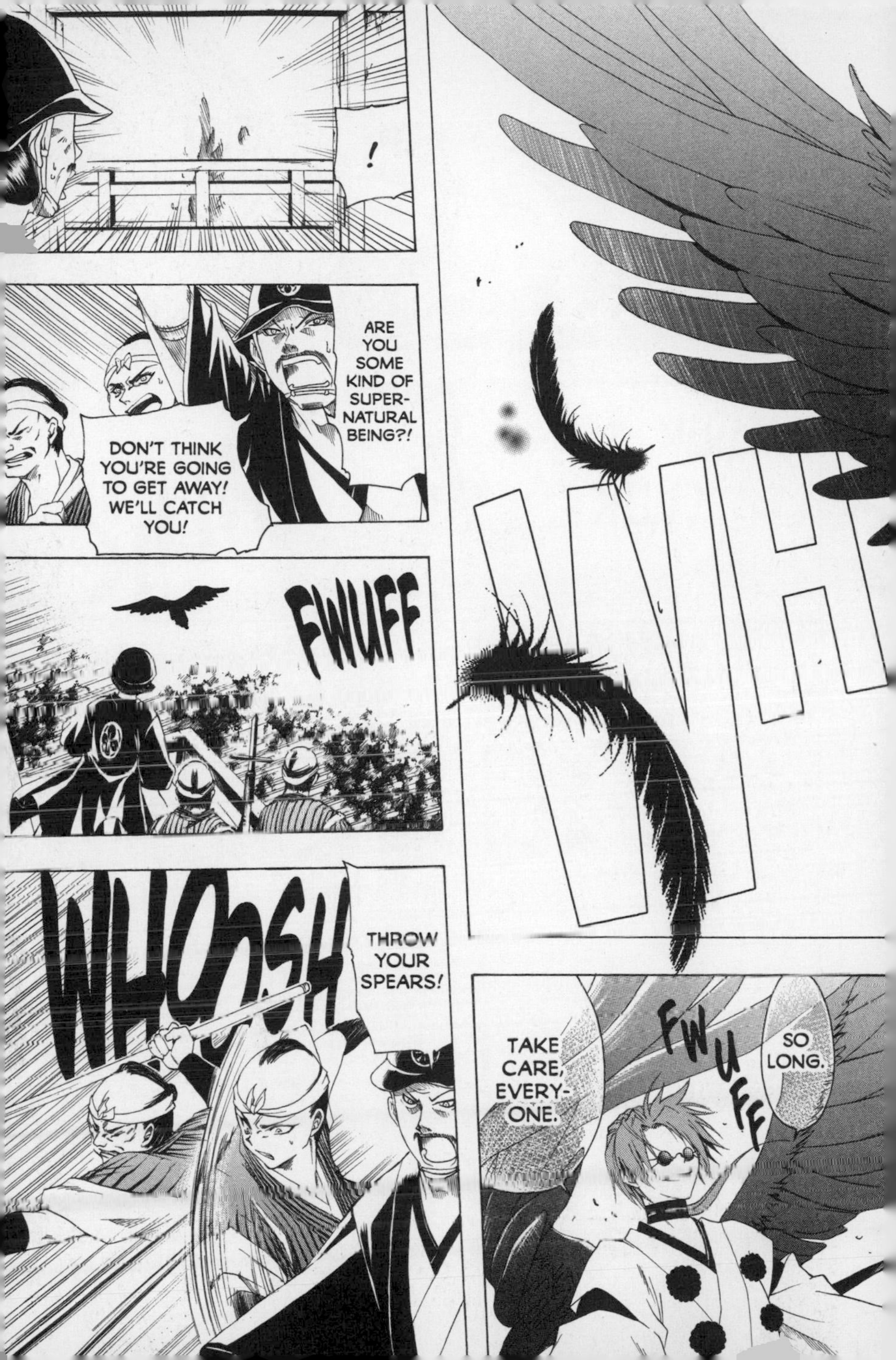
WHH
SO LONG.
TAKE CARE, EVERY-ONE.
FWUFF
!
ARE YOU SOME KIND OF SUPER-NATURAL BEING?!
DON'T THINK YOU'RE GOING TO GET AWAY! WE'LL CATCH YOU!
FWUFF
THROW YOUR SPEARS!
WHOOSH

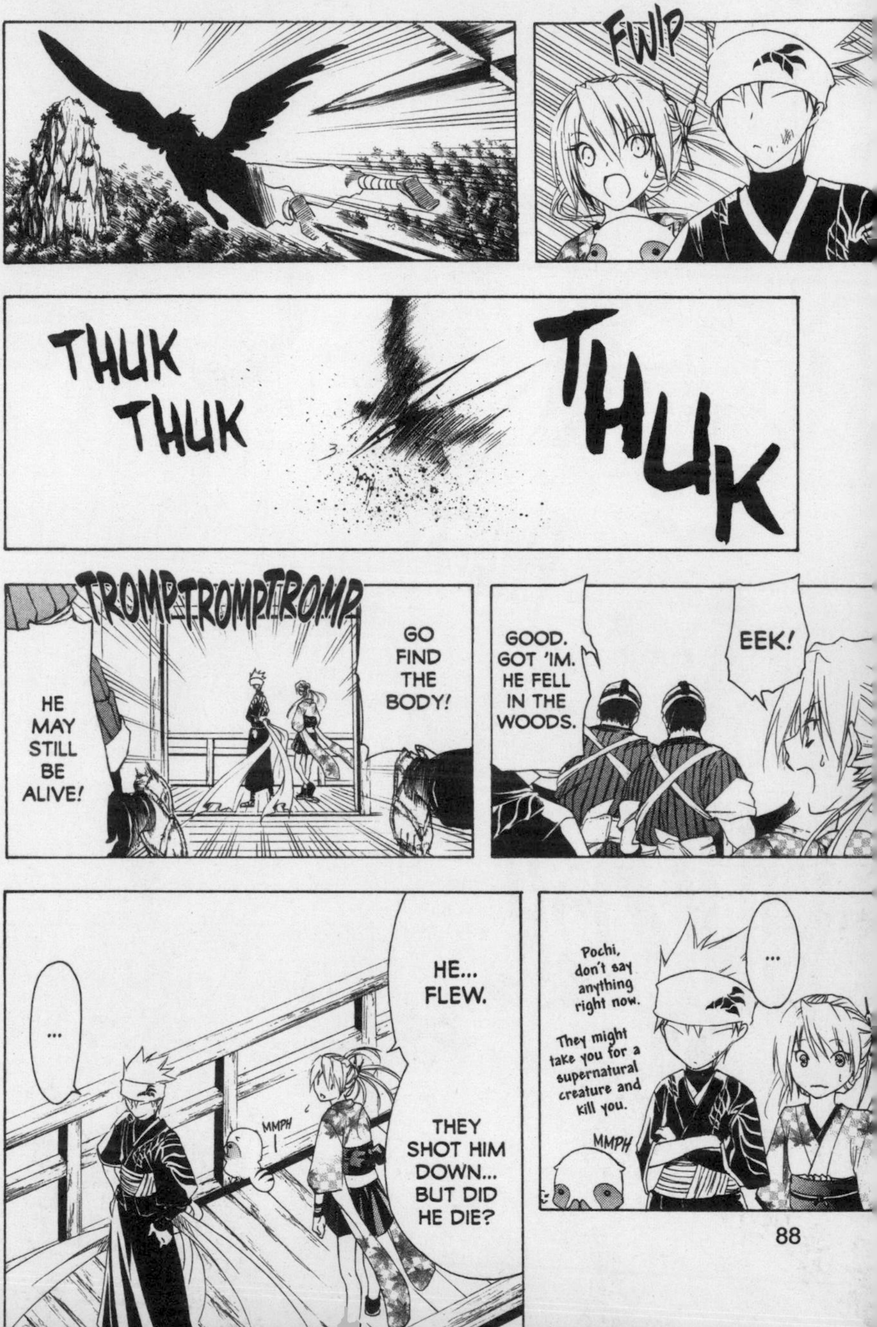
FWIP
THUK
THUK
THUK
EEK!
GOOD. GOT 'IM. HE FELL IN THE WOODS.
GO FIND THE BODY!
TROMP TROMP TROMP
HE MAY STILL BE ALIVE!
...
Pochi, don't say anything right now.
They might take you for a supernatural creature and kill you.
MMPH
HE... FLEW.
THEY SHOT HIM DOWN... BUT DID HE DIE?
MMPH
...

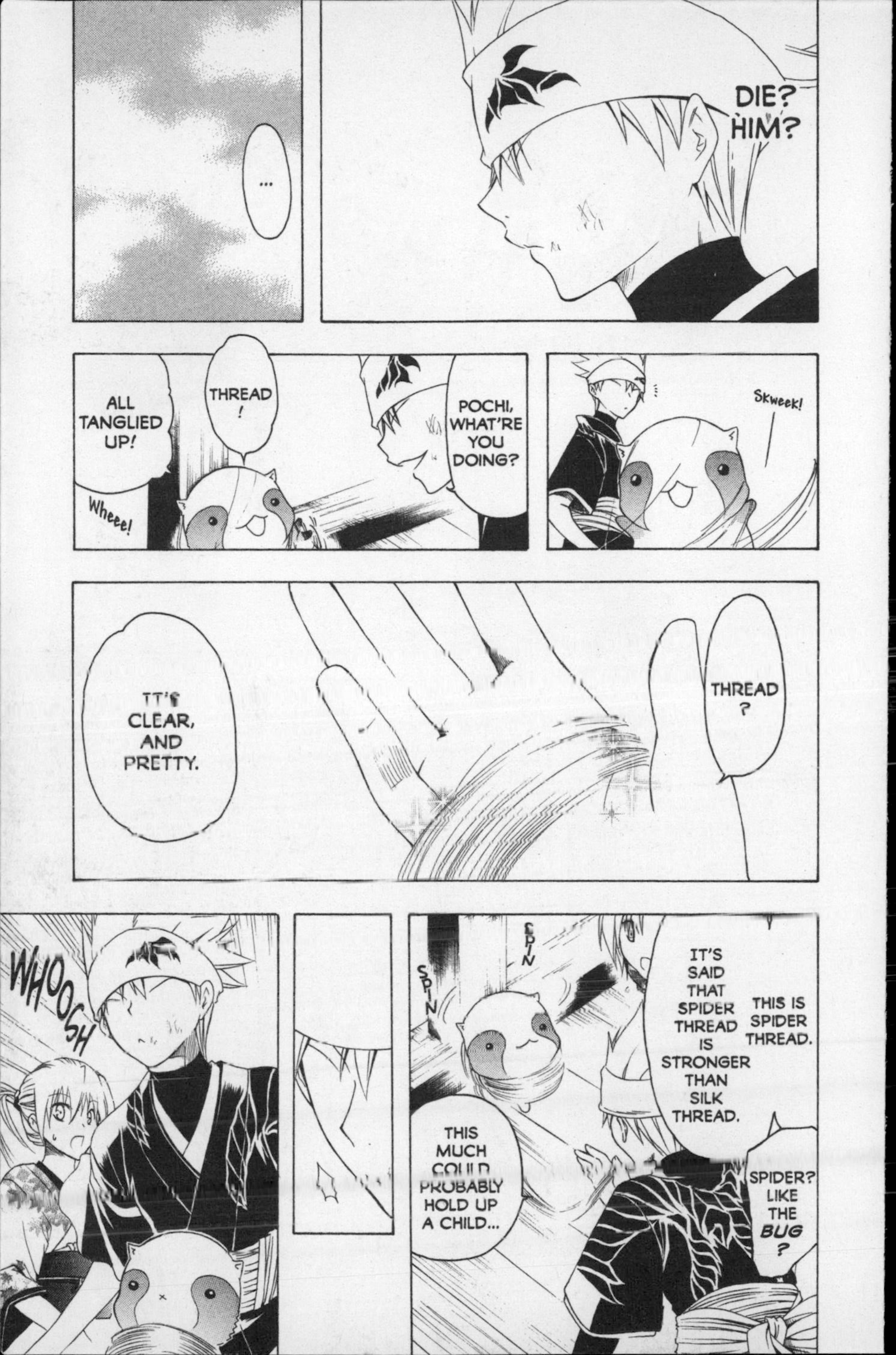
DIE? HIM?
...
Skweek!
POCHI, WHAT'RE YOU DOING?
THREAD!
ALL TANGLIED UP!
Wheee!
THREAD?
IT'S CLEAR, AND PRETTY.
THIS IS SPIDER THREAD.
IT'S SAID THAT SPIDER THREAD IS STRONGER THAN SILK THREAD.
SPIDER? LIKE THE BUG?
SPIN
SPIN
THIS MUCH COULD PROBABLY HOLD UP A CHILD...
WHOOSH

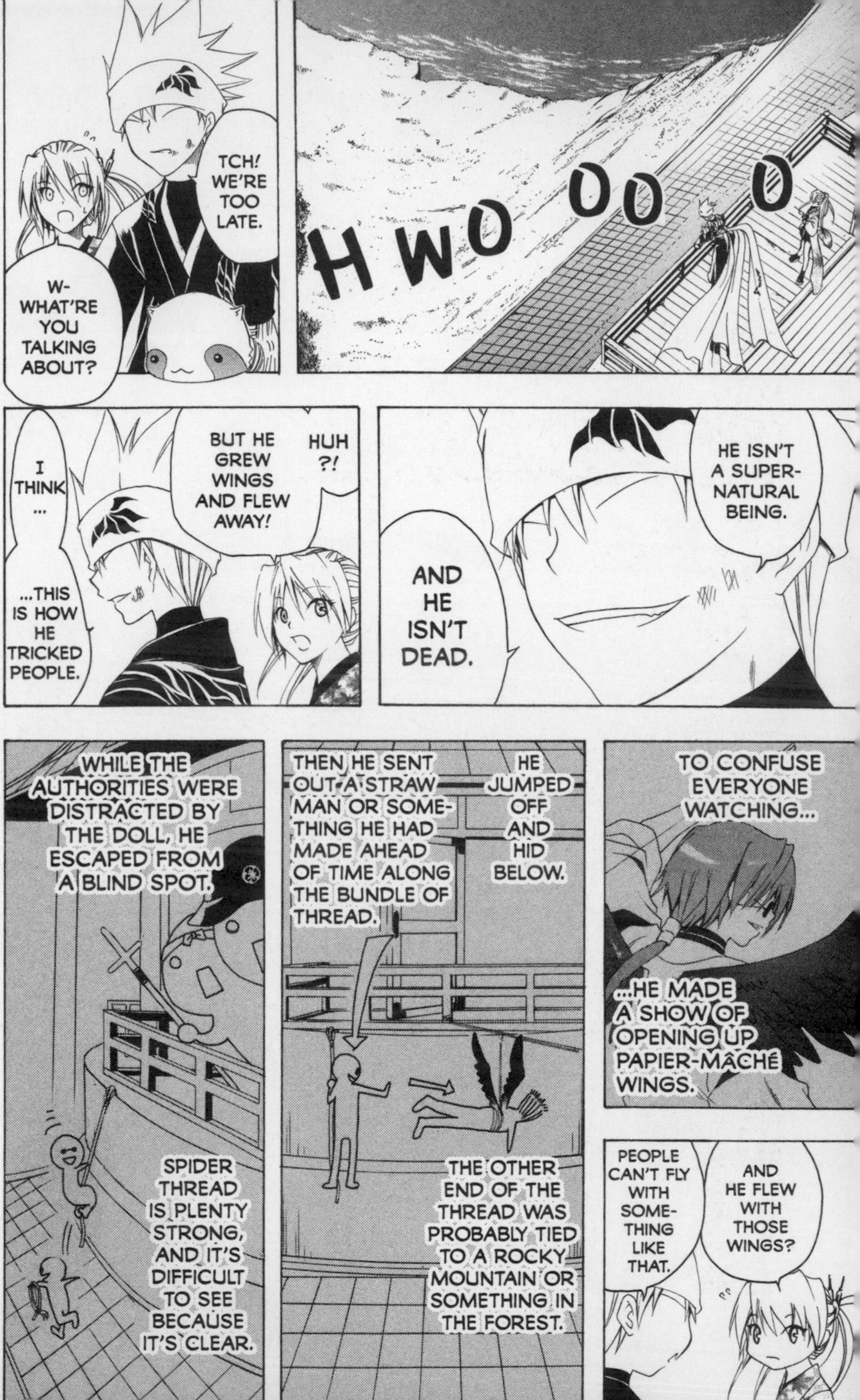
HWO OO O
TCH! WE'RE TOO LATE.
W-WHAT'RE YOU TALKING ABOUT?
HE ISN'T A SUPER-NATURAL BEING.
AND HE ISN'T DEAD.
HUH ?!
BUT HE GREW WINGS AND FLEW AWAY!
I THINK ...
...THIS IS HOW HE TRICKED PEOPLE.
TO CONFUSE EVERYONE WATCHING...
...HE MADE A SHOW OF OPENING UP PAPIER-MÂCHÉ WINGS.
AND HE FLEW WITH THOSE WINGS?
PEOPLE CAN'T FLY WITH SOME-THING LIKE THAT.
THEN HE SENT OUT A STRAW MAN OR SOME-THING HE HAD MADE AHEAD OF TIME ALONG THE BUNDLE OF THREAD.
HE JUMPED OFF AND HID BELOW.
THE OTHER END OF THE THREAD WAS PROBABLY TIED TO A ROCKY MOUNTAIN OR SOMETHING IN THE FOREST.
WHILE THE AUTHORITIES WERE DISTRACTED BY THE DOLL, HE ESCAPED FROM A BLIND SPOT.
SPIDER THREAD IS PLENTY STRONG, AND IT'S DIFFICULT TO SEE BECAUSE IT'S CLEAR.

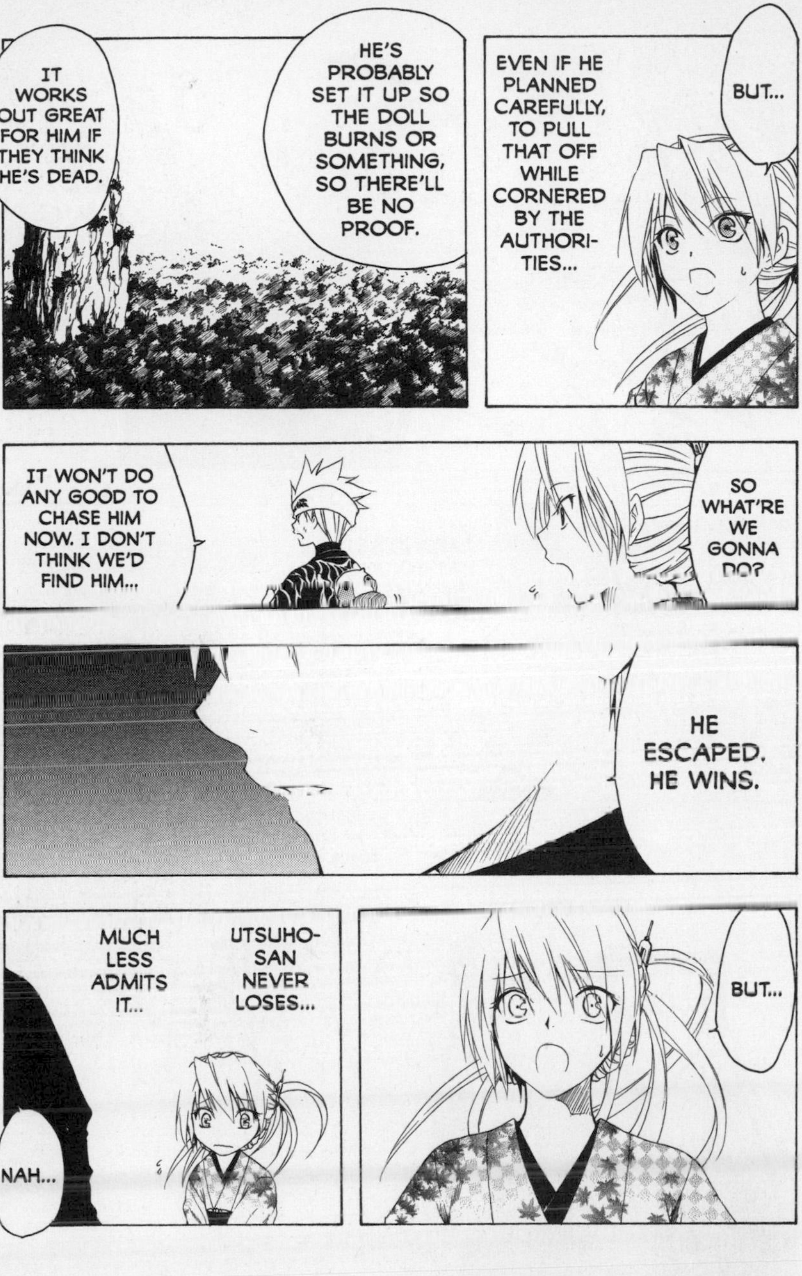
BUT...
EVEN IF HE PLANNED CAREFULLY, TO PULL THAT OFF WHILE CORNERED BY THE AUTHORITIES...
HE'S PROBABLY SET IT UP SO THE DOLL BURNS OR SOMETHING, SO THERE'LL BE NO PROOF.
IT WORKS OUT GREAT FOR HIM IF THEY THINK HE'S DEAD.
SO WHAT'RE WE GONNA DO?
IT WON'T DO ANY GOOD TO CHASE HIM NOW. I DON'T THINK WE'D FIND HIM...
HE ESCAPED. HE WINS.
BUT...
UTSUHO-SAN NEVER LOSES...
MUCH LESS ADMITS IT...
NAH...

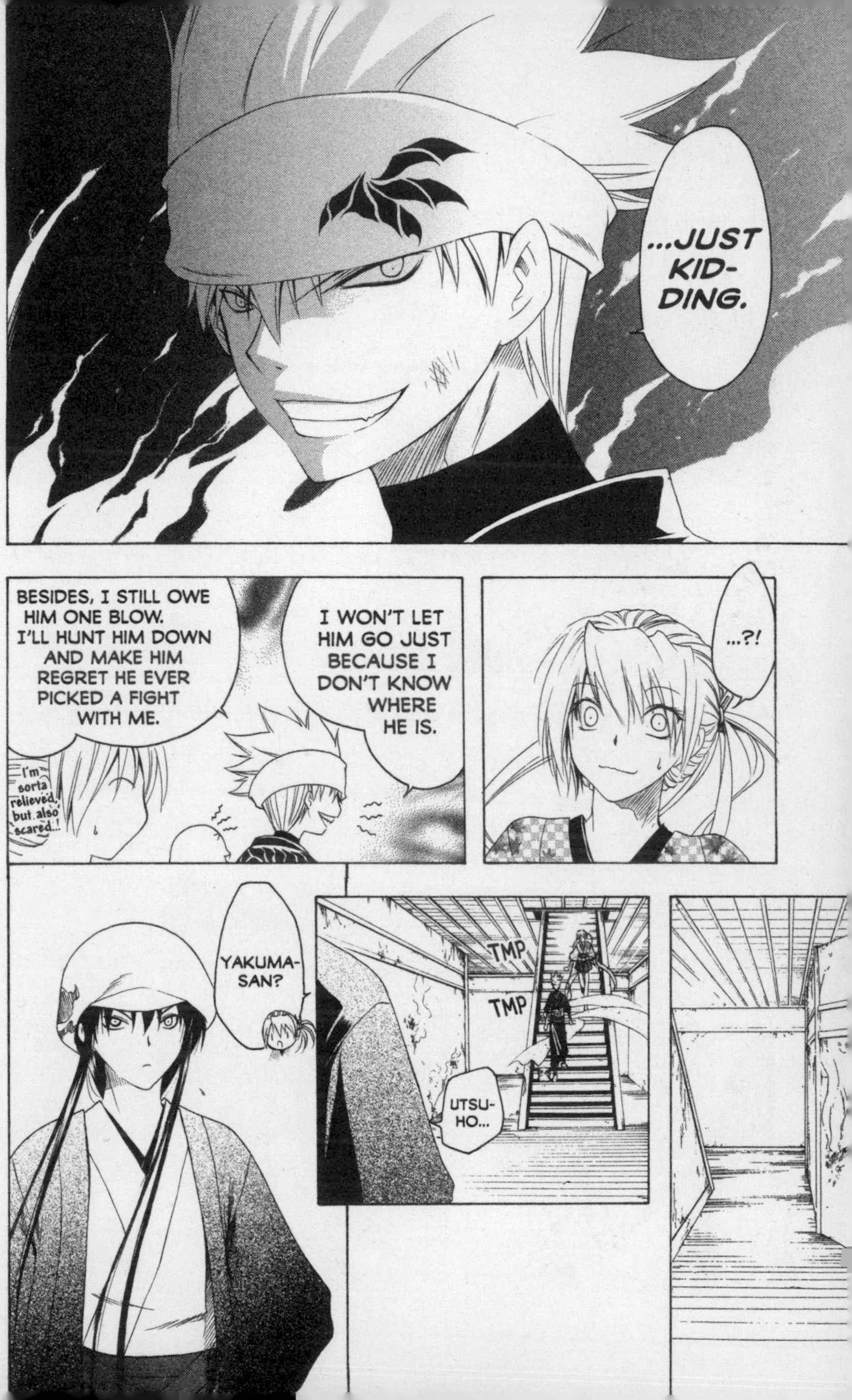
...JUST KID-DING.
...?!
I WON'T LET HIM GO JUST BECAUSE I DON'T KNOW WHERE HE IS.
BESIDES, I STILL OWE HIM ONE BLOW. I'LL HUNT HIM DOWN AND MAKE HIM REGRET HE EVER PICKED A FIGHT WITH ME.
I'm sorta relieved, but also scared...
TMP
TMP
UTSU-HO...
YAKUMA-SAN?

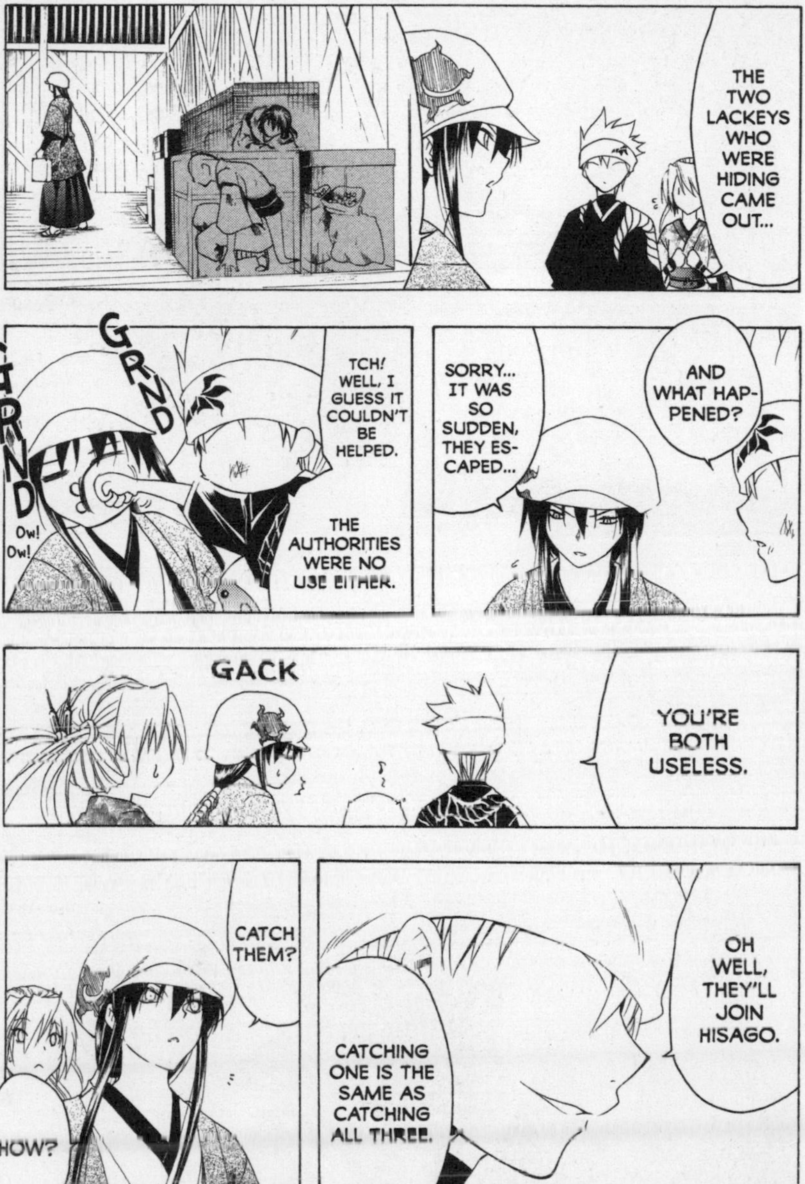
THE TWO LACKEYS WHO WERE HIDING CAME OUT...
AND WHAT HAPPENED?
SORRY... IT WAS SO SUDDEN, THEY ESCAPED...
TCH! WELL, I GUESS IT COULDN'T BE HELPED.
THE AUTHORITIES WERE NO USE EITHER.
GRND GRND
Ow! Ow!
YOU'RE BOTH USELESS.
GACK
OH WELL, THEY'LL JOIN HISAGO.
CATCHING ONE IS THE SAME AS CATCHING ALL THREE.
CATCH THEM?
HOW?

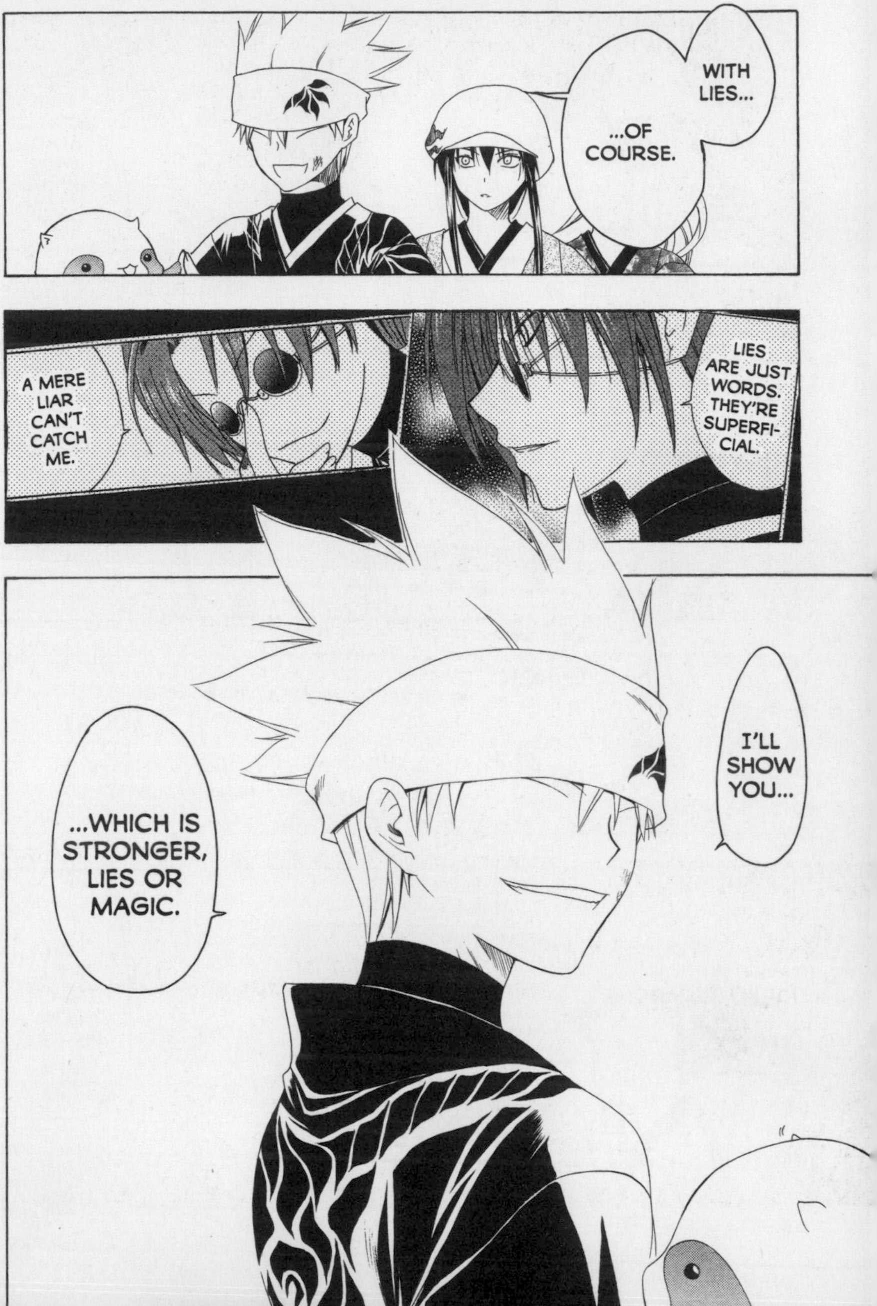
WITH LIES... ...OF COURSE.
LIES ARE JUST WORDS. THEY'RE SUPERFI-CIAL.
A MERE LIAR CAN'T CATCH ME.
I'LL SHOW YOU...
...WHICH IS STRONGER, LIES OR MAGIC.

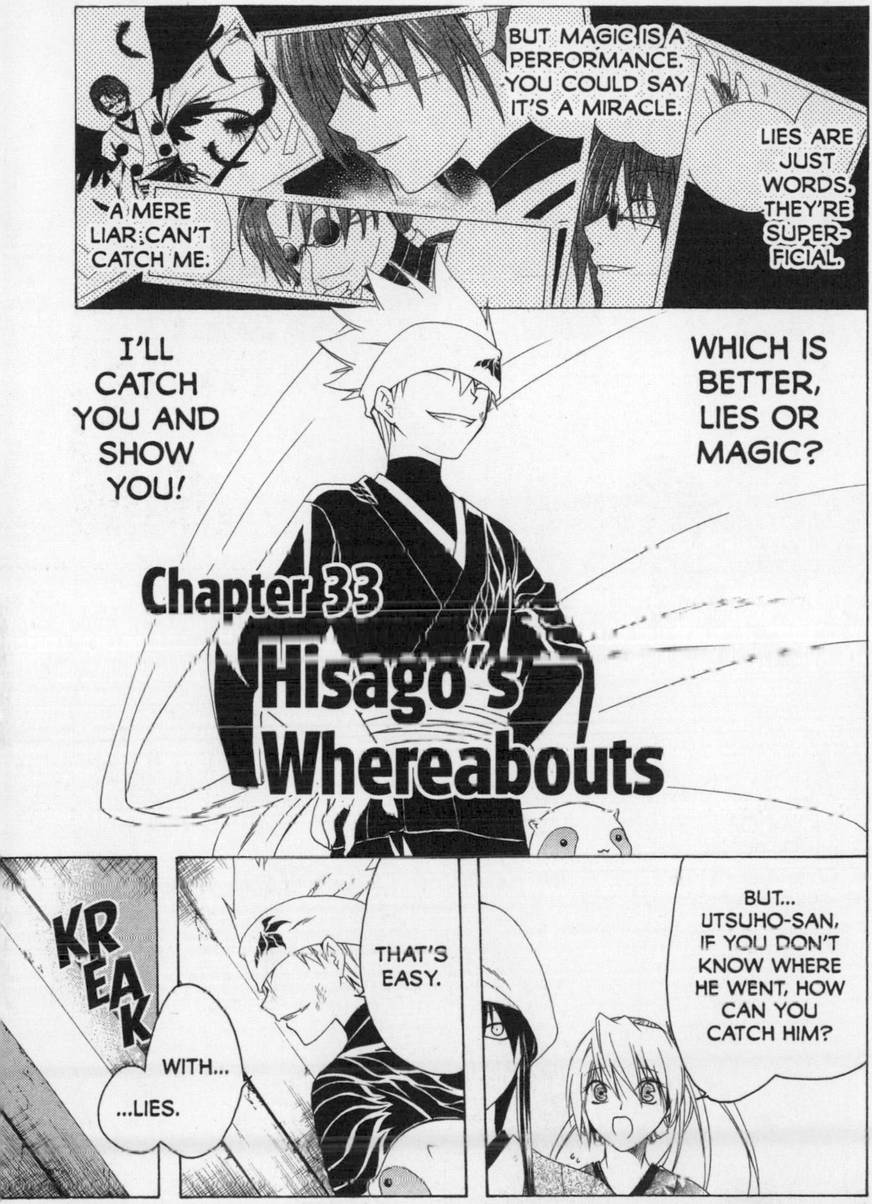
LIES ARE JUST WORDS. THEY'RE SUPER-FICIAL.
BUT MAGIC IS A PERFORMANCE. YOU COULD SAY IT'S A MIRACLE.
A MERE LIAR CAN'T CATCH ME.
WHICH IS BETTER, LIES OR MAGIC?
I'LL CATCH YOU AND SHOW YOU!
Chapter 33
Hisago's Whereabouts
BUT... UTSUHO-SAN, IF YOU DON'T KNOW WHERE HE WENT, HOW CAN YOU CATCH HIM?
THAT'S EASY.
KREAK
WITH...
...LIES.

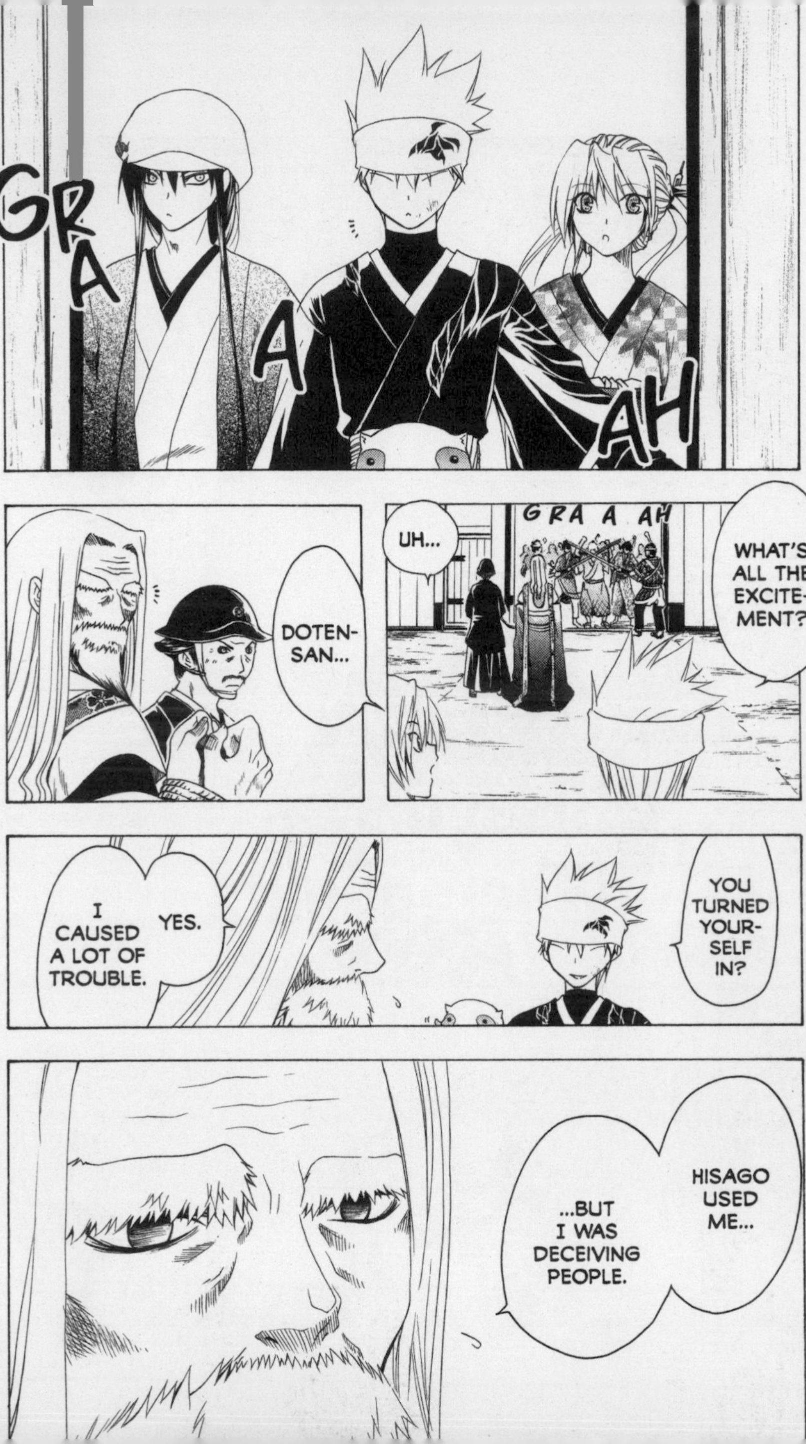
GRA
A
AH
WHAT'S ALL THE EXCITE- MENT?
GRA A AH
UH...
DOTEN- SAN...
YOU TURNED YOUR- SELF IN?
YES.
I CAUSED A LOT OF TROUBLE.
HISAGO USED ME...
...BUT I WAS DECEIVING PEOPLE.

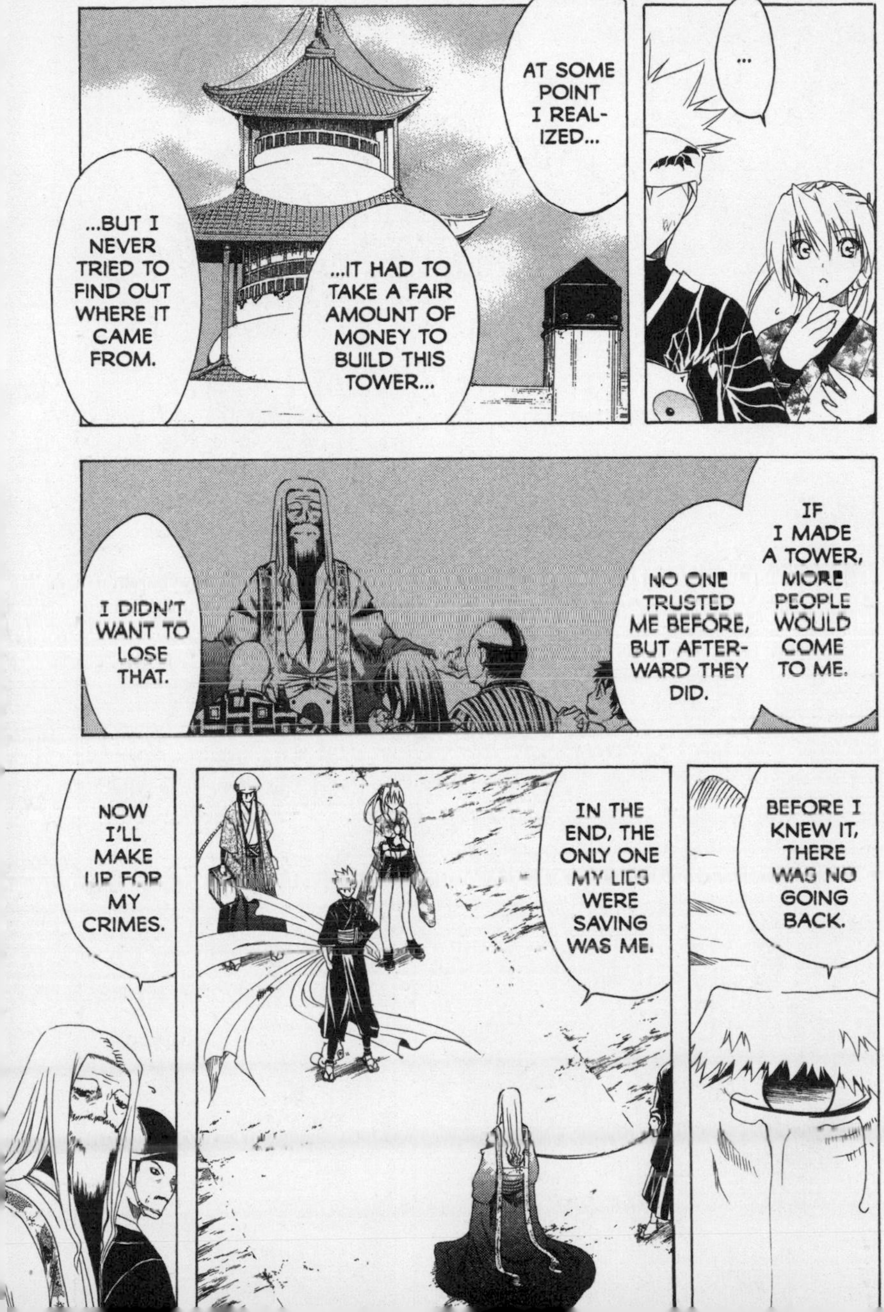
...
AT SOME POINT I REAL-IZED...
...IT HAD TO TAKE A FAIR AMOUNT OF MONEY TO BUILD THIS TOWER...
...BUT I NEVER TRIED TO FIND OUT WHERE IT CAME FROM.
IF I MADE A TOWER, MORE PEOPLE WOULD COME TO ME.
NO ONE TRUSTED ME BEFORE, BUT AFTER-WARD THEY DID.
I DIDN'T WANT TO LOSE THAT.
BEFORE I KNEW IT, THERE WAS NO GOING BACK.
IN THE END, THE ONLY ONE MY LIES WERE SAVING WAS ME.
NOW I'LL MAKE UP FOR MY CRIMES.

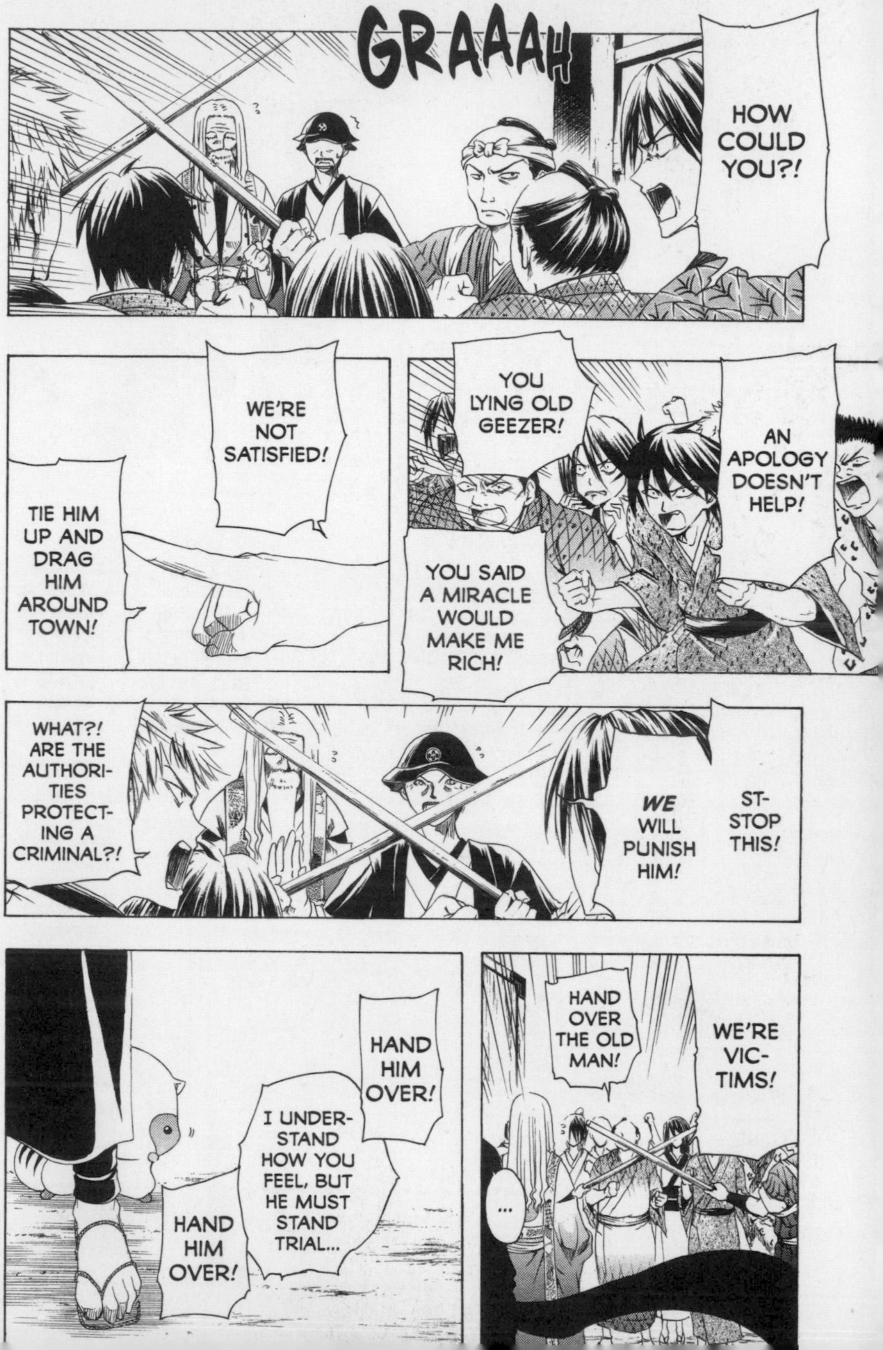
GRAAAH
HOW COULD YOU?!
AN APOLOGY DOESN'T HELP!
YOU LYING OLD GEEZER!
YOU SAID A MIRACLE WOULD MAKE ME RICH!
WE'RE NOT SATISFIED!
TIE HIM UP AND DRAG HIM AROUND TOWN!
ST-STOP THIS!
WE WILL PUNISH HIM!
WHAT?! ARE THE AUTHORITIES PROTECTING A CRIMINAL?!
WE'RE VICTIMS!
HAND OVER THE OLD MAN!
...
HAND HIM OVER!
I UNDERSTAND HOW YOU FEEL, BUT HE MUST STAND TRIAL...
HAND HIM OVER!

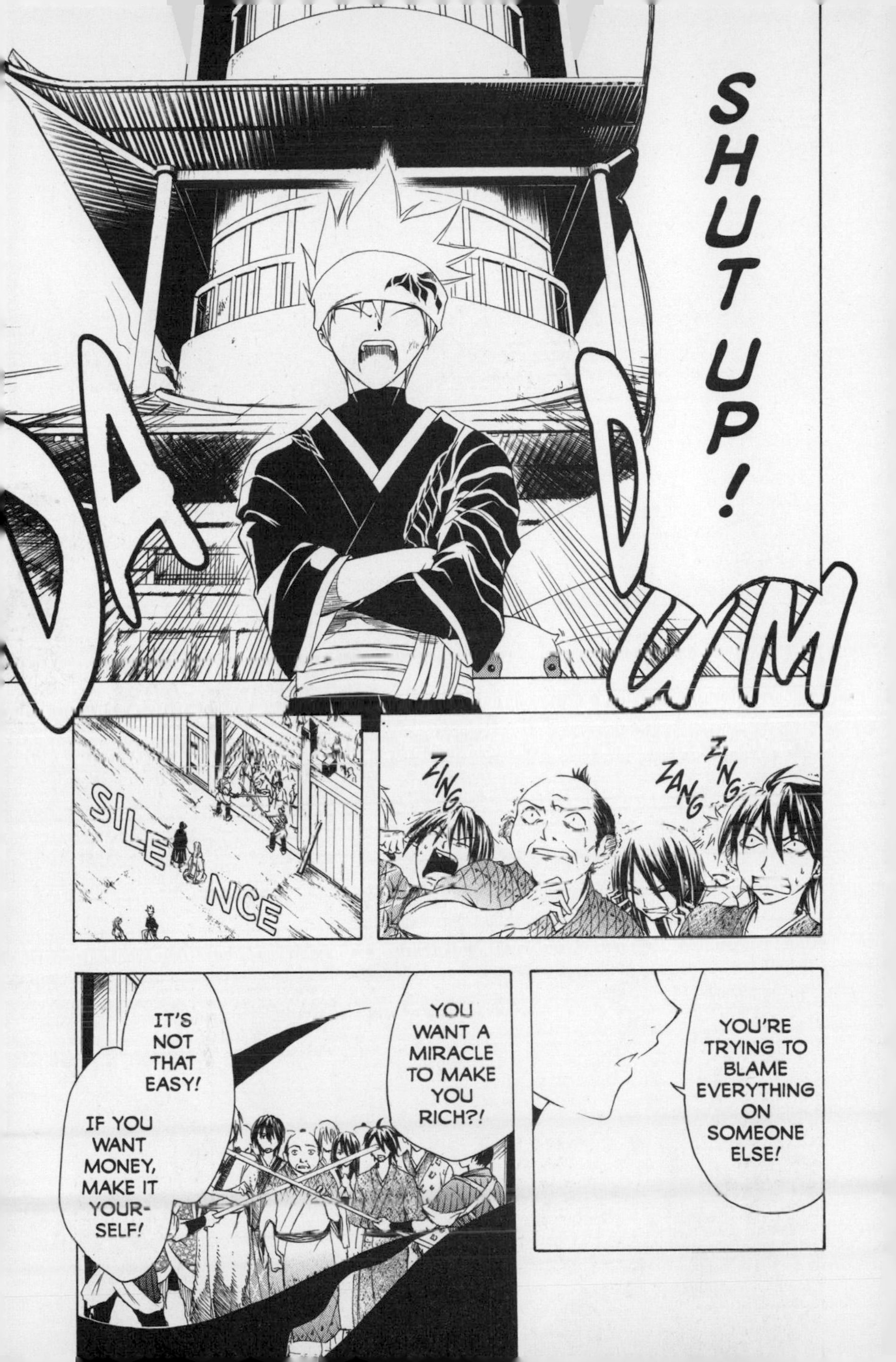
SHUT UP!
DADUM
ZING
ZANG
ZING
SILENCE
YOU'RE TRYING TO BLAME EVERYTHING ON SOMEONE ELSE!
YOU WANT A MIRACLE TO MAKE YOU RICH?!
IT'S NOT THAT EASY!
IF YOU WANT MONEY, MAKE IT YOURSELF!

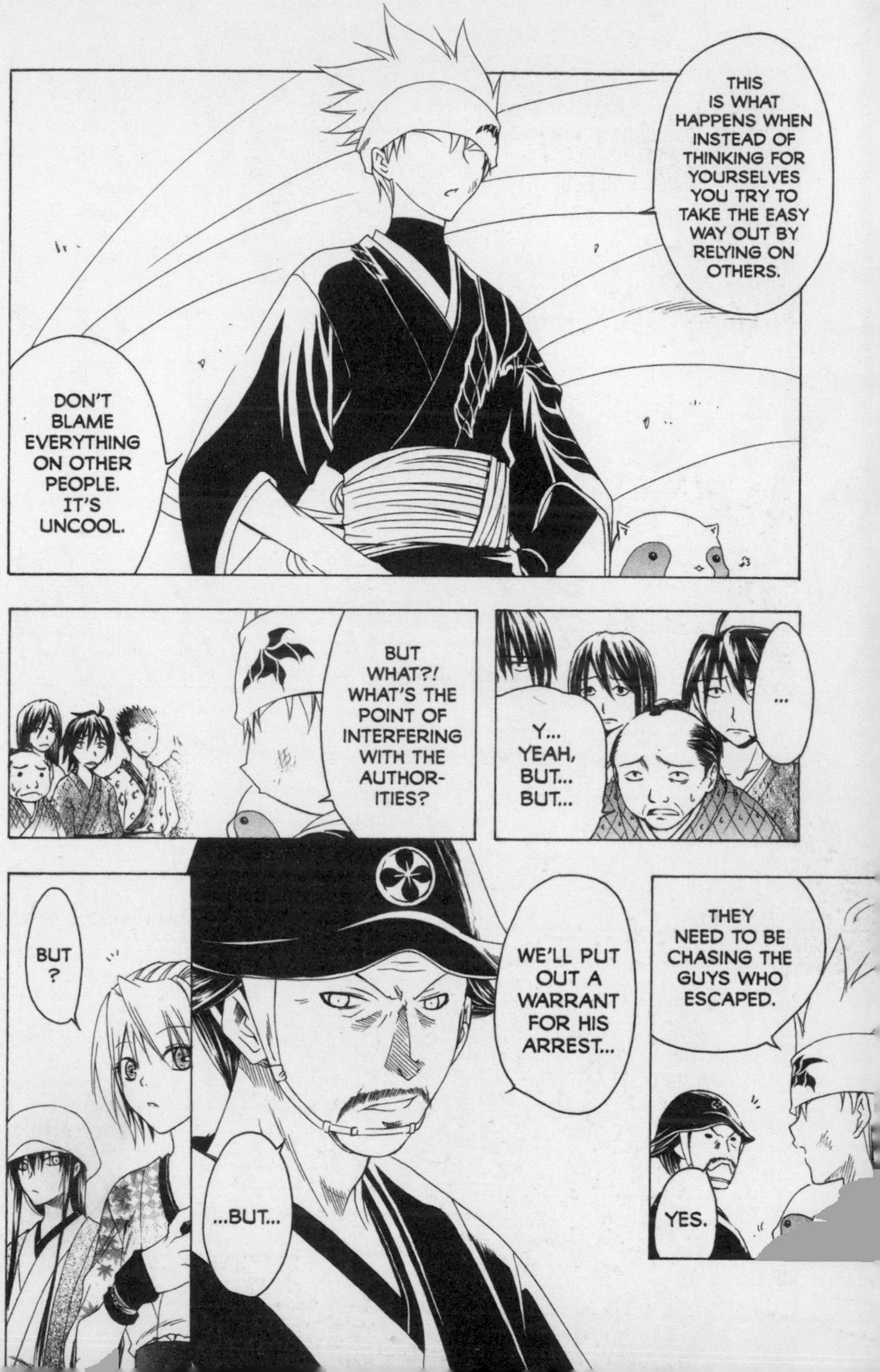
THIS IS WHAT HAPPENS WHEN INSTEAD OF THINKING FOR YOURSELVES YOU TRY TO TAKE THE EASY WAY OUT BY RELYING ON OTHERS.
DON'T BLAME EVERYTHING ON OTHER PEOPLE. IT'S UNCOOL.
...
Y... YEAH, BUT... BUT...
BUT WHAT?! WHAT'S THE POINT OF INTERFERING WITH THE AUTHOR-ITIES?
THEY NEED TO BE CHASING THE GUYS WHO ESCAPED.
YES.
WE'LL PUT OUT A WARRANT FOR HIS ARREST...
...BUT...
BUT ?

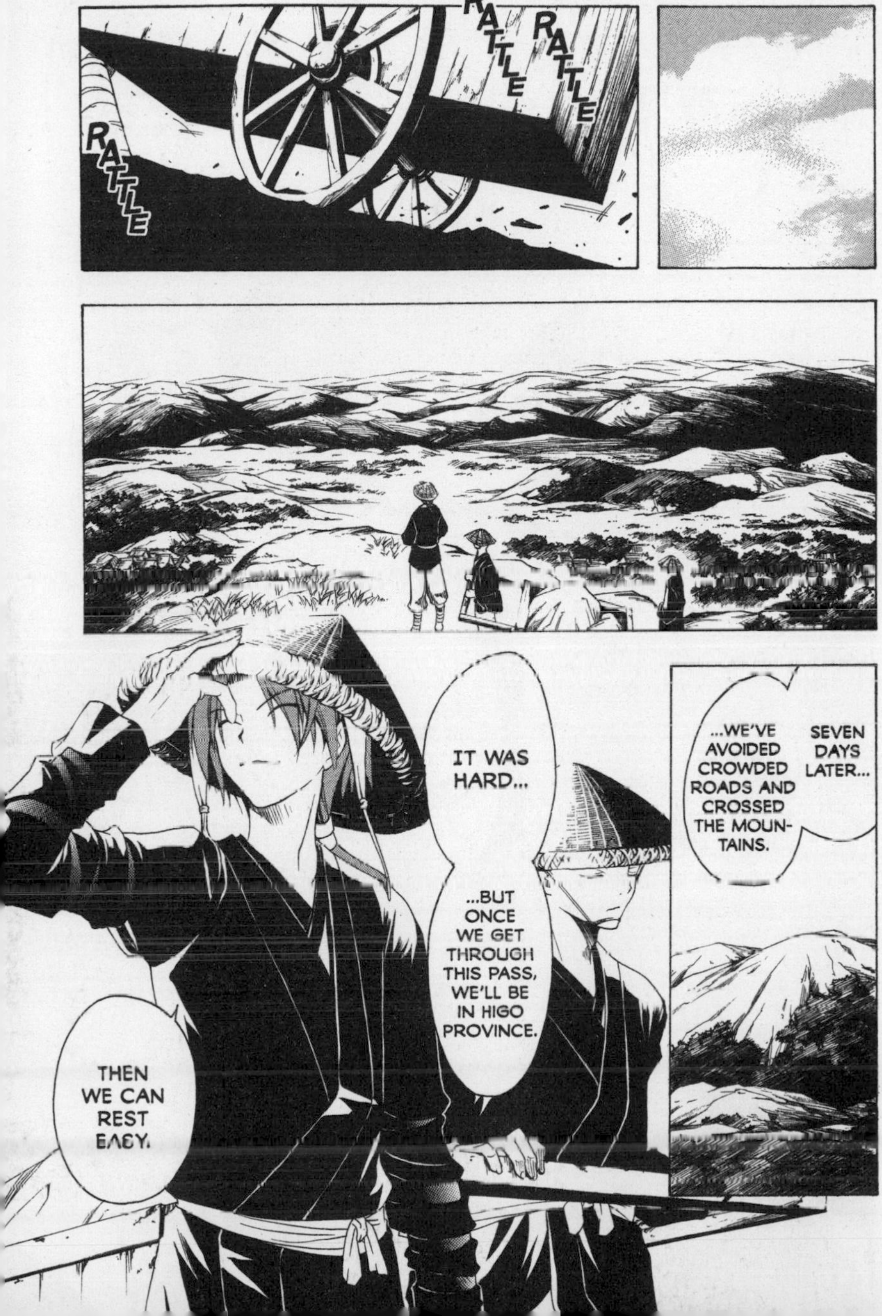
RATTLE RATTLE
RATTLE
SEVEN DAYS LATER...
...WE'VE AVOIDED CROWDED ROADS AND CROSSED THE MOUNTAINS.
IT WAS HARD...
...BUT ONCE WE GET THROUGH THIS PASS, WE'LL BE IN HIGO PROVINCE.
THEN WE CAN REST EASY.

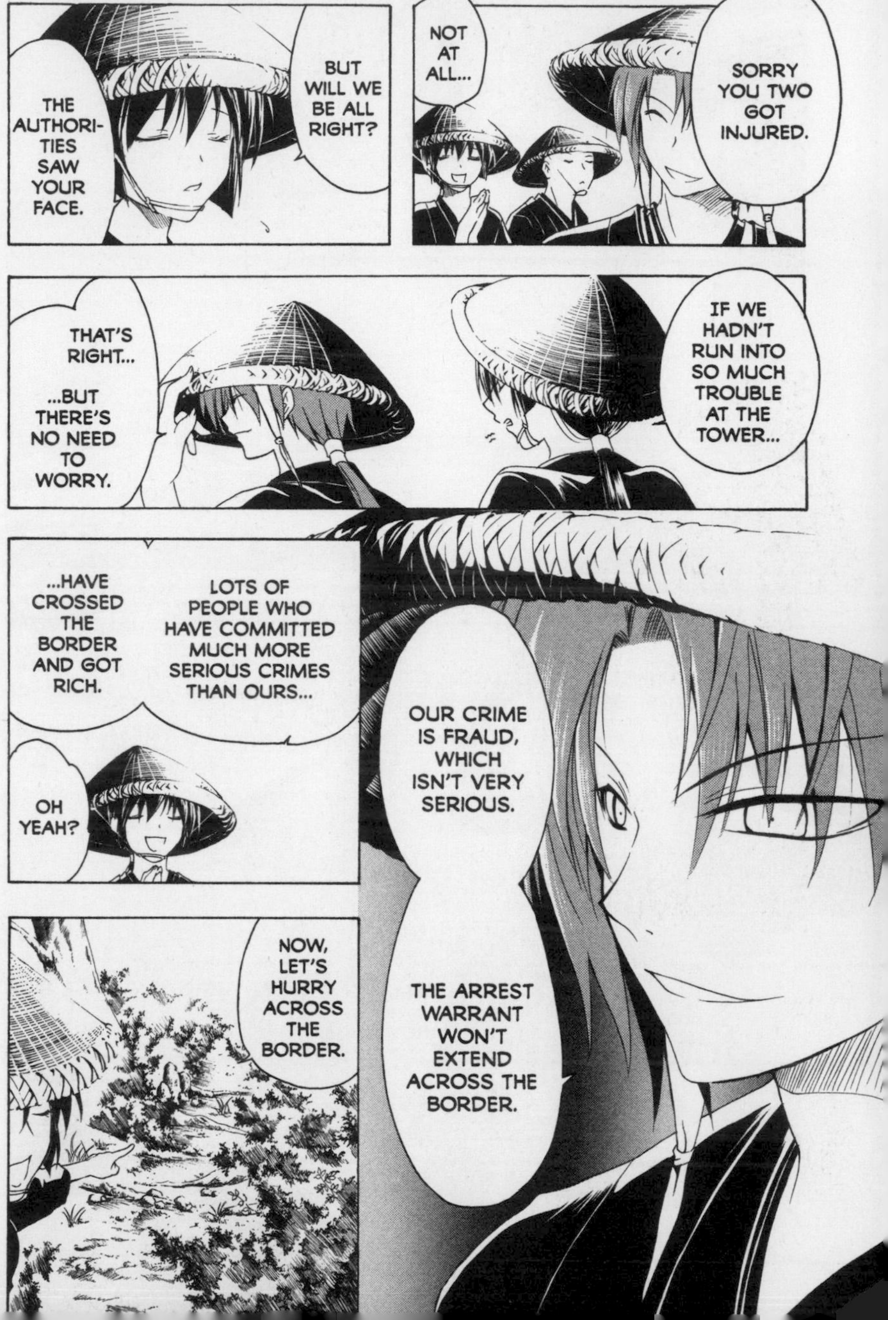
SORRY YOU TWO GOT INJURED.
NOT AT ALL...
BUT WILL WE BE ALL RIGHT?
THE AUTHORITIES SAW YOUR FACE.
IF WE HADN'T RUN INTO SO MUCH TROUBLE AT THE TOWER...
THAT'S RIGHT...
...BUT THERE'S NO NEED TO WORRY.
OUR CRIME IS FRAUD, WHICH ISN'T VERY SERIOUS.
THE ARREST WARRANT WON'T EXTEND ACROSS THE BORDER.
LOTS OF PEOPLE WHO HAVE COMMITTED MUCH MORE SERIOUS CRIMES THAN OURS...
...HAVE CROSSED THE BORDER AND GOT RICH.
OH YEAH?
NOW, LET'S HURRY ACROSS THE BORDER.

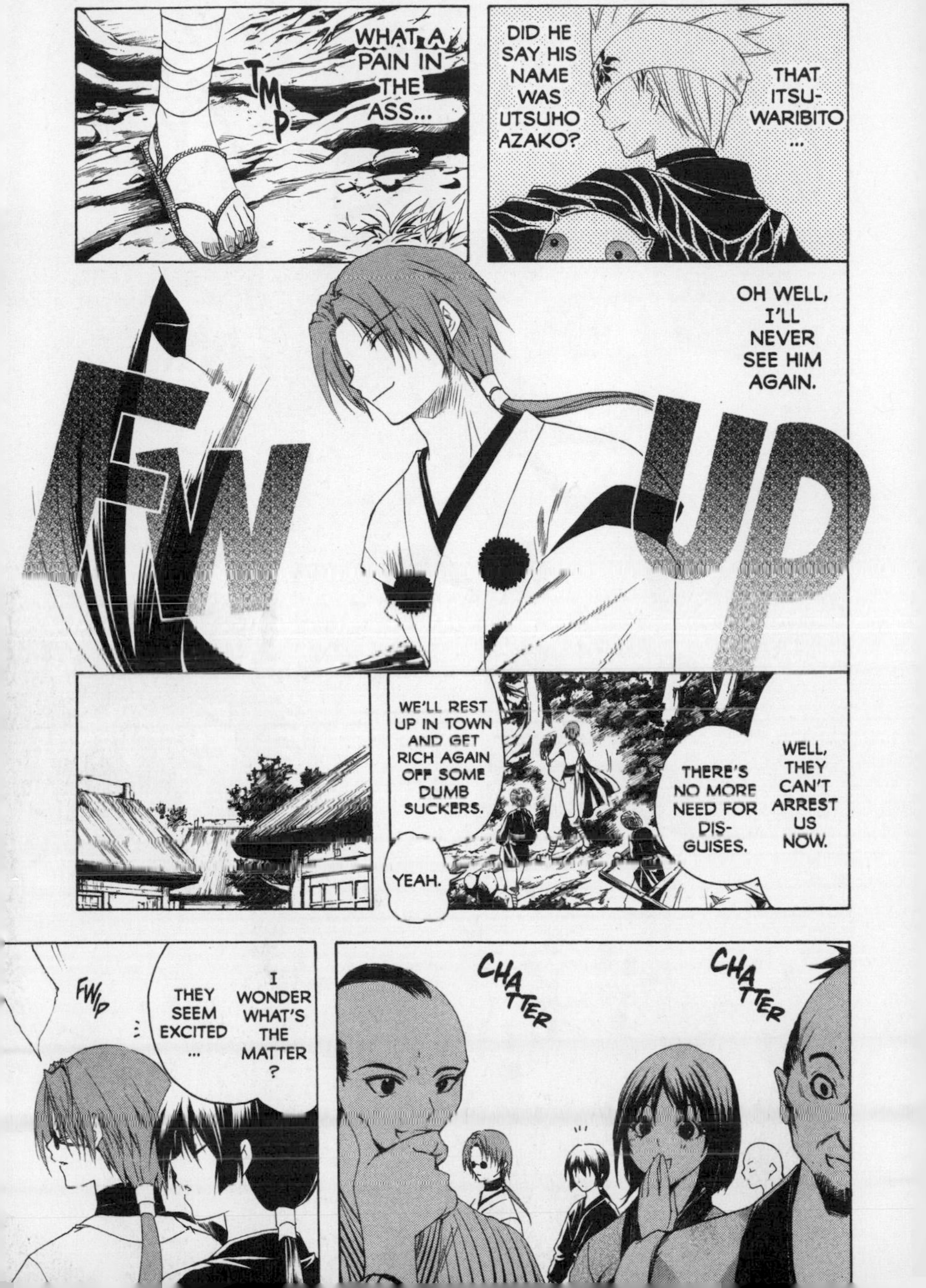
DID HE SAY HIS NAME WAS UTSUHO AZAKO?
THAT ITSU-WARIBITO ...
WHAT A PAIN IN THE ASS...
TMP
OH WELL, I'LL NEVER SEE HIM AGAIN.
FWUP
WELL, THEY CAN'T ARREST US NOW.
THERE'S NO MORE NEED FOR DIS-GUISES.
WE'LL REST UP IN TOWN AND GET RICH AGAIN OFF SOME DUMB SUCKERS.
YEAH.
CHATTER
CHATTER
I WONDER WHAT'S THE MATTER ?
THEY SEEM EXCITED ...
FWIP

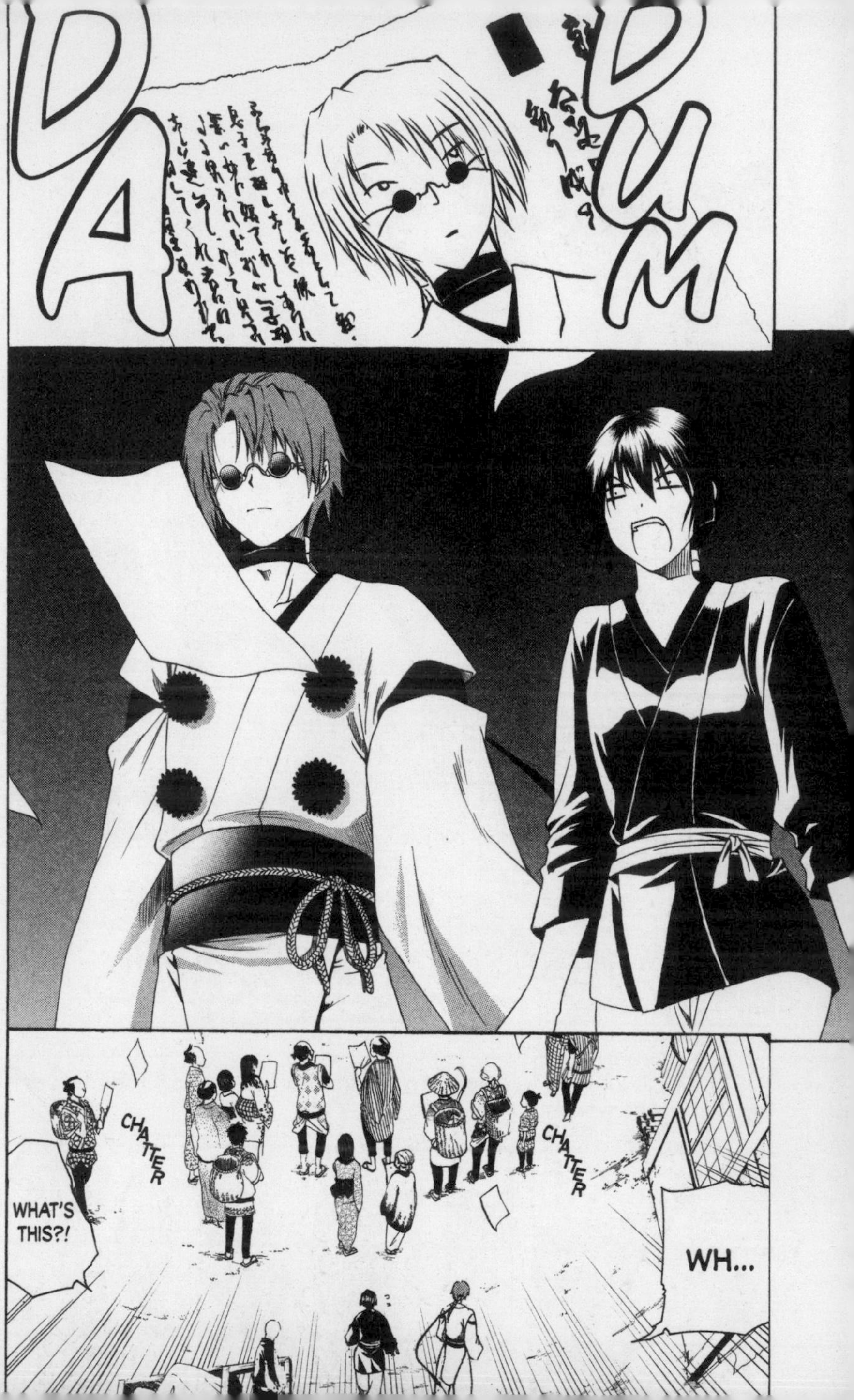
DA DUM
CHATTER
WH...
CHATTER
WHAT'S THIS?!

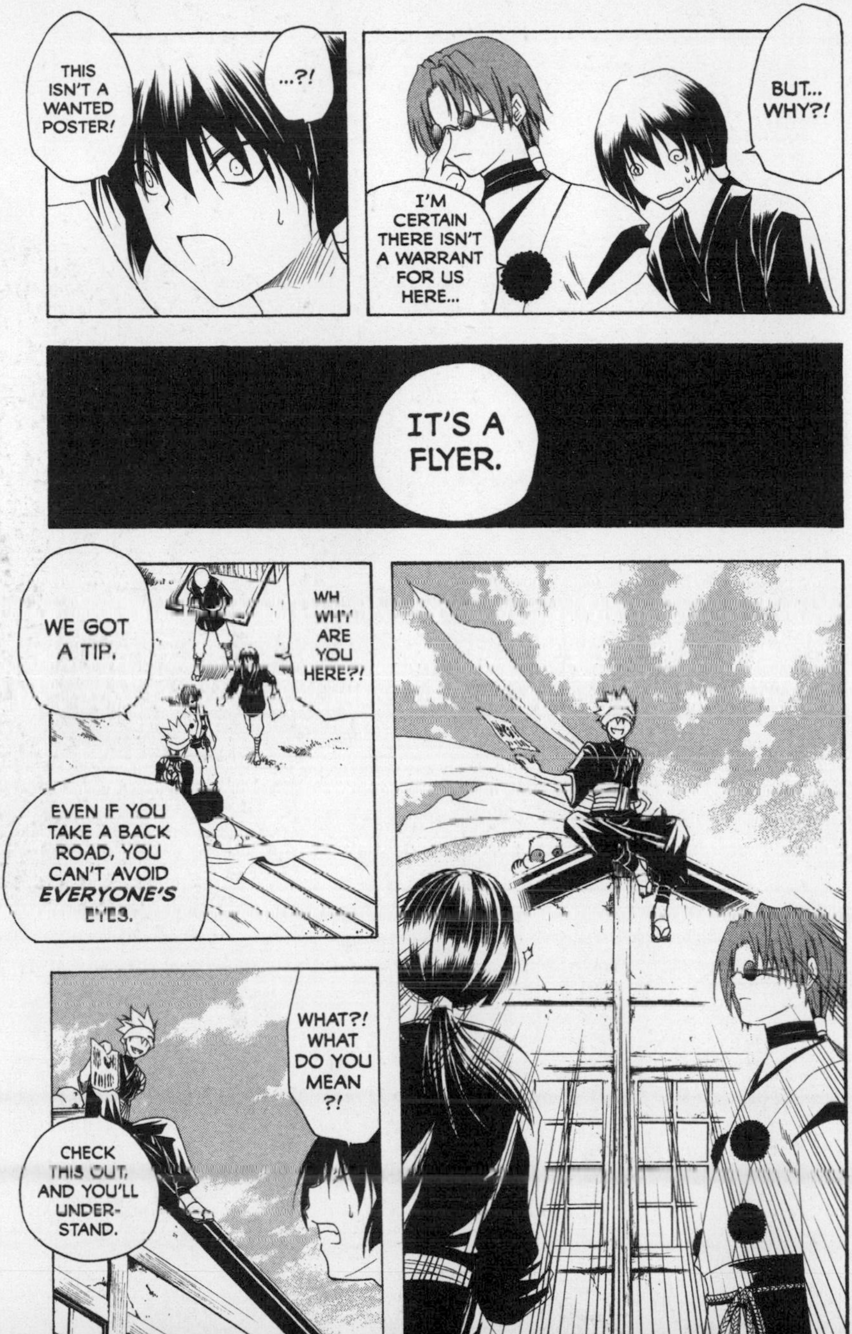
BUT... WHY?!
I'M CERTAIN THERE ISN'T A WARRANT FOR US HERE...
THIS ISN'T A WANTED POSTER!
...?!
IT'S A FLYER.
WH WHY ARE YOU HERE?!
WE GOT A TIP.
EVEN IF YOU TAKE A BACK ROAD, YOU CAN'T AVOID *EVERYONE'S* EYES.
WHAT?! WHAT DO YOU MEAN ?!
CHECK THIS OUT, AND YOU'LL UNDER-STAND.

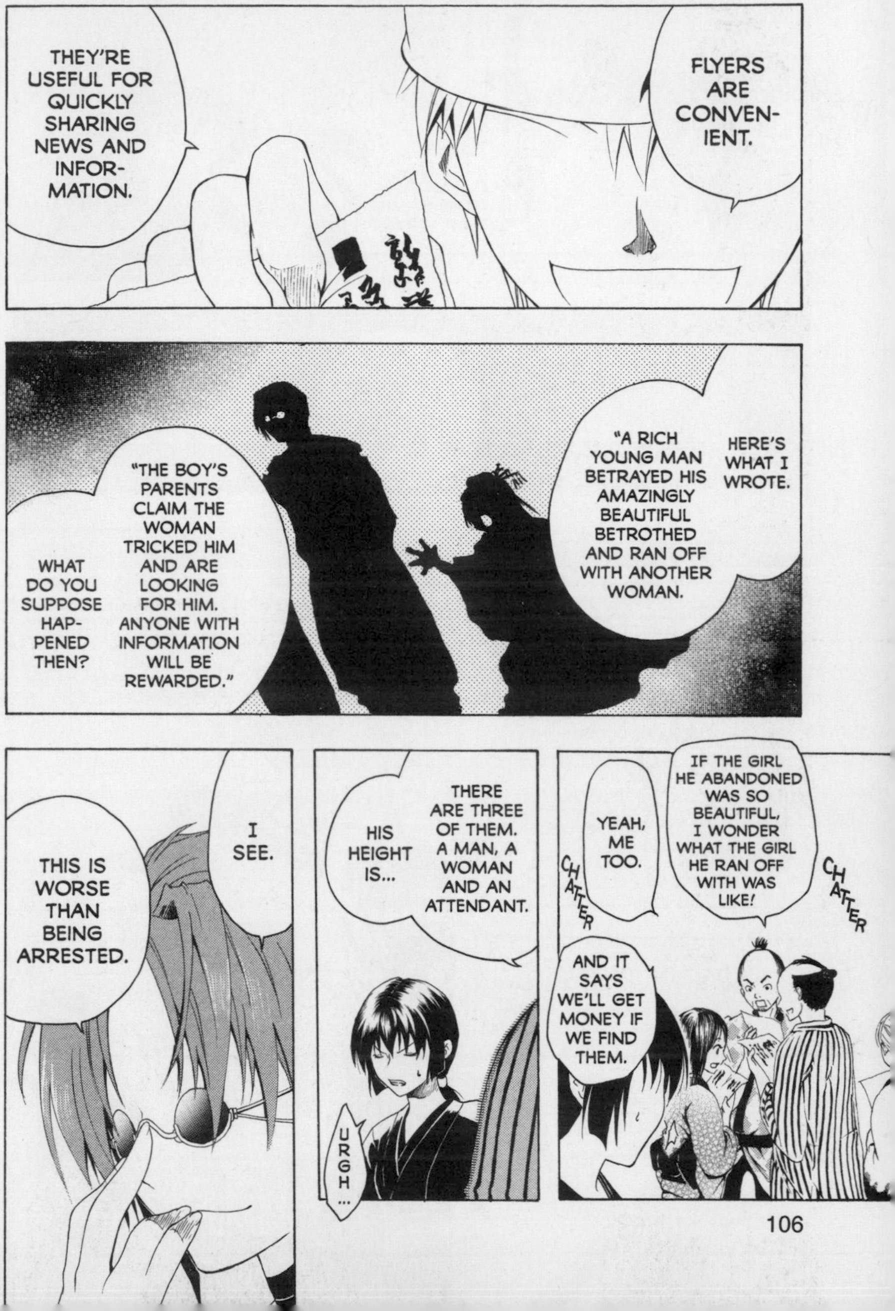
FLYERS ARE CONVEN-IENT.
THEY'RE USEFUL FOR QUICKLY SHARING NEWS AND INFOR-MATION.
HERE'S WHAT I WROTE.
"A RICH YOUNG MAN BETRAYED HIS AMAZINGLY BEAUTIFUL BETROTHED AND RAN OFF WITH ANOTHER WOMAN.
"THE BOY'S PARENTS CLAIM THE WOMAN TRICKED HIM AND ARE LOOKING FOR HIM. ANYONE WITH INFORMATION WILL BE REWARDED."
WHAT DO YOU SUPPOSE HAP-PENED THEN?
CHATTER
IF THE GIRL HE ABANDONED WAS SO BEAUTIFUL, I WONDER WHAT THE GIRL HE RAN OFF WITH WAS LIKE!
YEAH, ME TOO.
CHATTER
AND IT SAYS WE'LL GET MONEY IF WE FIND THEM.
THERE ARE THREE OF THEM. A MAN, A WOMAN AND AN ATTENDANT.
HIS HEIGHT IS...
URGH...
I SEE.
THIS IS WORSE THAN BEING ARRESTED.

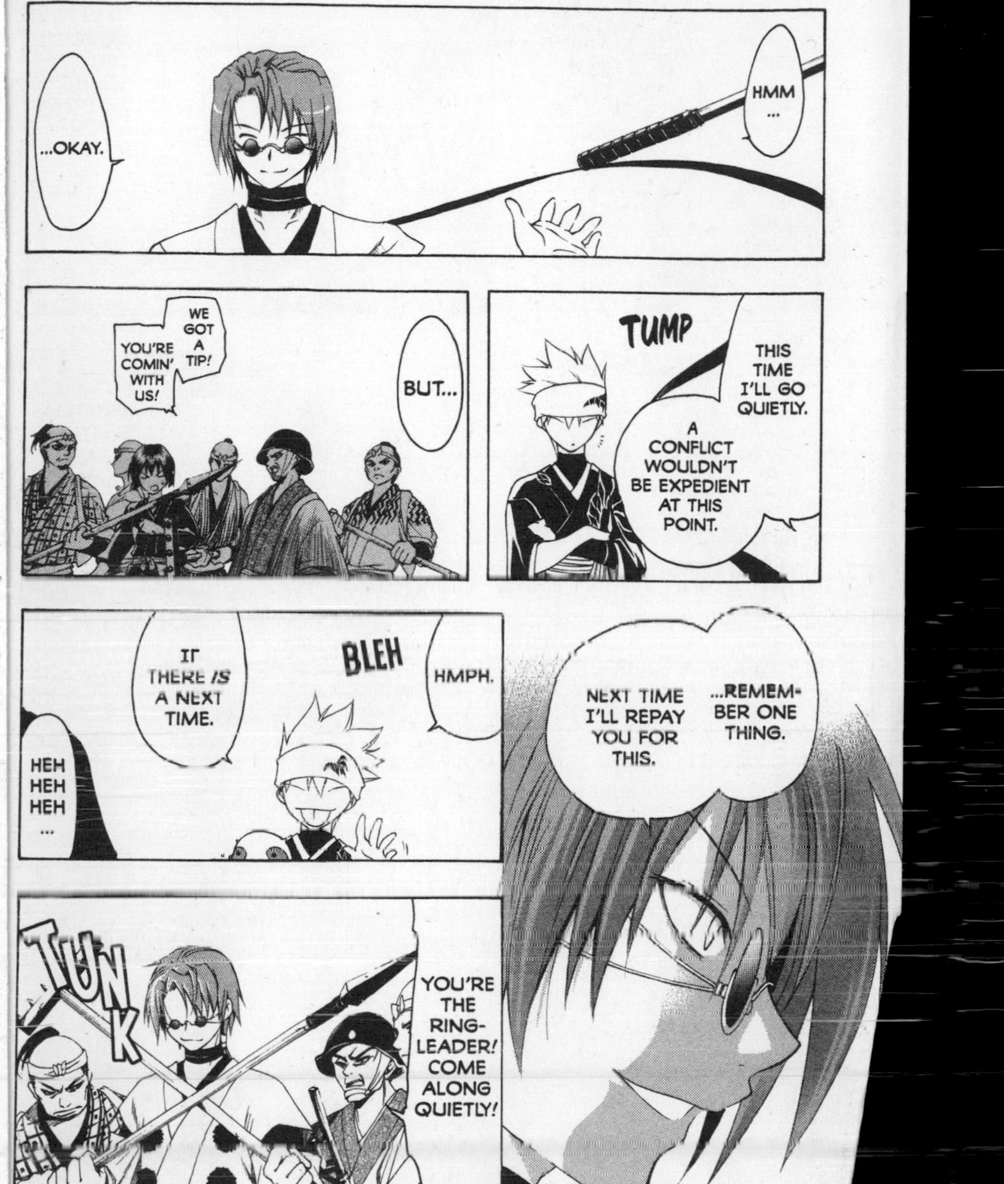
HMM ...
...OKAY.
TUMP
THIS TIME I'LL GO QUIETLY.
A CONFLICT WOULDN'T BE EXPEDIENT AT THIS POINT.
BUT...
WE GOT A TIP!
YOU'RE COMIN' WITH US!
...REMEMBER ONE THING.
NEXT TIME I'LL REPAY YOU FOR THIS.
HMPH.
BLEH
IF THERE IS A NEXT TIME.
HEH HEH HEH ...
TUNK
YOU'RE THE RINGLEADER! COME ALONG QUIETLY!

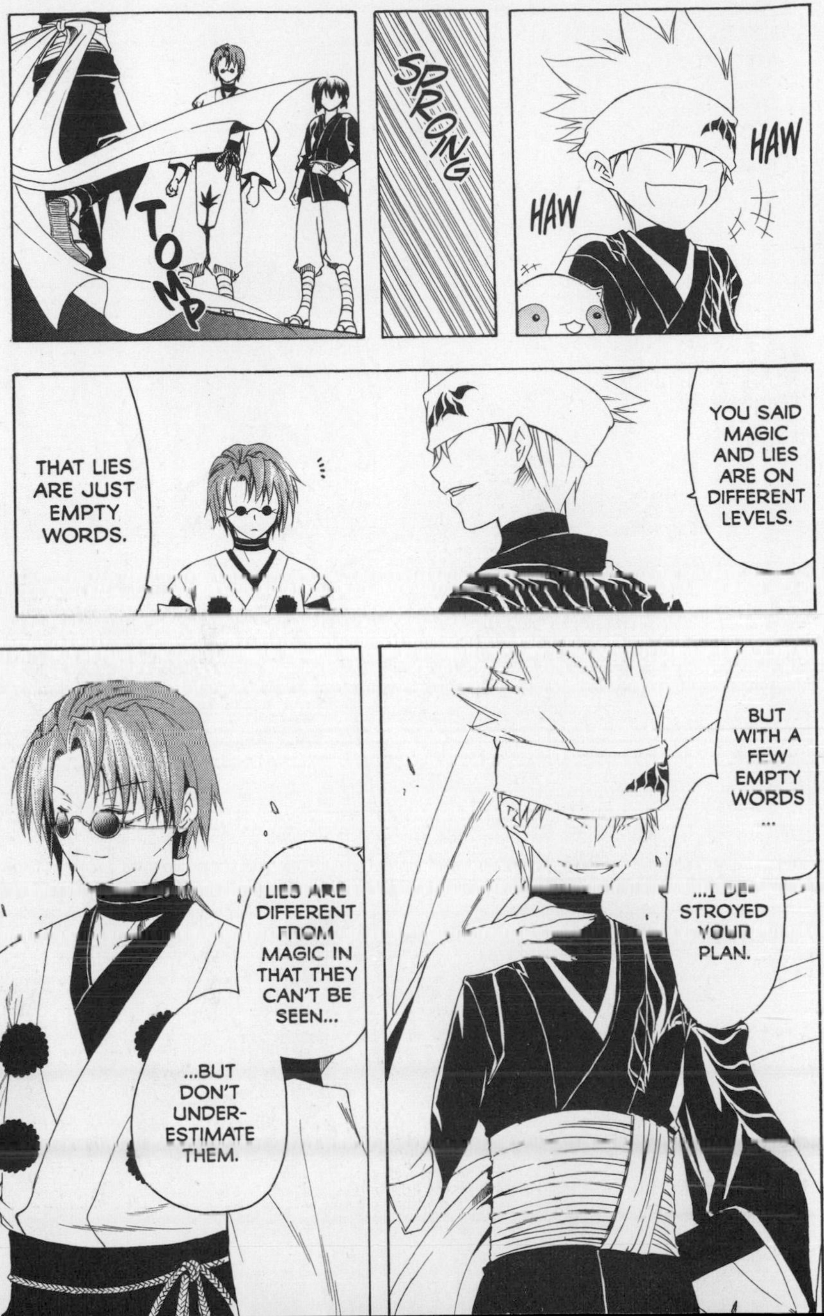
HAW
HAW
SPRONG
TOMP
YOU SAID MAGIC AND LIES ARE ON DIFFERENT LEVELS.
THAT LIES ARE JUST EMPTY WORDS.
BUT WITH A FEW EMPTY WORDS ...
...I DESTROYED YOUR PLAN.
LIES ARE DIFFERENT FROM MAGIC IN THAT THEY CAN'T BE SEEN...
...BUT DON'T UNDERESTIMATE THEM.

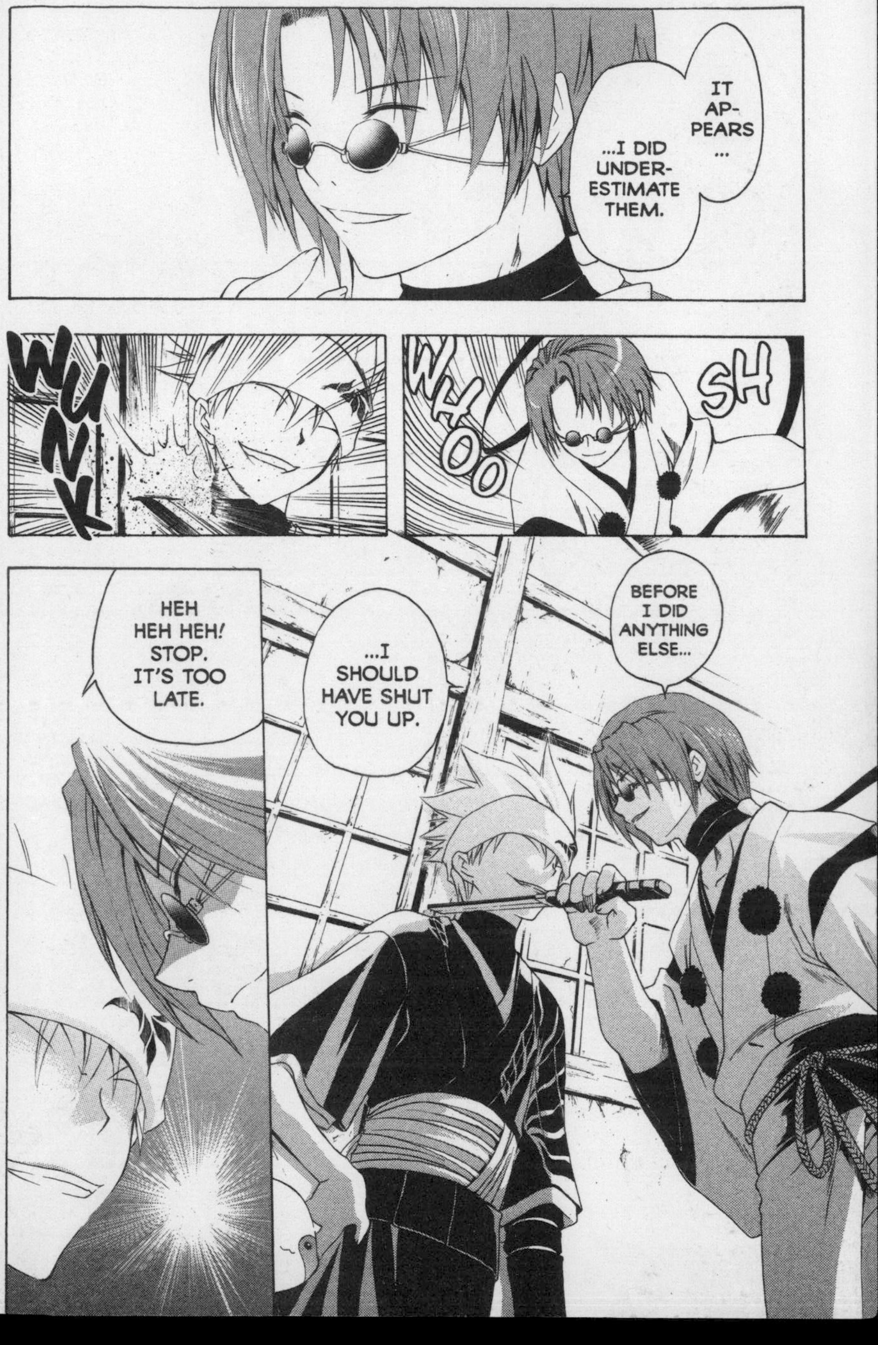
IT AP- PEARS ...
...I DID UNDER- ESTIMATE THEM.
WHOOSH
WUNK
BEFORE I DID ANYTHING ELSE...
...I SHOULD HAVE SHUT YOU UP.
HEH HEH HEH! STOP. IT'S TOO LATE.

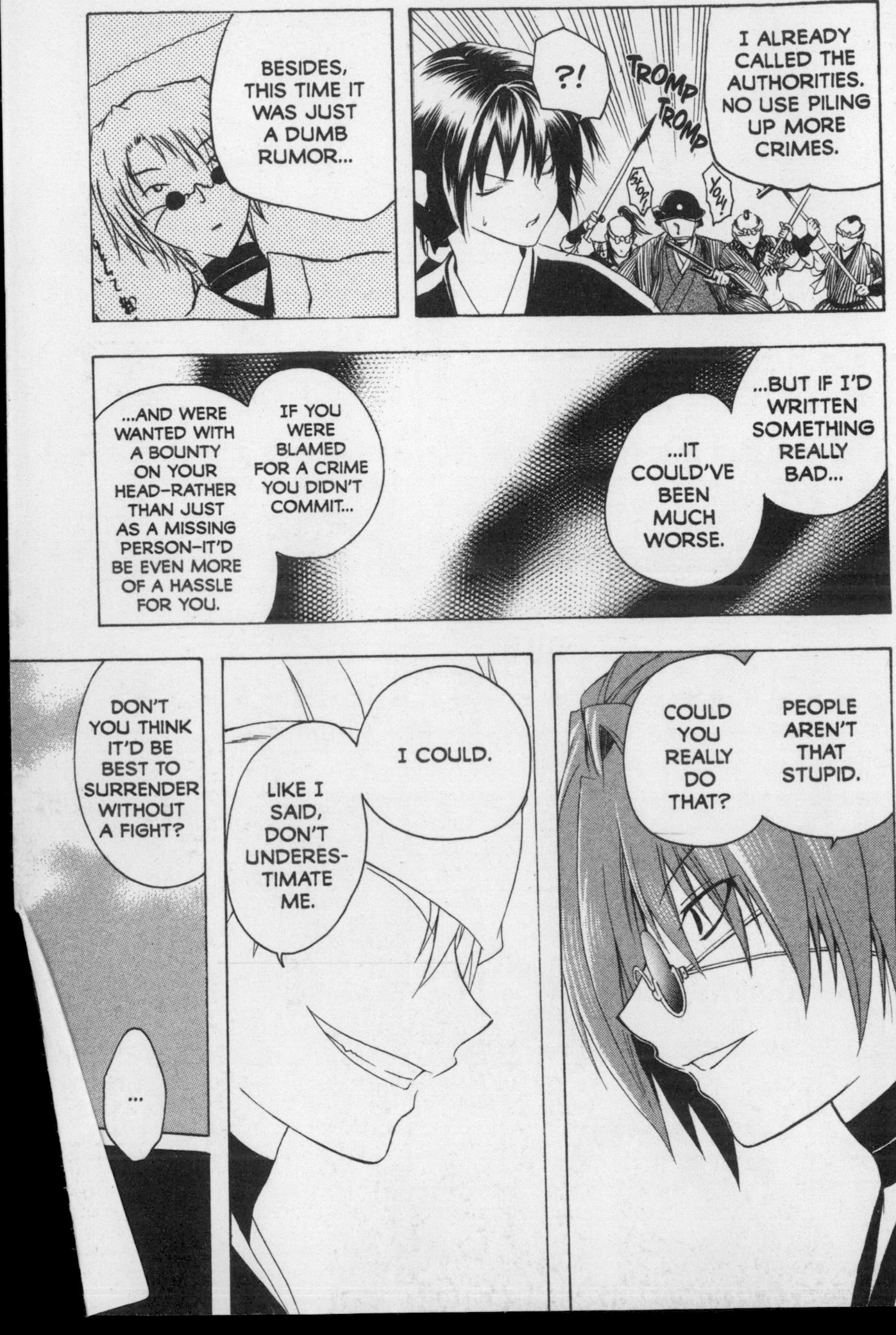
I ALREADY CALLED THE AUTHORITIES. NO USE PILING UP MORE CRIMES.
?!
TROMP TROMP
BESIDES, THIS TIME IT WAS JUST A DUMB RUMOR...
...BUT IF I'D WRITTEN SOMETHING REALLY BAD...
...IT COULD'VE BEEN MUCH WORSE.
IF YOU WERE BLAMED FOR A CRIME YOU DIDN'T COMMIT...
...AND WERE WANTED WITH A BOUNTY ON YOUR HEAD–RATHER THAN JUST AS A MISSING PERSON–IT'D BE EVEN MORE OF A HASSLE FOR YOU.
PEOPLE AREN'T THAT STUPID.
COULD YOU REALLY DO THAT?
I COULD.
LIKE I SAID, DON'T UNDERES- TIMATE ME.
DON'T YOU THINK IT'D BE BEST TO SURRENDER WITHOUT A FIGHT?
...

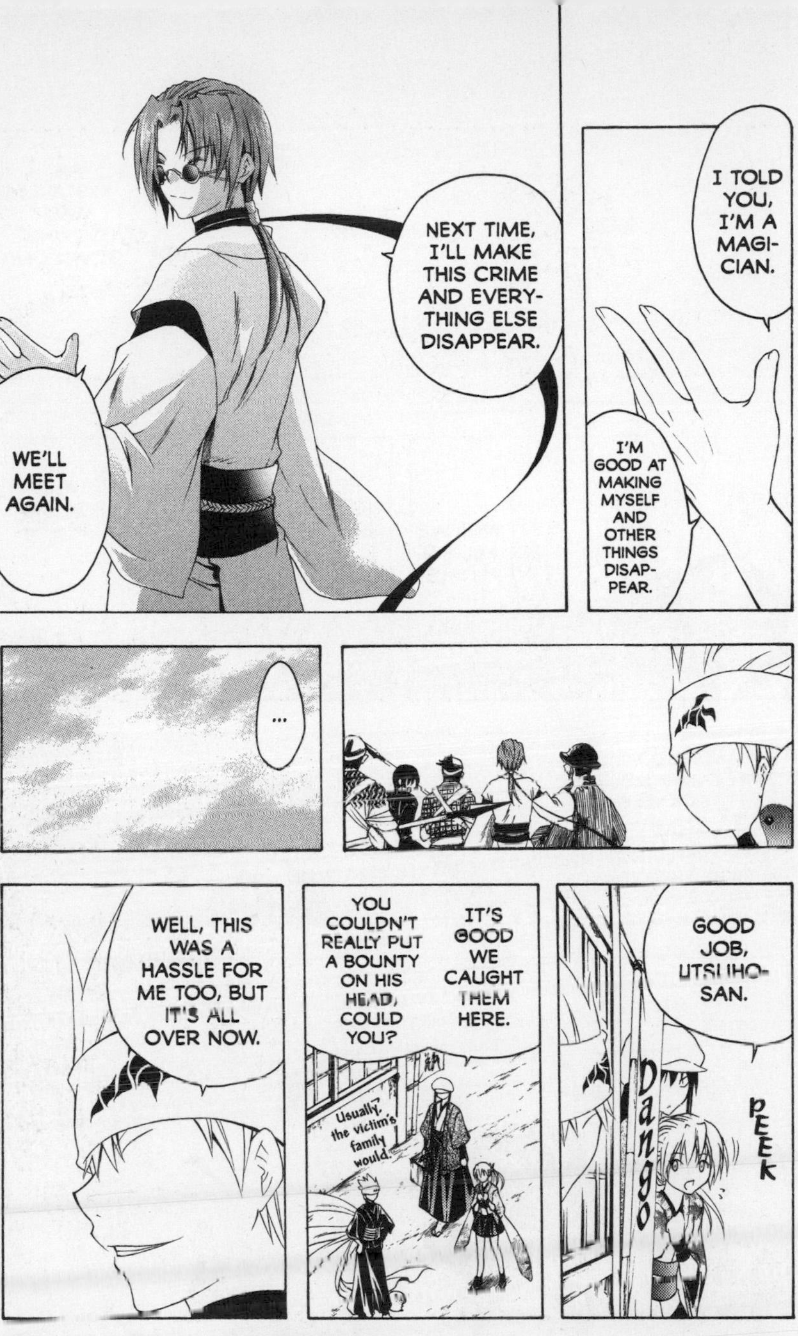
I TOLD YOU, I'M A MAGI-CIAN.
I'M GOOD AT MAKING MYSELF AND OTHER THINGS DISAP-PEAR.
NEXT TIME, I'LL MAKE THIS CRIME AND EVERY-THING ELSE DISAPPEAR.
WE'LL MEET AGAIN.
...
GOOD JOB, UTSUHO-SAN.
Dango
PEEK
IT'S GOOD WE CAUGHT THEM HERE.
YOU COULDN'T REALLY PUT A BOUNTY ON HIS HEAD, COULD YOU?
Usually, the victim's family would.
WELL, THIS WAS A HASSLE FOR ME TOO, BUT IT'S ALL OVER NOW.

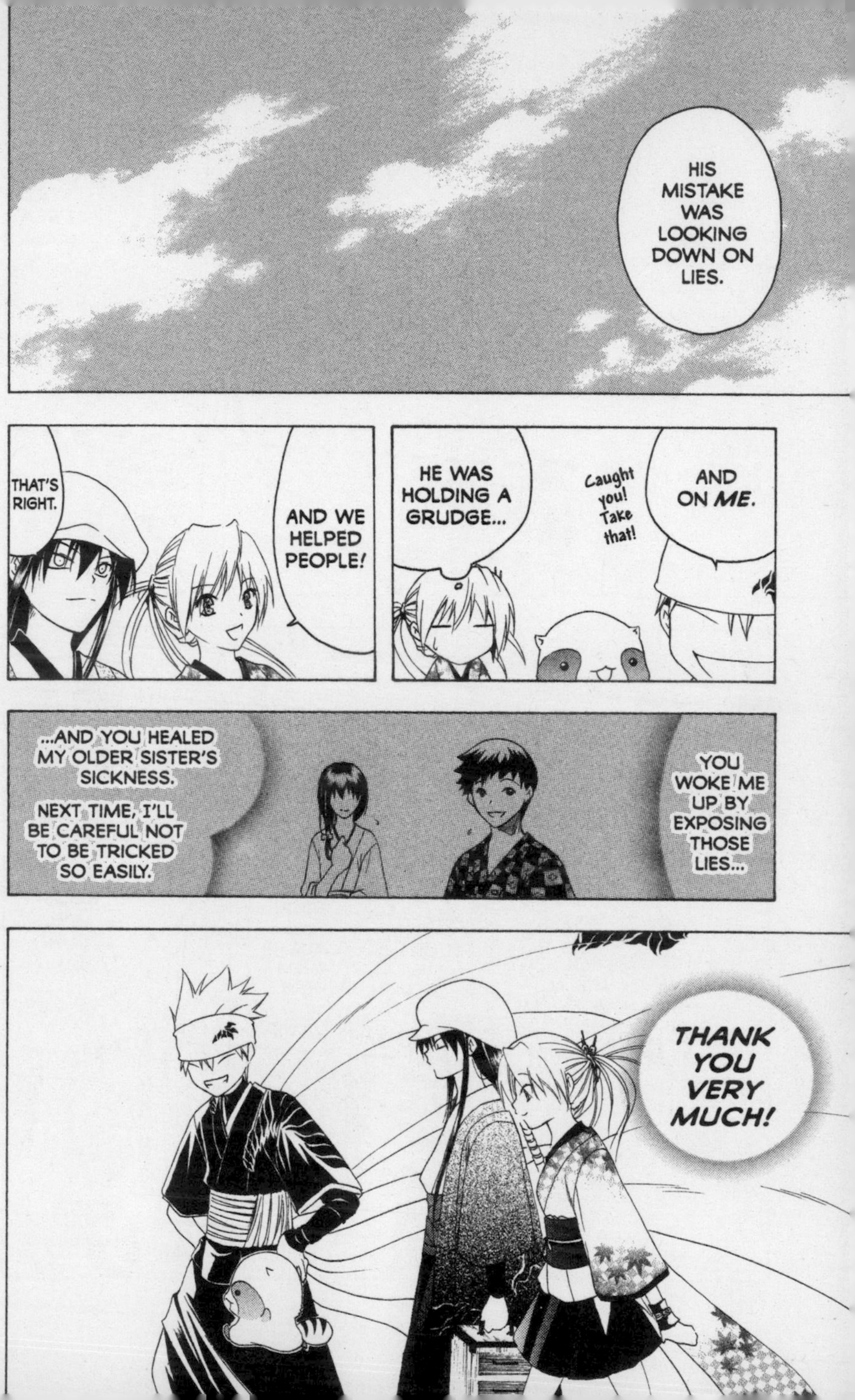
HIS MISTAKE WAS LOOKING DOWN ON LIES.
AND ON *ME*.
Caught you! Take that!
HE WAS HOLDING A GRUDGE...
AND WE HELPED PEOPLE!
THAT'S RIGHT.
YOU WOKE ME UP BY EXPOSING THOSE LIES...
...AND YOU HEALED MY OLDER SISTER'S SICKNESS.
NEXT TIME, I'LL BE CAREFUL NOT TO BE TRICKED SO EASILY.
THANK YOU VERY MUCH!

Itsuwaribito◆空◆

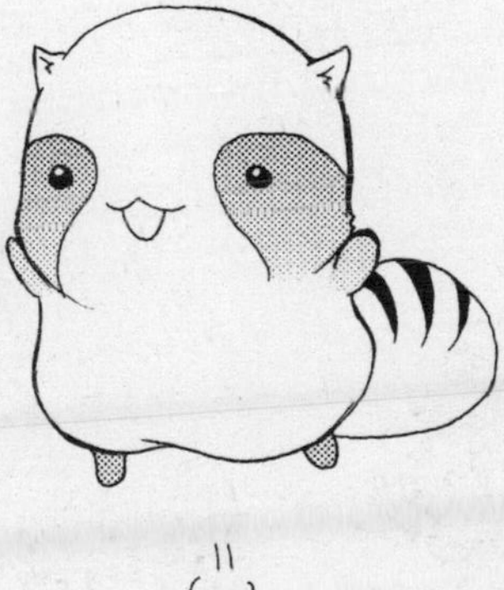

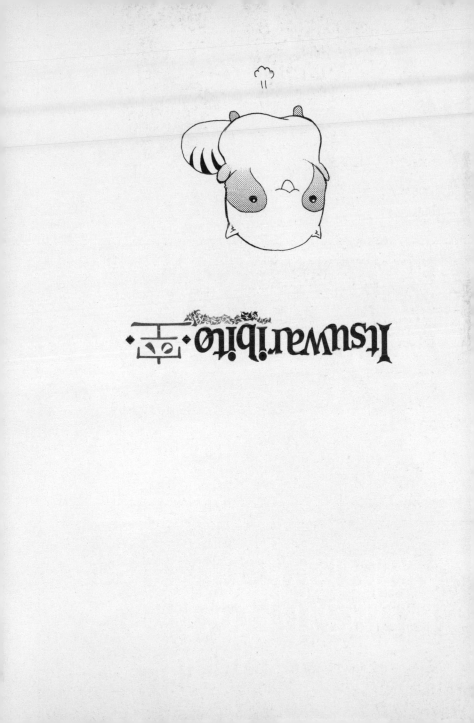

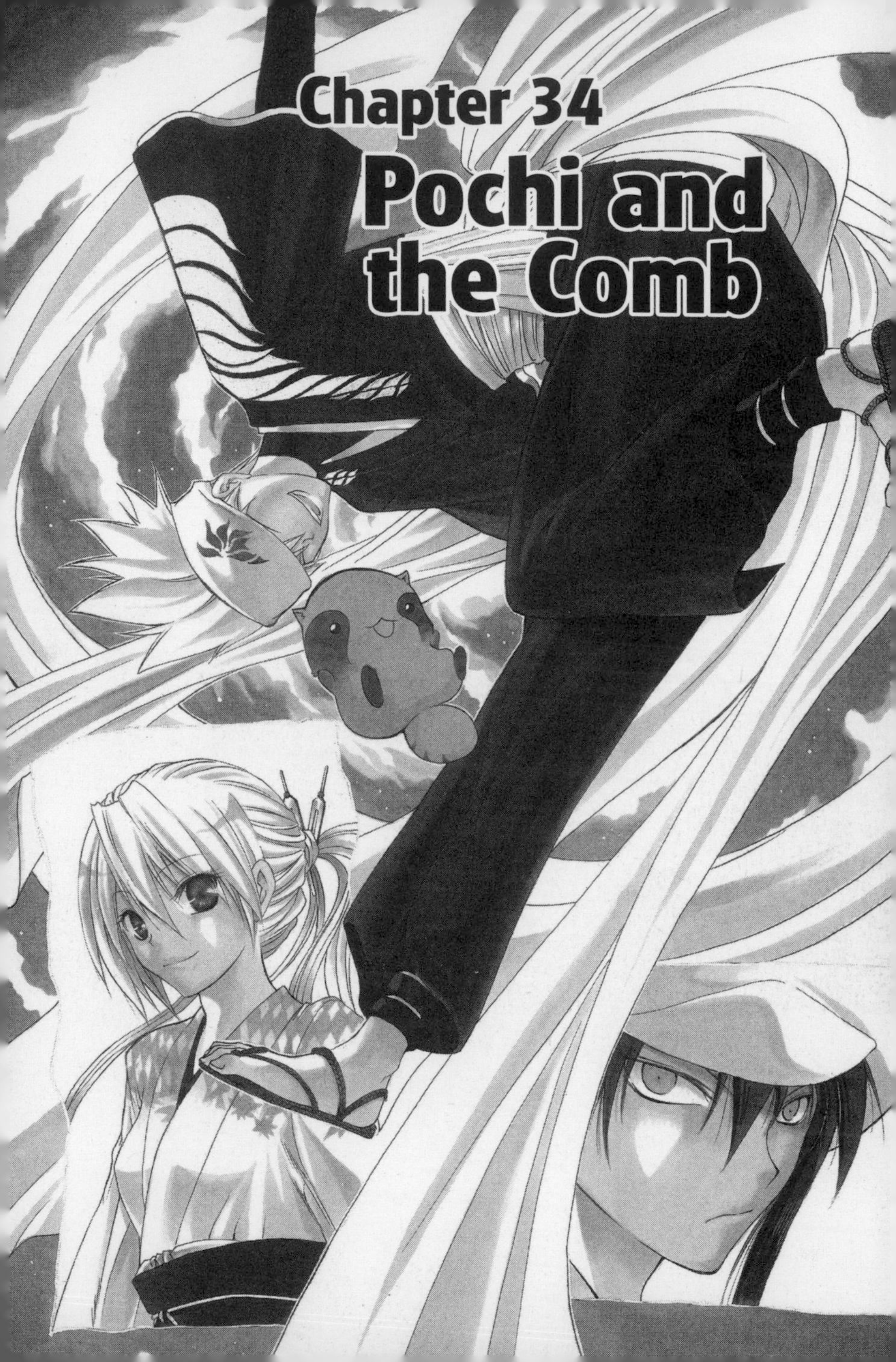
Chapter 34
Pochi and the Comb

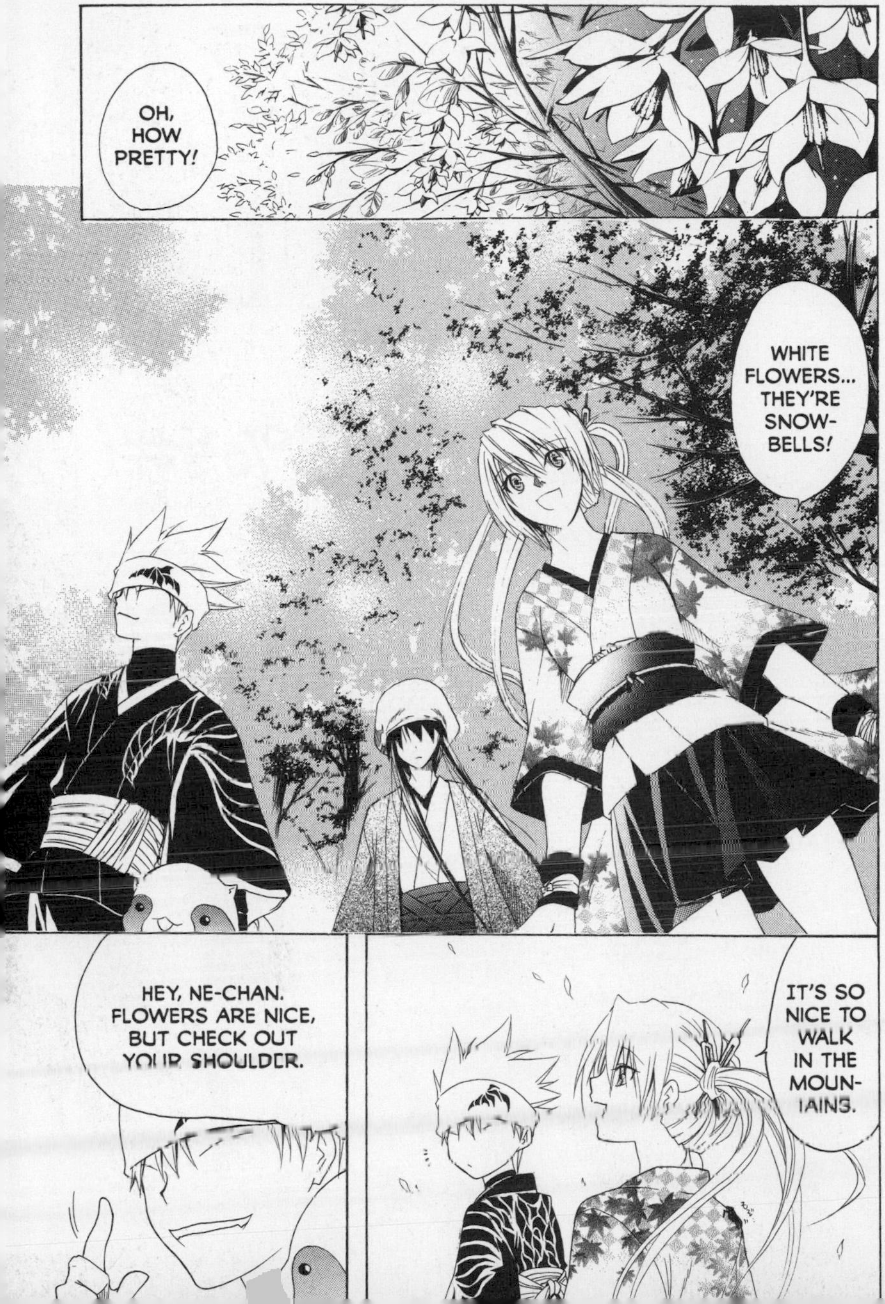
OH, HOW PRETTY!
WHITE FLOWERS... THEY'RE SNOW-BELLS!
IT'S SO NICE TO WALK IN THE MOUN-TAINS.
HEY, NE-CHAN. FLOWERS ARE NICE, BUT CHECK OUT YOUR SHOULDER.

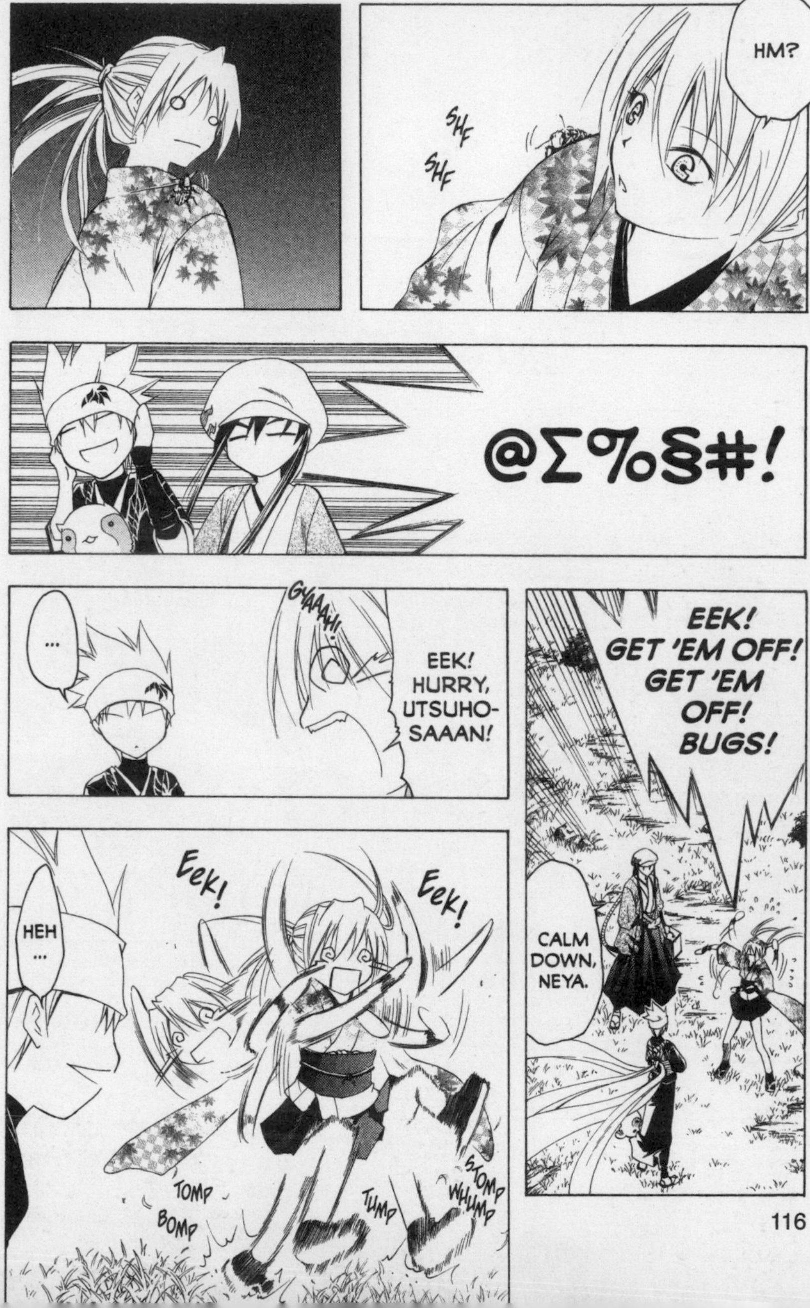
HM?
SHF
SHF
@Σ%§#!
EEK! GET 'EM OFF! GET 'EM OFF! BUGS!
CALM DOWN, NEYA.
GYAAAH!
EEK! HURRY, UTSUHO-SAAAN!
...
Eek!
Eek!
HEH ...
STOMP
WHUMP
TUMP
TOMP
BOMP

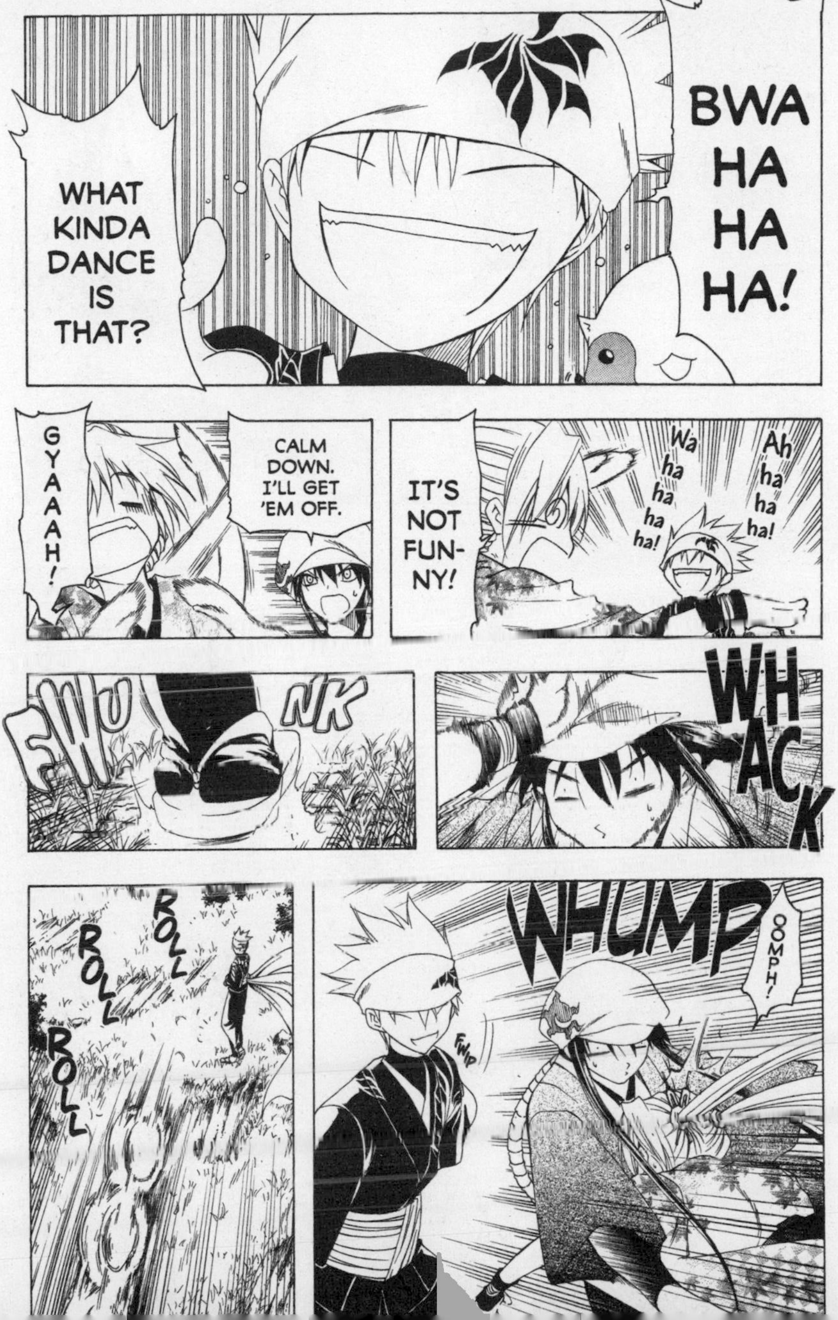
BWA HA HA HA!
WHAT KINDA DANCE IS THAT?
Ah ha ha ha ha!
Wa ha ha ha ha!
IT'S NOT FUN-NY!
CALM DOWN. I'LL GET 'EM OFF.
GYAAAAH!
WHACK
FWUNK
WHUMP
OOMPH!
FWIP
ROLL
ROLL
ROLL
ROLL

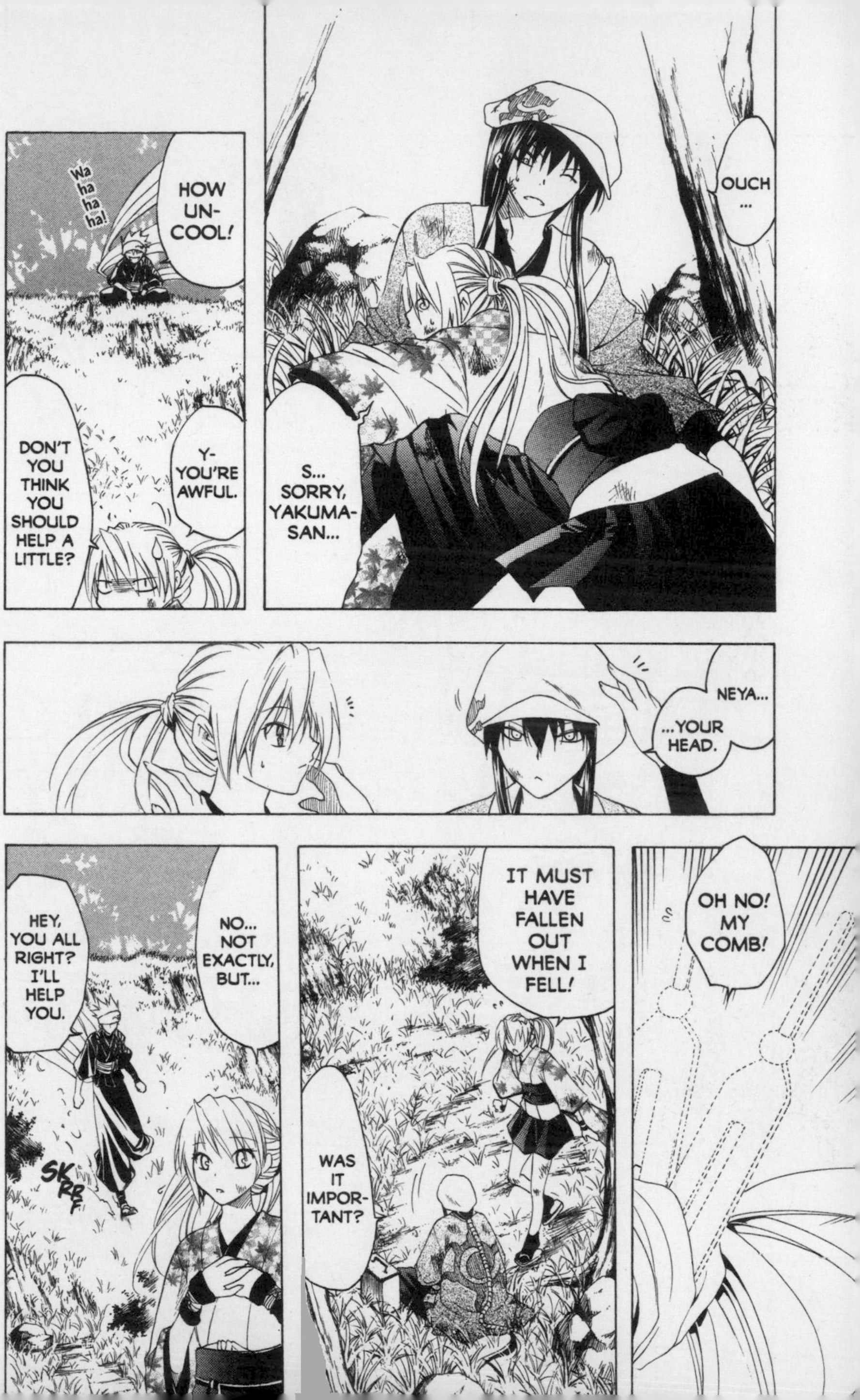
OUCH ...
S... SORRY, YAKUMA-SAN...
HOW UN-COOL!
Wa ha ha ha!
Y-YOU'RE AWFUL.
DON'T YOU THINK YOU SHOULD HELP A LITTLE?
NEYA... ...YOUR HEAD.
OH NO! MY COMB!
IT MUST HAVE FALLEN OUT WHEN I FELL!
WAS IT IMPORTANT?
NO... NOT EXACTLY, BUT...
HEY, YOU ALL RIGHT? I'LL HELP YOU.
SKRRF

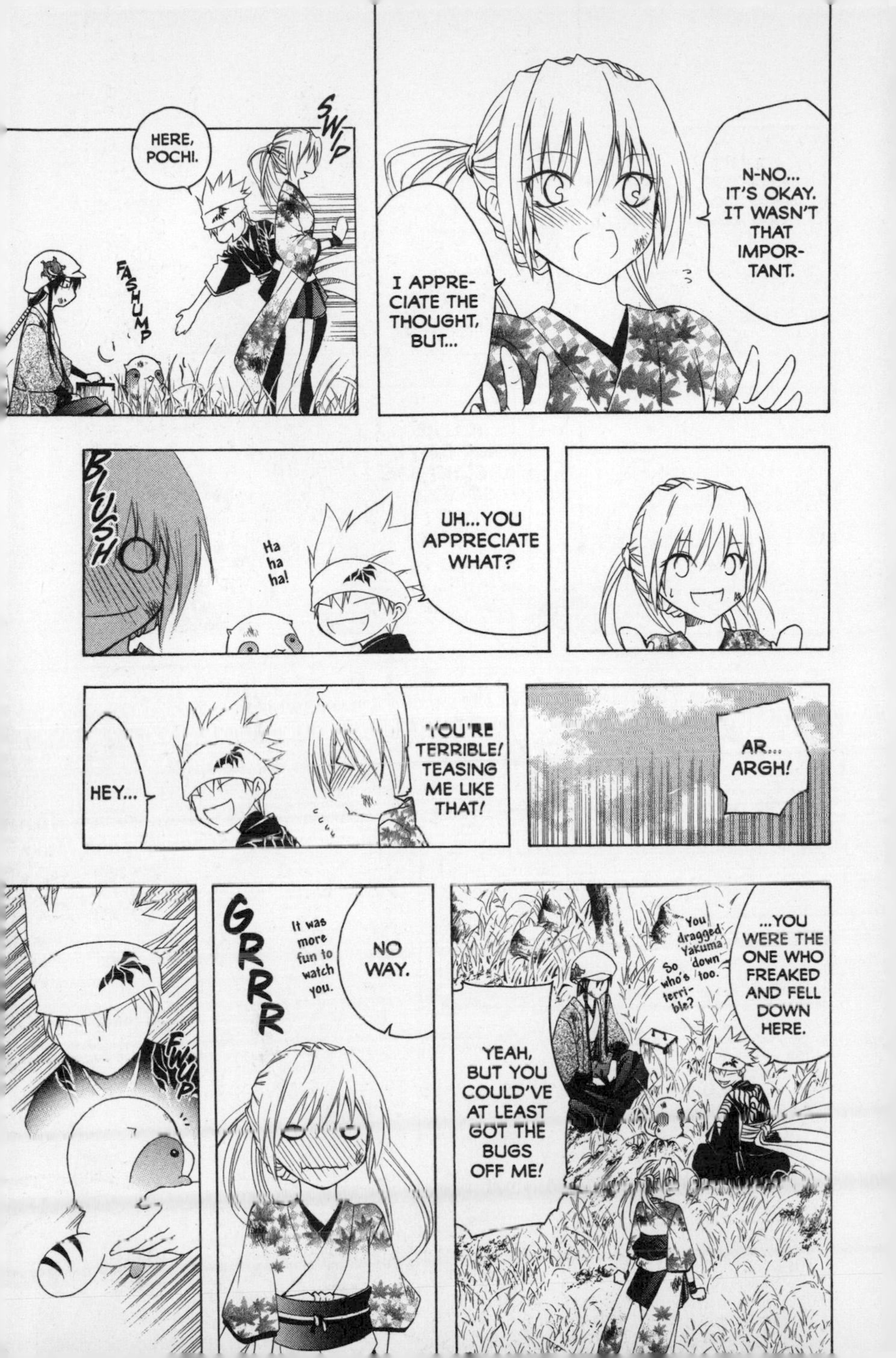
N-NO... IT'S OKAY. IT WASN'T THAT IMPOR-TANT.
I APPRE-CIATE THE THOUGHT, BUT...
SWIP
HERE, POCHI.
FASHUMP
UH...YOU APPRECIATE WHAT?
Ha ha ha!
BLUSH
AR... ARGH!
YOU'RE TERRIBLE! TEASING ME LIKE THAT!
HEY...
...YOU WERE THE ONE WHO FREAKED AND FELL DOWN HERE.
You dragged Yakuma down too.
So who's terri-ble?
YEAH, BUT YOU COULD'VE AT LEAST GOT THE BUGS OFF ME!
NO WAY.
It was more fun to watch you.
GRRR
FWUP

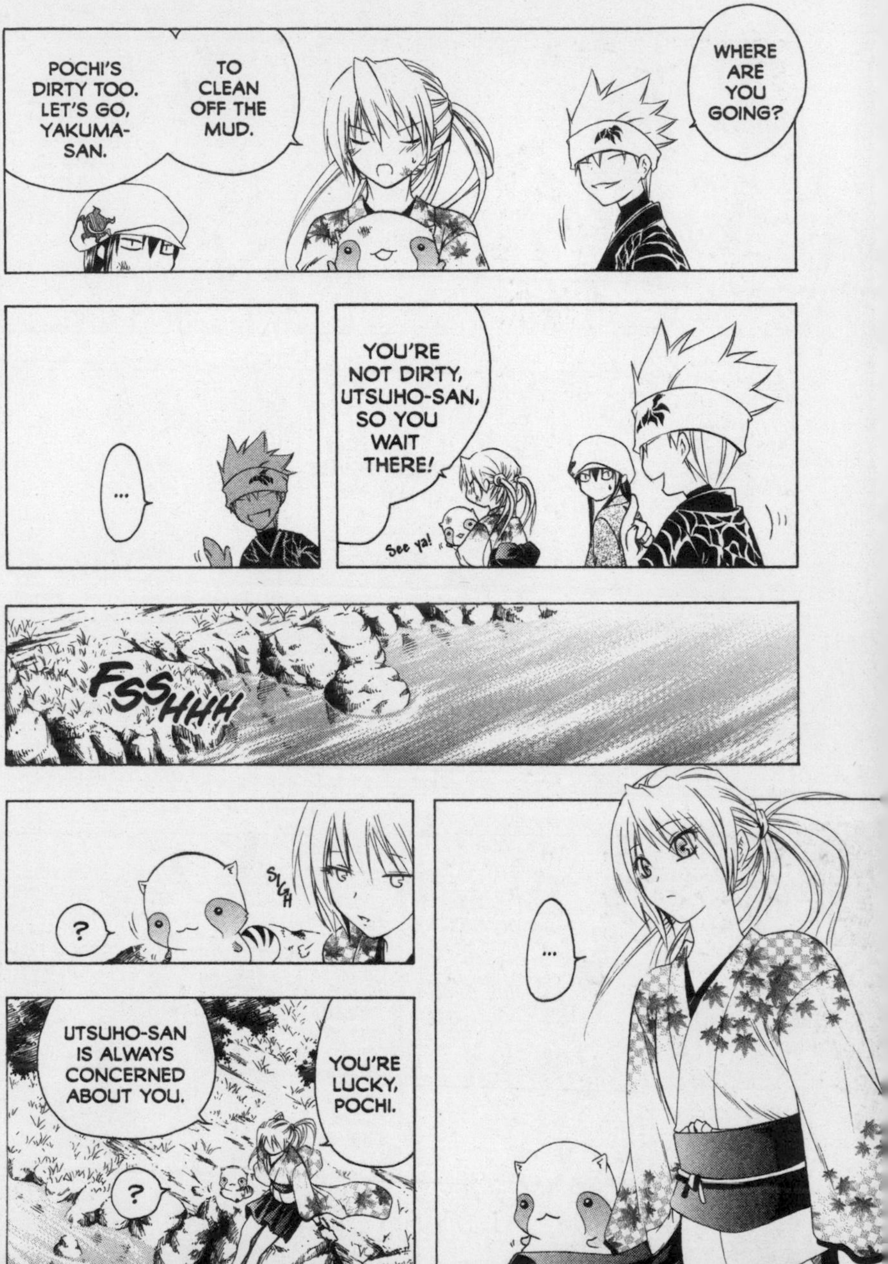
WHERE ARE YOU GOING?
TO CLEAN OFF THE MUD.
POCHI'S DIRTY TOO. LET'S GO, YAKUMA-SAN.
YOU'RE NOT DIRTY, UTSUHO-SAN, SO YOU WAIT THERE!
See ya!
...
FSSHHH
...
SIGH
?
YOU'RE LUCKY, POCHI.
UTSUHO-SAN IS ALWAYS CONCERNED ABOUT YOU.
?

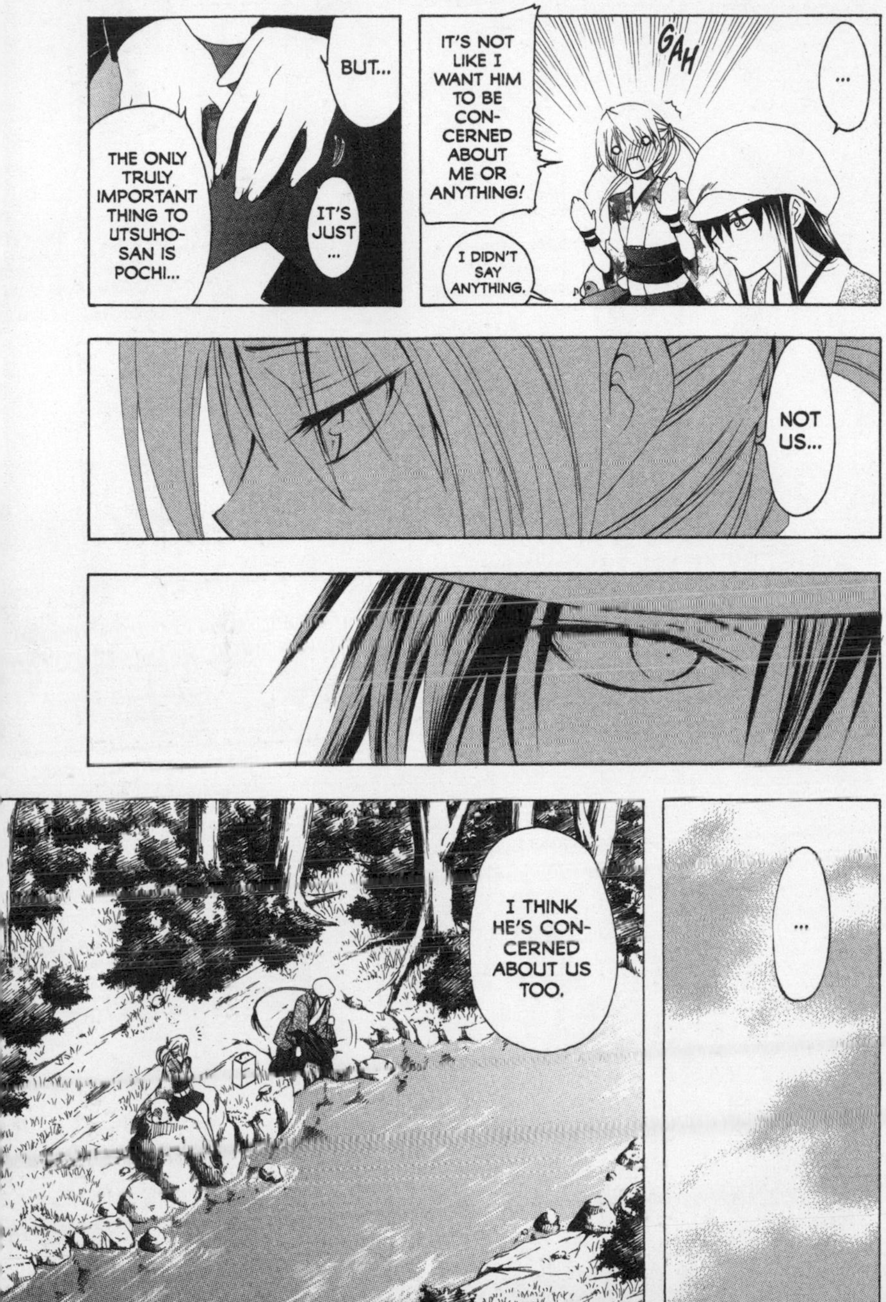
...
GAH
IT'S NOT LIKE I WANT HIM TO BE CON-CERNED ABOUT ME OR ANYTHING!
I DIDN'T SAY ANYTHING.
BUT...
IT'S JUST ...
THE ONLY TRULY IMPORTANT THING TO UTSUHO-SAN IS POCHI...
NOT US...
...
I THINK HE'S CON-CERNED ABOUT US TOO.

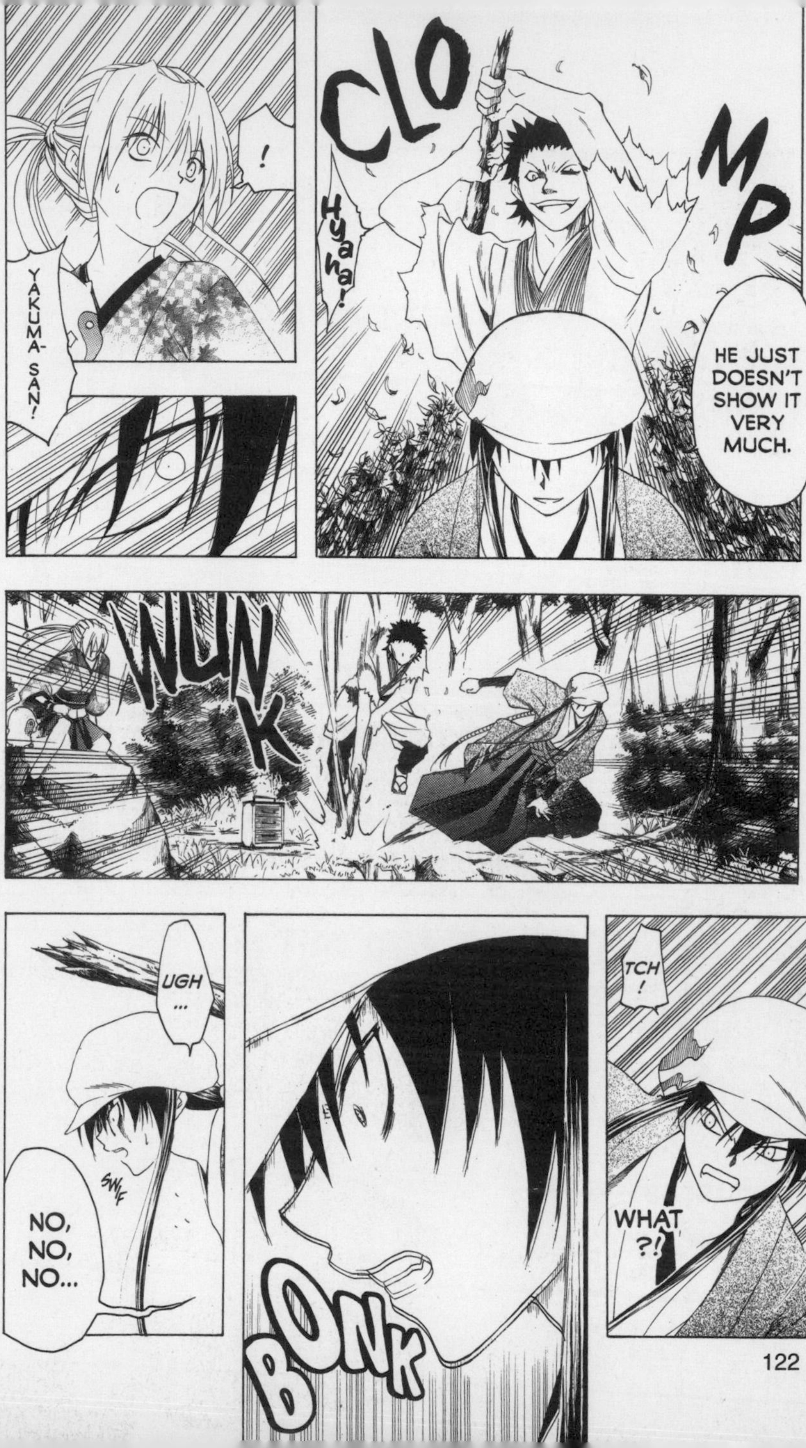
HE JUST DOESN'T SHOW IT VERY MUCH.
CLOMP
Hyana!
!
YAKUMA-SAN!
WUNK
TCH!
WHAT?!
BONK
UGH...
SNIF
NO, NO, NO...

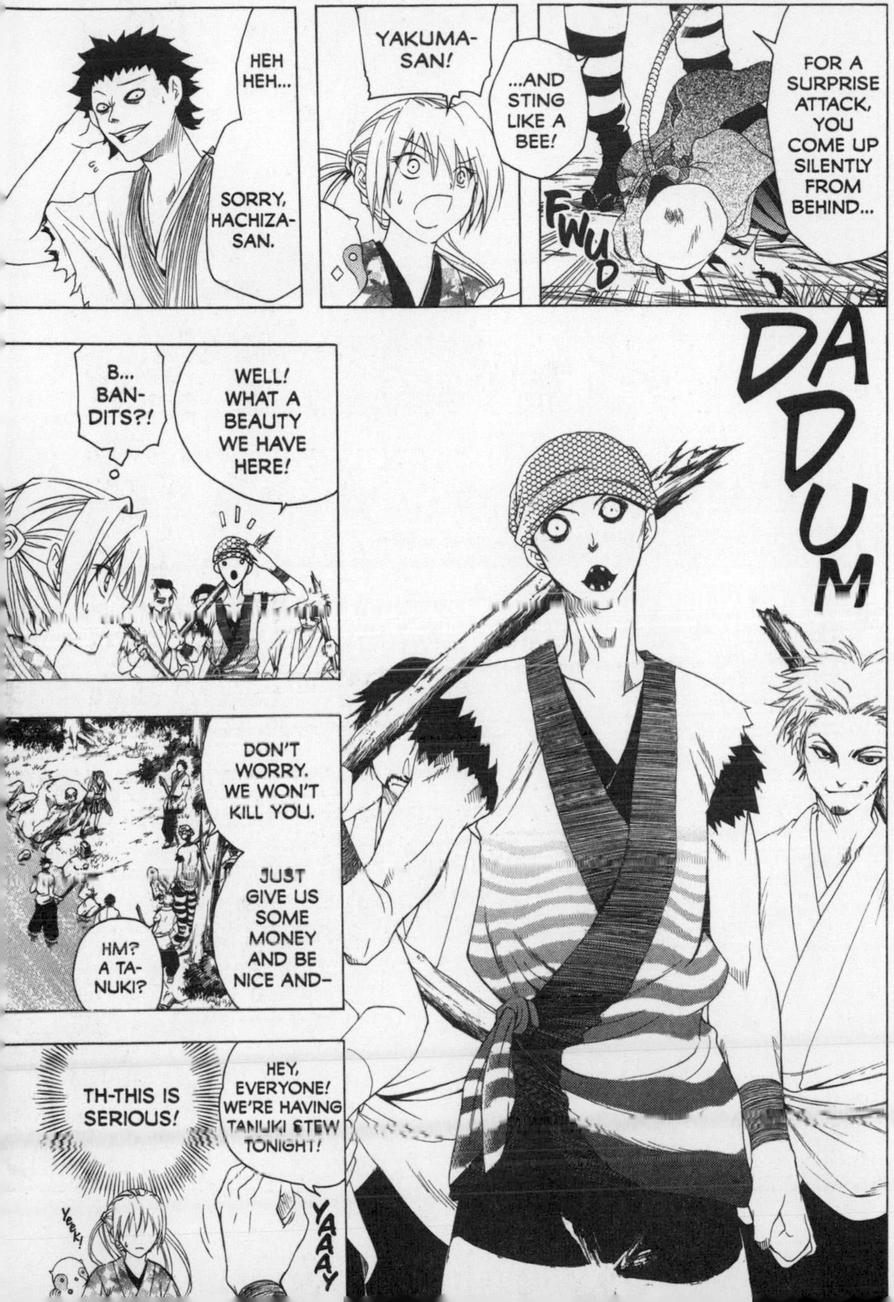
FOR A SURPRISE ATTACK, YOU COME UP SILENTLY FROM BEHIND...
FWUD
...AND STING LIKE A BEE!
YAKUMA-SAN!
HEH HEH...
SORRY, HACHIZA-SAN.
DADUM
WELL! WHAT A BEAUTY WE HAVE HERE!
B... BAN-DITS?!
DON'T WORRY. WE WON'T KILL YOU.
JUST GIVE US SOME MONEY AND BE NICE AND–
HM? A TA-NUKI?
HEY, EVERYONE! WE'RE HAVING TANUKI STEW TONIGHT!
TH-THIS IS SERIOUS!
YAAAY
Yeeek!

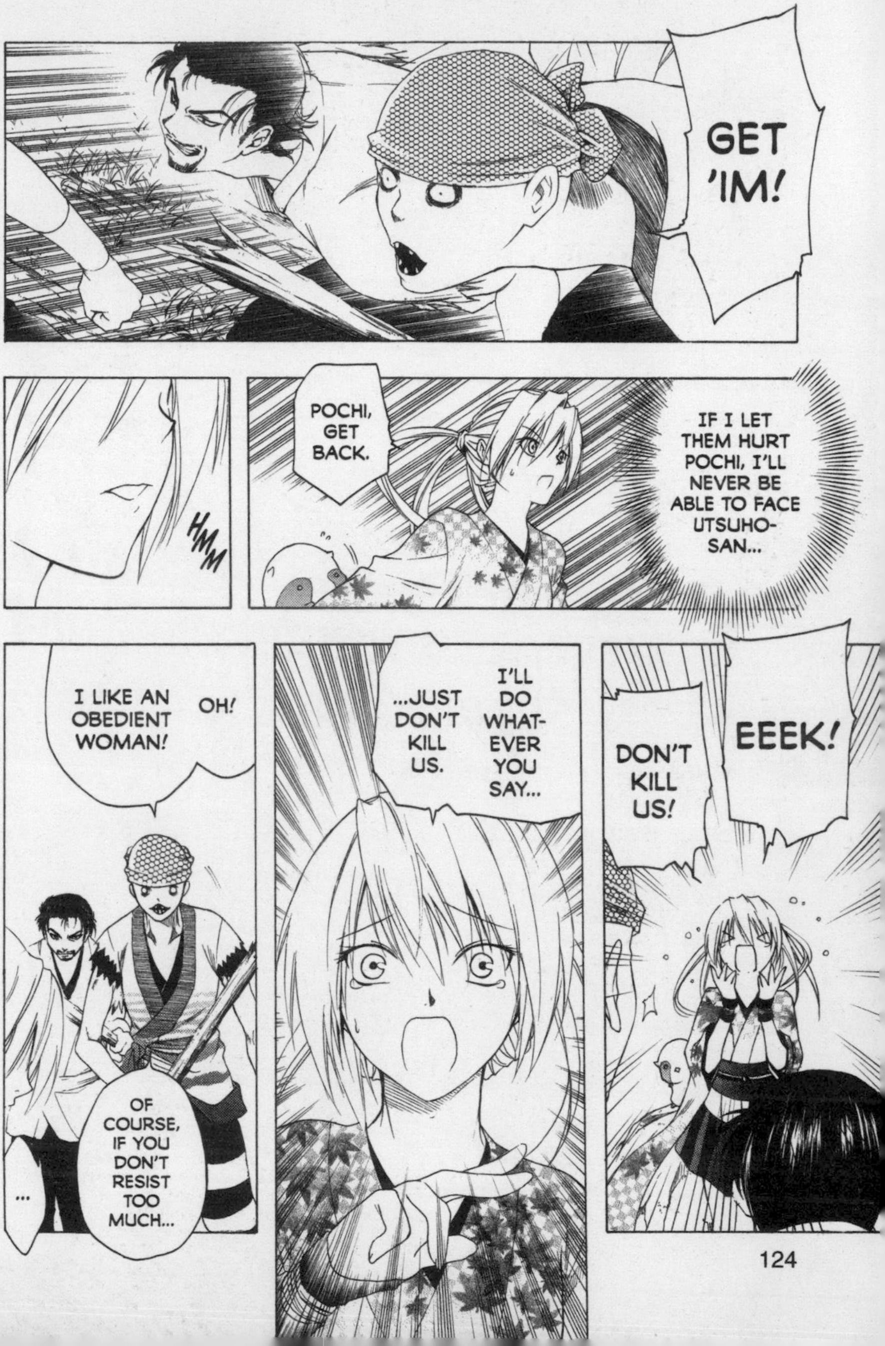
GET 'IM!
IF I LET THEM HURT POCHI, I'LL NEVER BE ABLE TO FACE UTSUHO-SAN...
POCHI, GET BACK.
HMM
EEEK!
DON'T KILL US!
I'LL DO WHAT-EVER YOU SAY...
...JUST DON'T KILL US.
OH!
I LIKE AN OBEDIENT WOMAN!
OF COURSE, IF YOU DON'T RESIST TOO MUCH...
...

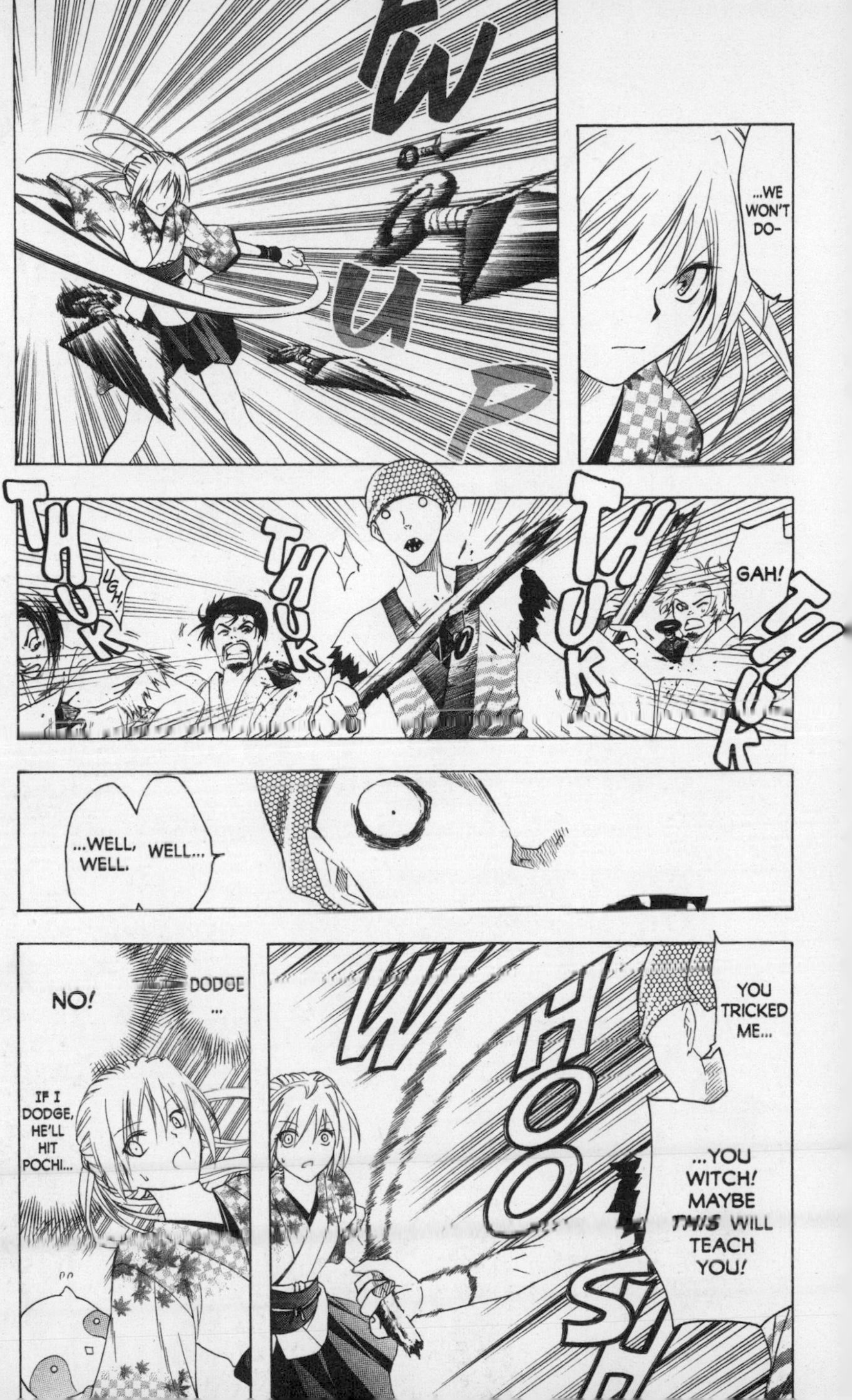
...WE WON'T DO-
TWOUP
THUK
GAH!
THUK
THUK
UGH!
THUK
...WELL, WELL.
WELL...
YOU TRICKED ME...
...YOU WITCH! MAYBE THIS WILL TEACH YOU!
WHOOSH
DODGE...
NO!
IF I DODGE, HE'LL HIT POCHI...

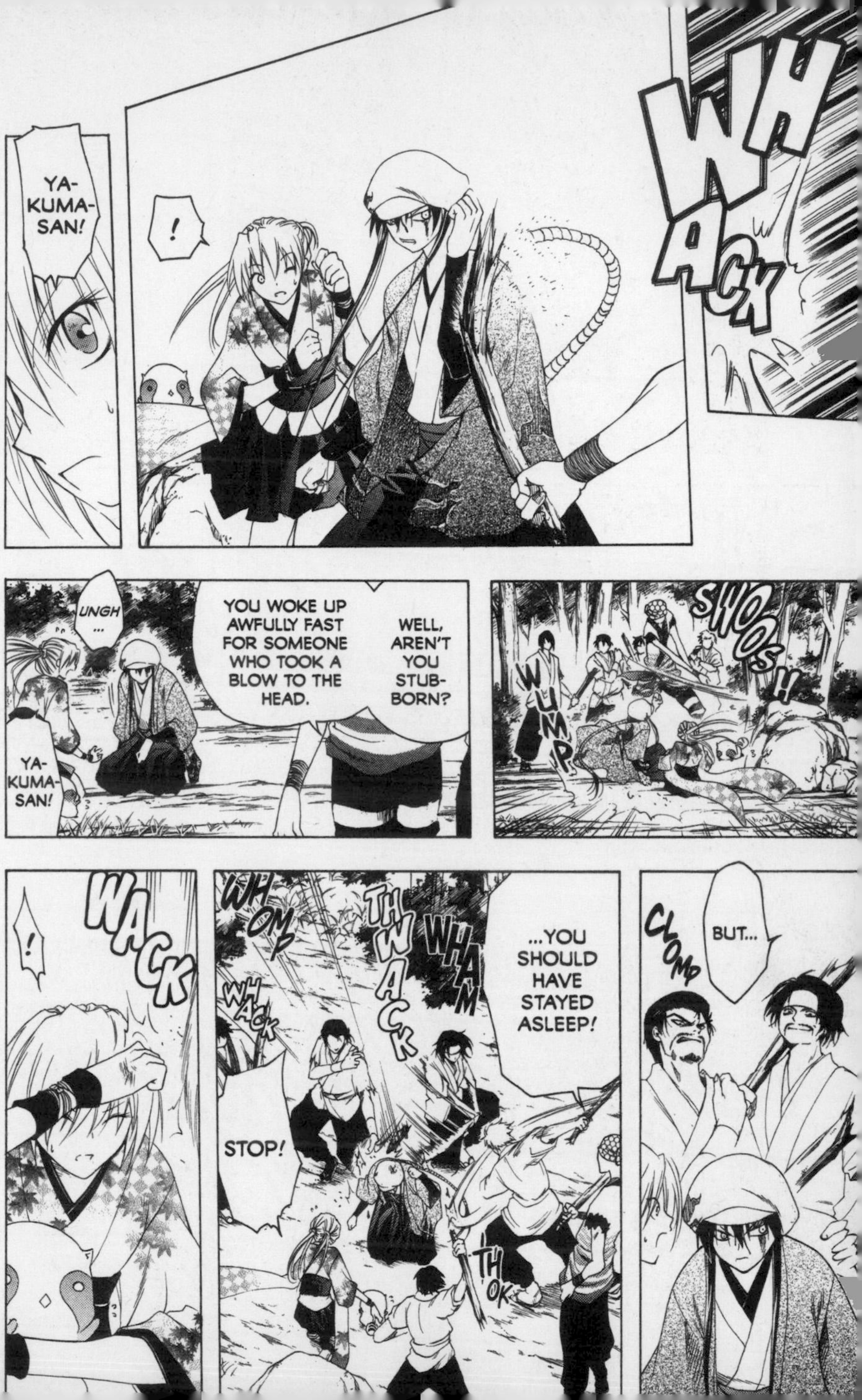
WHACK
!
YA-KUMA-SAN!
SHOOSH
WUMP
WELL, AREN'T YOU STUBBORN?
YOU WOKE UP AWFULLY FAST FOR SOMEONE WHO TOOK A BLOW TO THE HEAD.
UNGH...
YA-KUMA-SAN!
BUT...
CLOMP
...YOU SHOULD HAVE STAYED ASLEEP!
WHAM
THWACK
WHOMP
WHACK
STOP!
THOK
WACK
!

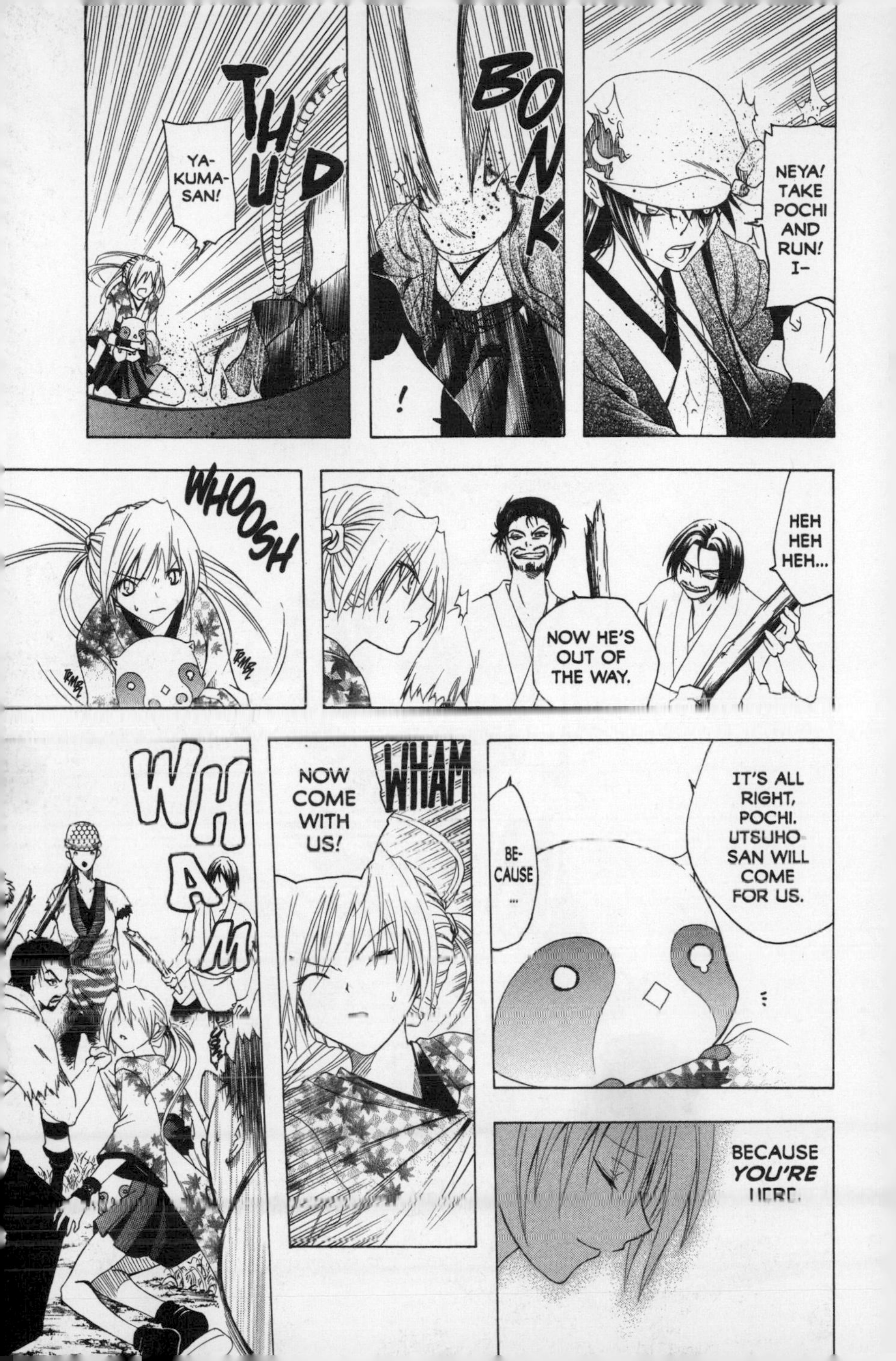
NEYA! TAKE POCHI AND RUN! I–
BONK
!
THUD
YA-KUMA-SAN!
HEH HEH HEH...
NOW HE'S OUT OF THE WAY.
WHOOSH
IT'S ALL RIGHT, POCHI. UTSUHO-SAN WILL COME FOR US.
BE-CAUSE ...
BECAUSE YOU'RE HERE.
WHAM
NOW COME WITH US!
WHAM

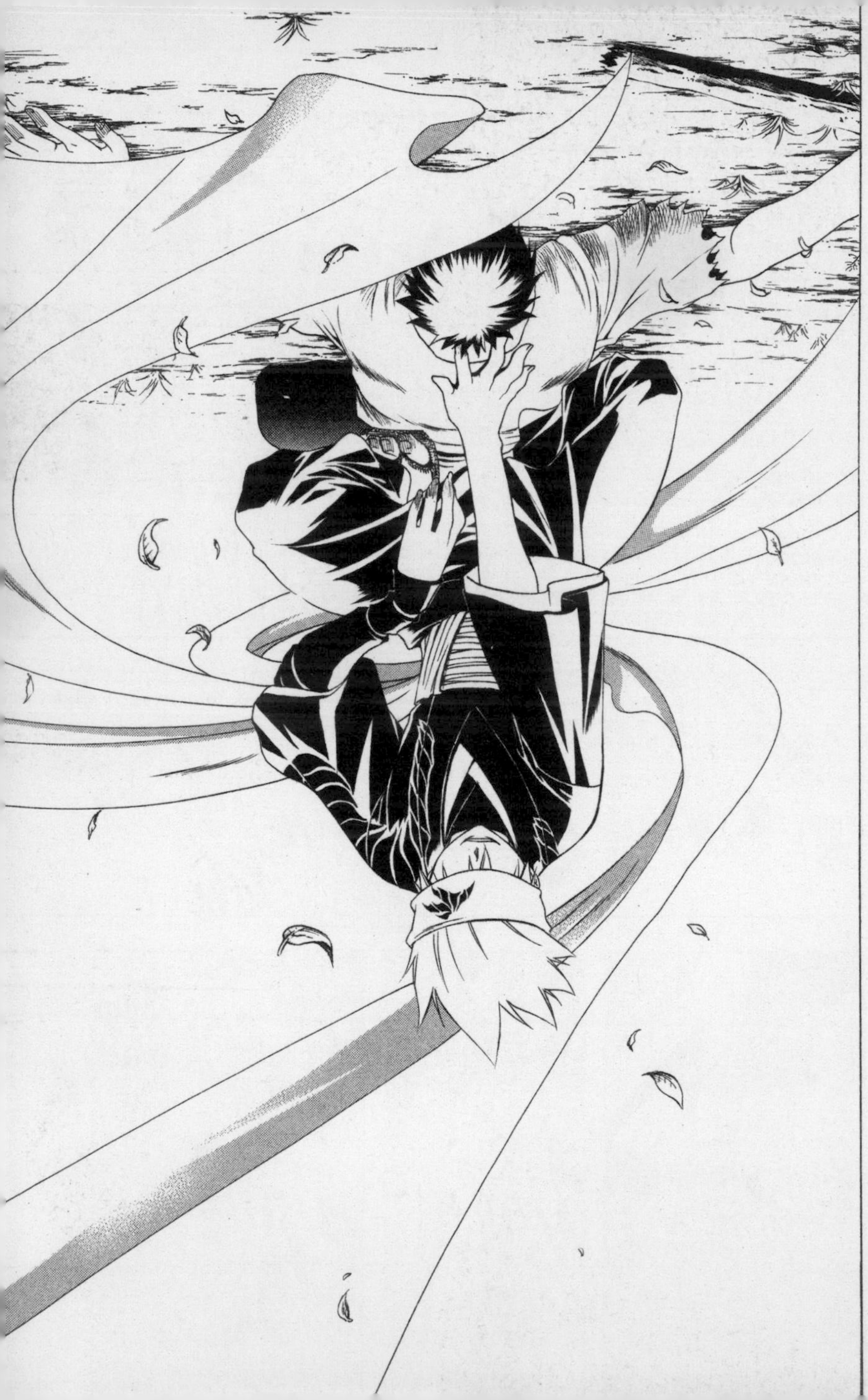

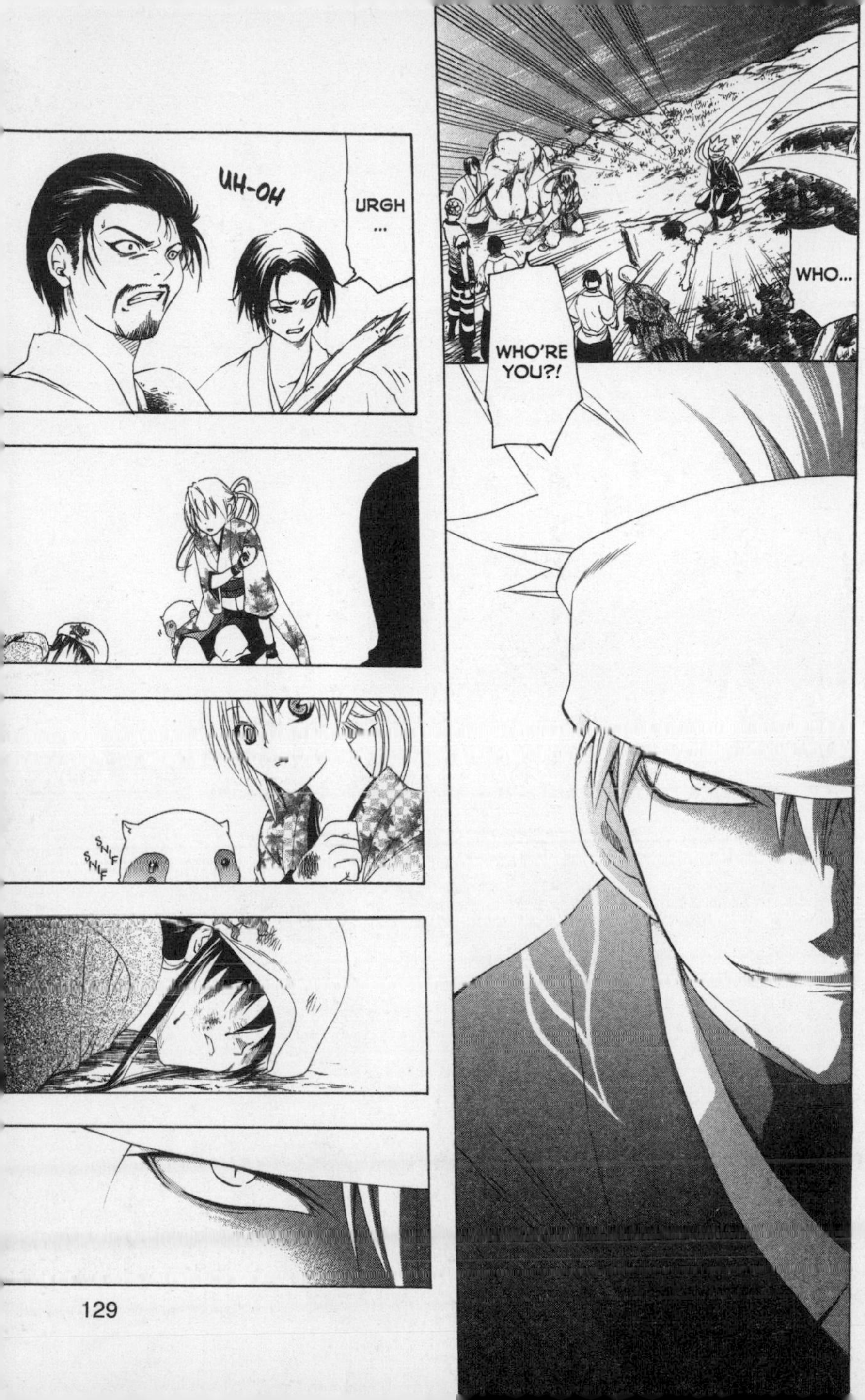
WHO...
WHO'RE YOU?!
URGH ...
UH-OH
SNIF SNIF

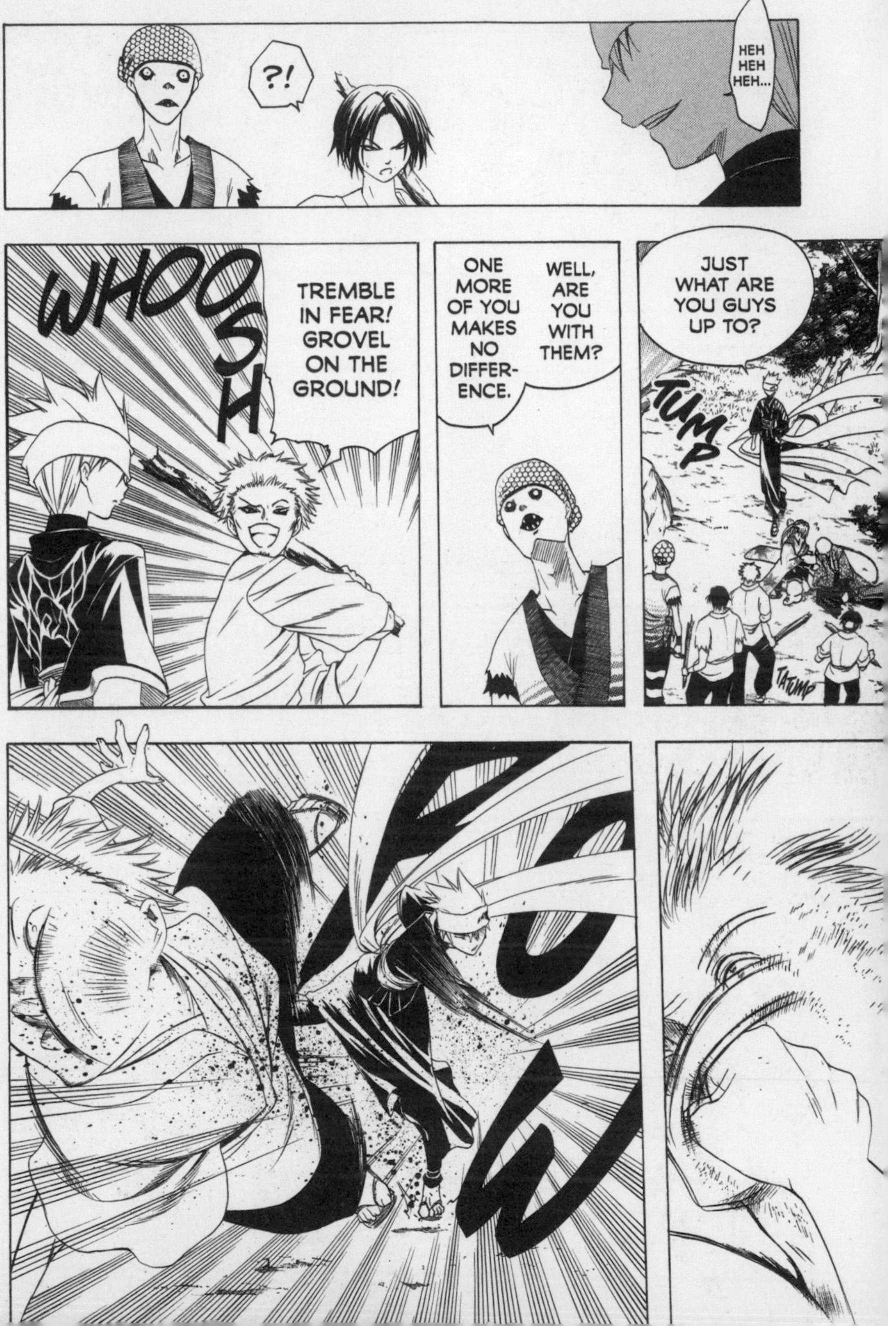
HEH HEH HEH...
?!
JUST WHAT ARE YOU GUYS UP TO?
TUMP
TATUMP
WELL, ARE YOU WITH THEM?
ONE MORE OF YOU MAKES NO DIFFER-ENCE.
TREMBLE IN FEAR! GROVEL ON THE GROUND!
WHOOSH

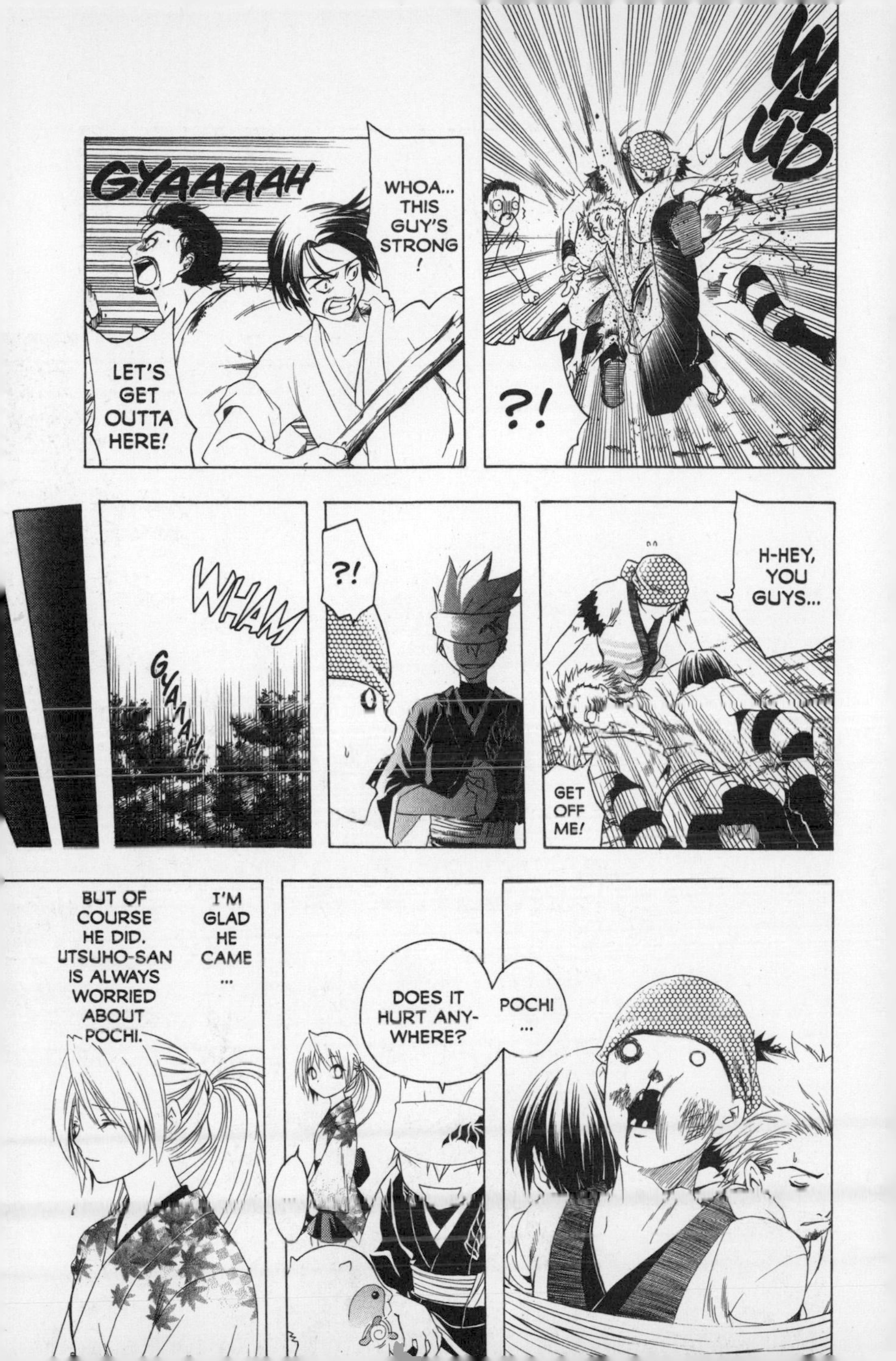
WHUD
?!
GYAAAAH
WHOA... THIS GUY'S STRONG!
LET'S GET OUTTA HERE!
H-HEY, YOU GUYS...
GET OFF ME!
?!
WHAM
GYAAAAH!
POCHI...
DOES IT HURT ANY-WHERE?
I'M GLAD HE CAME...
BUT OF COURSE HE DID. UTSUHO-SAN IS ALWAYS WORRIED ABOUT POCHI.

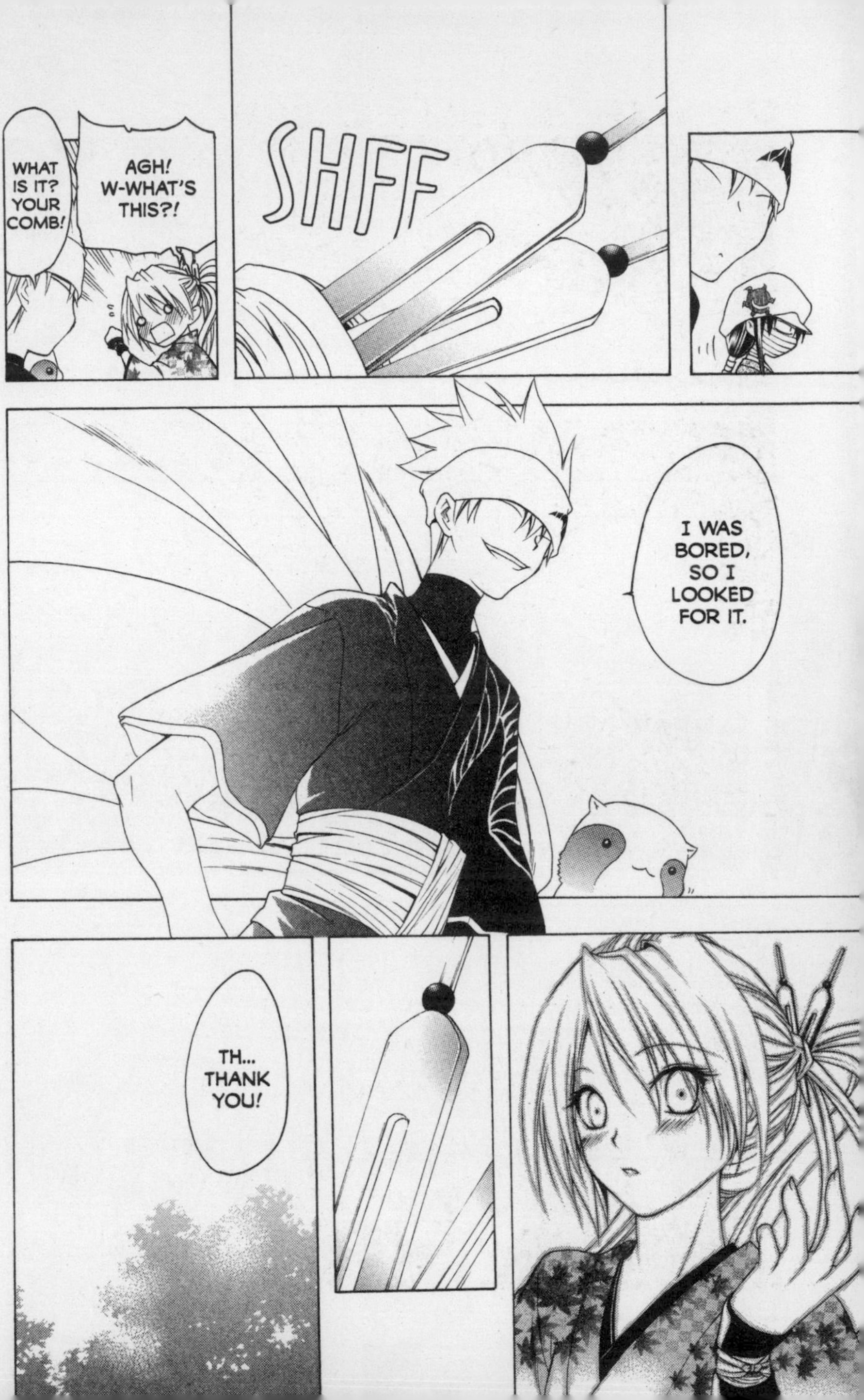
SHFF
AGH! W-WHAT'S THIS?!
WHAT IS IT? YOUR COMB!
I WAS BORED, SO I LOOKED FOR IT.
TH... THANK YOU!

Chapter 35 Yakuma's Choice

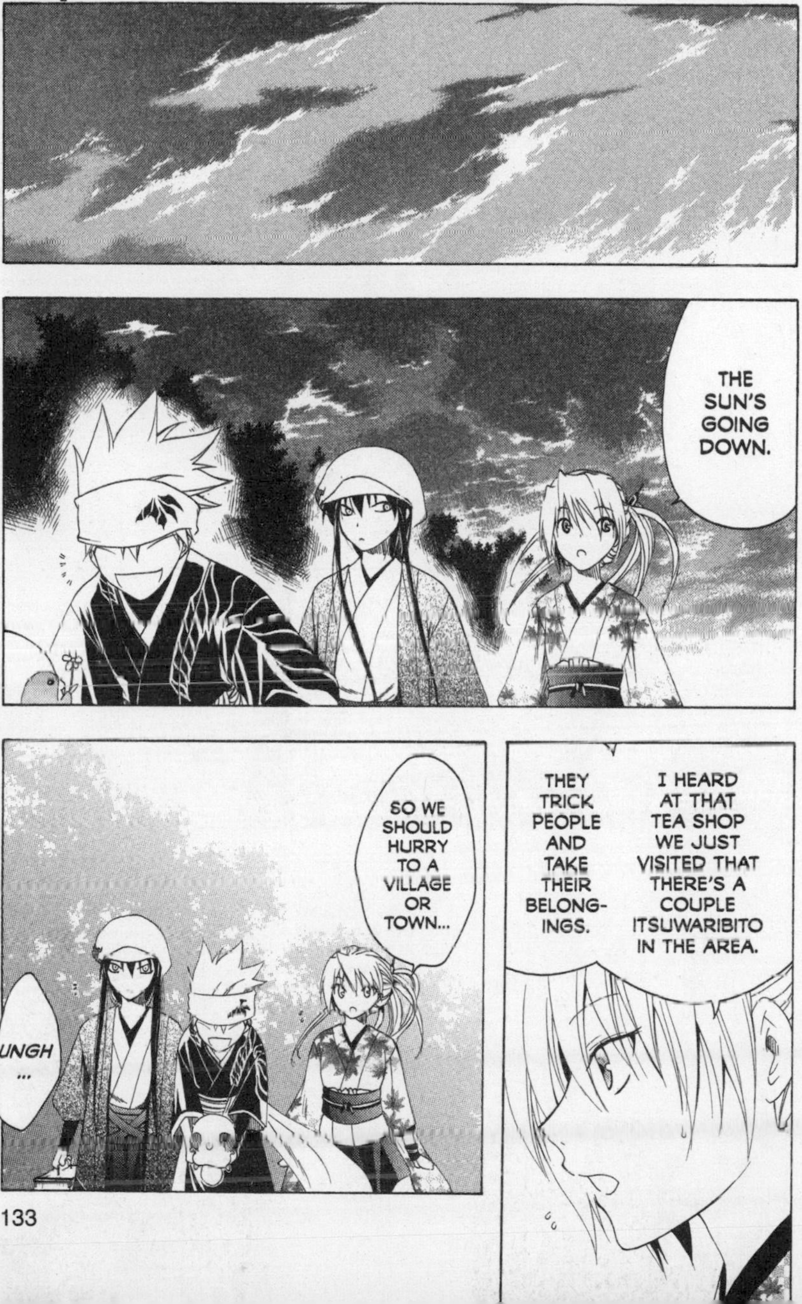
THE SUN'S GOING DOWN.
I HEARD AT THAT TEA SHOP WE JUST VISITED THAT THERE'S A COUPLE ITSUWARIBITO IN THE AREA.
THEY TRICK PEOPLE AND TAKE THEIR BELONG-INGS.
SO WE SHOULD HURRY TO A VILLAGE OR TOWN...
UNGH ...

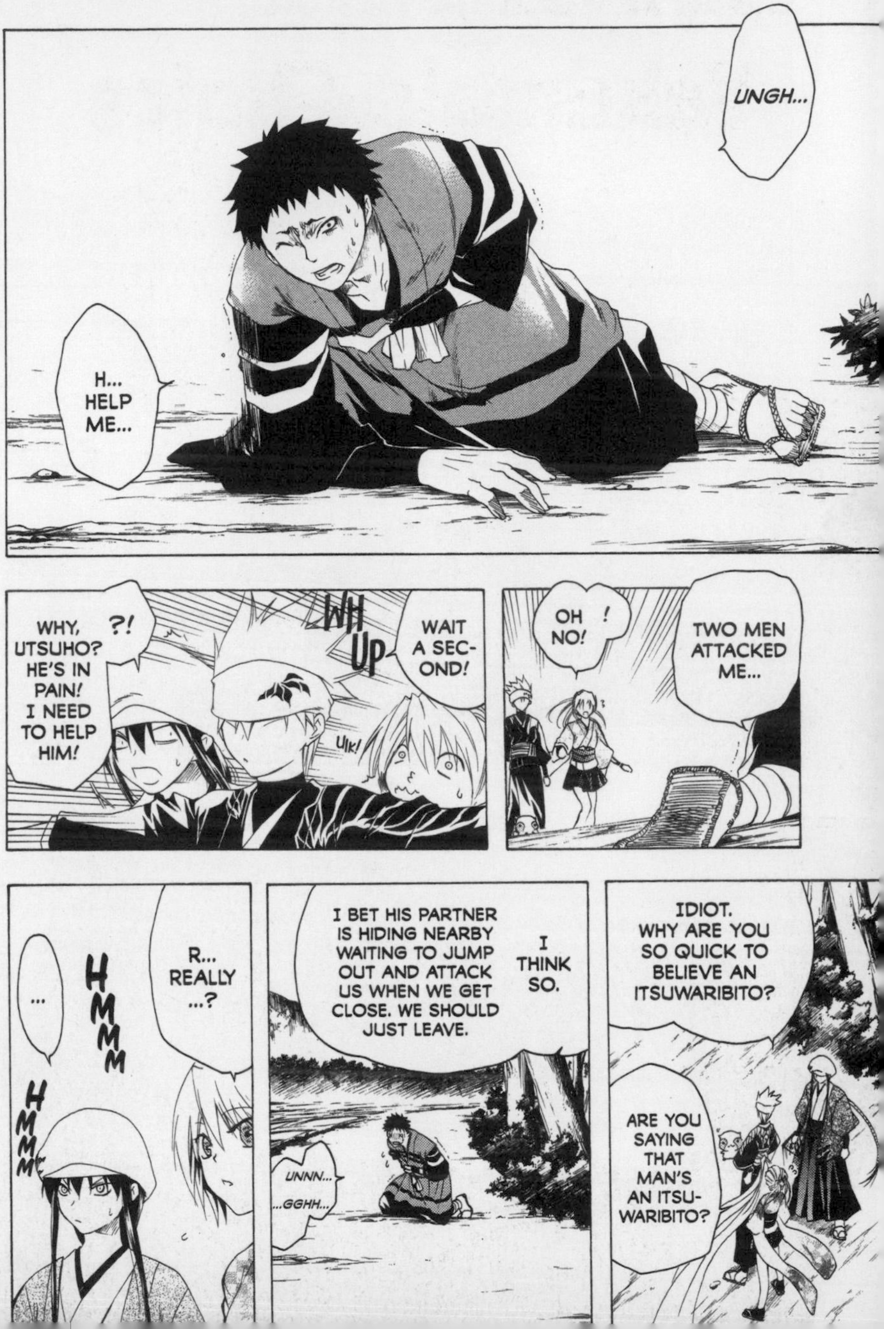
UNGH...
H... HELP ME...
TWO MEN ATTACKED ME...
OH NO!
!
WAIT A SEC-OND!
WH UP
UIK!
?!
WHY, UTSUHO? HE'S IN PAIN! I NEED TO HELP HIM!
IDIOT. WHY ARE YOU SO QUICK TO BELIEVE AN ITSUWARIBITO?
ARE YOU SAYING THAT MAN'S AN ITSU-WARIBITO?
I THINK SO.
I BET HIS PARTNER IS HIDING NEARBY WAITING TO JUMP OUT AND ATTACK US WHEN WE GET CLOSE. WE SHOULD JUST LEAVE.
UNNN...
...GGHH...
R... REALLY ...?
HMMM
...
HMMM

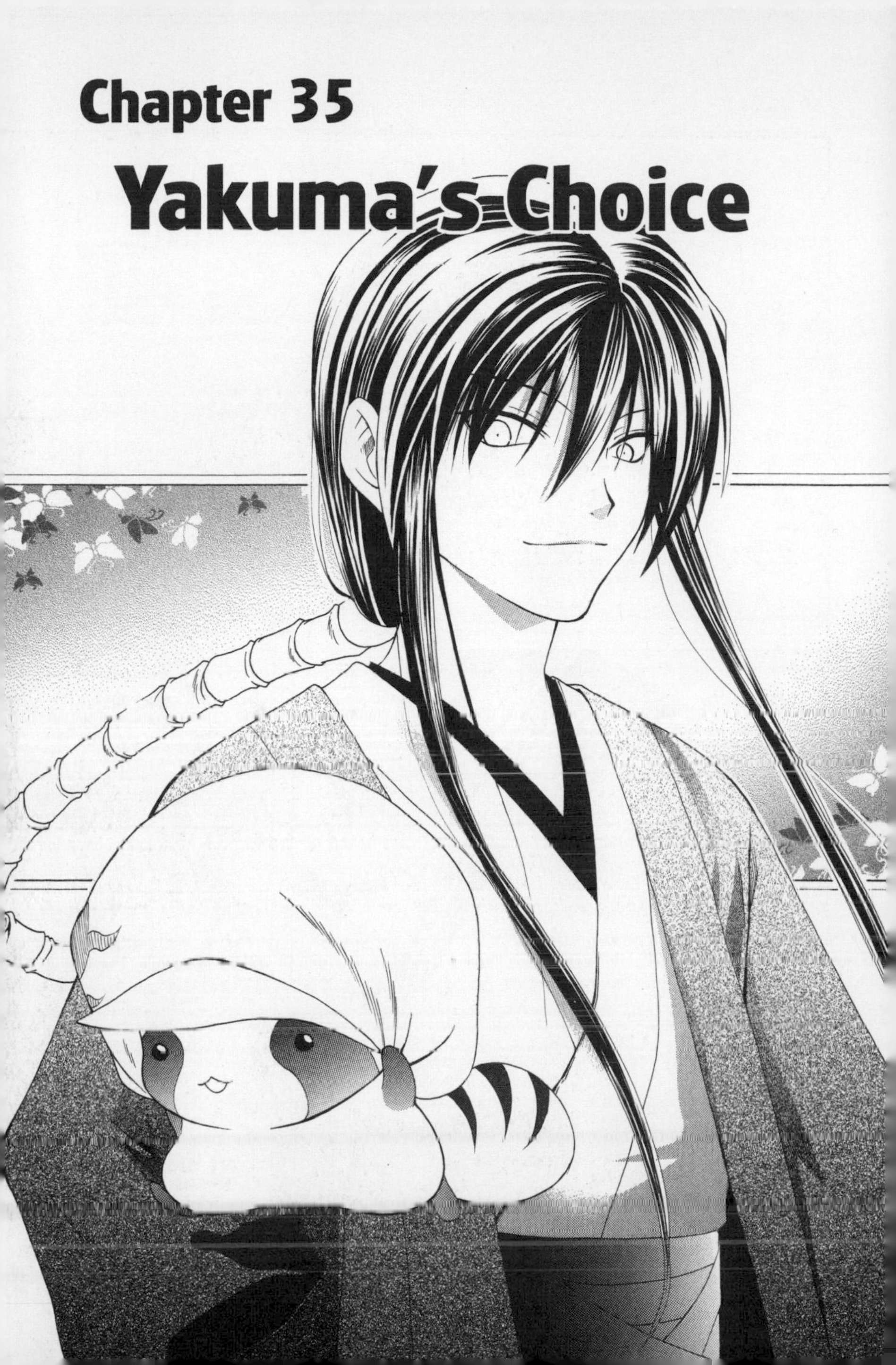
Chapter 35
Yakuma's Choice

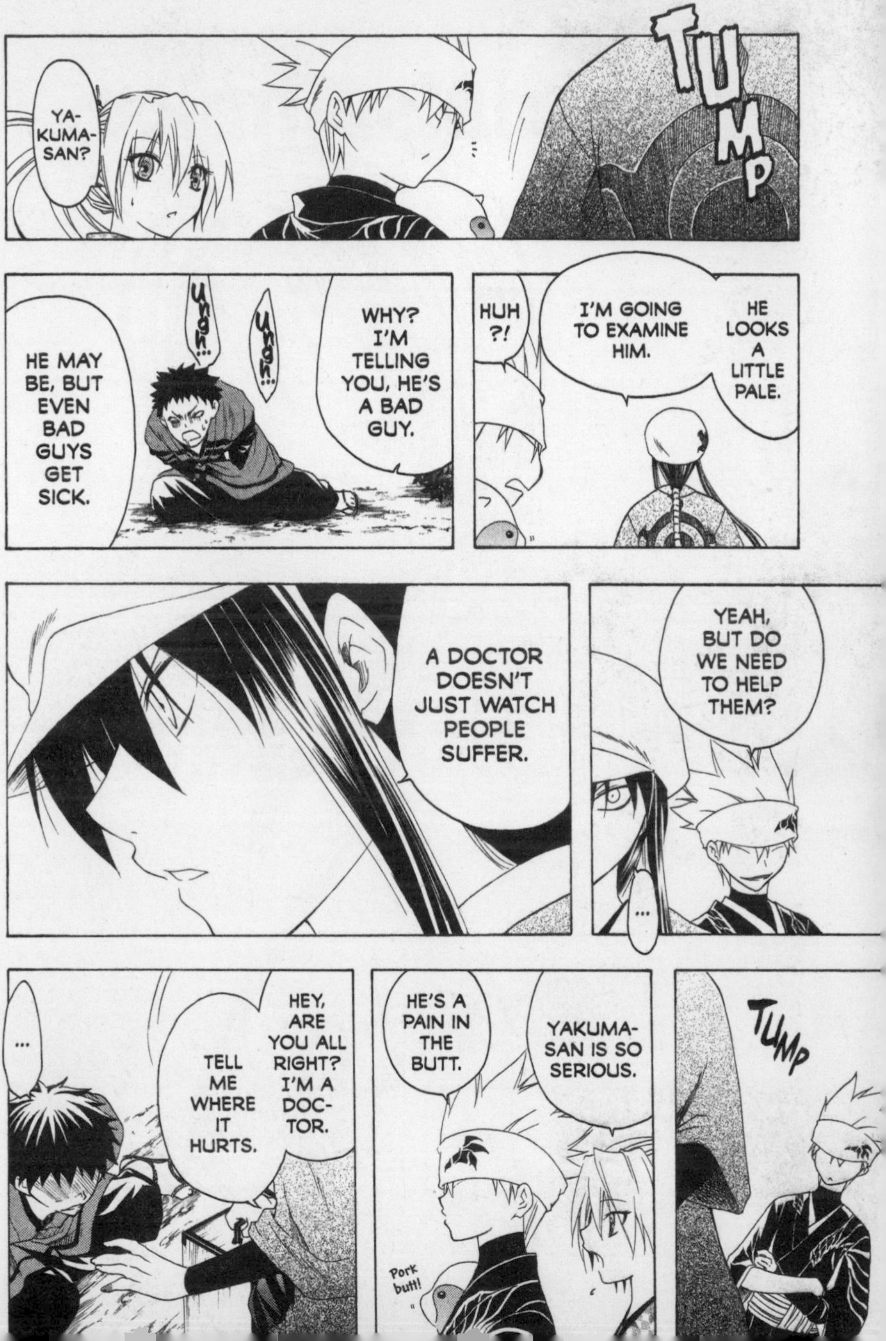
TUMP
YA-KUMA-SAN?
HE LOOKS A LITTLE PALE.
I'M GOING TO EXAMINE HIM.
HUH ?!
WHY? I'M TELLING YOU, HE'S A BAD GUY.
Ungh...
Ungh...
HE MAY BE, BUT EVEN BAD GUYS GET SICK.
YEAH, BUT DO WE NEED TO HELP THEM?
...
A DOCTOR DOESN'T JUST WATCH PEOPLE SUFFER.
TUMP
YAKUMA-SAN IS SO SERIOUS.
HE'S A PAIN IN THE BUTT.
Pork butt!
HEY, ARE YOU ALL RIGHT? I'M A DOC-TOR.
TELL ME WHERE IT HURTS.
...

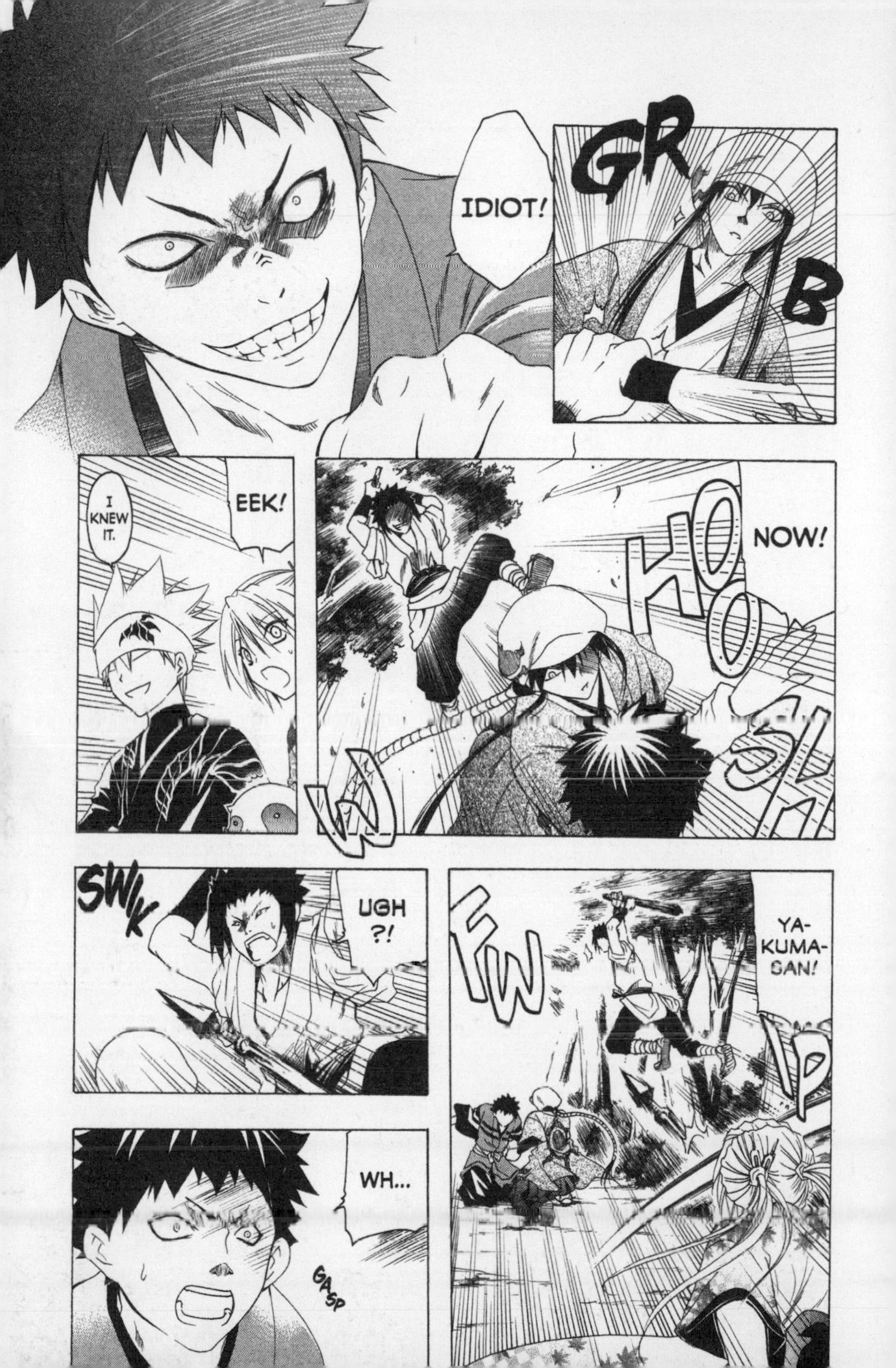
GRAB
IDIOT!
NOW!
WHOOSH
WHAM
EEK!
I KNEW IT.
YA-KUMA-SAN!
FWIP
UGH ?!
SWIK
WH...
GASP

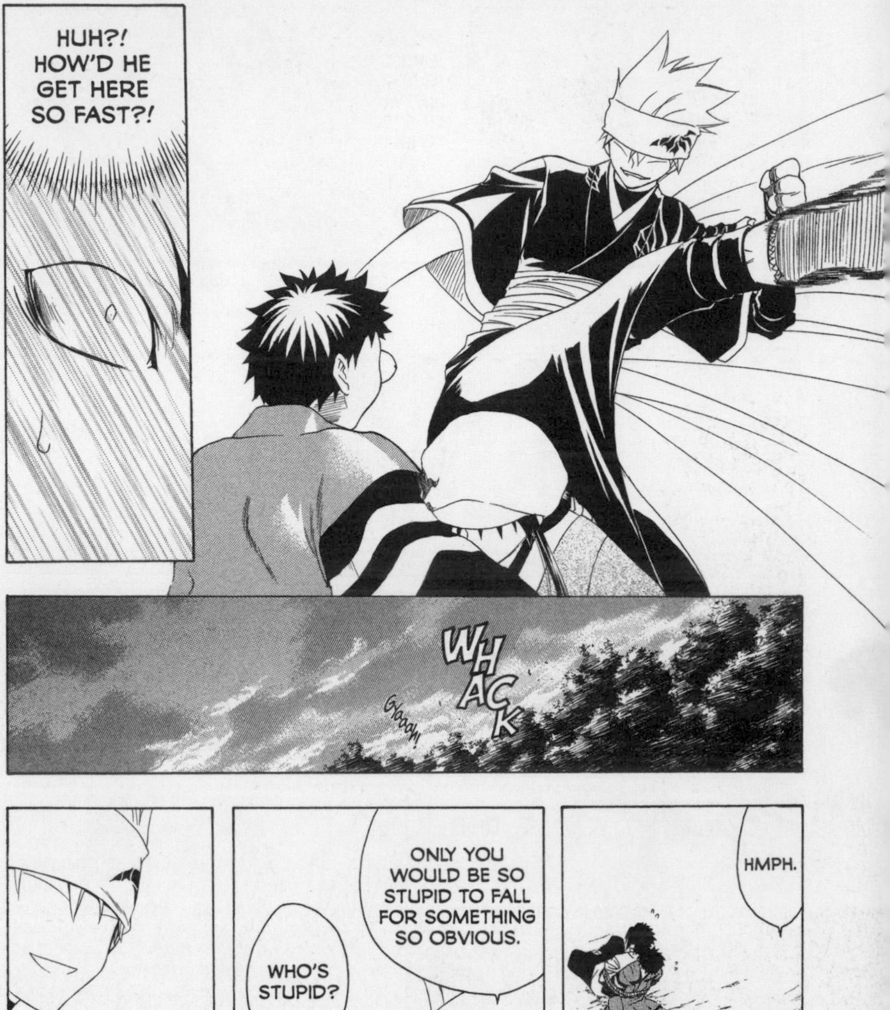
HUH?! HOW'D HE GET HERE SO FAST?!
WHACK
Gyaaah!
HMPH.
JUST LIKE I THOUGHT. HOW UNCOOL.
ONLY YOU WOULD BE SO STUPID TO FALL FOR SOMETHING SO OBVIOUS.
WHO'S STUPID?
Me too.

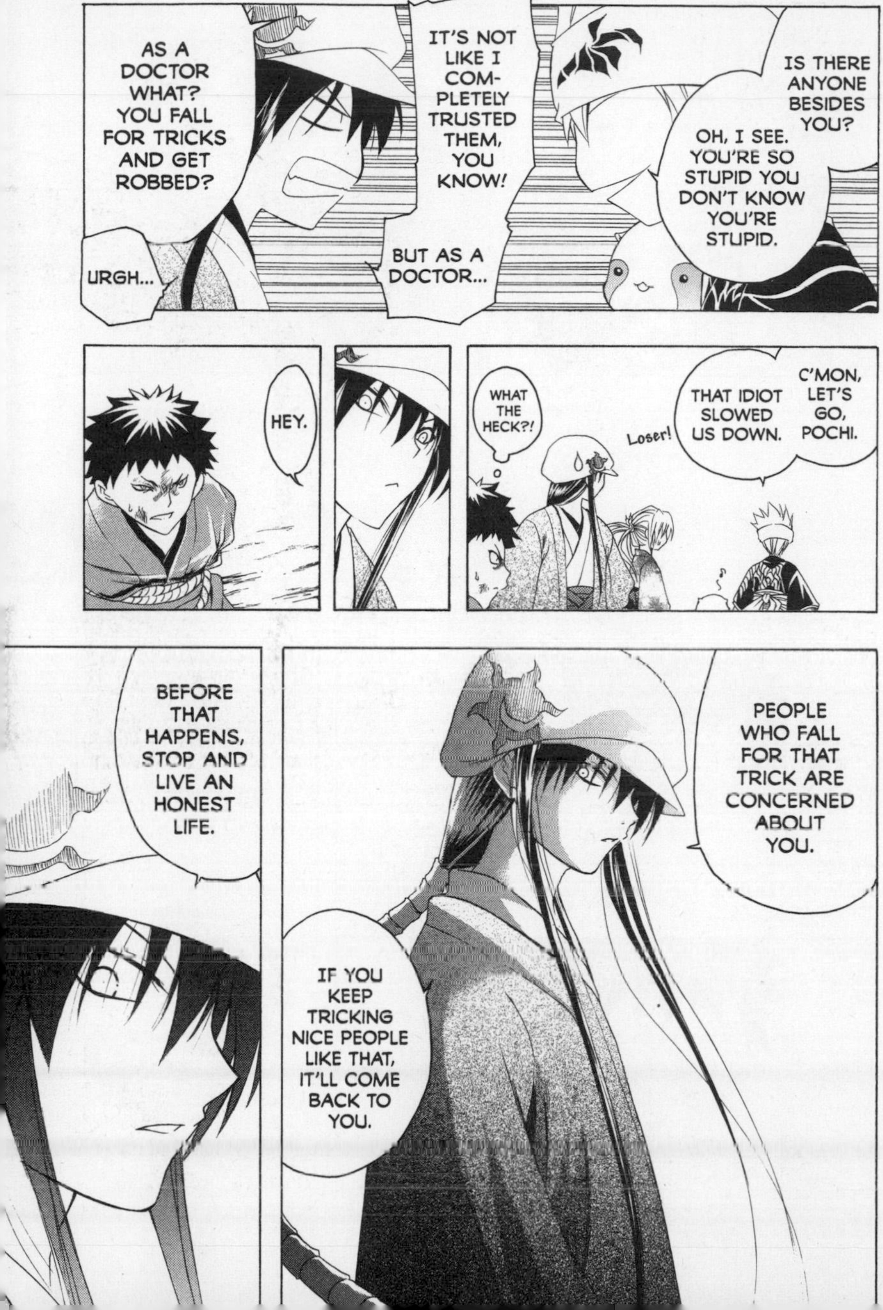
IS THERE ANYONE BESIDES YOU?
OH, I SEE. YOU'RE SO STUPID YOU DON'T KNOW YOU'RE STUPID.
IT'S NOT LIKE I COM-PLETELY TRUSTED THEM, YOU KNOW!
BUT AS A DOCTOR...
AS A DOCTOR WHAT? YOU FALL FOR TRICKS AND GET ROBBED?
URGH...
C'MON, LET'S GO, POCHI.
THAT IDIOT SLOWED US DOWN.
Loser!
WHAT THE HECK?!
HEY.
PEOPLE WHO FALL FOR THAT TRICK ARE CONCERNED ABOUT YOU.
IF YOU KEEP TRICKING NICE PEOPLE LIKE THAT, IT'LL COME BACK TO YOU.
BEFORE THAT HAPPENS, STOP AND LIVE AN HONEST LIFE.

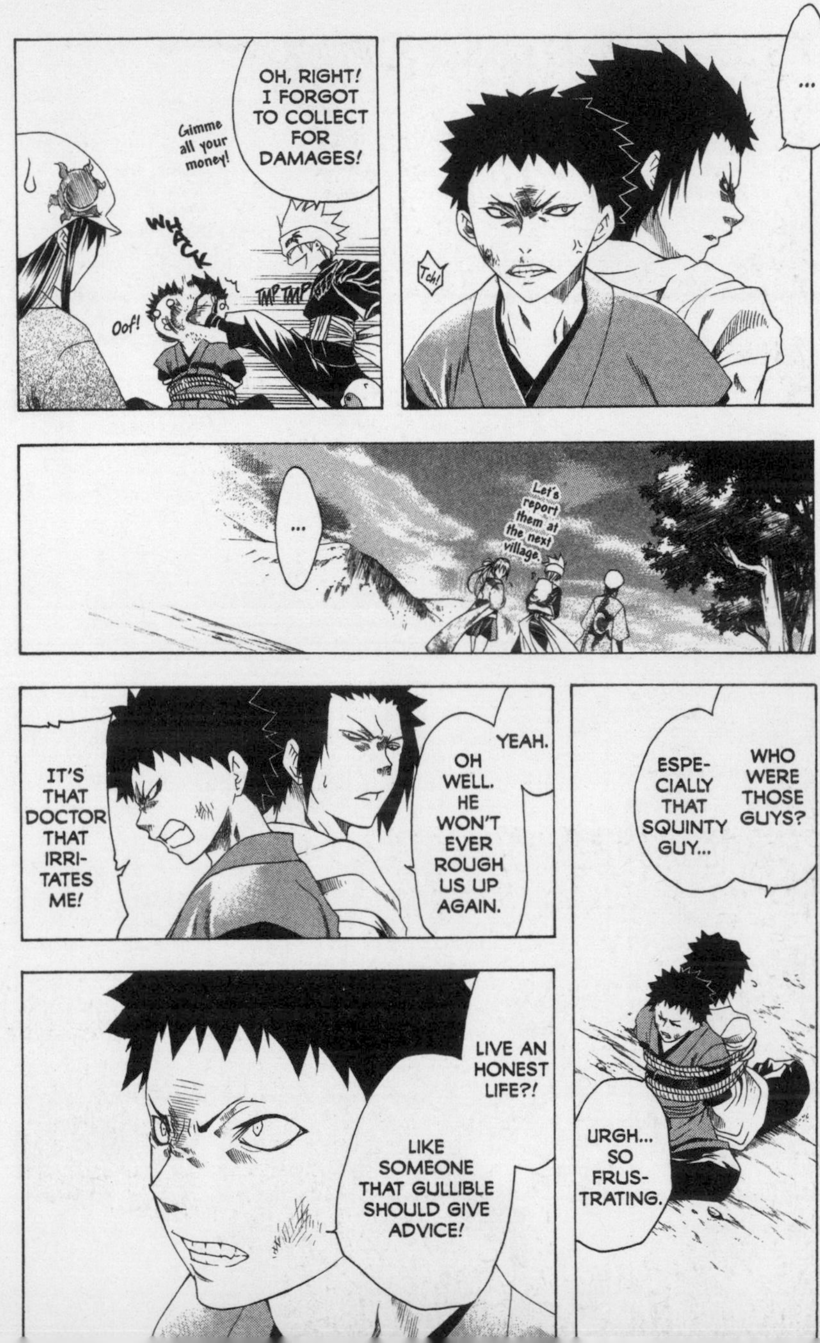
...
Tch!
OH, RIGHT! I FORGOT TO COLLECT FOR DAMAGES!
Gimme all your money!
WHACK
TMP TMP
Oof!
Let's report them at the next village.
...
WHO WERE THOSE GUYS?
ESPECIALLY THAT SQUINTY GUY...
URGH... SO FRUSTRATING.
YEAH.
OH WELL. HE WON'T EVER ROUGH US UP AGAIN.
IT'S THAT DOCTOR THAT IRRITATES ME!
LIVE AN HONEST LIFE?!
LIKE SOMEONE THAT GULLIBLE SHOULD GIVE ADVICE!

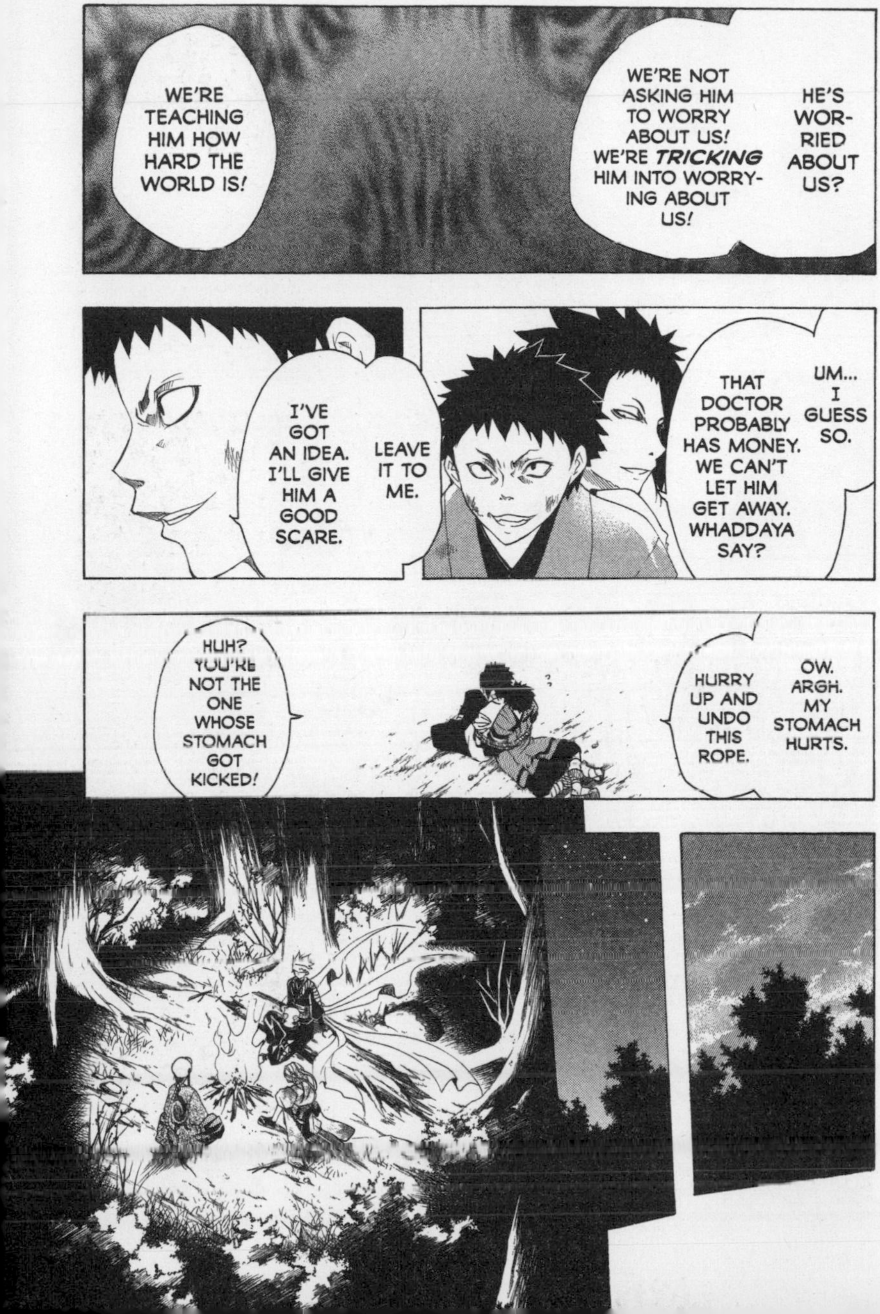
HE'S WOR-RIED ABOUT US?
WE'RE NOT ASKING HIM TO WORRY ABOUT US! WE'RE TRICKING HIM INTO WORRY-ING ABOUT US!
WE'RE TEACHING HIM HOW HARD THE WORLD IS!
UM... I GUESS SO.
THAT DOCTOR PROBABLY HAS MONEY. WE CAN'T LET HIM GET AWAY. WHADDAYA SAY?
LEAVE IT TO ME.
I'VE GOT AN IDEA. I'LL GIVE HIM A GOOD SCARE.
OW. ARGH. MY STOMACH HURTS.
HURRY UP AND UNDO THIS ROPE.
HUH? YOU'RE NOT THE ONE WHOSE STOMACH GOT KICKED!

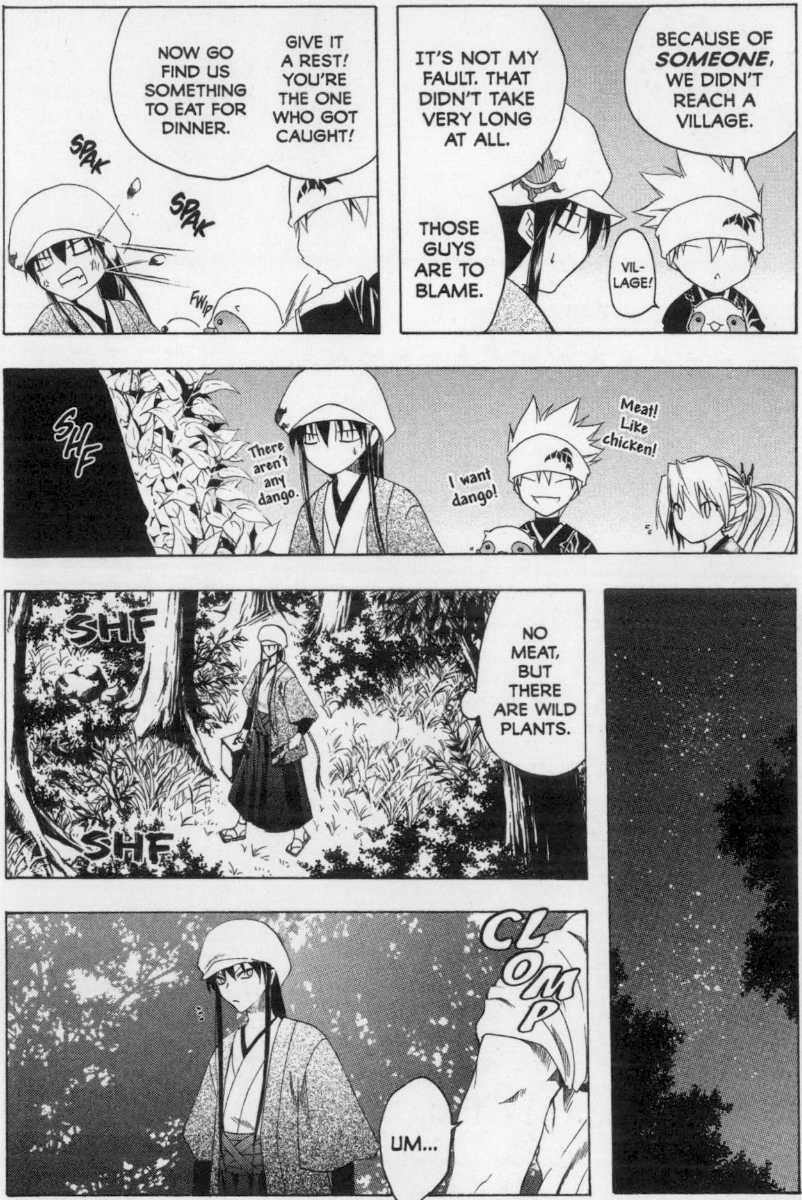
BECAUSE OF *SOMEONE*, WE DIDN'T REACH A VILLAGE.
VIL-LAGE!
IT'S NOT MY FAULT. THAT DIDN'T TAKE VERY LONG AT ALL.
THOSE GUYS ARE TO BLAME.
GIVE IT A REST! YOU'RE THE ONE WHO GOT CAUGHT!
NOW GO FIND US SOMETHING TO EAT FOR DINNER.
SPAK
SPAK
FWIP
Meat! Like chicken!
I want dango!
There aren't any dango.
SHF
NO MEAT, BUT THERE ARE WILD PLANTS.
SHF
SHF
CLOMP
UM...

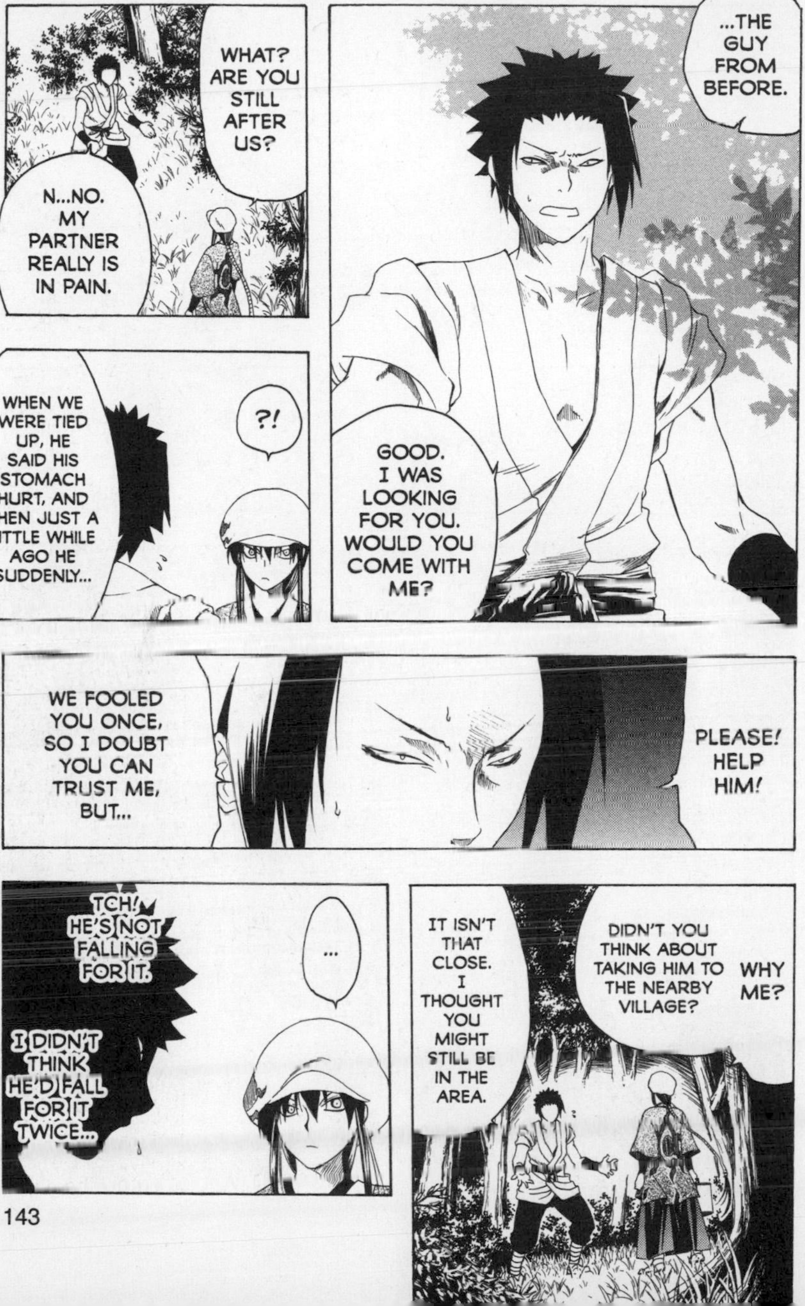
...THE GUY FROM BEFORE.
GOOD. I WAS LOOKING FOR YOU. WOULD YOU COME WITH ME?
WHAT? ARE YOU STILL AFTER US?
N...NO. MY PARTNER REALLY IS IN PAIN.
?!
WHEN WE WERE TIED UP, HE SAID HIS STOMACH HURT, AND THEN JUST A LITTLE WHILE AGO HE SUDDENLY...
PLEASE! HELP HIM!
WE FOOLED YOU ONCE, SO I DOUBT YOU CAN TRUST ME, BUT...
WHY ME?
DIDN'T YOU THINK ABOUT TAKING HIM TO THE NEARBY VILLAGE?
IT ISN'T THAT CLOSE. I THOUGHT YOU MIGHT STILL BE IN THE AREA.
...
TCH! HE'S NOT FALLING FOR IT.
I DIDN'T THINK HE'D FALL FOR IT TWICE...

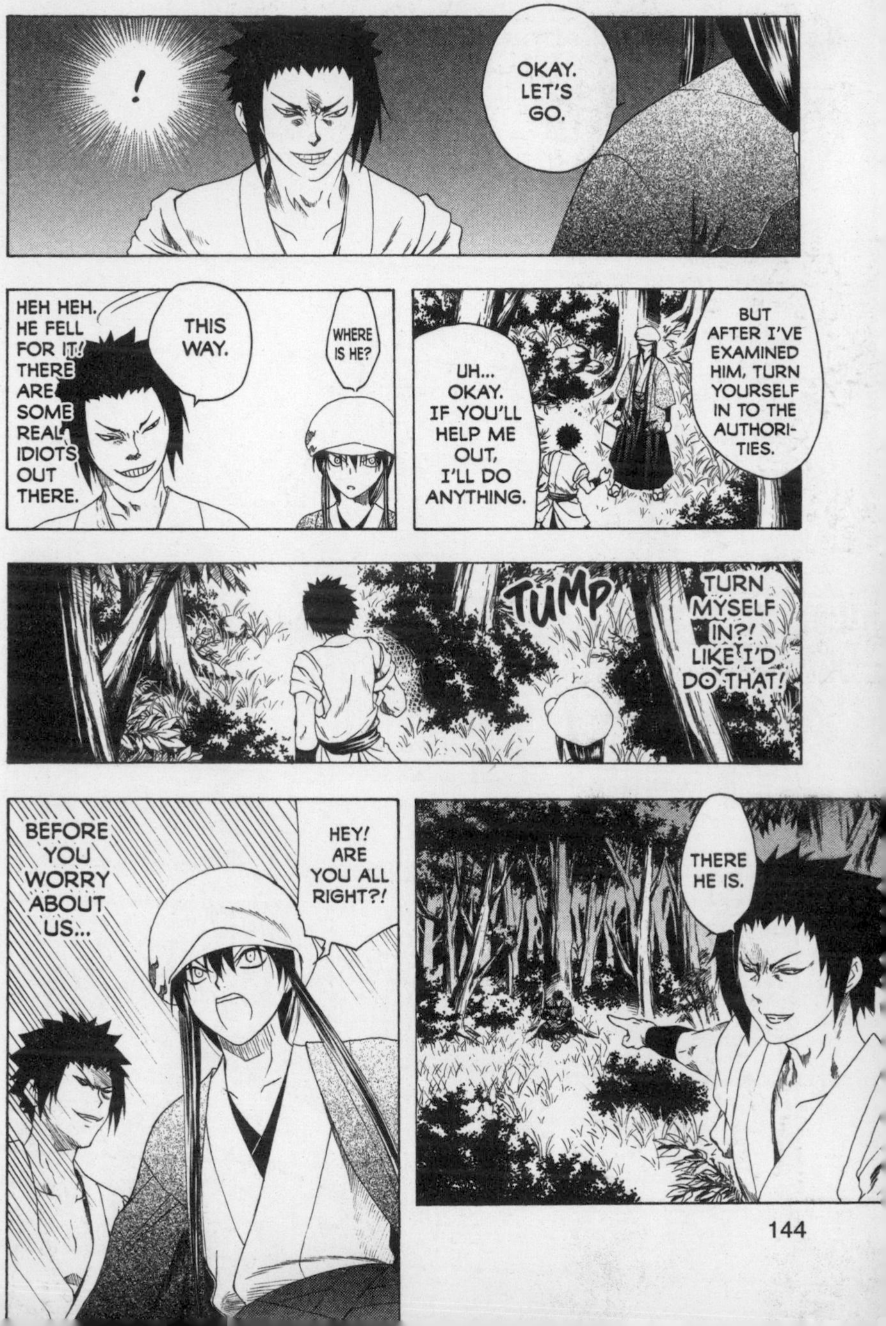
OKAY. LET'S GO.
!
BUT AFTER I'VE EXAMINED HIM, TURN YOURSELF IN TO THE AUTHORITIES.
UH... OKAY. IF YOU'LL HELP ME OUT, I'LL DO ANYTHING.
WHERE IS HE?
THIS WAY.
HEH HEH. HE FELL FOR IT! THERE ARE SOME REAL IDIOTS OUT THERE.
TURN MYSELF IN?! LIKE I'D DO THAT!
TUMP
THERE HE IS.
HEY! ARE YOU ALL RIGHT?!
BEFORE YOU WORRY ABOUT US...

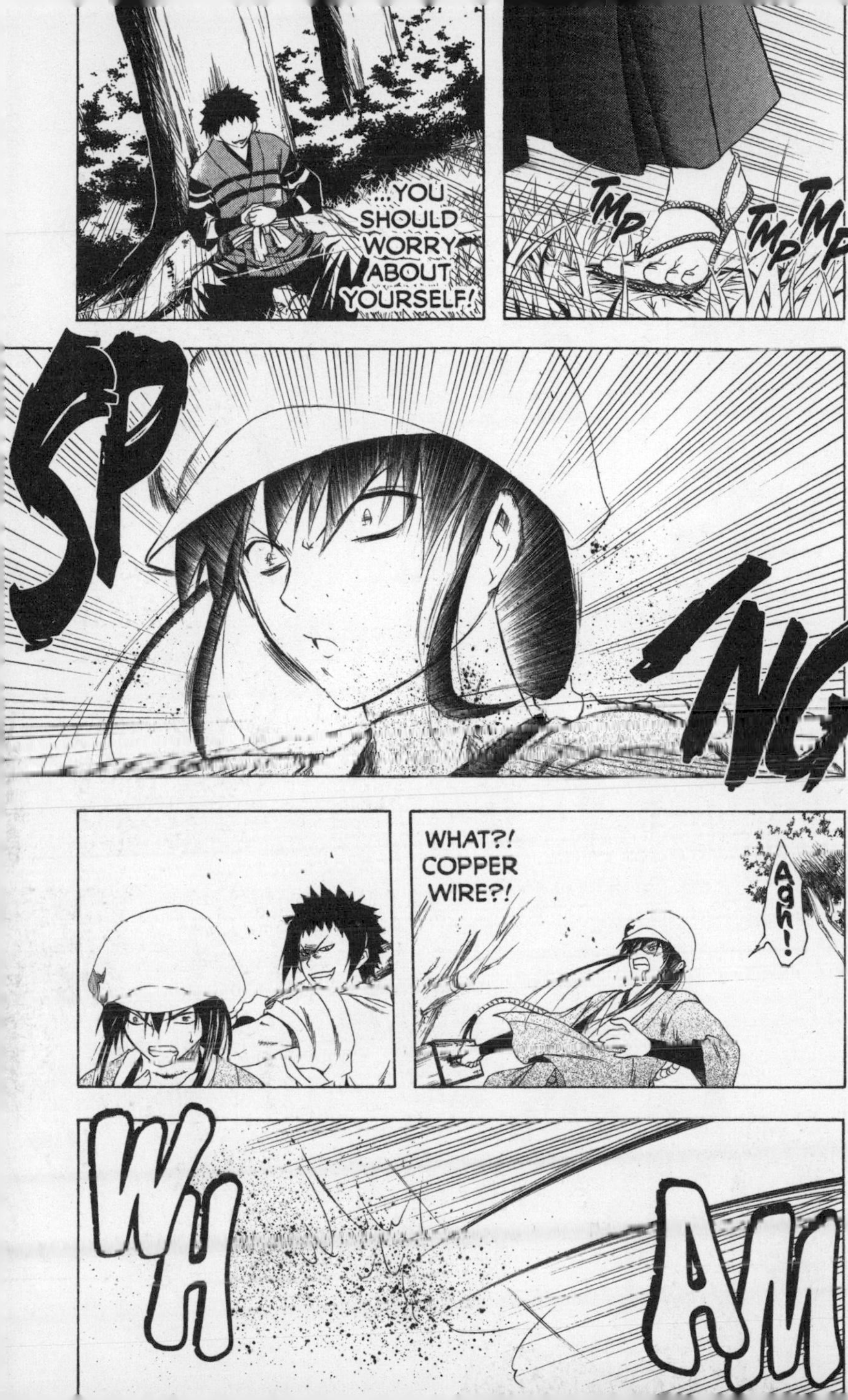
TMP TMP
TMP
...YOU SHOULD WORRY ABOUT YOURSELF!
SPANG
Agh!
WHAT?! COPPER WIRE?!
WHAM

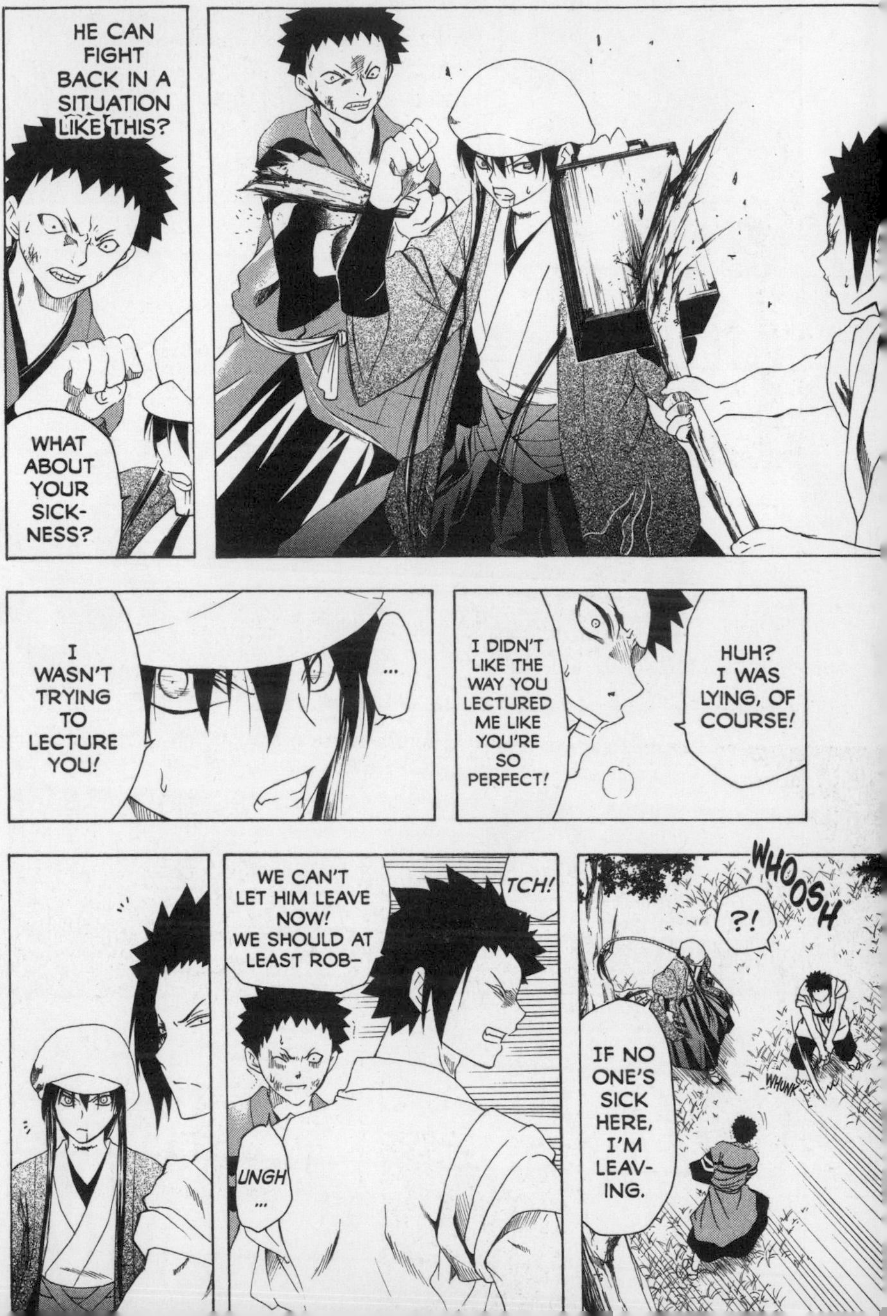
HE CAN FIGHT BACK IN A SITUATION LIKE THIS?
WHAT ABOUT YOUR SICK-NESS?
HUH? I WAS LYING, OF COURSE!
I DIDN'T LIKE THE WAY YOU LECTURED ME LIKE YOU'RE SO PERFECT!
...
I WASN'T TRYING TO LECTURE YOU!
WHOOSH
?!
WHUNK
IF NO ONE'S SICK HERE, I'M LEAV-ING.
TCH!
WE CAN'T LET HIM LEAVE NOW! WE SHOULD AT LEAST ROB–
UNGH ...

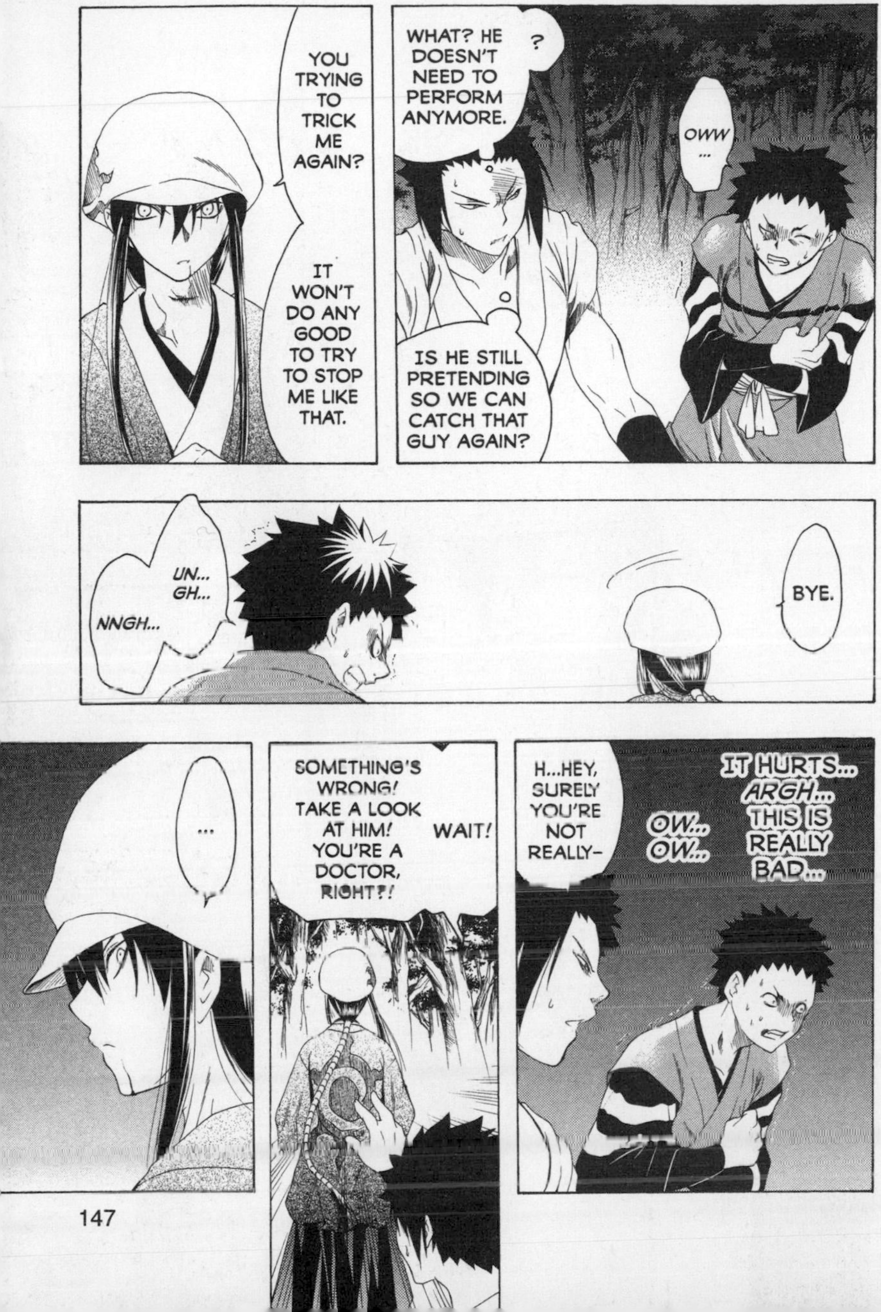
?
WHAT? HE DOESN'T NEED TO PERFORM ANYMORE.
IS HE STILL PRETENDING SO WE CAN CATCH THAT GUY AGAIN?
OWW ...
YOU TRYING TO TRICK ME AGAIN?
IT WON'T DO ANY GOOD TO TRY TO STOP ME LIKE THAT.
BYE.
UN... GH...
NNGH...
IT HURTS... ARGH... THIS IS REALLY BAD...
OW... OW...
H...HEY, SURELY YOU'RE NOT REALLY-
WAIT!
SOMETHING'S WRONG! TAKE A LOOK AT HIM! YOU'RE A DOCTOR, RIGHT?!
...

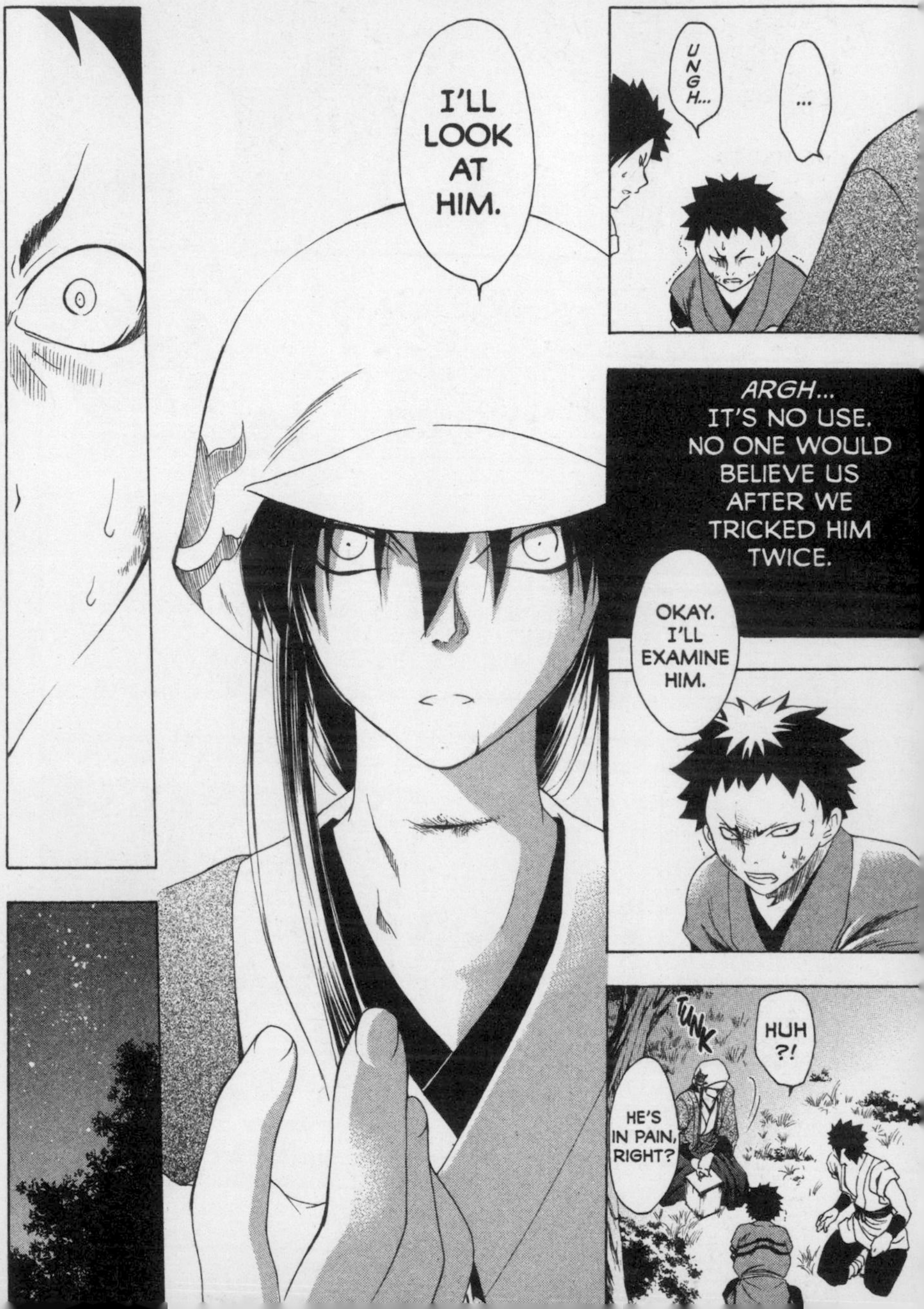
...
UNGH...
ARGH... IT'S NO USE. NO ONE WOULD BELIEVE US AFTER WE TRICKED HIM TWICE.
OKAY. I'LL EXAMINE HIM.
HUH ?!
TUNK
HE'S IN PAIN, RIGHT?
I'LL LOOK AT HIM.

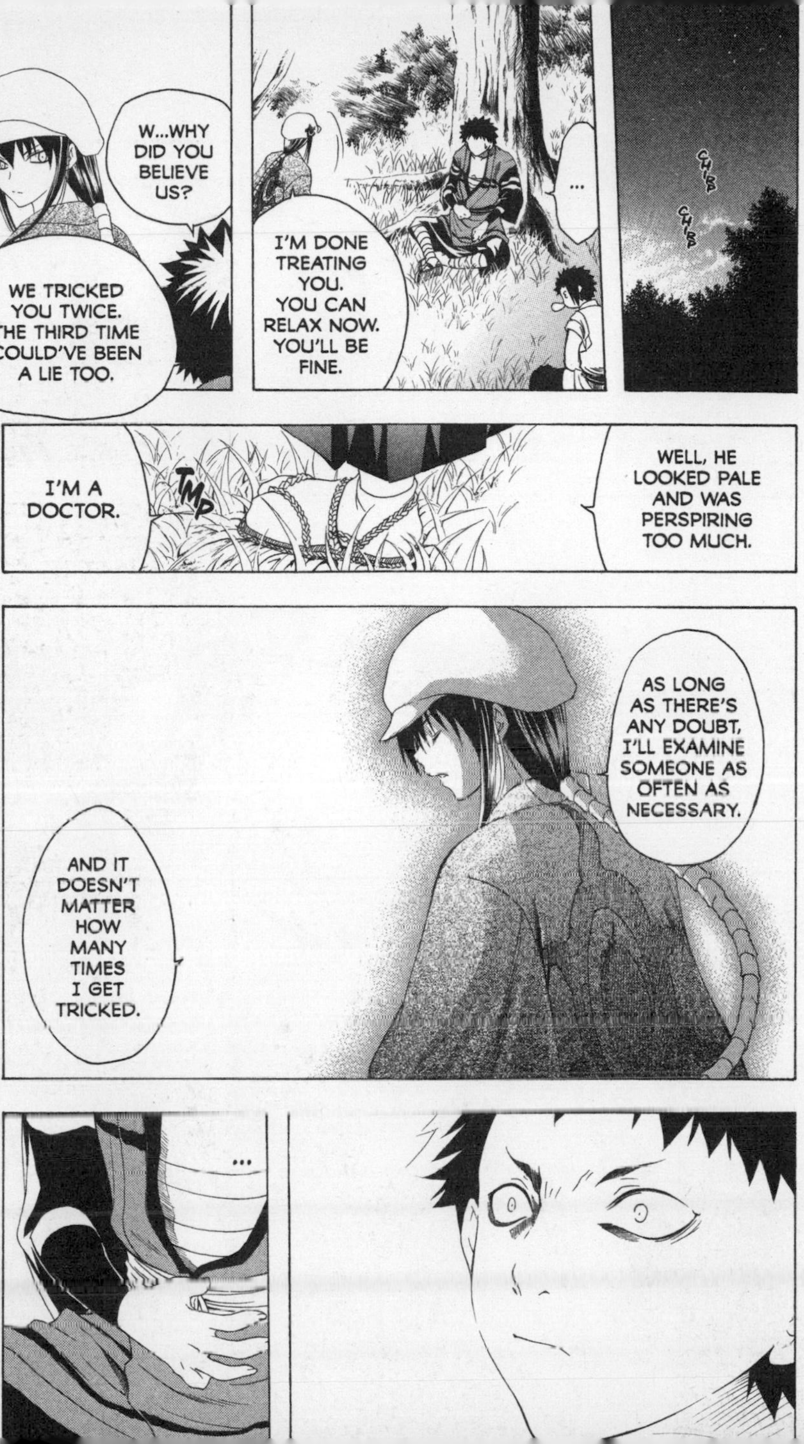
CHIRP
CHIRP
...
I'M DONE TREATING YOU. YOU CAN RELAX NOW. YOU'LL BE FINE.
W...WHY DID YOU BELIEVE US?
WE TRICKED YOU TWICE. THE THIRD TIME COULD'VE BEEN A LIE TOO.
WELL, HE LOOKED PALE AND WAS PERSPIRING TOO MUCH.
TMP
I'M A DOCTOR.
AS LONG AS THERE'S ANY DOUBT, I'LL EXAMINE SOMEONE AS OFTEN AS NECESSARY.
AND IT DOESN'T MATTER HOW MANY TIMES I GET TRICKED.
...

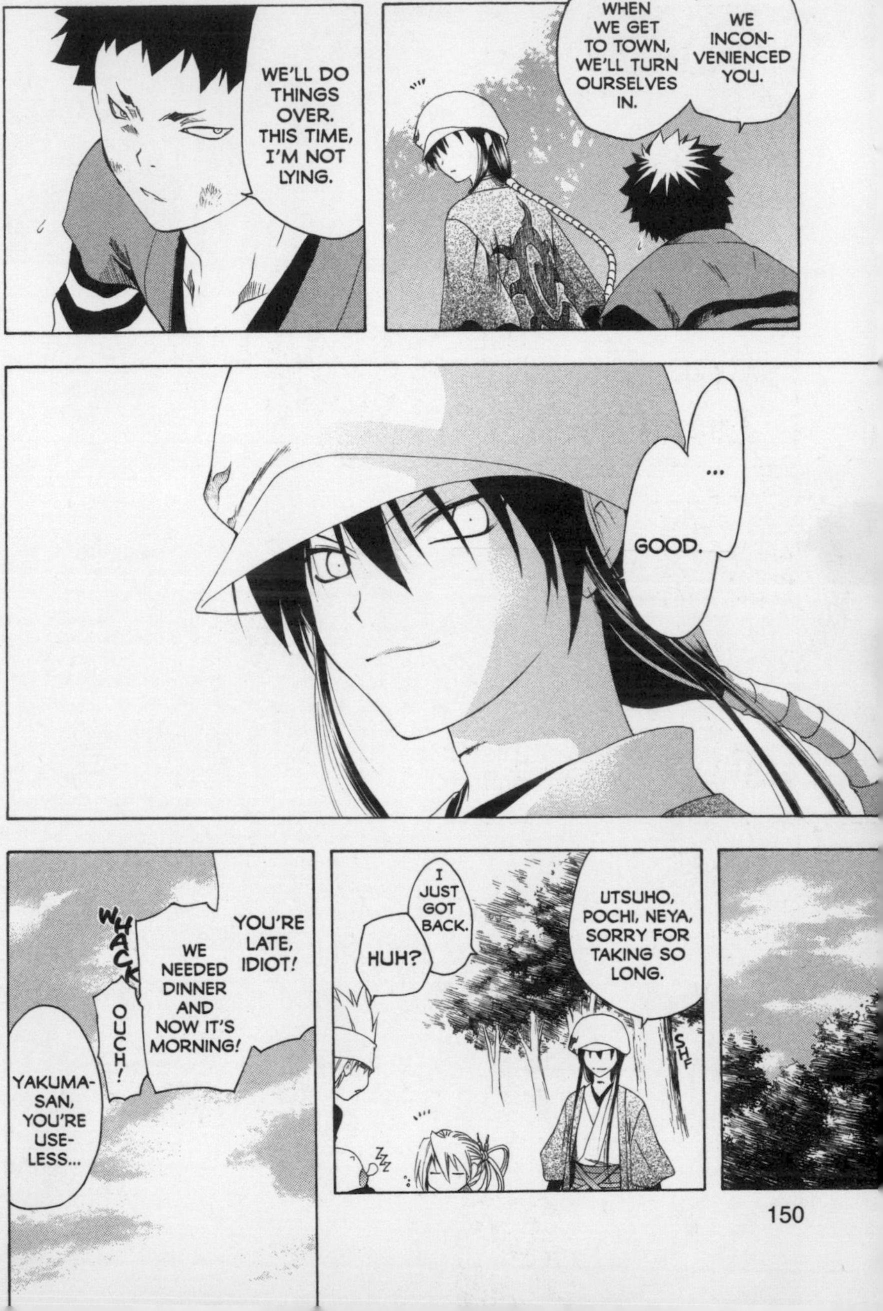
WE INCON-VENIENCED YOU.
WHEN WE GET TO TOWN, WE'LL TURN OURSELVES IN.
WE'LL DO THINGS OVER. THIS TIME, I'M NOT LYING.
...
GOOD.
UTSUHO, POCHI, NEYA, SORRY FOR TAKING SO LONG.
SHF
I JUST GOT BACK.
HUH?
YOU'RE LATE, IDIOT!
WE NEEDED DINNER AND NOW IT'S MORNING!
WHACK
OUCH!
YAKUMA-SAN, YOU'RE USE-LESS...

Chapter 36

Town of Explosives

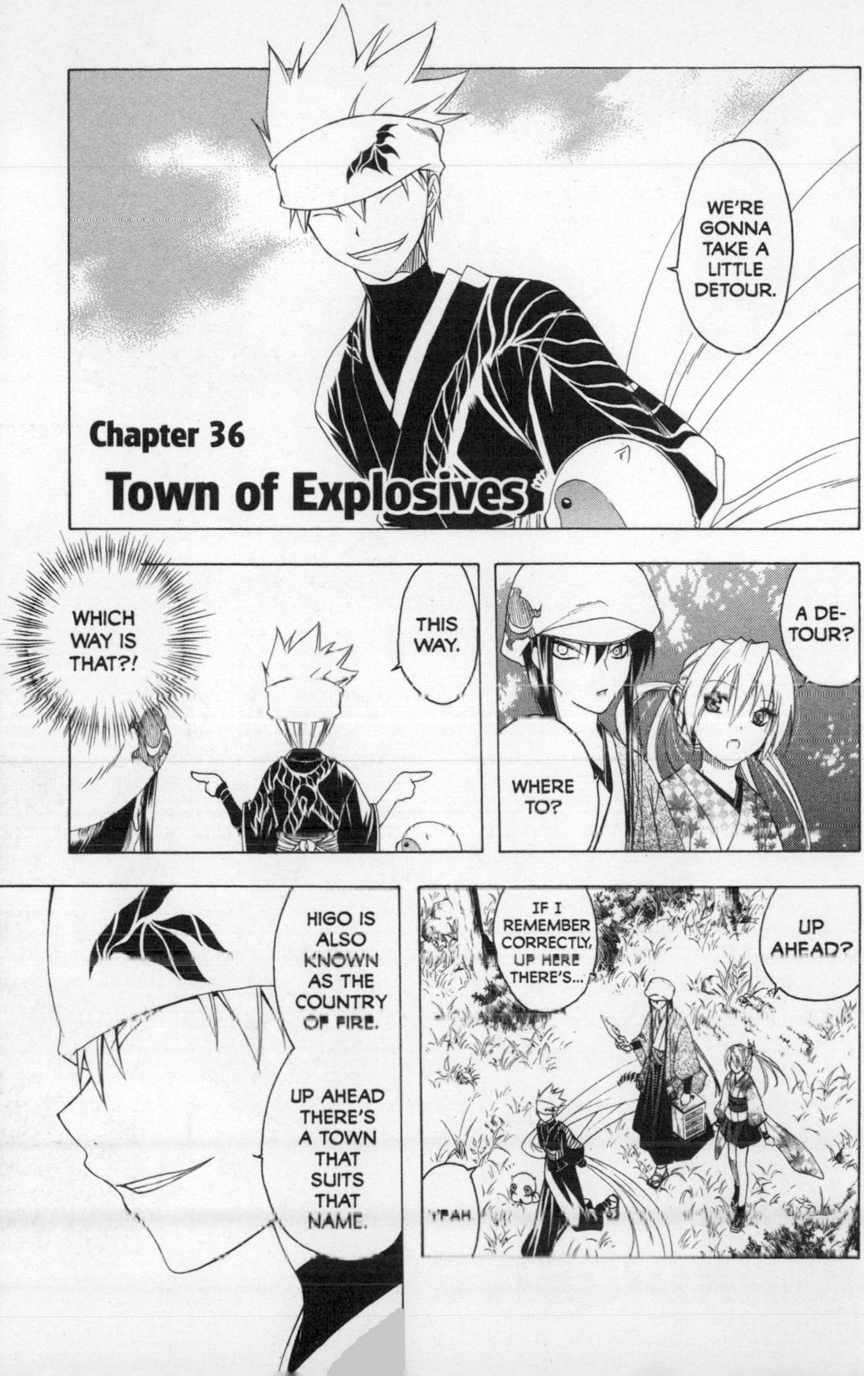
WE'RE GONNA TAKE A LITTLE DETOUR.
A DE-TOUR?
WHERE TO?
THIS WAY.
WHICH WAY IS THAT?!
UP AHEAD?
IF I REMEMBER CORRECTLY, UP HERE THERE'S...
YEAH
HIGO IS ALSO KNOWN AS THE COUNTRY OF FIRE.
UP AHEAD THERE'S A TOWN THAT SUITS THAT NAME.

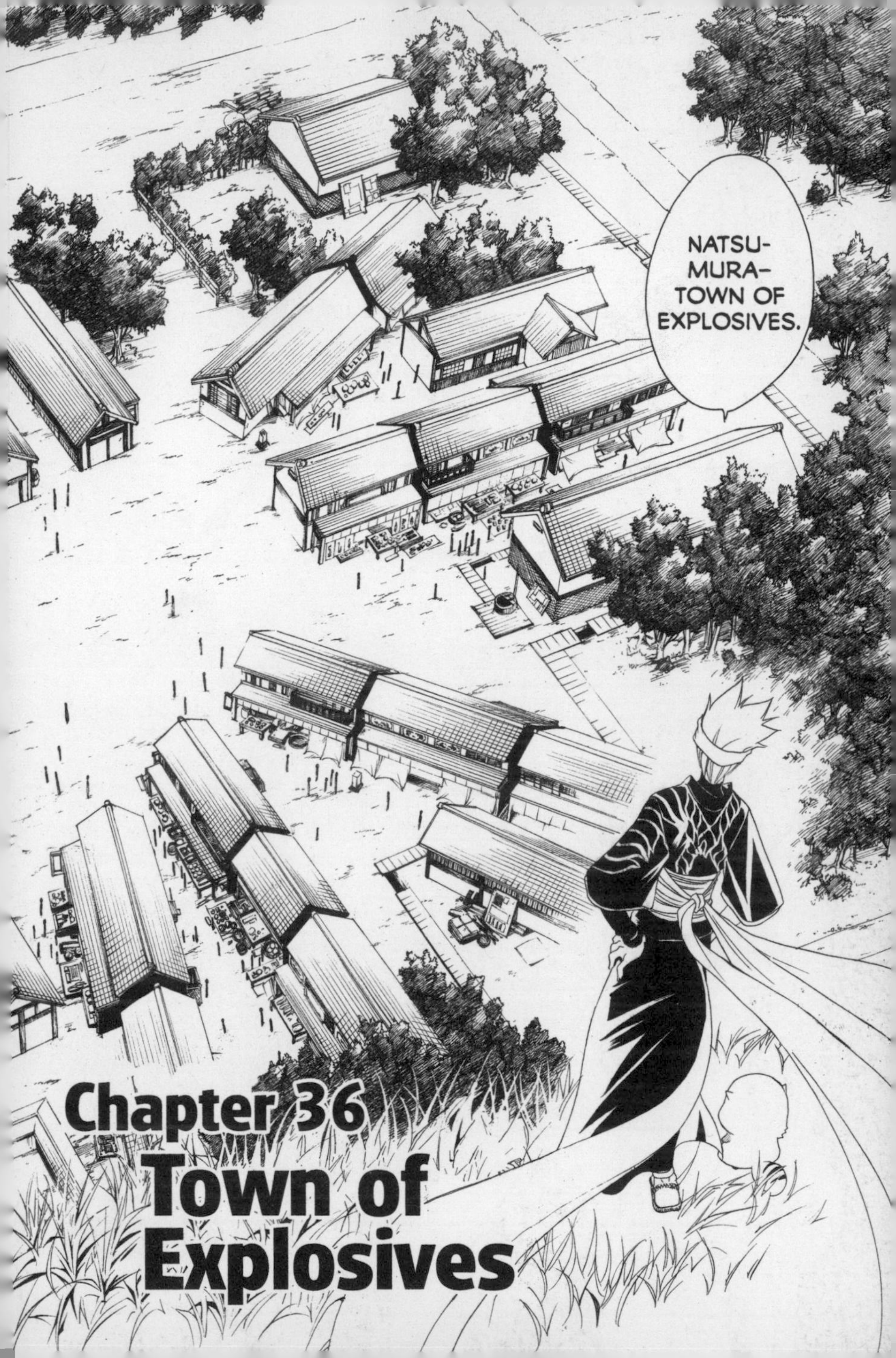
NATSU-MURA-TOWN OF EXPLOSIVES.
Chapter 36
Town of Explosives

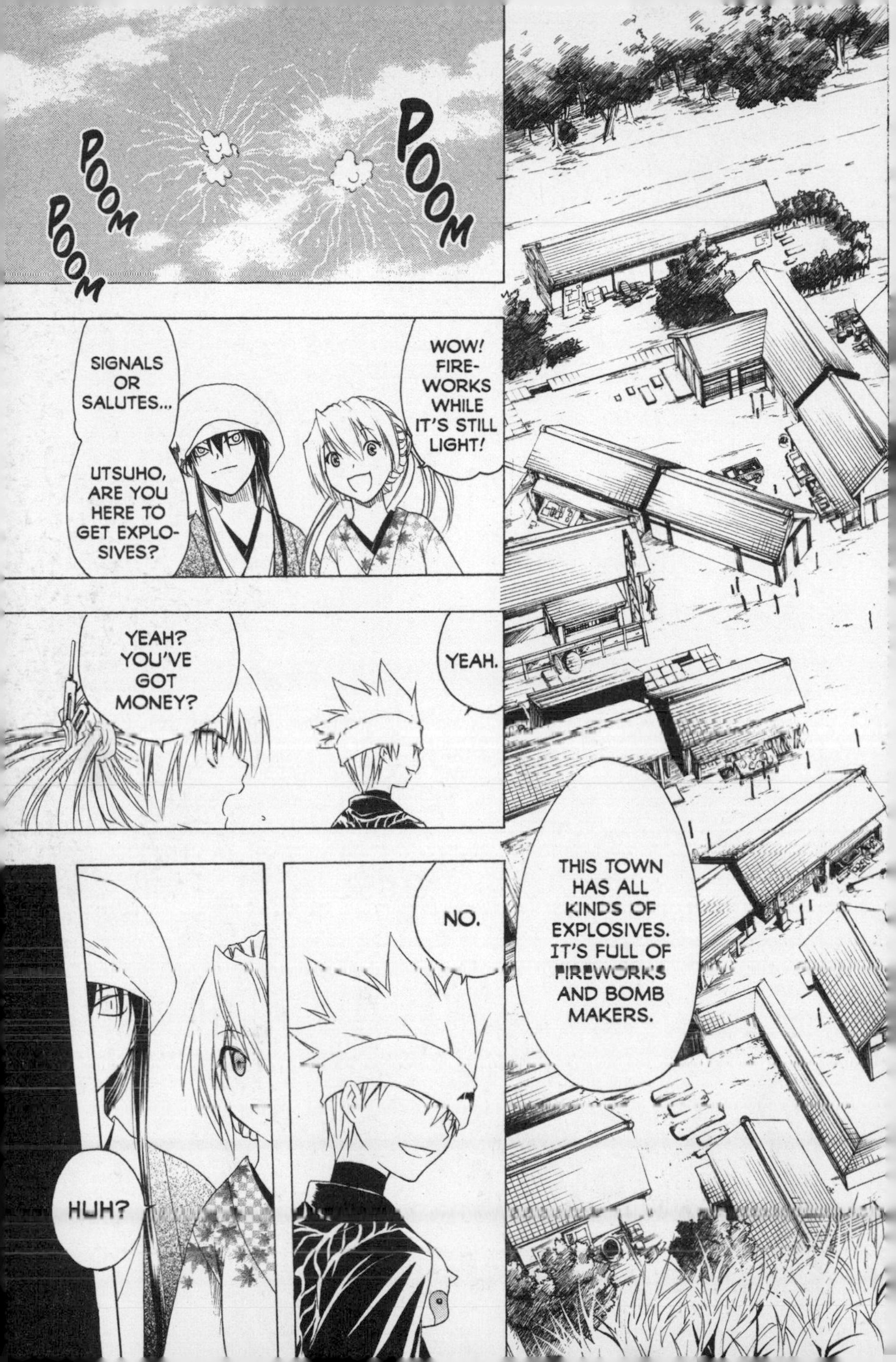
THIS TOWN HAS ALL KINDS OF EXPLOSIVES. IT'S FULL OF FIREWORKS AND BOMB MAKERS.
POOM
POOM
POOM
WOW! FIRE-WORKS WHILE IT'S STILL LIGHT!
SIGNALS OR SALUTES...
UTSUHO, ARE YOU HERE TO GET EXPLO-SIVES?
YEAH.
YEAH? YOU'VE GOT MONEY?
NO.
HUH?

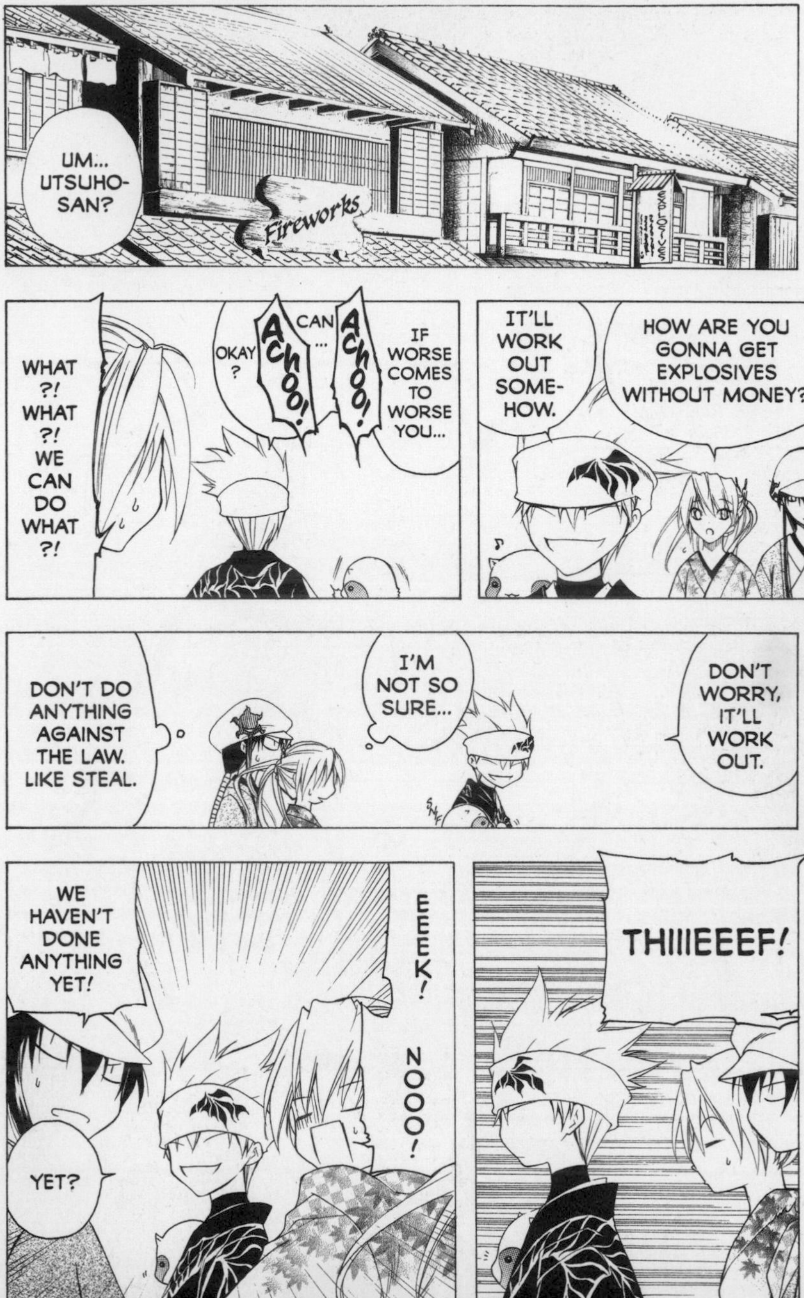
Fireworks
EXPLOSIVES
UM... UTSUHO-SAN?
HOW ARE YOU GONNA GET EXPLOSIVES WITHOUT MONEY?
IT'LL WORK OUT SOME-HOW.
IF WORSE COMES TO WORSE YOU...
ACHOO!
CAN ...
ACHOO!
OKAY ?
WHAT ?! WHAT ?! WE CAN DO WHAT ?!
DON'T WORRY, IT'LL WORK OUT.
I'M NOT SO SURE...
DON'T DO ANYTHING AGAINST THE LAW. LIKE STEAL.
THIIIEEEF!
EEEK! NOOO!
WE HAVEN'T DONE ANYTHING YET!
YET?

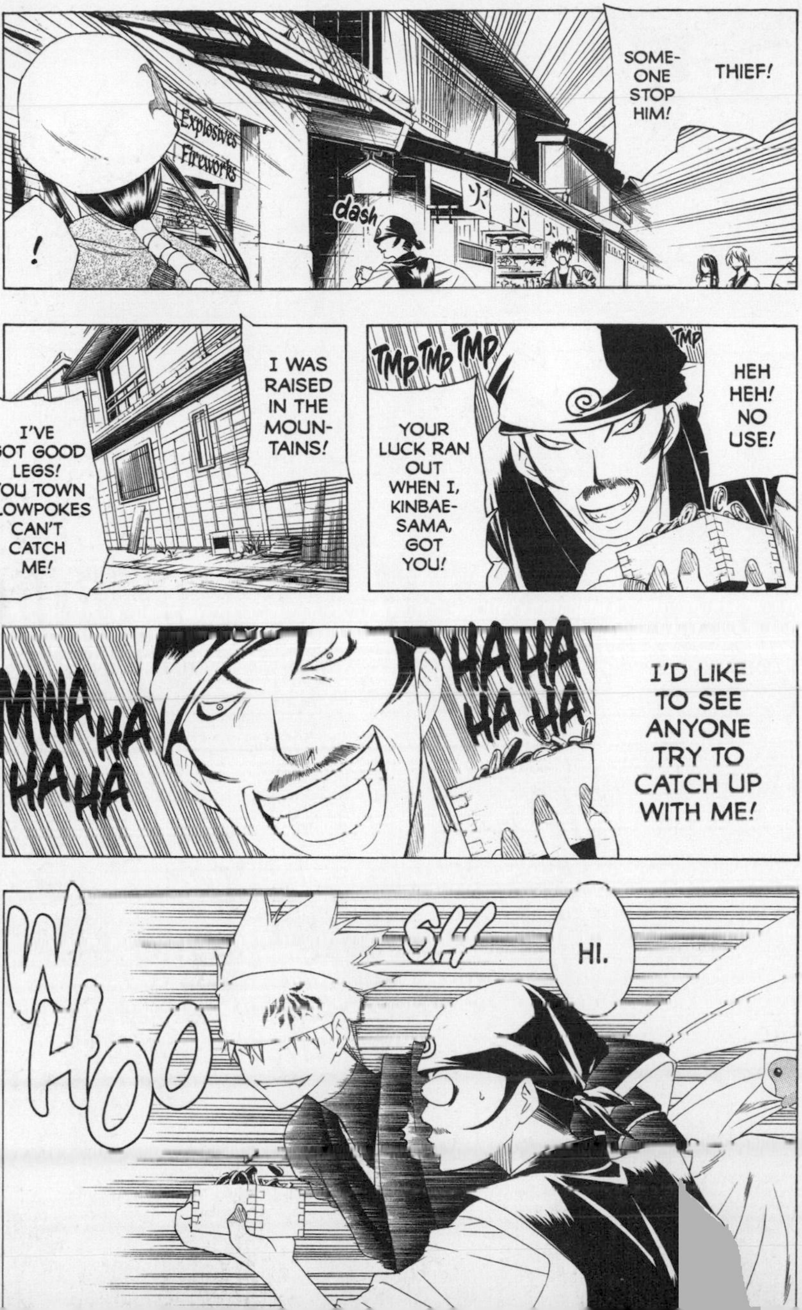
THIEF!
SOME-ONE STOP HIM!
Explosives Fireworks
dash
!
HEH HEH! NO USE!
TMP TMP TMP TMP
YOUR LUCK RAN OUT WHEN I, KINBAE-SAMA, GOT YOU!
I WAS RAISED IN THE MOUN-TAINS!
I'VE GOT GOOD LEGS! YOU TOWN SLOWPOKES CAN'T CATCH ME!
I'D LIKE TO SEE ANYONE TRY TO CATCH UP WITH ME!
HA HA HA HA
MWA HA HA HA
HI.
SH
WHOO

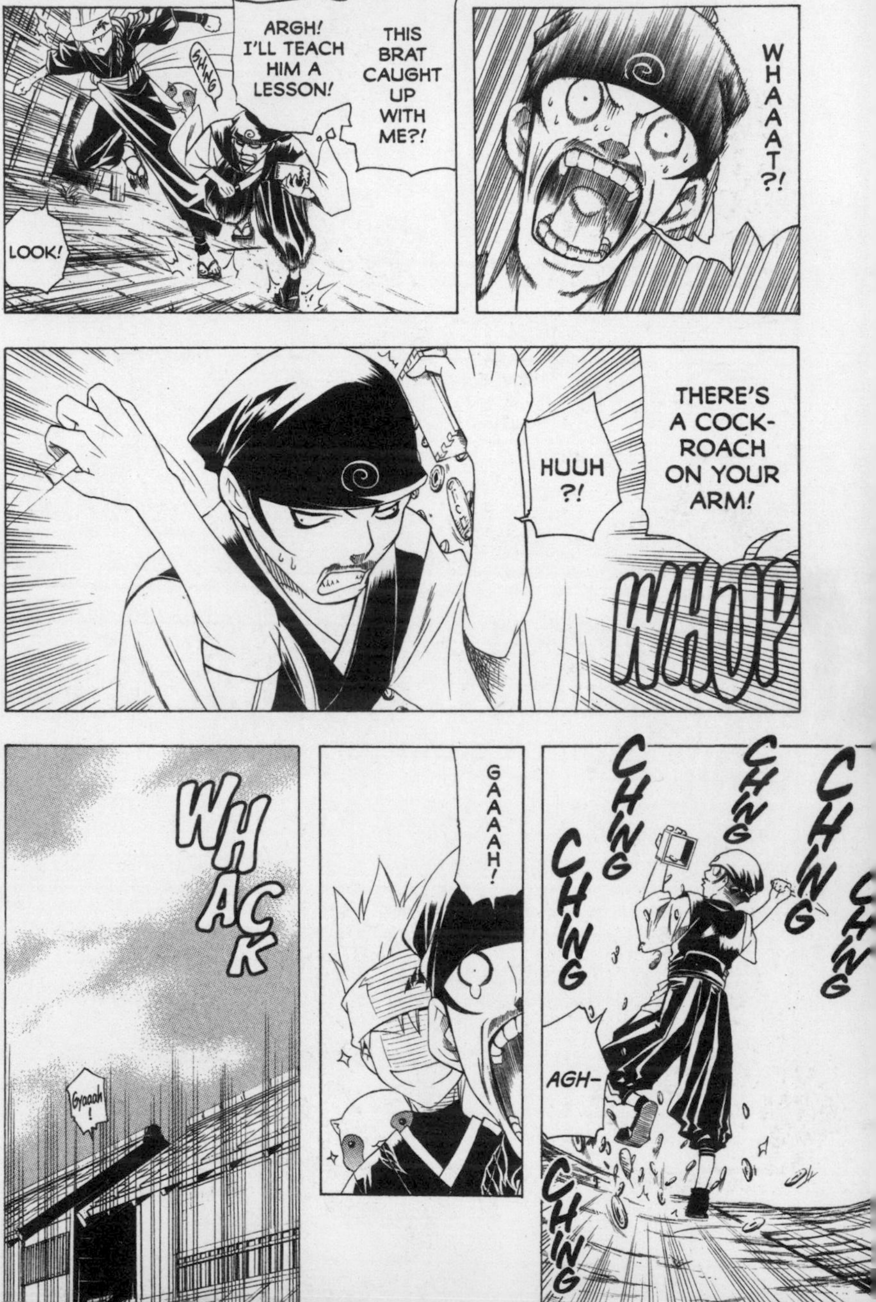
WHAAAAT?!
THIS BRAT CAUGHT UP WITH ME?!
ARGH! I'LL TEACH HIM A LESSON!
SHING
LOOK!
THERE'S A COCK-ROACH ON YOUR ARM!
HUUH ?!
WHOP
CHING
CHING
CHING
CHING
CHING
AGH-
CHING
GAAAAAH!
WHACK
Gyaaah!

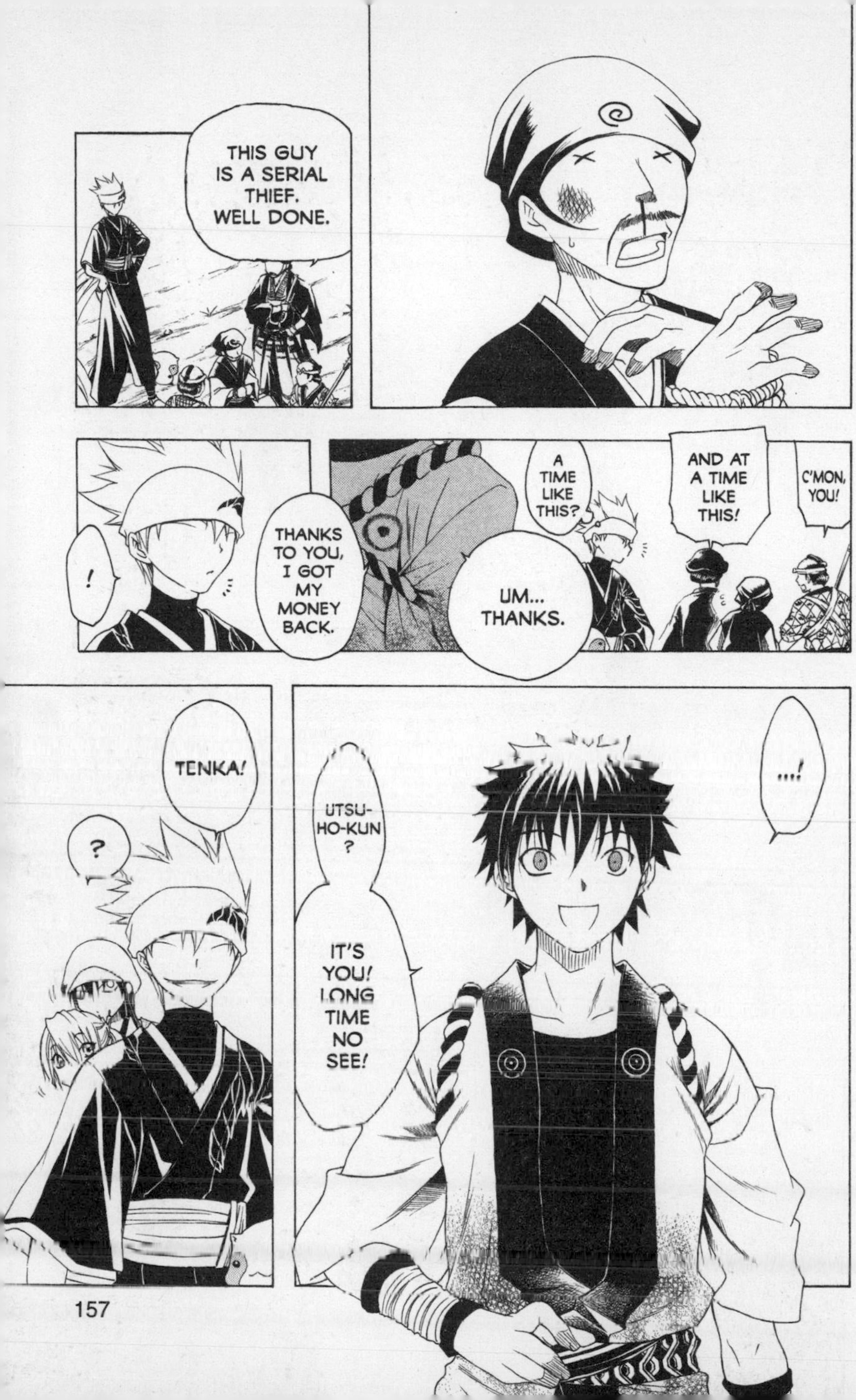
THIS GUY IS A SERIAL THIEF. WELL DONE.
C'MON, YOU!
AND AT A TIME LIKE THIS!
A TIME LIKE THIS?
UM... THANKS.
THANKS TO YOU, I GOT MY MONEY BACK.
!
...!
UTSU-HO-KUN?
IT'S YOU! LONG TIME NO SEE!
TENKA!
?

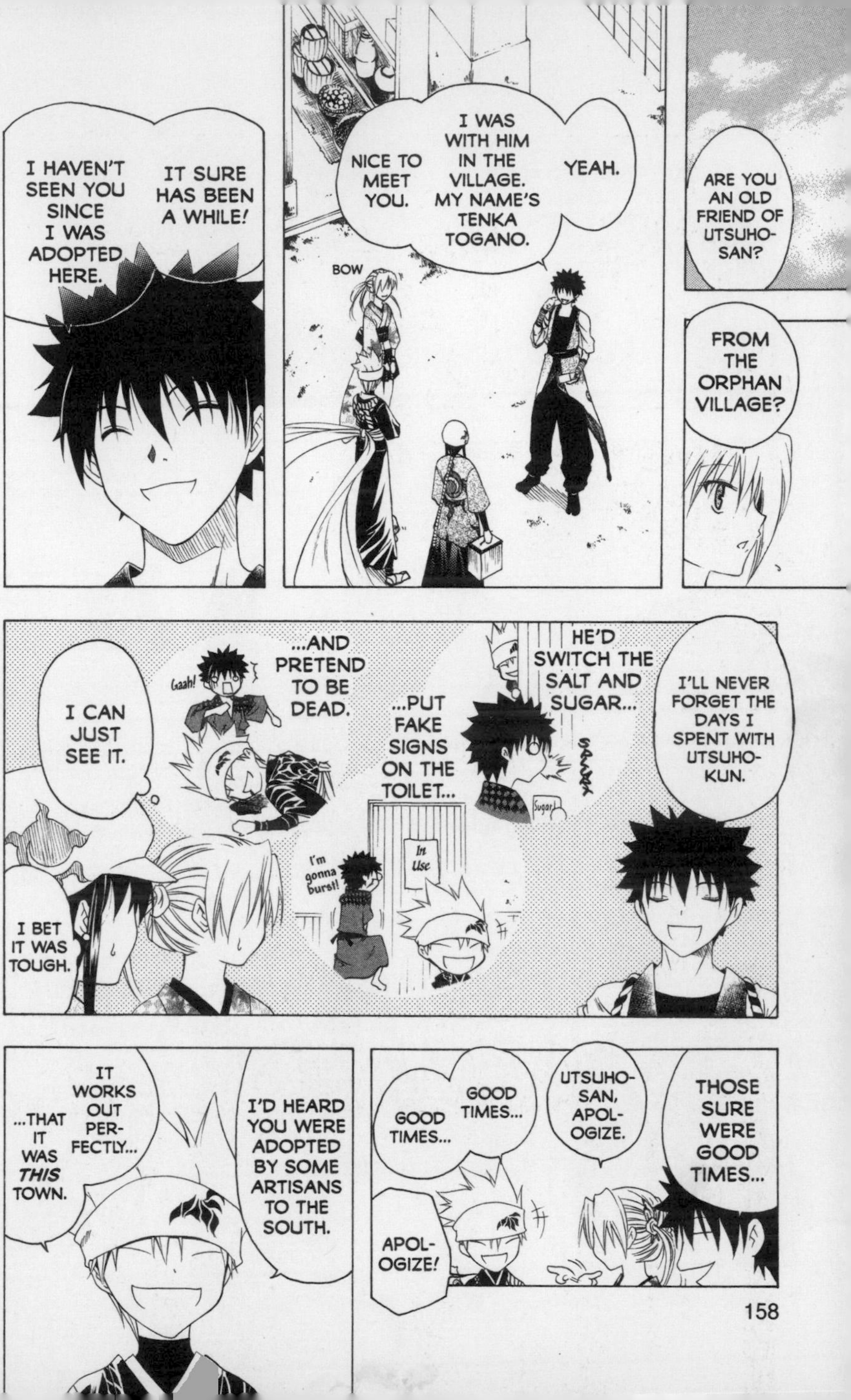

ARE YOU AN OLD FRIEND OF UTSUHO-SAN?
FROM THE ORPHAN VILLAGE?
YEAH.
I WAS WITH HIM IN THE VILLAGE. MY NAME'S TENKA TOGANO.
NICE TO MEET YOU.
BOW
IT SURE HAS BEEN A WHILE!
I HAVEN'T SEEN YOU SINCE I WAS ADOPTED HERE.
I'LL NEVER FORGET THE DAYS I SPENT WITH UTSUHO-KUN.
HE'D SWITCH THE SALT AND SUGAR...
Sugar!
...PUT FAKE SIGNS ON THE TOILET...
In Use
I'm gonna burst!
...AND PRETEND TO BE DEAD.
Gaah!
I CAN JUST SEE IT.
I BET IT WAS TOUGH.
THOSE SURE WERE GOOD TIMES...
UTSUHO-SAN, APOLOGIZE.
GOOD TIMES...
GOOD TIMES...
APOLOGIZE!
I'D HEARD YOU WERE ADOPTED BY SOME ARTISANS TO THE SOUTH.
IT WORKS OUT PERFECTLY...
...THAT IT WAS *THIS* TOWN.

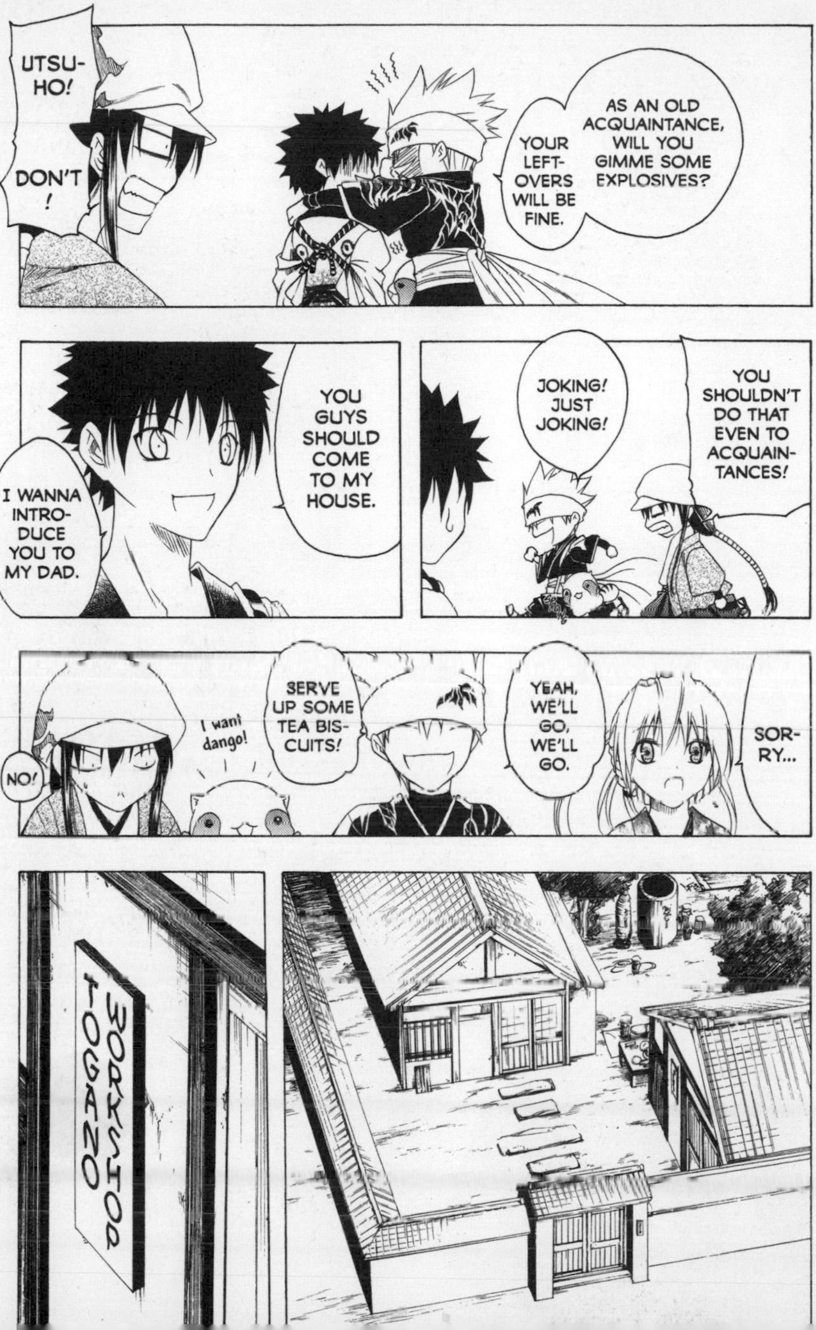
AS AN OLD ACQUAINTANCE, WILL YOU GIMME SOME EXPLOSIVES?
YOUR LEFT-OVERS WILL BE FINE.
UTSU-HO! DON'T!
YOU SHOULDN'T DO THAT EVEN TO ACQUAIN-TANCES!
JOKING! JUST JOKING!
YOU GUYS SHOULD COME TO MY HOUSE.
I WANNA INTRO-DUCE YOU TO MY DAD.
SOR-RY...
YEAH, WE'LL GO, WE'LL GO.
SERVE UP SOME TEA BIS-CUITS!
I want dango!
NO!
TOGANO WORKSHOP

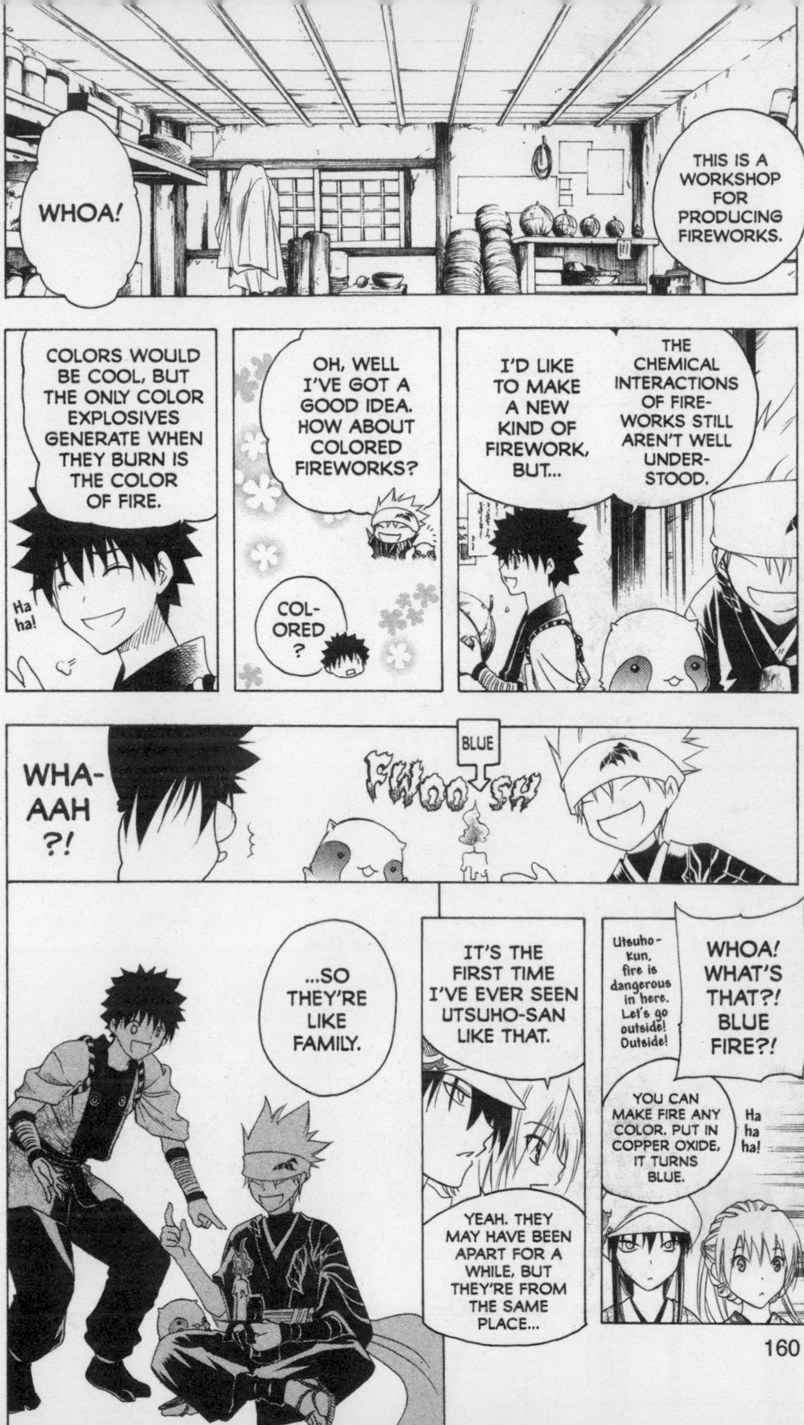
THIS IS A WORKSHOP FOR PRODUCING FIREWORKS.
WHOA!
THE CHEMICAL INTERACTIONS OF FIRE-WORKS STILL AREN'T WELL UNDER-STOOD.
I'D LIKE TO MAKE A NEW KIND OF FIREWORK, BUT...
OH, WELL I'VE GOT A GOOD IDEA. HOW ABOUT COLORED FIREWORKS?
COL-ORED ?
COLORS WOULD BE COOL, BUT THE ONLY COLOR EXPLOSIVES GENERATE WHEN THEY BURN IS THE COLOR OF FIRE.
Ha ha!
BLUE
FWOOSH
WHA-AAH ?!
WHOA! WHAT'S THAT?! BLUE FIRE?!
Utsuho-kun, fire is dangerous in here. Let's go outside! Outside!
YOU CAN MAKE FIRE ANY COLOR. PUT IN COPPER OXIDE, IT TURNS BLUE.
Ha ha ha!
IT'S THE FIRST TIME I'VE EVER SEEN UTSUHO-SAN LIKE THAT.
YEAH. THEY MAY HAVE BEEN APART FOR A WHILE, BUT THEY'RE FROM THE SAME PLACE...
...SO THEY'RE LIKE FAMILY.

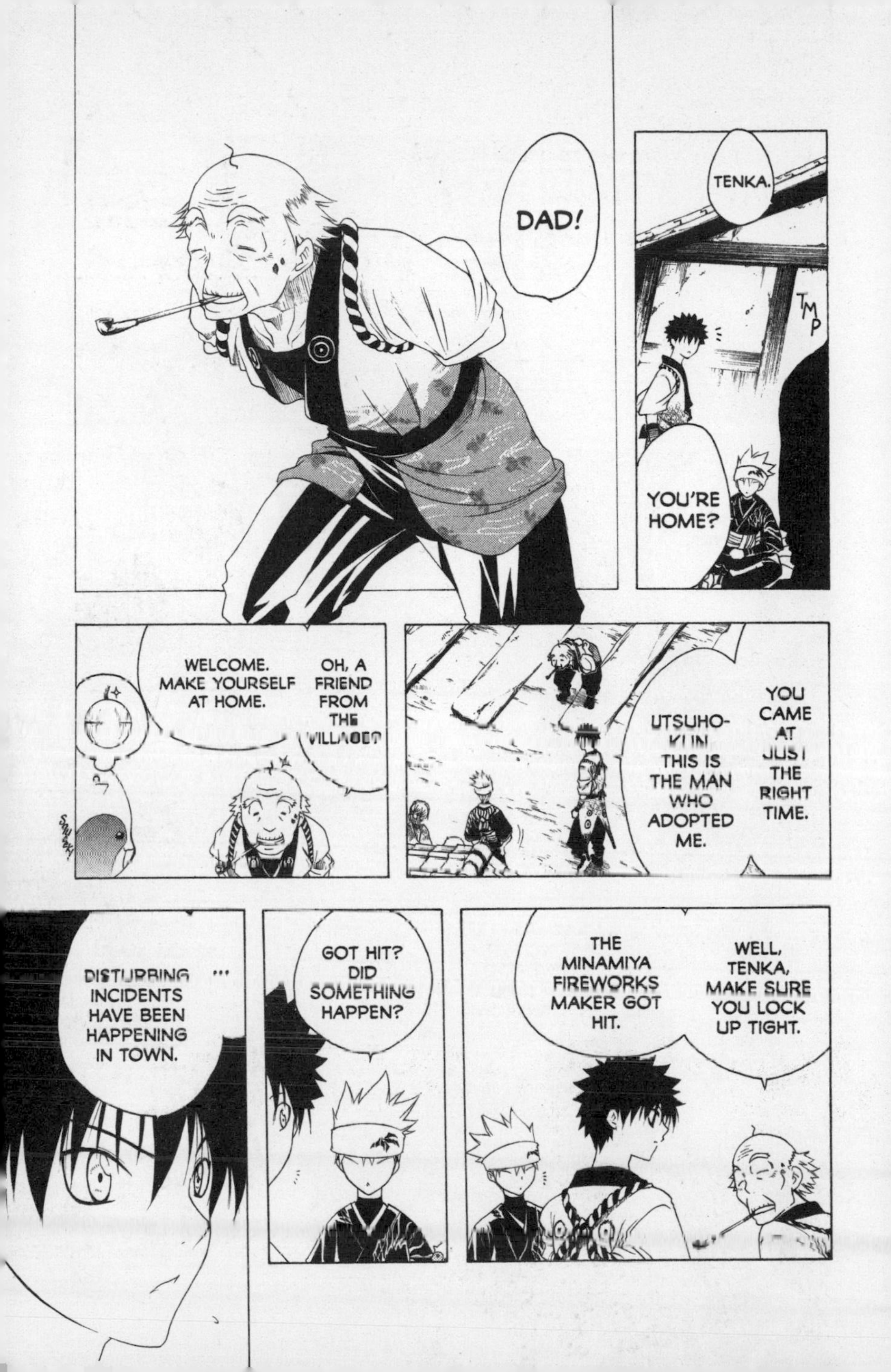
TENKA.
TMP
YOU'RE HOME?
DAD!
YOU CAME AT JUST THE RIGHT TIME.
UTSUHO-KUN THIS IS THE MAN WHO ADOPTED ME.
OH, A FRIEND FROM THE VILLAGE?
WELCOME. MAKE YOURSELF AT HOME.
WELL, TENKA, MAKE SURE YOU LOCK UP TIGHT.
THE MINAMIYA FIREWORKS MAKER GOT HIT.
GOT HIT? DID SOMETHING HAPPEN?
...
DISTURBING INCIDENTS HAVE BEEN HAPPENING IN TOWN.

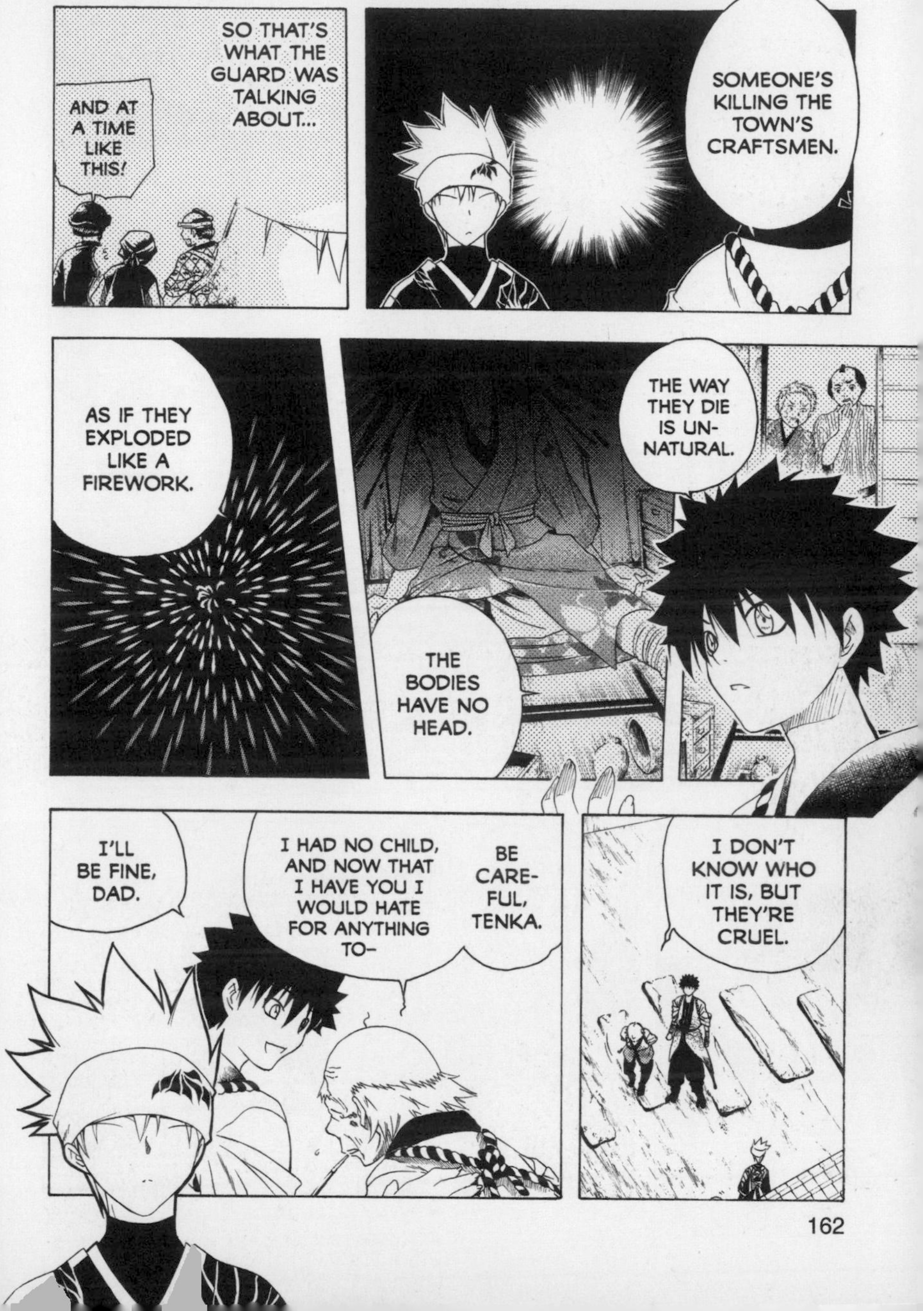
SOMEONE'S KILLING THE TOWN'S CRAFTSMEN.
SO THAT'S WHAT THE GUARD WAS TALKING ABOUT...
AND AT A TIME LIKE THIS!
THE WAY THEY DIE IS UN-NATURAL.
THE BODIES HAVE NO HEAD.
AS IF THEY EXPLODED LIKE A FIREWORK.
I DON'T KNOW WHO IT IS, BUT THEY'RE CRUEL.
BE CARE-FUL, TENKA.
I HAD NO CHILD, AND NOW THAT I HAVE YOU I WOULD HATE FOR ANYTHING TO–
I'LL BE FINE, DAD.

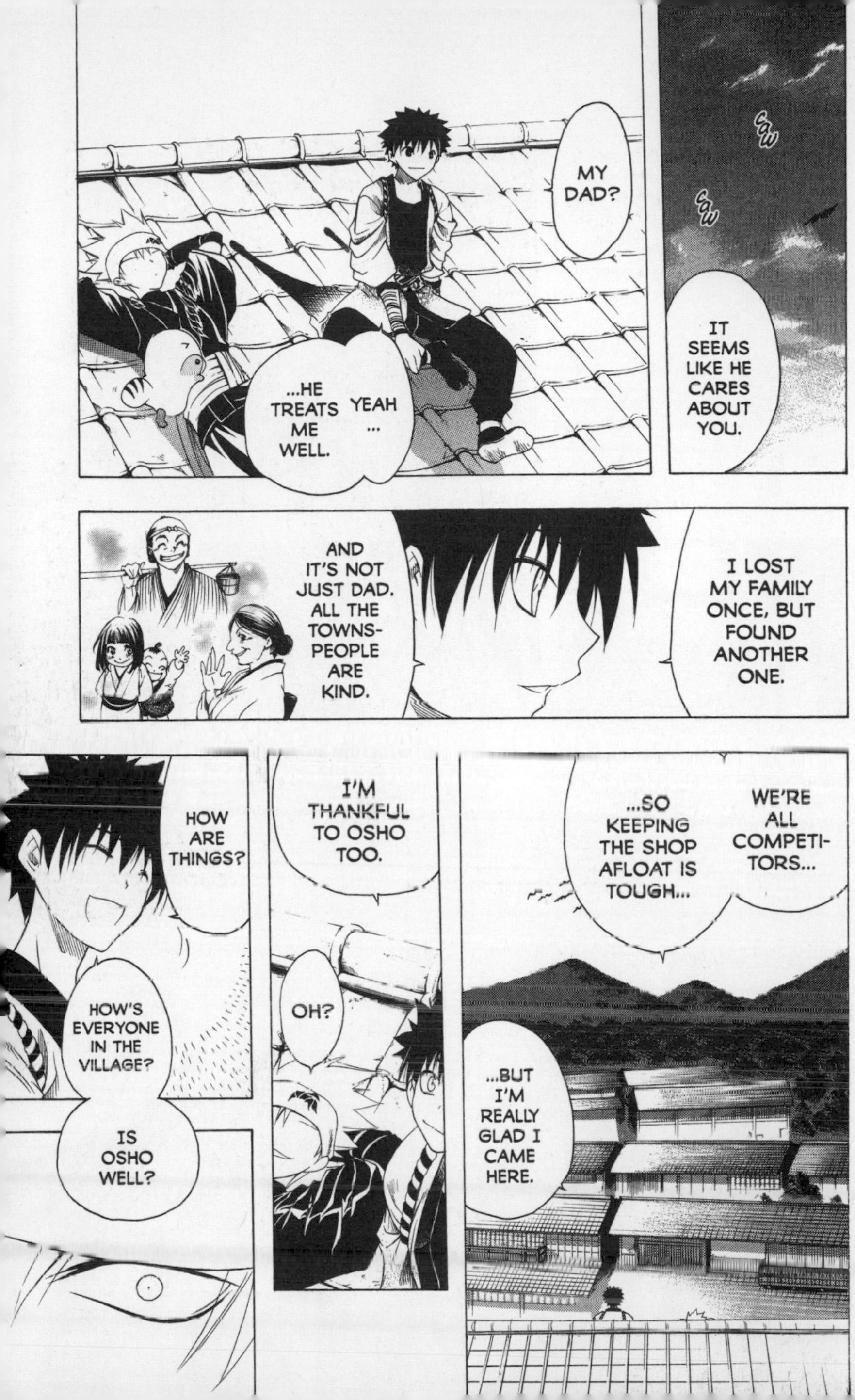
caw
caw
IT SEEMS LIKE HE CARES ABOUT YOU.
MY DAD?
YEAH ...
...HE TREATS ME WELL.
I LOST MY FAMILY ONCE, BUT FOUND ANOTHER ONE.
AND IT'S NOT JUST DAD. ALL THE TOWNS-PEOPLE ARE KIND.
WE'RE ALL COMPETI-TORS...
...SO KEEPING THE SHOP AFLOAT IS TOUGH...
...BUT I'M REALLY GLAD I CAME HERE.
I'M THANKFUL TO OSHO TOO.
OH?
HOW ARE THINGS?
HOW'S EVERYONE IN THE VILLAGE?
IS OSHO WELL?

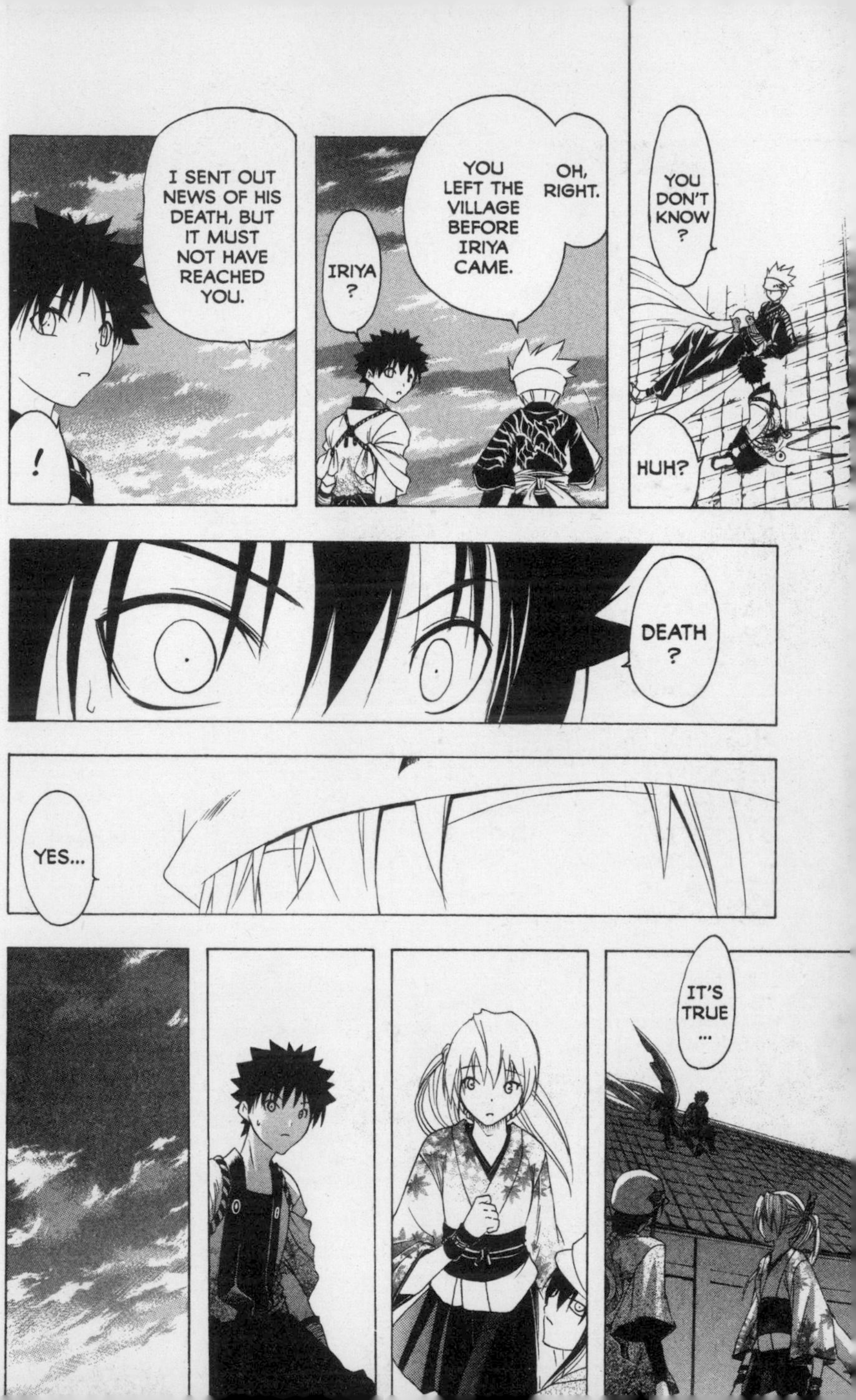
YOU DON'T KNOW?
HUH?
OH, RIGHT.
YOU LEFT THE VILLAGE BEFORE IRIYA CAME.
IRIYA?
I SENT OUT NEWS OF HIS DEATH, BUT IT MUST NOT HAVE REACHED YOU.
!
DEATH?
YES...
IT'S TRUE...

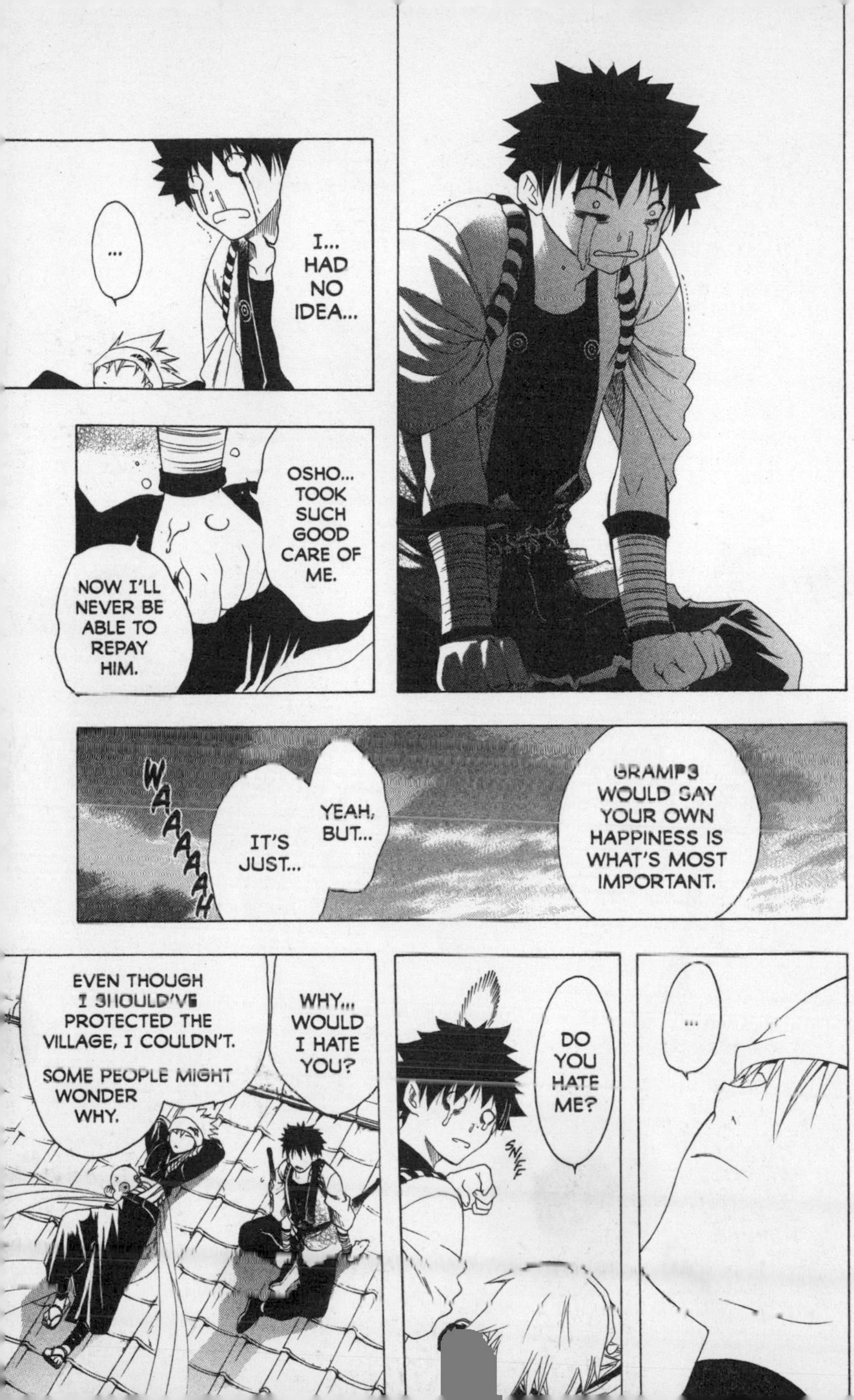
I... HAD NO IDEA...
...
OSHO... TOOK SUCH GOOD CARE OF ME.
NOW I'LL NEVER BE ABLE TO REPAY HIM.
GRAMPS WOULD SAY YOUR OWN HAPPINESS IS WHAT'S MOST IMPORTANT.
YEAH, BUT...
IT'S JUST...
WAAAAAH
...
DO YOU HATE ME?
SNIFF
WHY... WOULD I HATE YOU?
EVEN THOUGH I SHOULD'VE PROTECTED THE VILLAGE, I COULDN'T.
SOME PEOPLE MIGHT WONDER WHY.

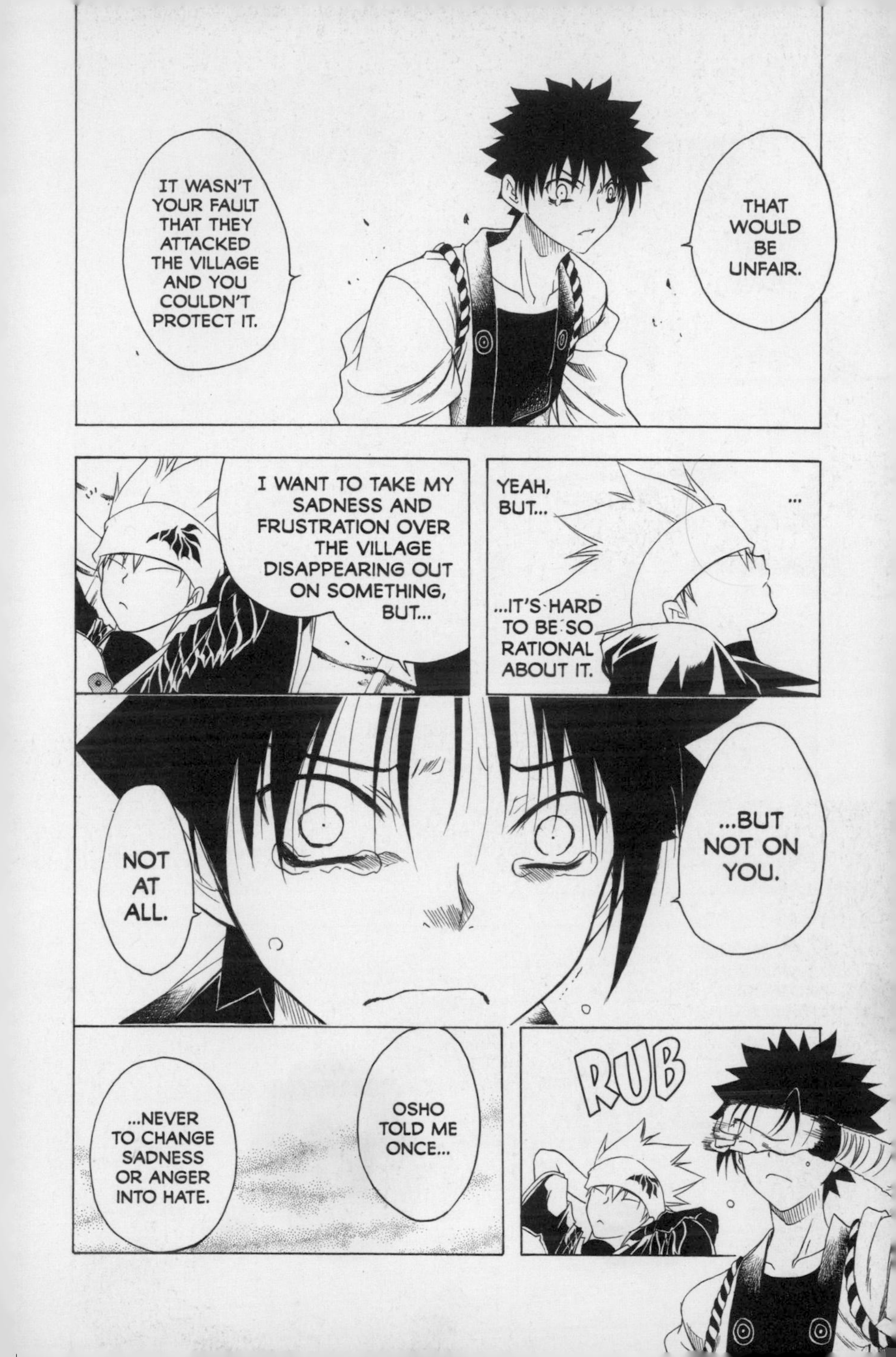
THAT WOULD BE UNFAIR.
IT WASN'T YOUR FAULT THAT THEY ATTACKED THE VILLAGE AND YOU COULDN'T PROTECT IT.
...
YEAH, BUT...
...IT'S HARD TO BE SO RATIONAL ABOUT IT.
I WANT TO TAKE MY SADNESS AND FRUSTRATION OVER THE VILLAGE DISAPPEARING OUT ON SOMETHING, BUT...
...BUT NOT ON YOU.
NOT AT ALL.
RUB
OSHO TOLD ME ONCE...
...NEVER TO CHANGE SADNESS OR ANGER INTO HATE.

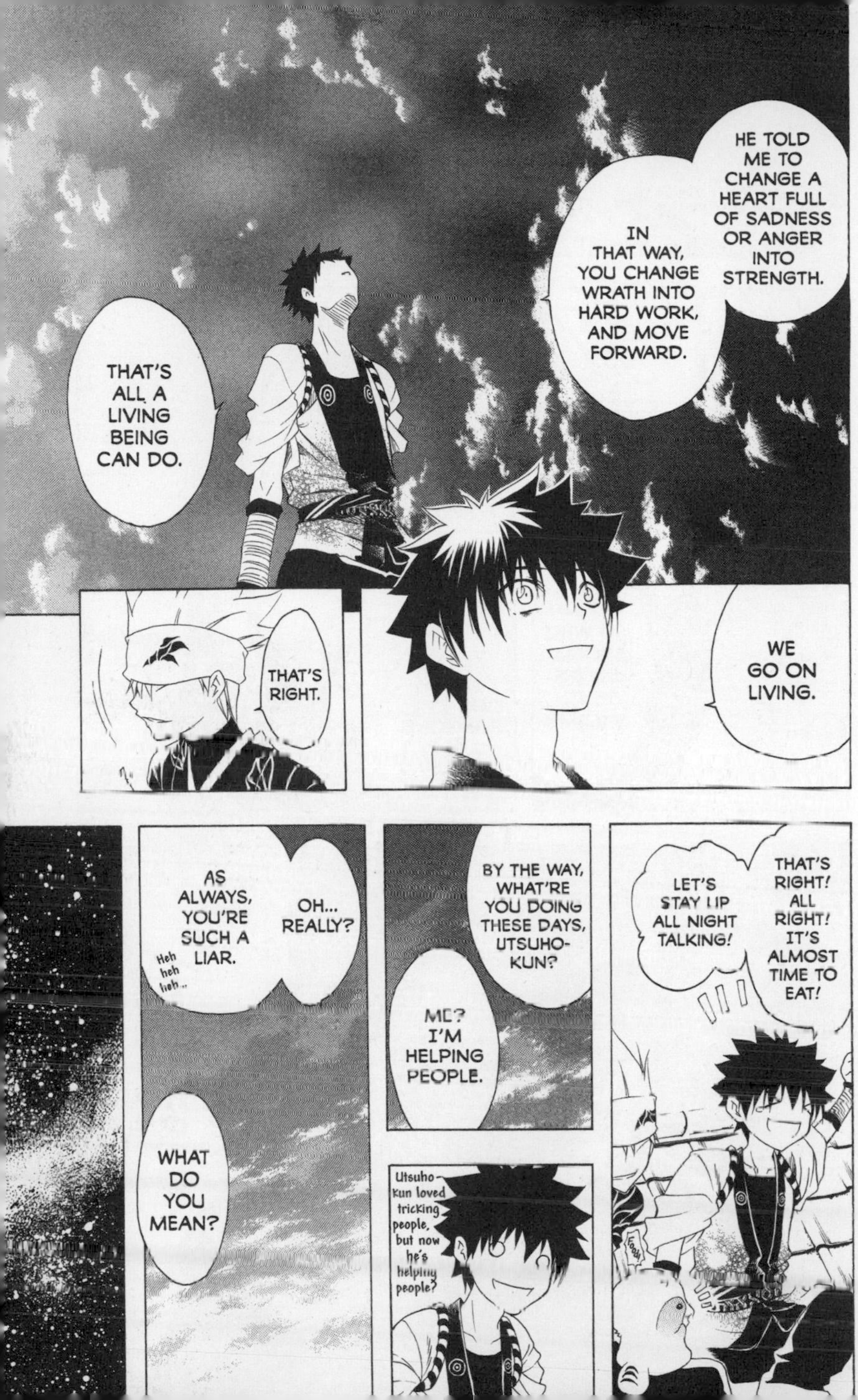
HE TOLD ME TO CHANGE A HEART FULL OF SADNESS OR ANGER INTO STRENGTH.
IN THAT WAY, YOU CHANGE WRATH INTO HARD WORK, AND MOVE FORWARD.
THAT'S ALL A LIVING BEING CAN DO.
WE GO ON LIVING.
THAT'S RIGHT.
THAT'S RIGHT! ALL RIGHT! IT'S ALMOST TIME TO EAT!
LET'S STAY UP ALL NIGHT TALKING!
Utsuho-kun loved tricking people, but now he's helping people?
BY THE WAY, WHAT'RE YOU DOING THESE DAYS, UTSUHO-KUN?
ME? I'M HELPING PEOPLE.
OH... REALLY?
AS ALWAYS, YOU'RE SUCH A LIAR.
Heh heh heh...
WHAT DO YOU MEAN?

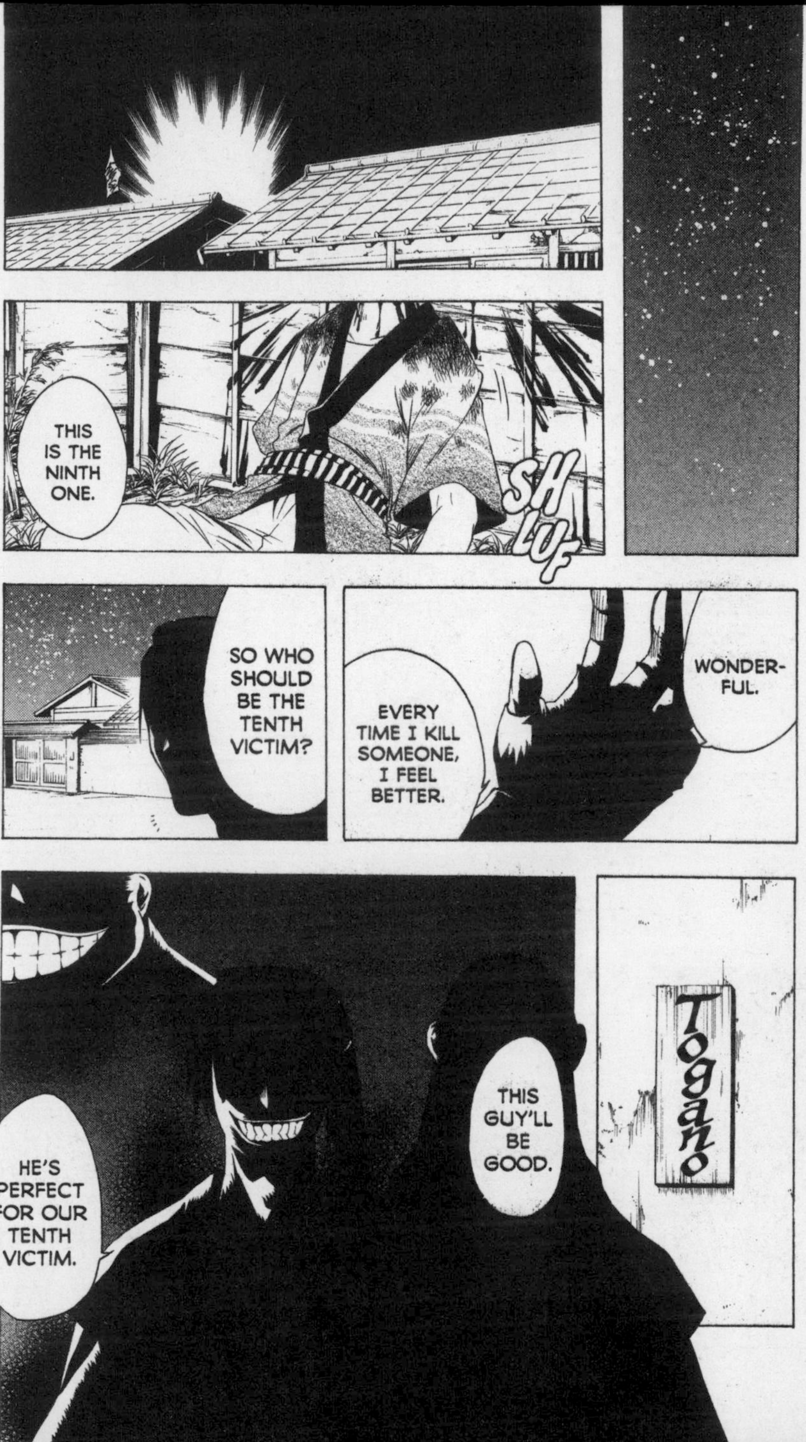
THIS IS THE NINTH ONE.
SHLUF
WONDERFUL.
EVERY TIME I KILL SOMEONE, I FEEL BETTER.
SO WHO SHOULD BE THE TENTH VICTIM?
Togano
THIS GUY'LL BE GOOD.
HE'S PERFECT FOR OUR TENTH VICTIM.

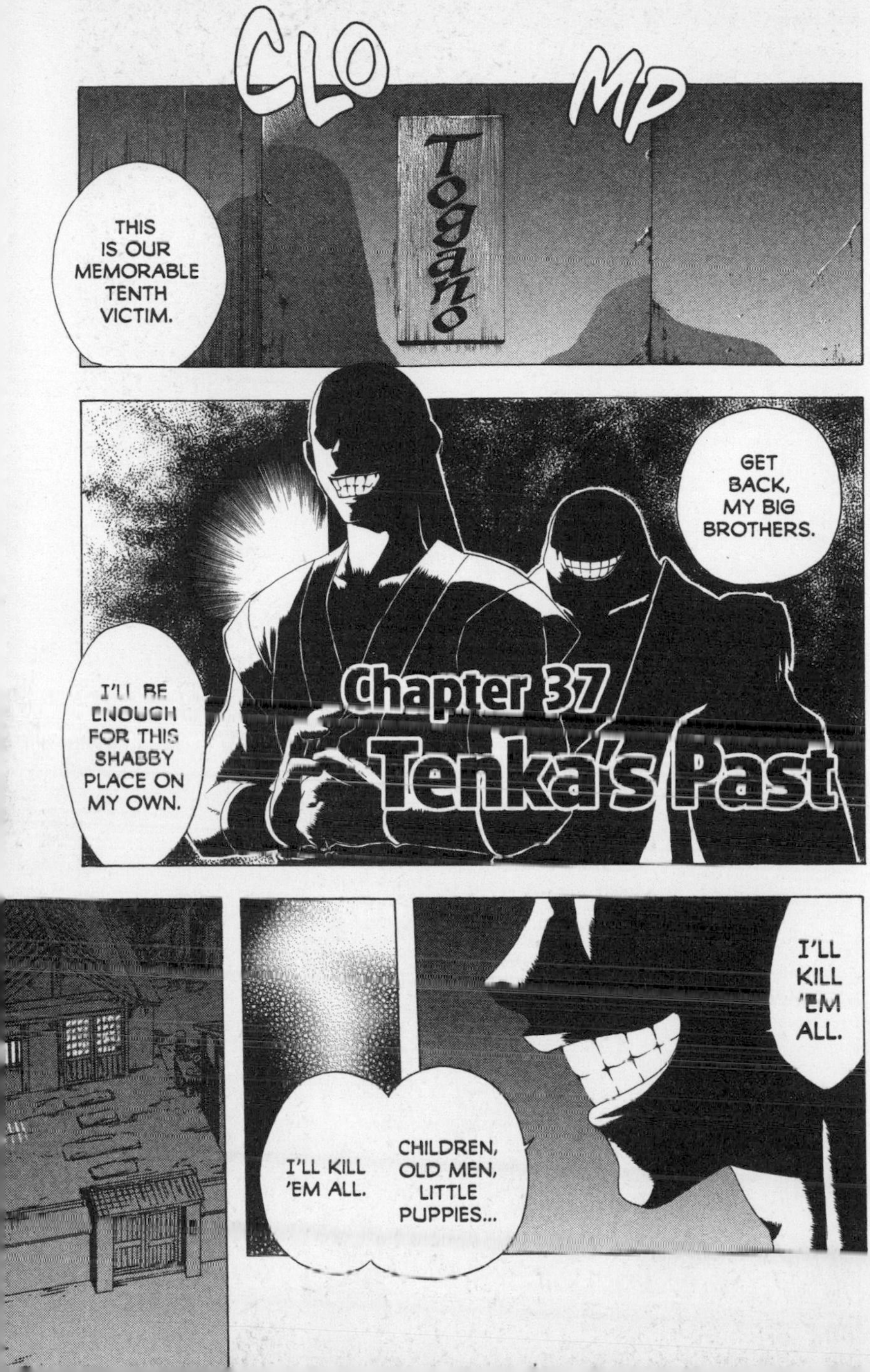
CLOMP
Togano
THIS IS OUR MEMORABLE TENTH VICTIM.
GET BACK, MY BIG BROTHERS.
I'LL BE ENOUGH FOR THIS SHABBY PLACE ON MY OWN.
Chapter 37
Tenka's Past
I'LL KILL 'EM ALL.
CHILDREN, OLD MEN, LITTLE PUPPIES...
I'LL KILL 'EM ALL.

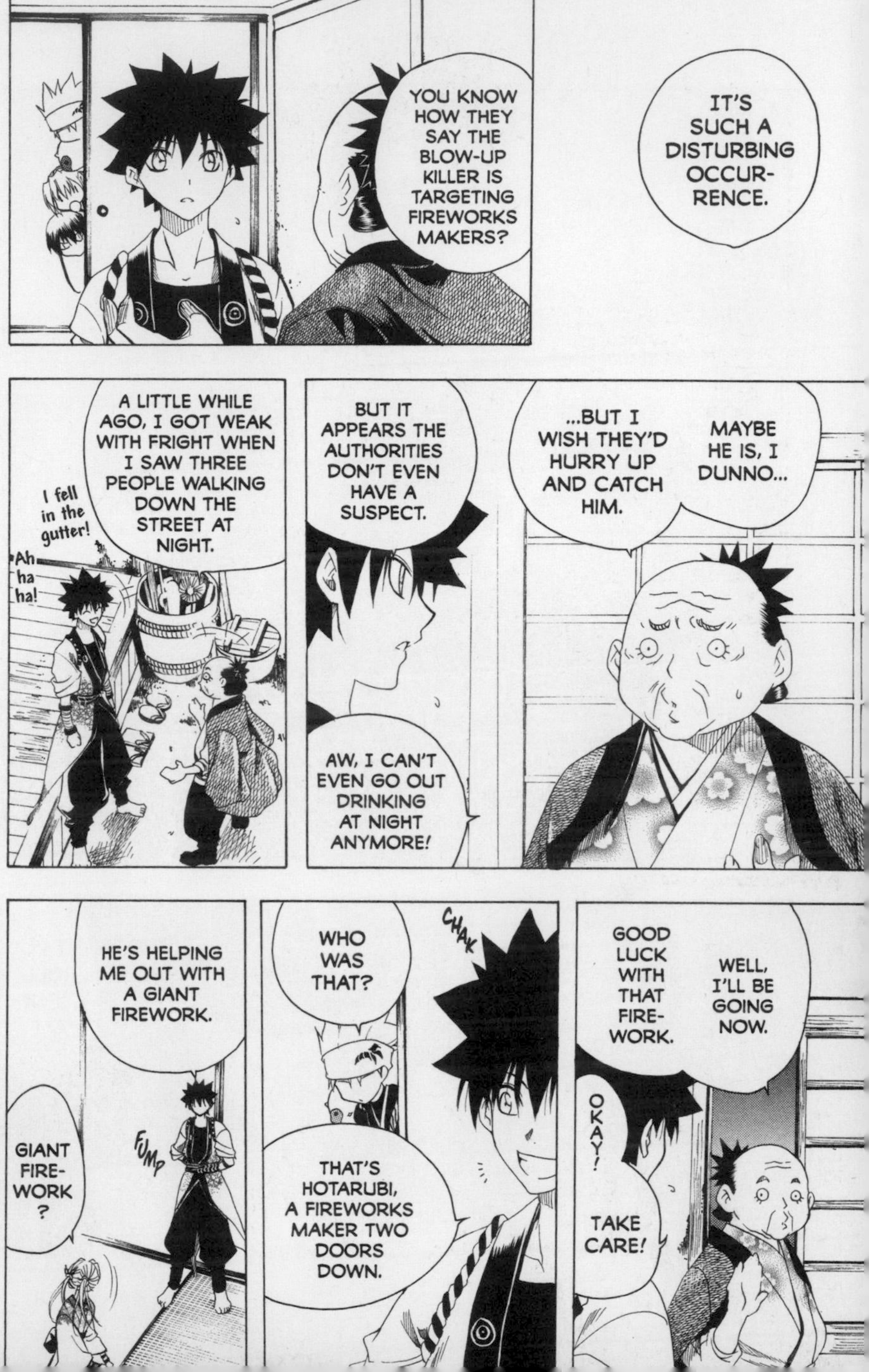
IT'S SUCH A DISTURBING OCCUR-RENCE.
YOU KNOW HOW THEY SAY THE BLOW-UP KILLER IS TARGETING FIREWORKS MAKERS?
MAYBE HE IS, I DUNNO...
...BUT I WISH THEY'D HURRY UP AND CATCH HIM.
BUT IT APPEARS THE AUTHORITIES DON'T EVEN HAVE A SUSPECT.
AW, I CAN'T EVEN GO OUT DRINKING AT NIGHT ANYMORE!
A LITTLE WHILE AGO, I GOT WEAK WITH FRIGHT WHEN I SAW THREE PEOPLE WALKING DOWN THE STREET AT NIGHT.
I fell in the gutter!
Ah ha ha!
WELL, I'LL BE GOING NOW.
GOOD LUCK WITH THAT FIRE-WORK.
OKAY!
TAKE CARE!
CHAK
WHO WAS THAT?
THAT'S HOTARUBI, A FIREWORKS MAKER TWO DOORS DOWN.
HE'S HELPING ME OUT WITH A GIANT FIREWORK.
FUMP
GIANT FIRE-WORK?

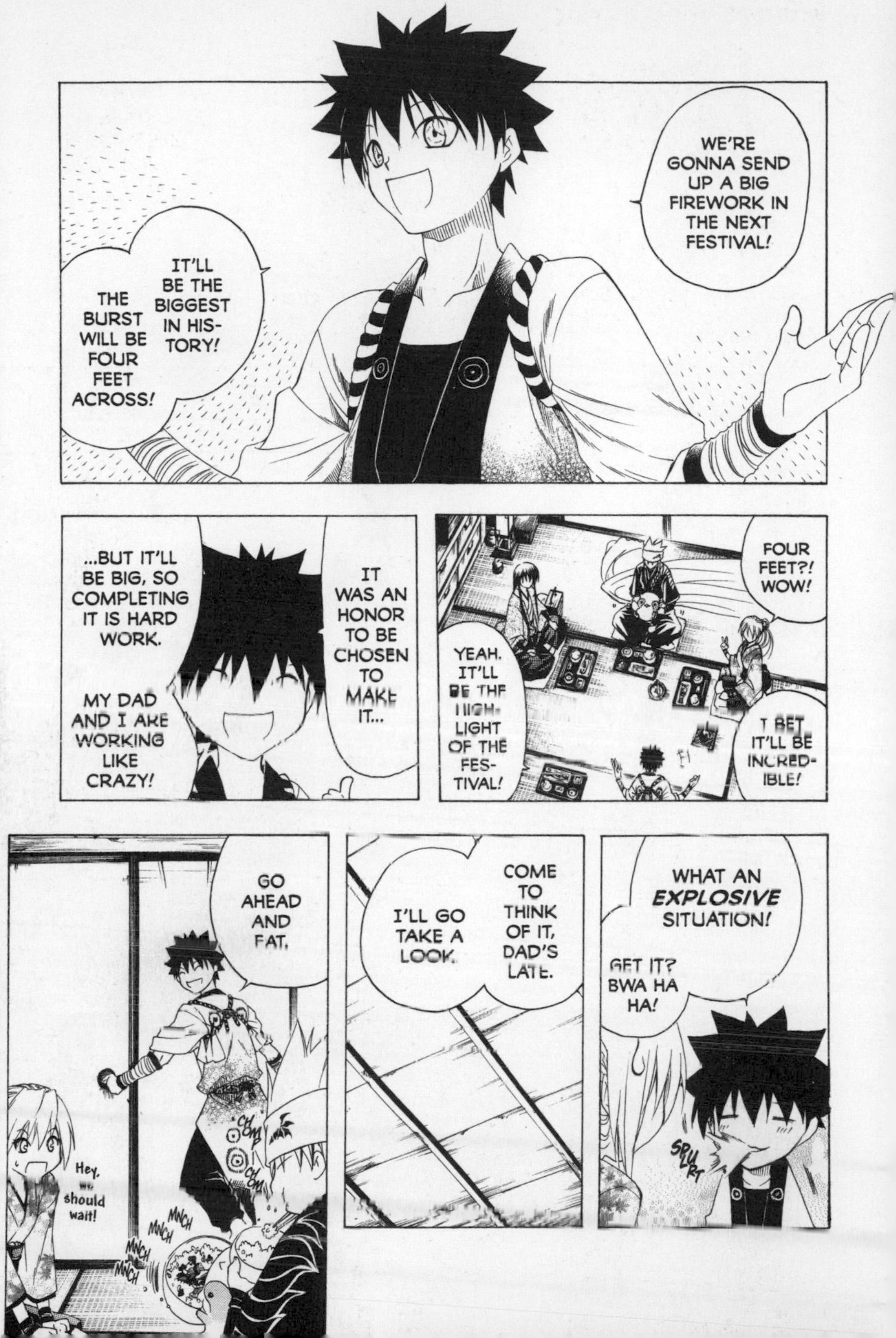
WE'RE GONNA SEND UP A BIG FIREWORK IN THE NEXT FESTIVAL!
IT'LL BE THE BIGGEST IN HISTORY!
THE BURST WILL BE FOUR FEET ACROSS!
FOUR FEET?! WOW!
YEAH. IT'LL BE THE HIGHLIGHT OF THE FESTIVAL!
I BET IT'LL BE INCREDIBLE!
IT WAS AN HONOR TO BE CHOSEN TO MAKE IT...
...BUT IT'LL BE BIG, SO COMPLETING IT IS HARD WORK.
MY DAD AND I ARE WORKING LIKE CRAZY!
WHAT AN *EXPLOSIVE* SITUATION!
GET IT? BWA HA HA!
SPLURT
COME TO THINK OF IT, DAD'S LATE.
I'LL GO TAKE A LOOK.
GO AHEAD AND EAT.
CHOMP
CHOM
Hey, we should wait!
MNCH MNCH MNCH MNCH

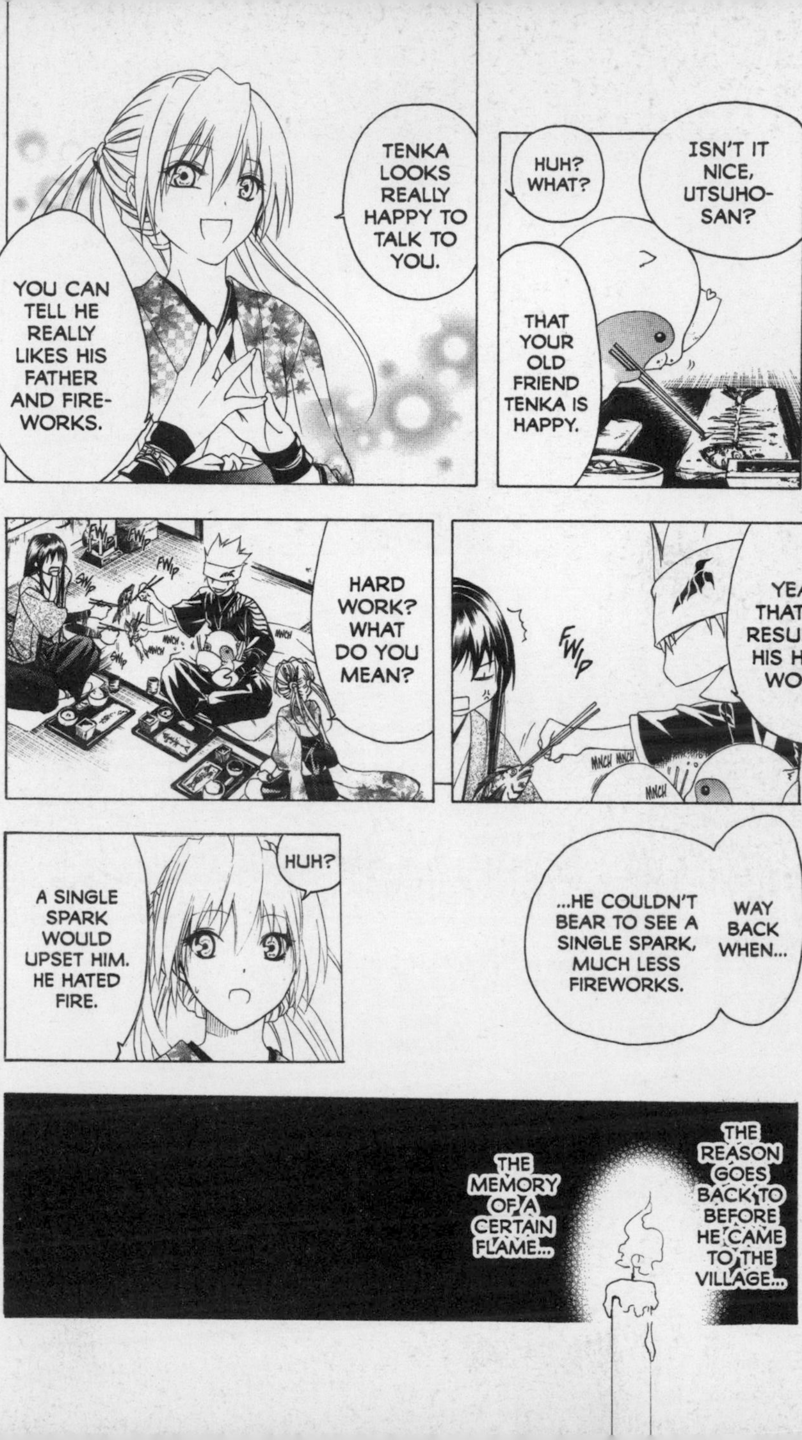
ISN'T IT NICE, UTSUHO-SAN?
HUH? WHAT?
THAT YOUR OLD FRIEND TENKA IS HAPPY.
TENKA LOOKS REALLY HAPPY TO TALK TO YOU.
YOU CAN TELL HE REALLY LIKES HIS FATHER AND FIRE-WORKS.
YEAH. THAT'S A RESULT OF HIS HARD WORK.
FWIP
MNCH MNCH
MNCH
HARD WORK? WHAT DO YOU MEAN?
FWIP
FWIP
FWIP
SWIP
MNCH
MNCH
MNCH
SWIP
WAY BACK WHEN...
...HE COULDN'T BEAR TO SEE A SINGLE SPARK, MUCH LESS FIREWORKS.
HUH?
A SINGLE SPARK WOULD UPSET HIM. HE HATED FIRE.
THE REASON GOES BACK TO BEFORE HE CAME TO THE VILLAGE...
THE MEMORY OF A CERTAIN FLAME...

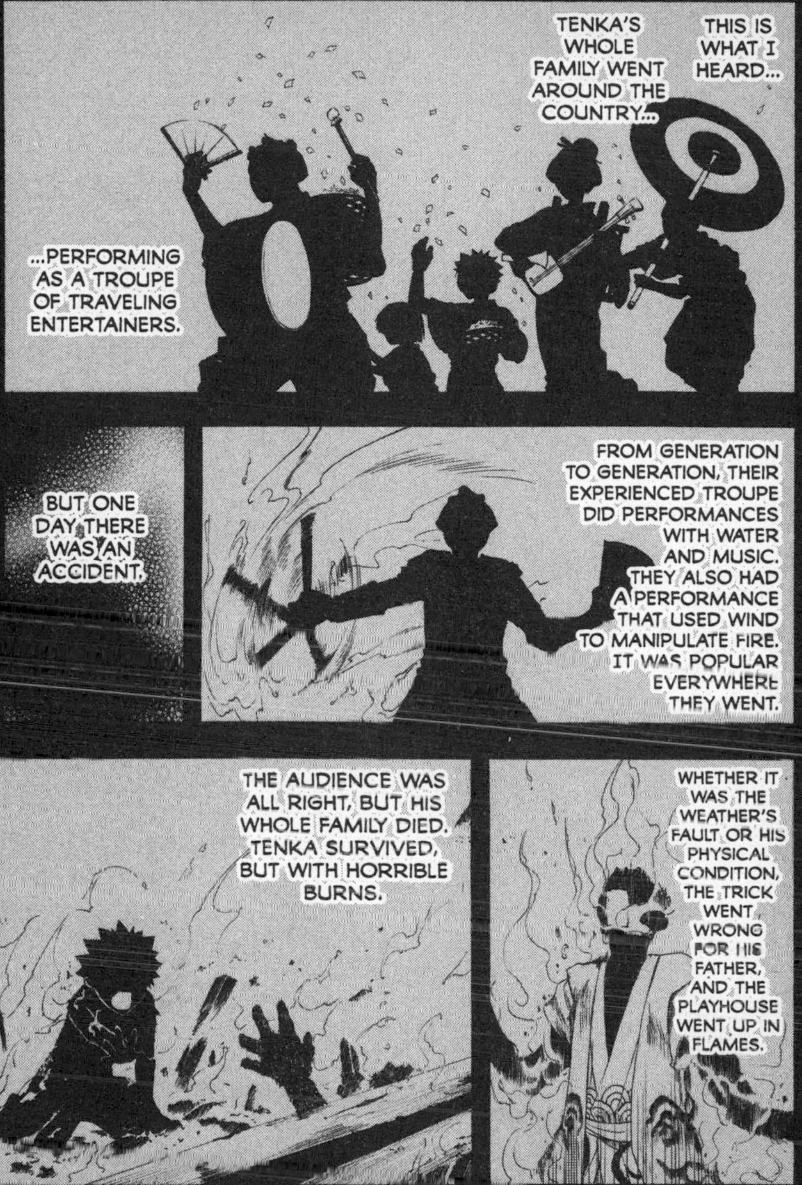
THIS IS WHAT I HEARD...
TENKA'S WHOLE FAMILY WENT AROUND THE COUNTRY...
...PERFORMING AS A TROUPE OF TRAVELING ENTERTAINERS.
FROM GENERATION TO GENERATION, THEIR EXPERIENCED TROUPE DID PERFORMANCES WITH WATER AND MUSIC. THEY ALSO HAD A PERFORMANCE THAT USED WIND TO MANIPULATE FIRE. IT WAS POPULAR EVERYWHERE THEY WENT.
BUT ONE DAY THERE WAS AN ACCIDENT.
WHETHER IT WAS THE WEATHER'S FAULT OR HIS PHYSICAL CONDITION, THE TRICK WENT WRONG FOR HIS FATHER, AND THE PLAYHOUSE WENT UP IN FLAMES.
THE AUDIENCE WAS ALL RIGHT, BUT HIS WHOLE FAMILY DIED. TENKA SURVIVED, BUT WITH HORRIBLE BURNS.

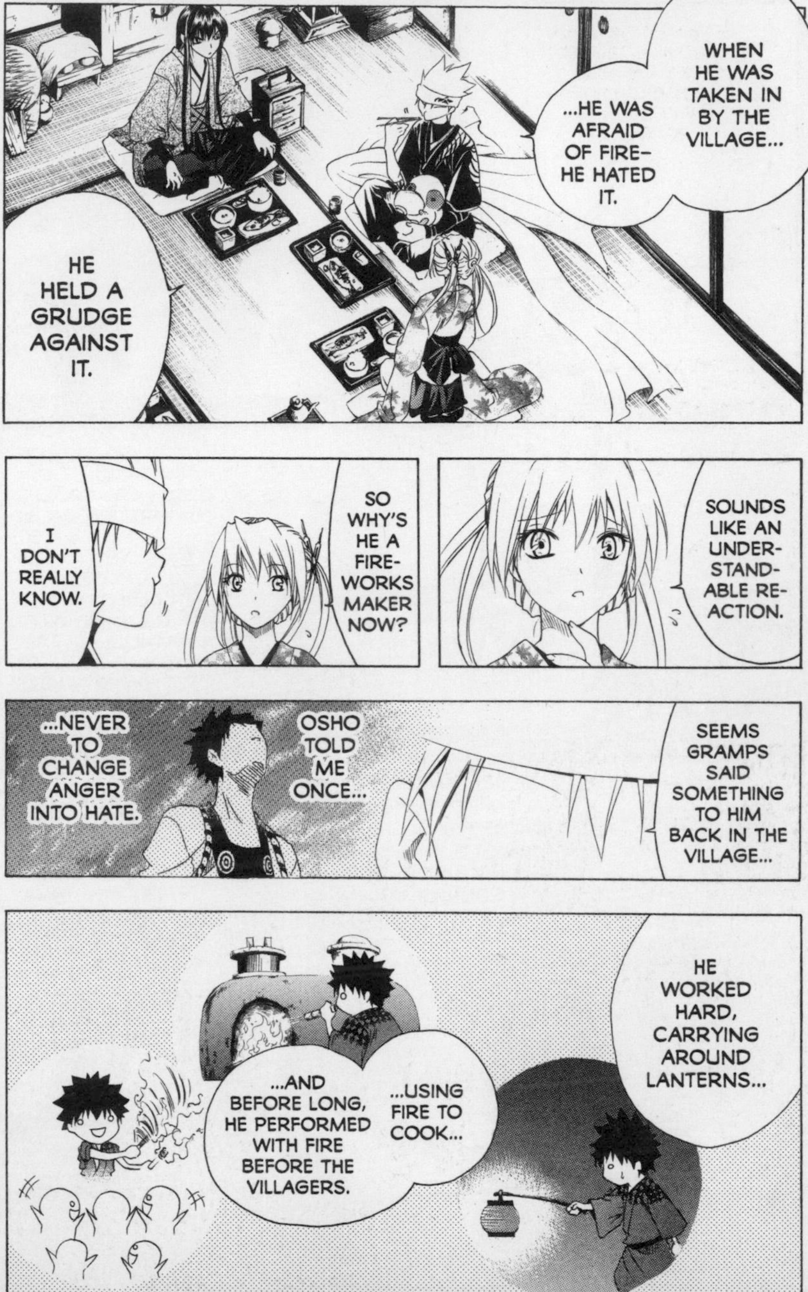
WHEN HE WAS TAKEN IN BY THE VILLAGE...
...HE WAS AFRAID OF FIRE— HE HATED IT.
HE HELD A GRUDGE AGAINST IT.
SOUNDS LIKE AN UNDER-STAND-ABLE RE-ACTION.
SO WHY'S HE A FIRE-WORKS MAKER NOW?
I DON'T REALLY KNOW.
SEEMS GRAMPS SAID SOMETHING TO HIM BACK IN THE VILLAGE...
OSHO TOLD ME ONCE...
...NEVER TO CHANGE ANGER INTO HATE.
HE WORKED HARD, CARRYING AROUND LANTERNS...
...USING FIRE TO COOK...
...AND BEFORE LONG, HE PERFORMED WITH FIRE BEFORE THE VILLAGERS.

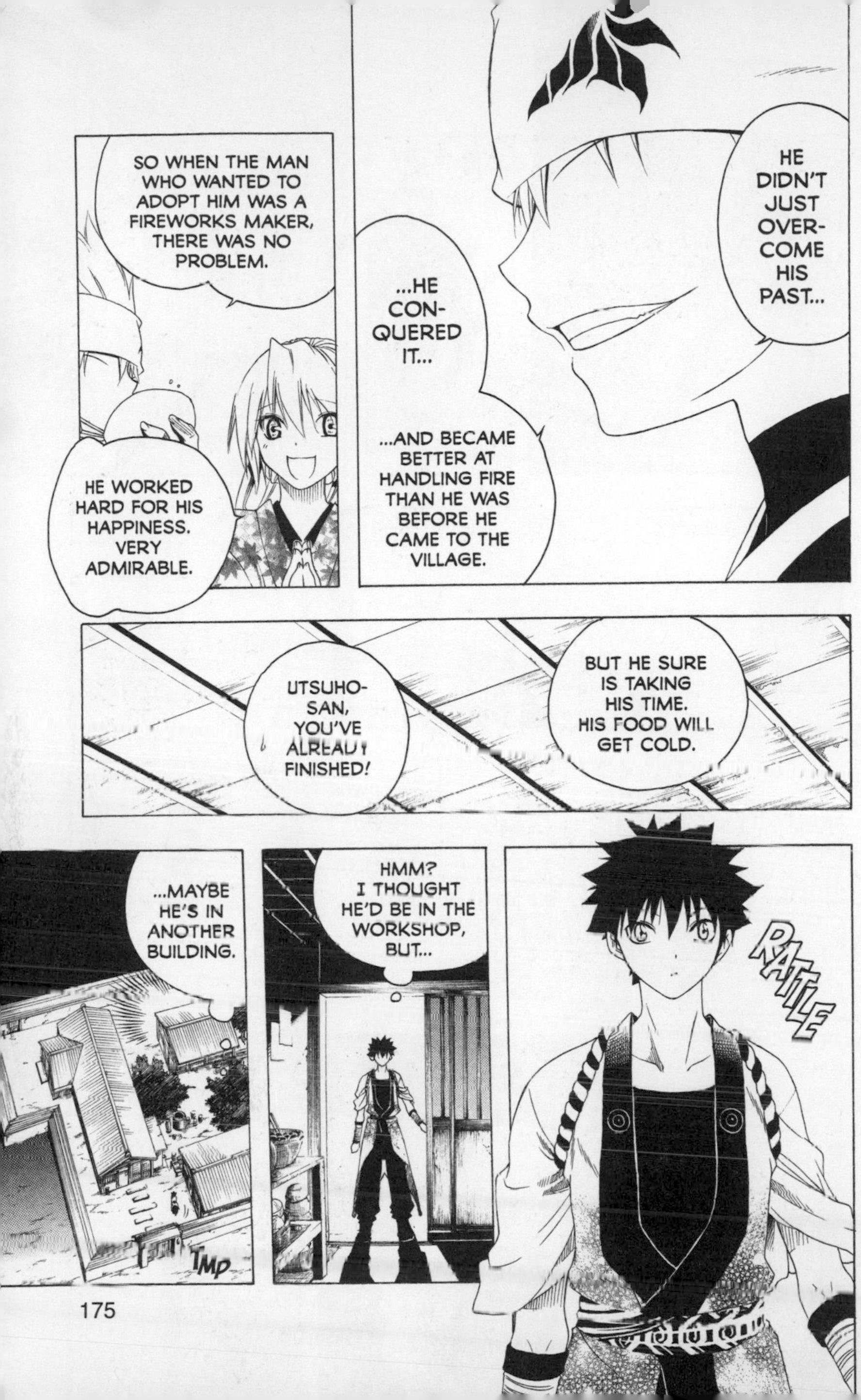
HE DIDN'T JUST OVER-COME HIS PAST...
...HE CON-QUERED IT...
...AND BECAME BETTER AT HANDLING FIRE THAN HE WAS BEFORE HE CAME TO THE VILLAGE.
SO WHEN THE MAN WHO WANTED TO ADOPT HIM WAS A FIREWORKS MAKER, THERE WAS NO PROBLEM.
HE WORKED HARD FOR HIS HAPPINESS. VERY ADMIRABLE.
BUT HE SURE IS TAKING HIS TIME. HIS FOOD WILL GET COLD.
UTSUHO-SAN, YOU'VE ALREADY FINISHED!
RATTLE
HMM? I THOUGHT HE'D BE IN THE WORKSHOP, BUT...
...MAYBE HE'S IN ANOTHER BUILDING.
TMP

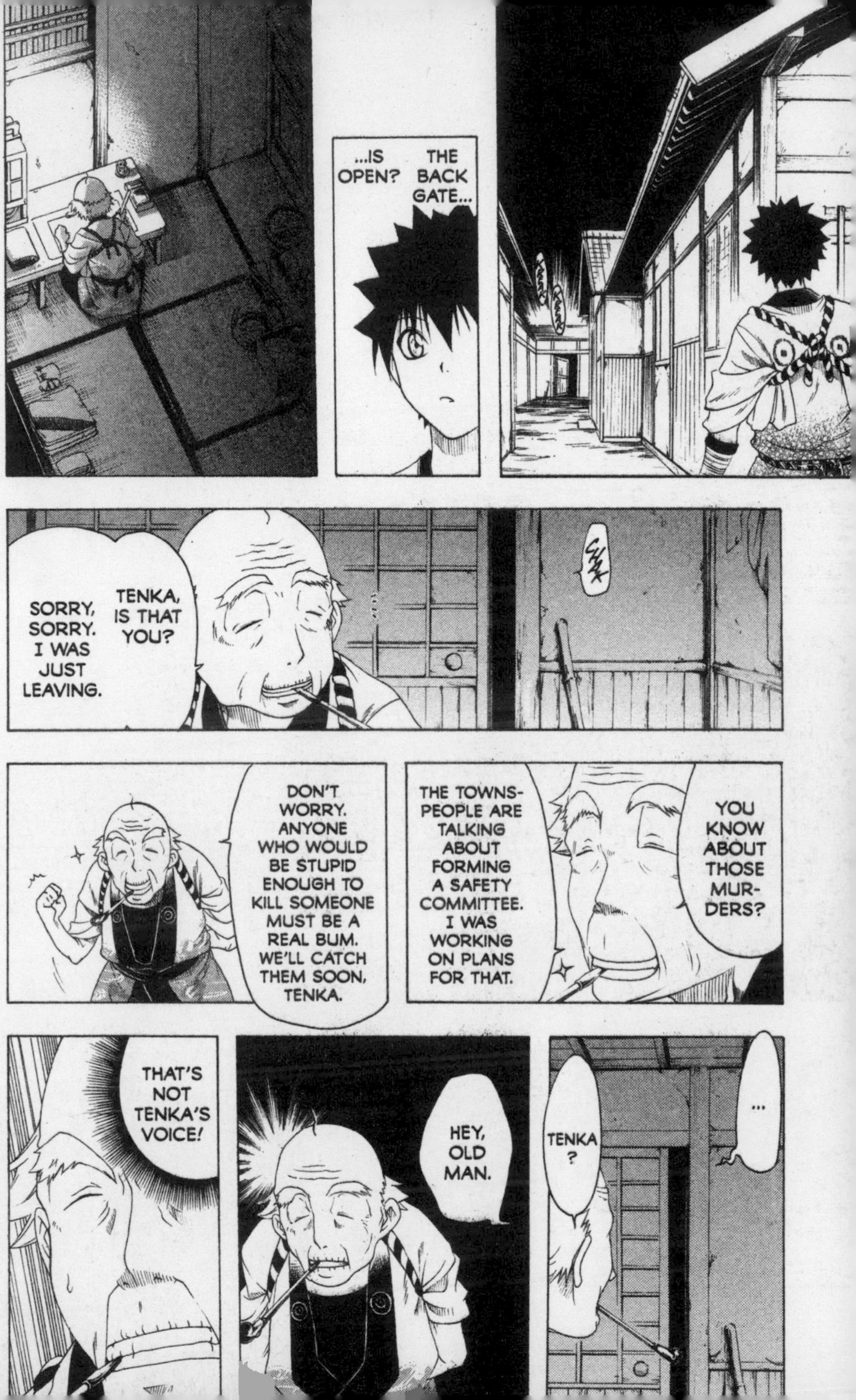
THE BACK GATE...
...IS OPEN?
TENKA, IS THAT YOU?
SORRY, SORRY. I WAS JUST LEAVING.
YOU KNOW ABOUT THOSE MUR-DERS?
THE TOWNS-PEOPLE ARE TALKING ABOUT FORMING A SAFETY COMMITTEE. I WAS WORKING ON PLANS FOR THAT.
DON'T WORRY. ANYONE WHO WOULD BE STUPID ENOUGH TO KILL SOMEONE MUST BE A REAL BUM. WE'LL CATCH THEM SOON, TENKA.
...
TENKA?
HEY, OLD MAN.
THAT'S NOT TENKA'S VOICE!

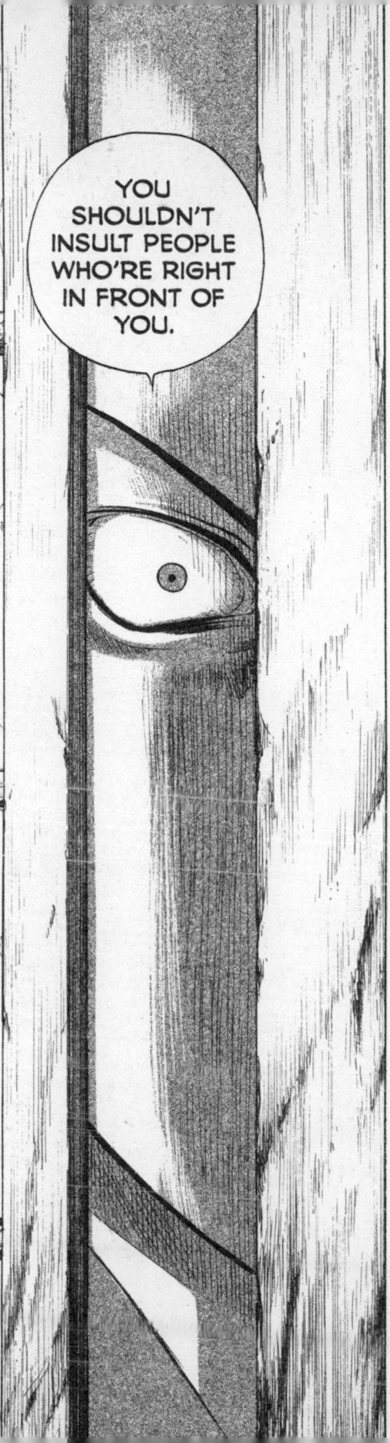
YOU SHOULDN'T INSULT PEOPLE WHO'RE RIGHT IN FRONT OF YOU.

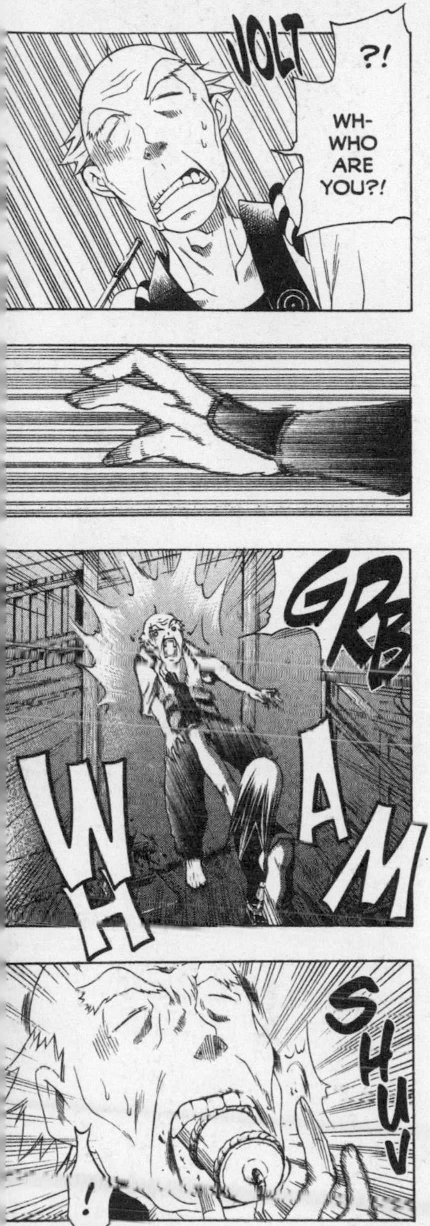
JOLT
?!
WH-WHO ARE YOU?!
GRB
WHAM
SHUV
!

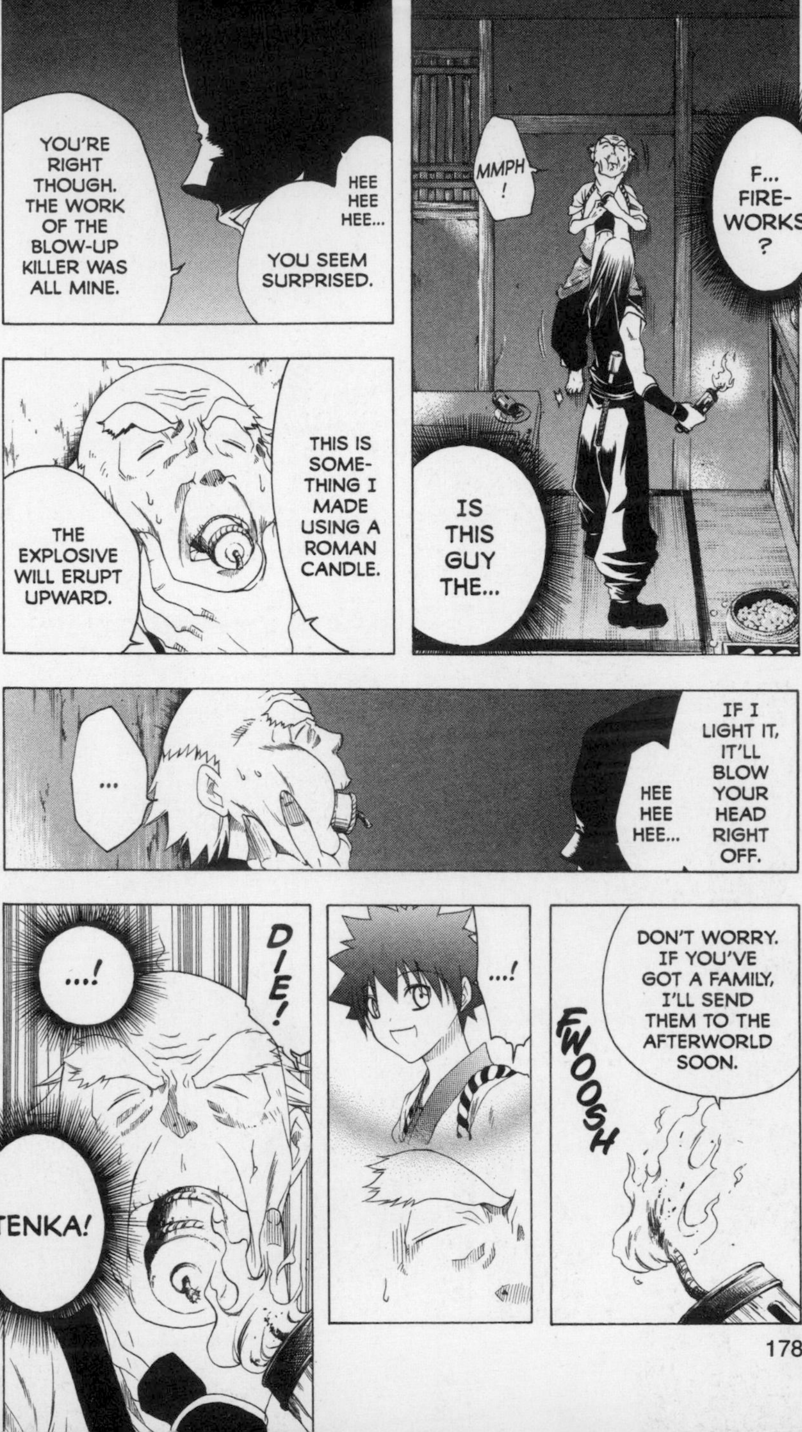
F... FIRE-WORKS?
MMPH!
IS THIS GUY THE...
HEE HEE HEE...
YOU SEEM SURPRISED.
YOU'RE RIGHT THOUGH. THE WORK OF THE BLOW-UP KILLER WAS ALL MINE.
THIS IS SOME-THING I MADE USING A ROMAN CANDLE.
THE EXPLOSIVE WILL ERUPT UPWARD.
IF I LIGHT IT, IT'LL BLOW YOUR HEAD RIGHT OFF.
HEE HEE HEE...
...
DON'T WORRY. IF YOU'VE GOT A FAMILY, I'LL SEND THEM TO THE AFTERWORLD SOON.
FWOOSH
...!
DIE!
...!
TENKA!

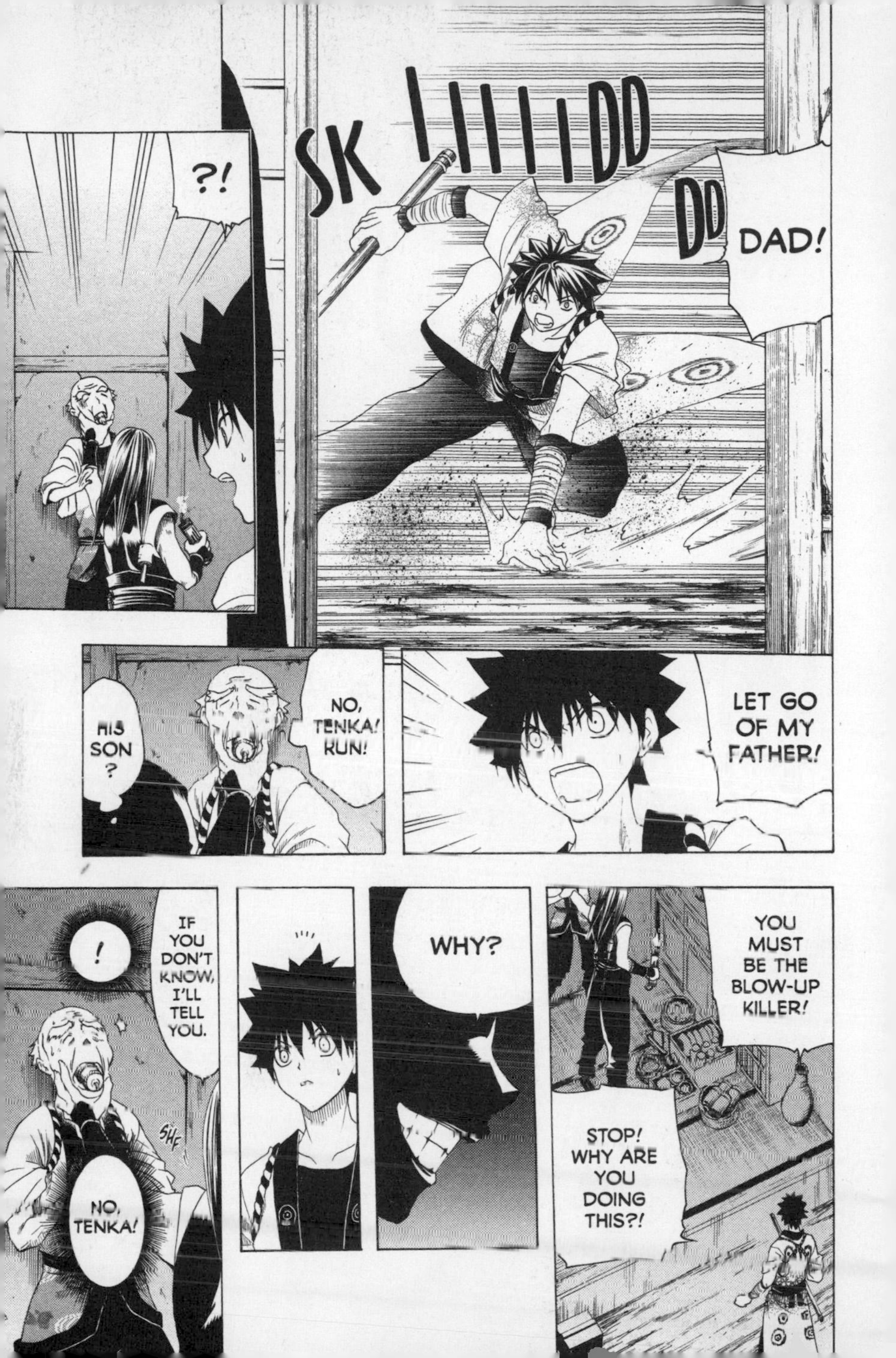
DAD!
SKIIIIIDD DD
?!
LET GO OF MY FATHER!
NO, TENKA! RUN!
HIS SON?
YOU MUST BE THE BLOW-UP KILLER!
STOP! WHY ARE YOU DOING THIS?!
WHY?
IF YOU DON'T KNOW, I'LL TELL YOU.
!
NO, TENKA!
SHF

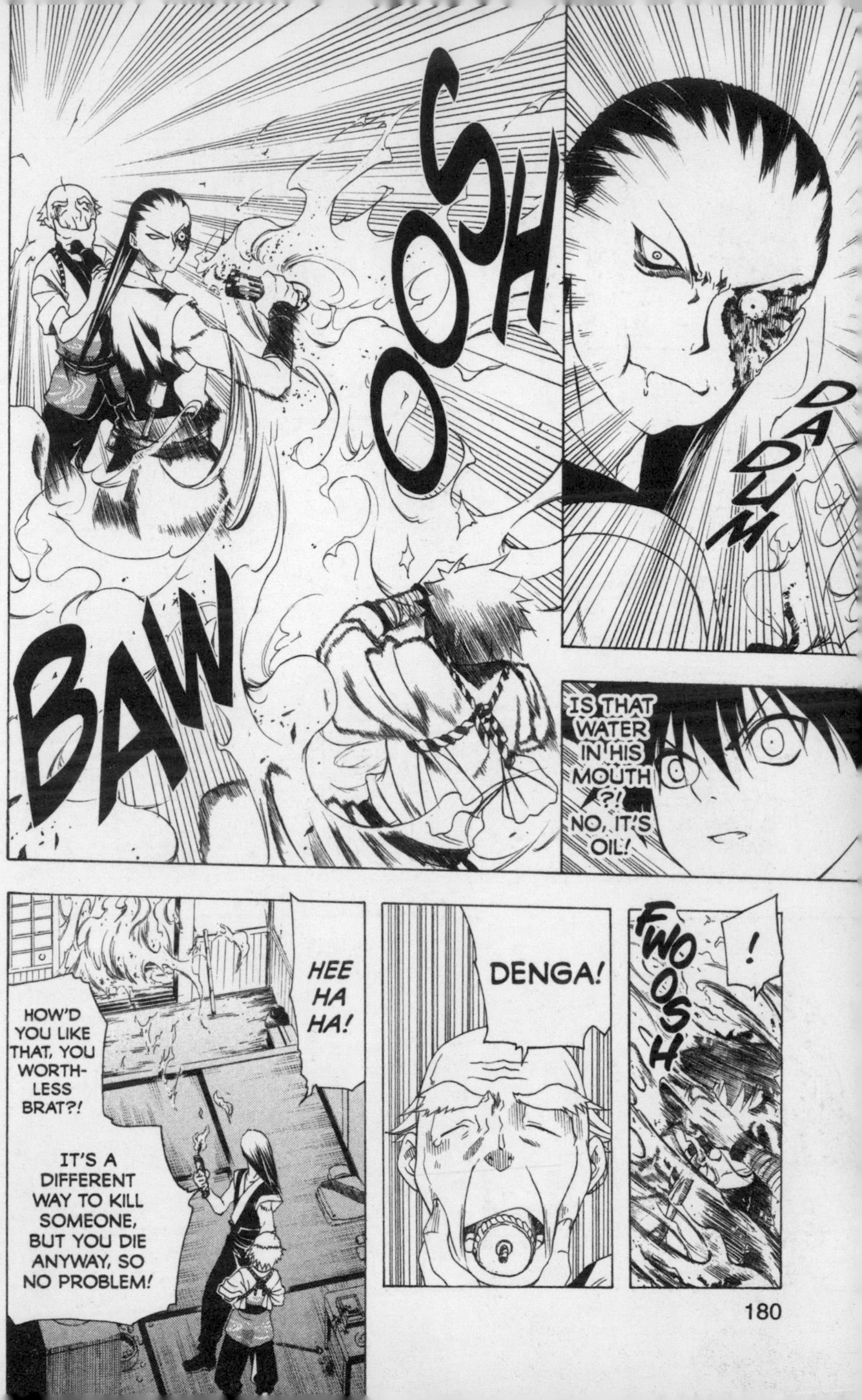
DADUM
IS THAT WATER IN HIS MOUTH ?!
NO, IT'S OIL!
SHOOO
BAW
!
FWOOSH
DENGA!
HEE HA HA!
HOW'D YOU LIKE THAT, YOU WORTH-LESS BRAT?!
IT'S A DIFFERENT WAY TO KILL SOMEONE, BUT YOU DIE ANYWAY, SO NO PROBLEM!

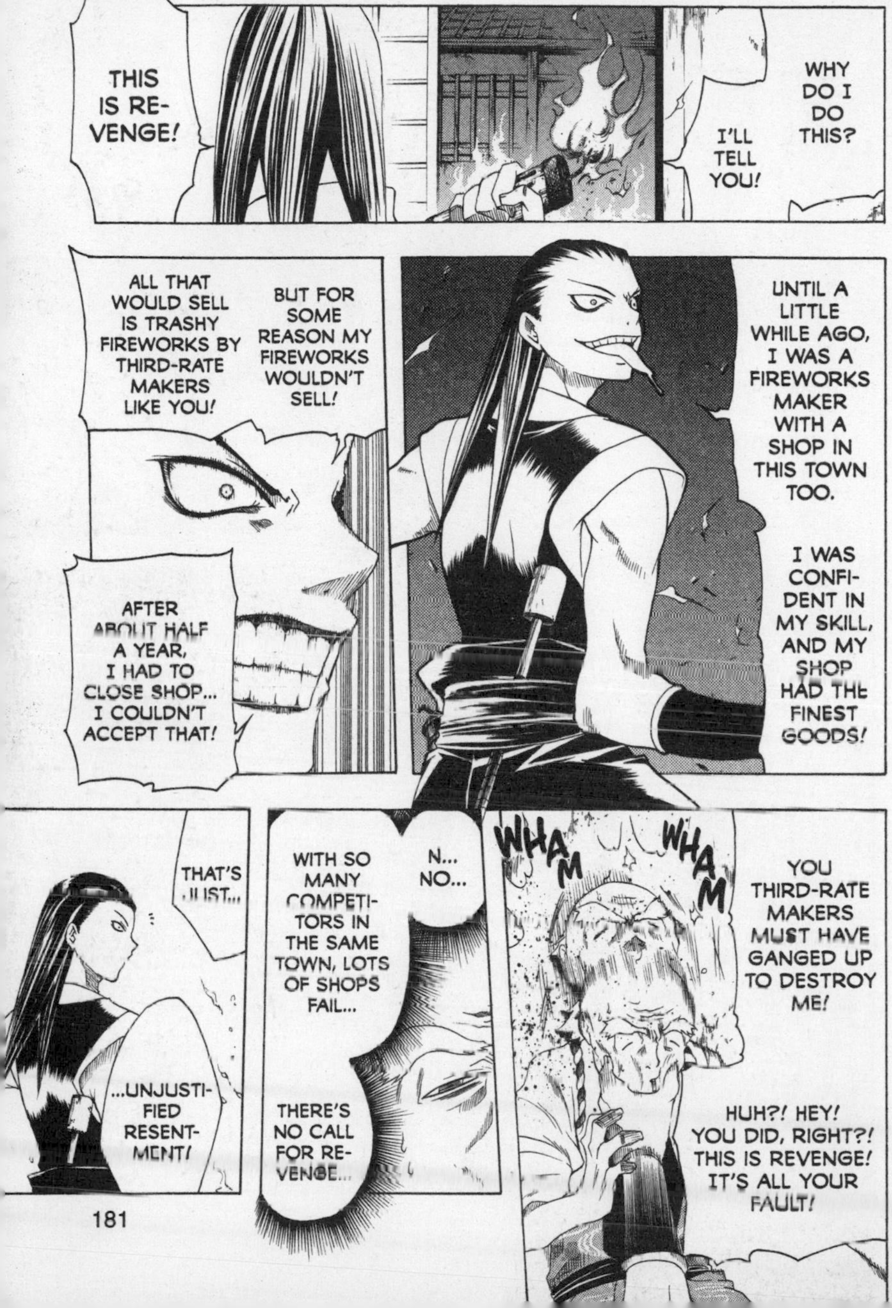
WHY DO I DO THIS?
I'LL TELL YOU!
THIS IS RE-VENGE!
UNTIL A LITTLE WHILE AGO, I WAS A FIREWORKS MAKER WITH A SHOP IN THIS TOWN TOO.
I WAS CONFI-DENT IN MY SKILL, AND MY SHOP HAD THE FINEST GOODS!
BUT FOR SOME REASON MY FIREWORKS WOULDN'T SELL!
ALL THAT WOULD SELL IS TRASHY FIREWORKS BY THIRD-RATE MAKERS LIKE YOU!
AFTER ABOUT HALF A YEAR, I HAD TO CLOSE SHOP... I COULDN'T ACCEPT THAT!
YOU THIRD-RATE MAKERS MUST HAVE GANGED UP TO DESTROY ME!
WHAM
WHAM
HUH?! HEY! YOU DID, RIGHT?! THIS IS REVENGE! IT'S ALL YOUR FAULT!
N... NO...
WITH SO MANY COMPETI-TORS IN THE SAME TOWN, LOTS OF SHOPS FAIL...
THERE'S NO CALL FOR RE-VENGE...
THAT'S JUST...
...UNJUSTI-FIED RESENT-MENT!

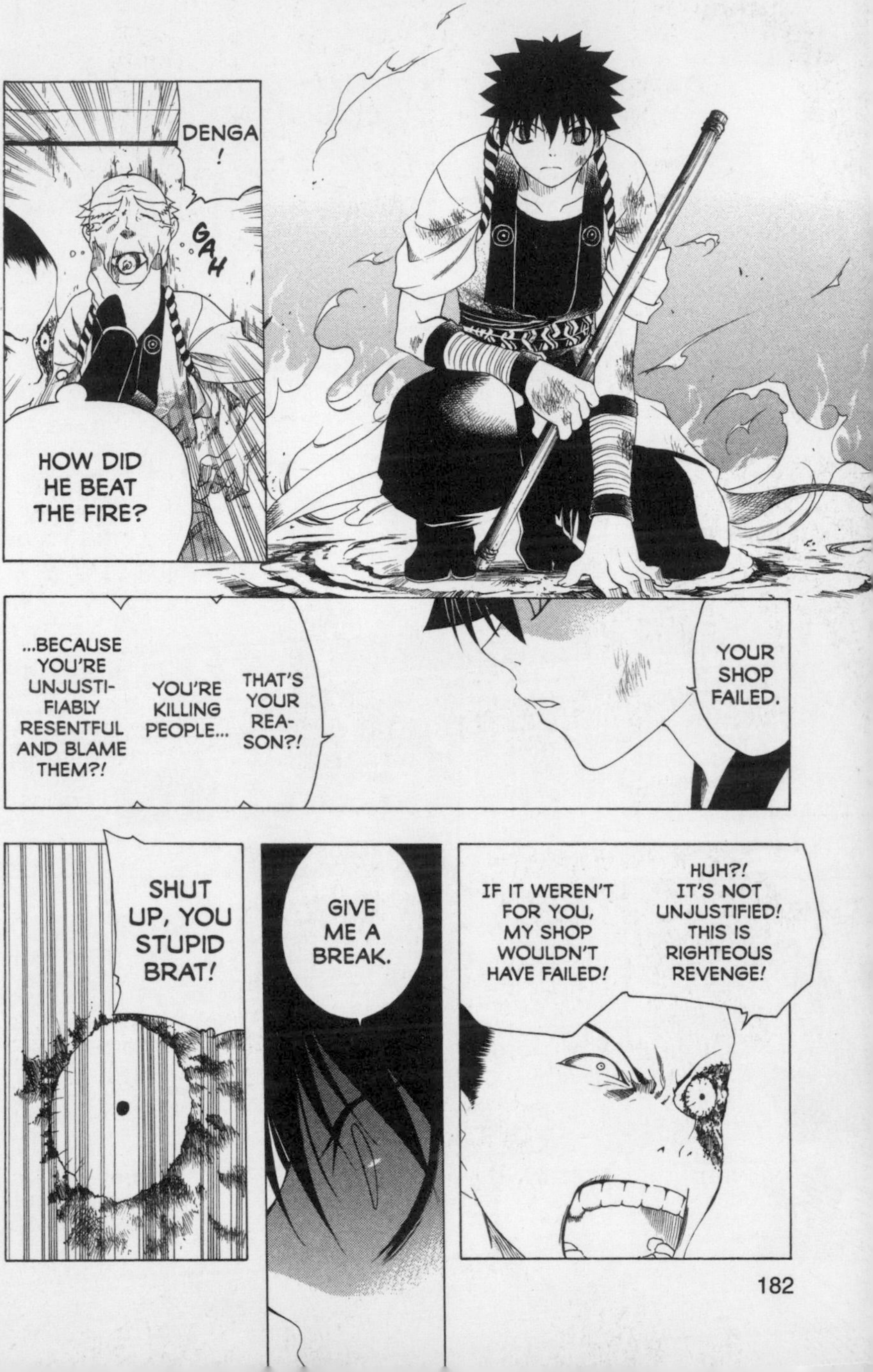
DENGA!
GAH
HOW DID HE BEAT THE FIRE?
YOUR SHOP FAILED.
THAT'S YOUR REA-SON?!
YOU'RE KILLING PEOPLE...
...BECAUSE YOU'RE UNJUSTI-FIABLY RESENTFUL AND BLAME THEM?!
HUH?! IT'S NOT UNJUSTIFIED! THIS IS RIGHTEOUS REVENGE!
IF IT WEREN'T FOR YOU, MY SHOP WOULDN'T HAVE FAILED!
GIVE ME A BREAK.
SHUT UP, YOU STUPID BRAT!

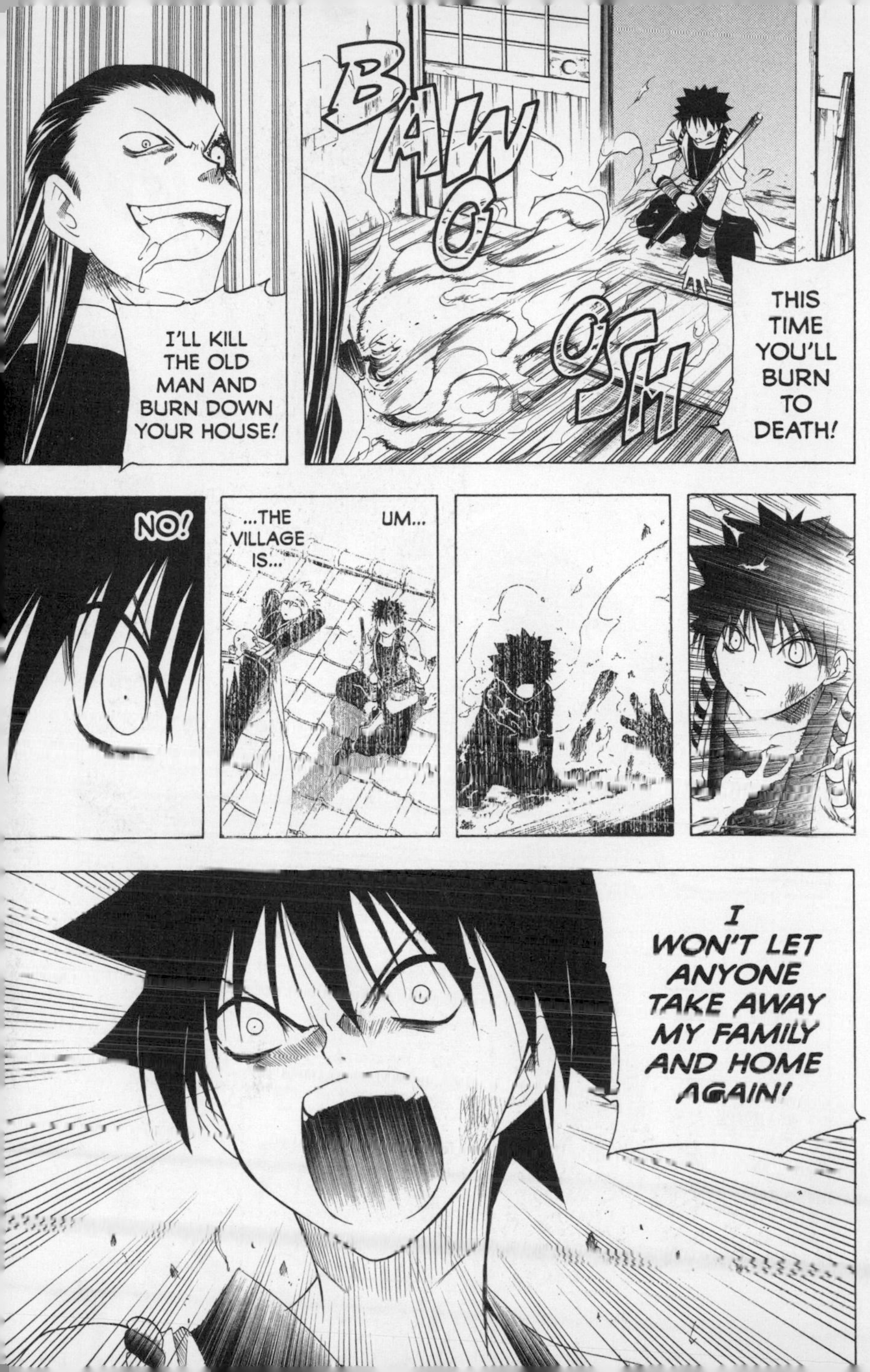
BAWOOSH
THIS TIME YOU'LL BURN TO DEATH!
I'LL KILL THE OLD MAN AND BURN DOWN YOUR HOUSE!
UM...
...THE VILLAGE IS...
NO!
I WON'T LET ANYONE TAKE AWAY MY FAMILY AND HOME AGAIN!

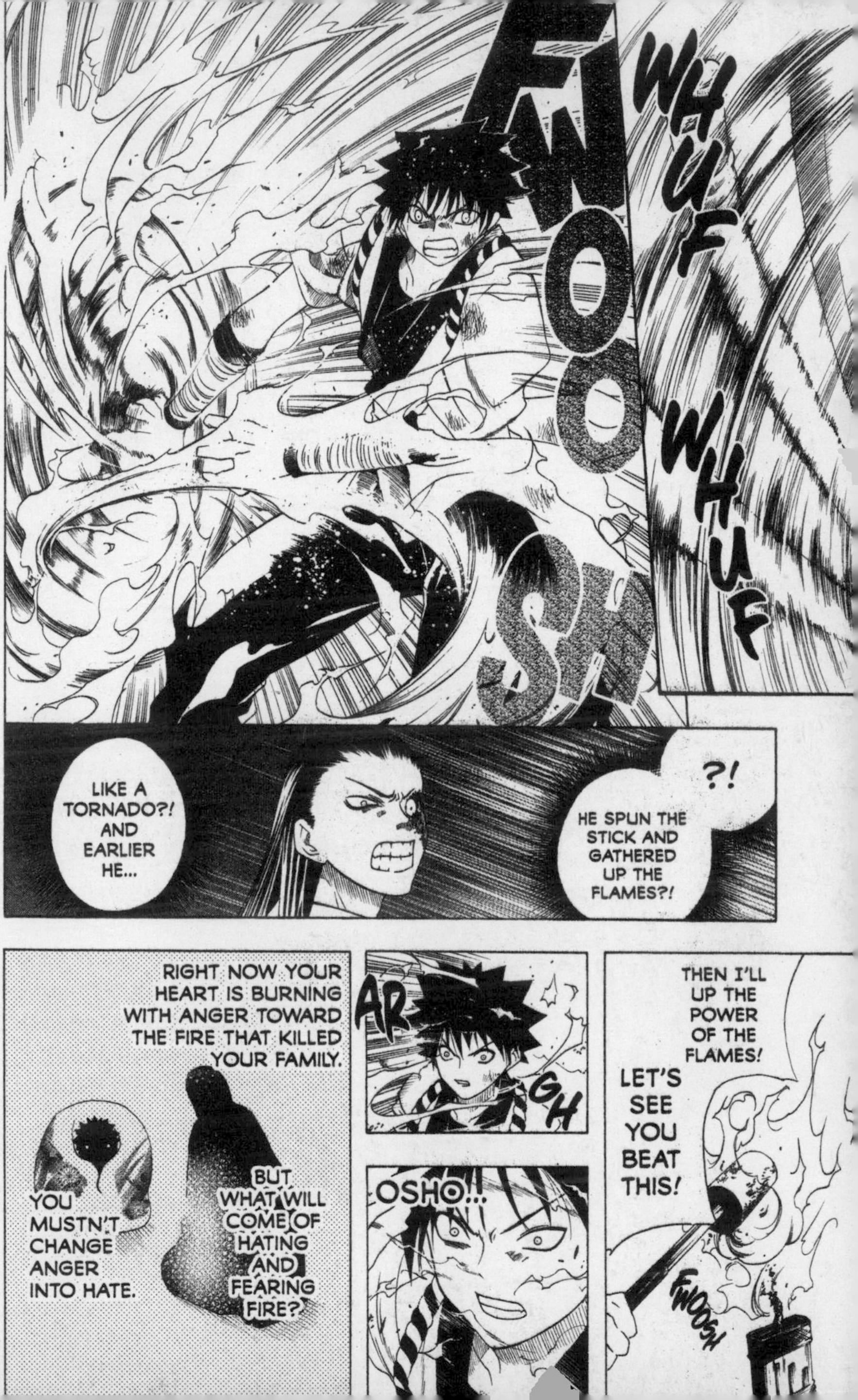
WHUF WHUF
FWOOOSH
WHUF WHUF
?!
HE SPUN THE STICK AND GATHERED UP THE FLAMES?!
LIKE A TORNADO?! AND EARLIER HE...
THEN I'LL UP THE POWER OF THE FLAMES!
LET'S SEE YOU BEAT THIS!
FWOOSH
ARGH
OSHO...!
RIGHT NOW YOUR HEART IS BURNING WITH ANGER TOWARD THE FIRE THAT KILLED YOUR FAMILY.
BUT WHAT WILL COME OF HATING AND FEARING FIRE?
YOU MUSTN'T CHANGE ANGER INTO HATE.

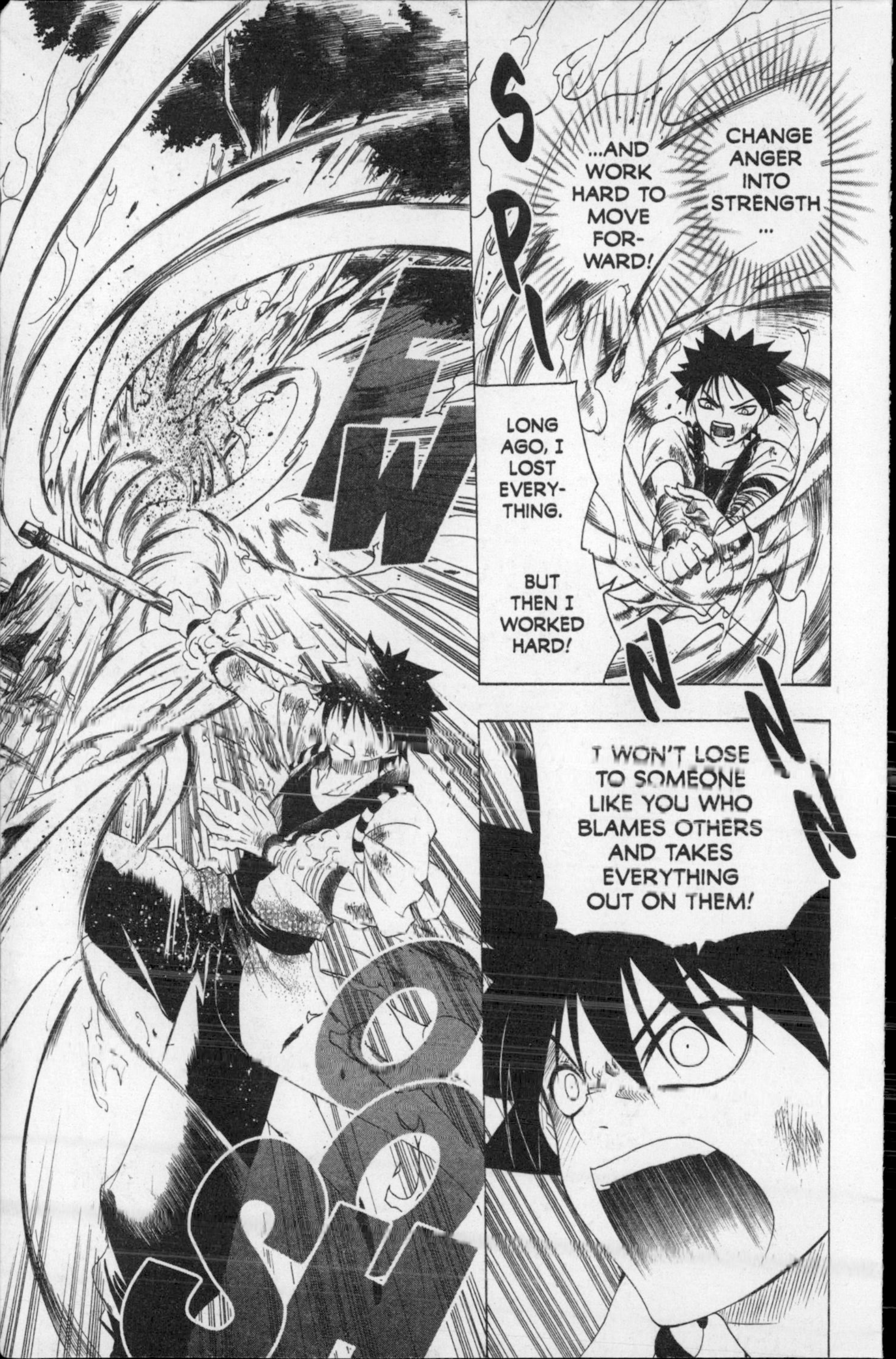
CHANGE ANGER INTO STRENGTH ...
...AND WORK HARD TO MOVE FOR-WARD!
SPINNNN
LONG AGO, I LOST EVERY-THING.
BUT THEN I WORKED HARD!
I WON'T LOSE TO SOMEONE LIKE YOU WHO BLAMES OTHERS AND TAKES EVERYTHING OUT ON THEM!
FW
SGO

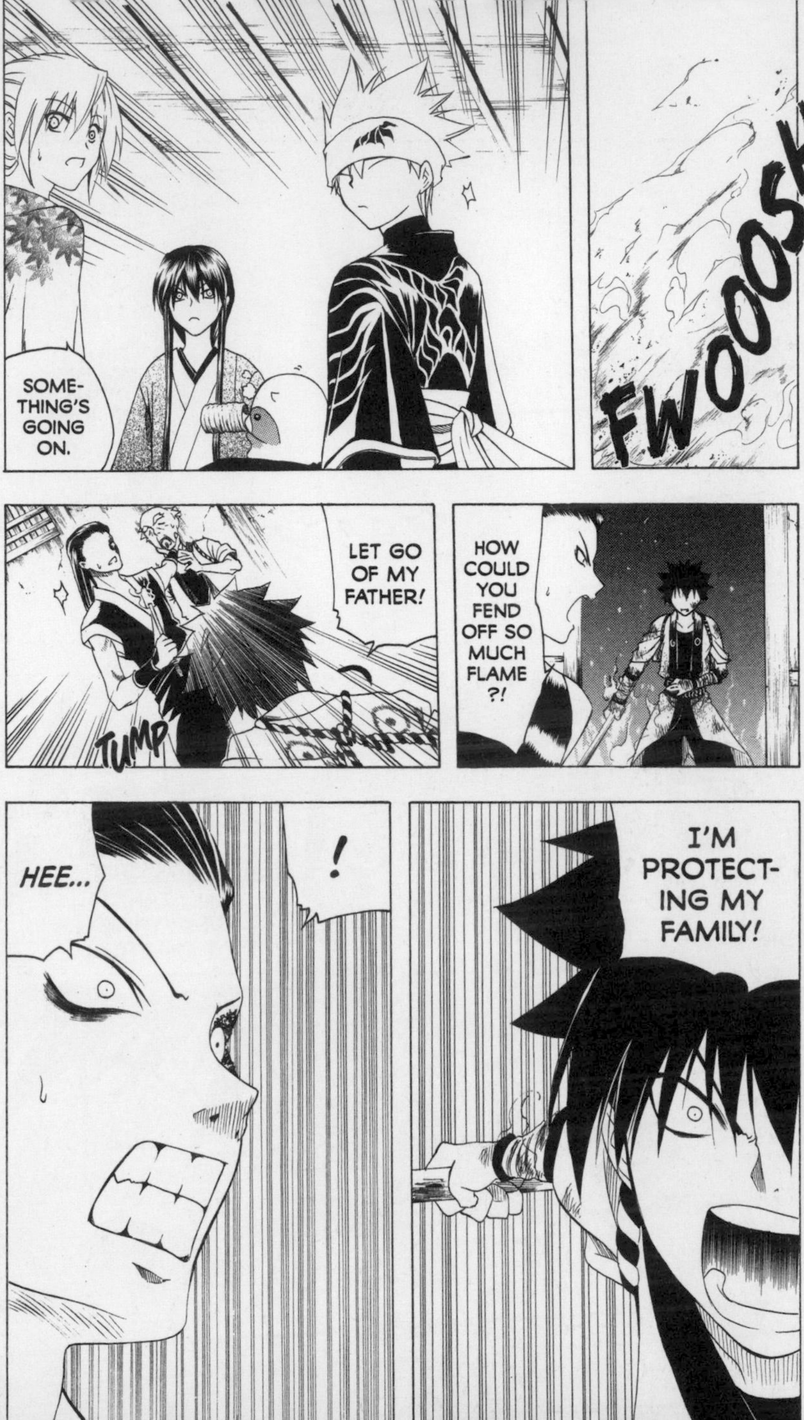
FWOOOSH
SOME-THING'S GOING ON.
HOW COULD YOU FEND OFF SO MUCH FLAME ?!
LET GO OF MY FATHER!
TUMP
I'M PROTECT-ING MY FAMILY!
!
HEE...

◆Bonus Manga◆

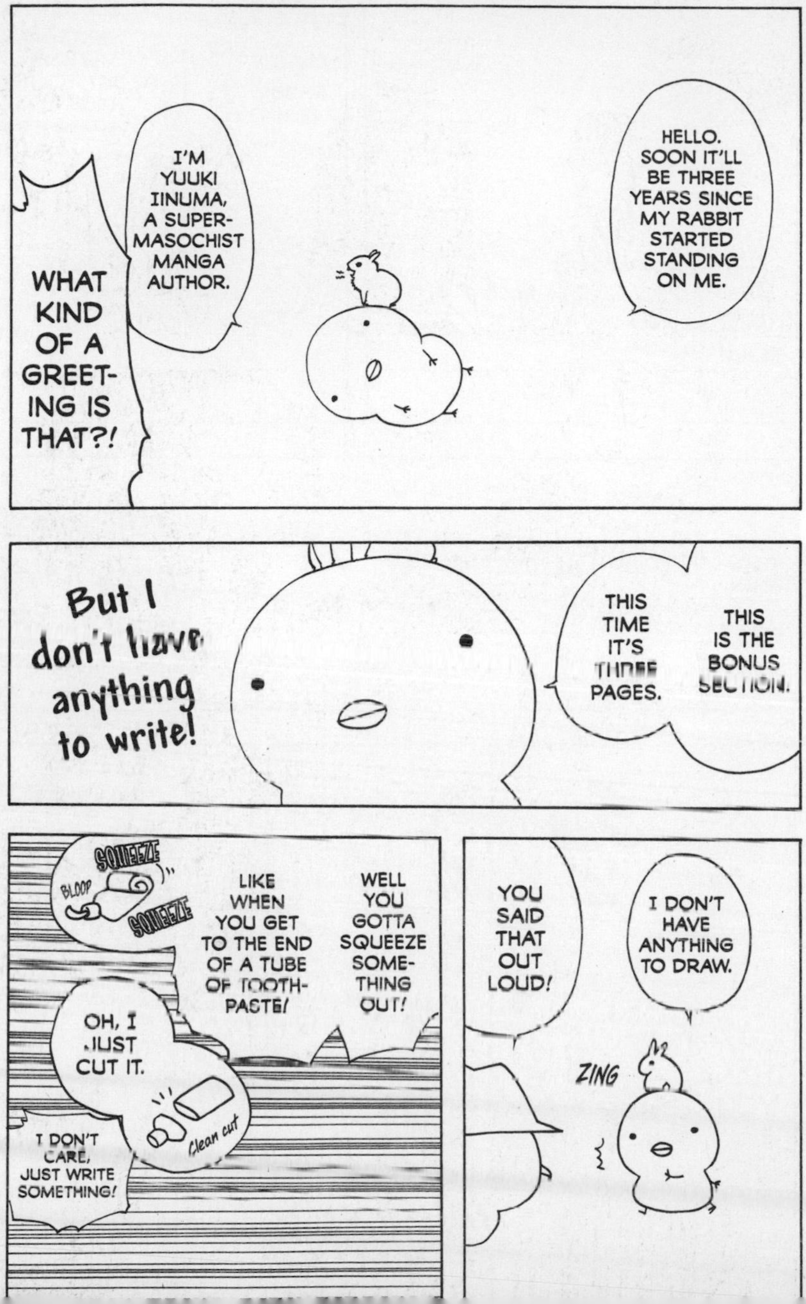
HELLO. SOON IT'LL BE THREE YEARS SINCE MY RABBIT STARTED STANDING ON ME.
I'M YUUKI IINUMA, A SUPER-MASOCHIST MANGA AUTHOR.
WHAT KIND OF A GREETING IS THAT?!
THIS IS THE BONUS SECTION.
THIS TIME IT'S THREE PAGES.
But I don't have anything to write!
I DON'T HAVE ANYTHING TO DRAW.
YOU SAID THAT OUT LOUD!
ZING
WELL YOU GOTTA SQUEEZE SOMETHING OUT!
LIKE WHEN YOU GET TO THE END OF A TUBE OF TOOTHPASTE!
SQUEEZE
BLOOP
SQUEEZE
OH, I JUST CUT IT.
Clean cut
I DON'T CARE, JUST WRITE SOMETHING!

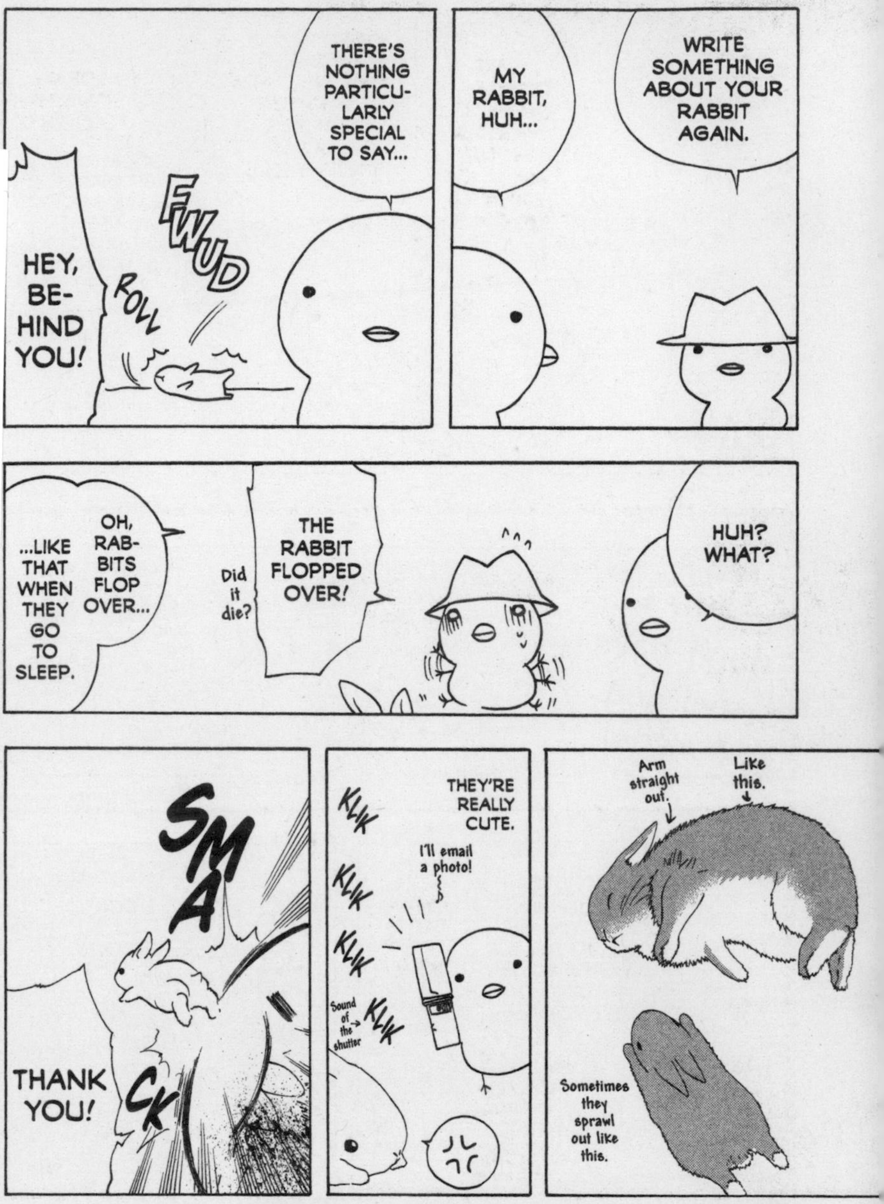
WRITE SOMETHING ABOUT YOUR RABBIT AGAIN.
MY RABBIT, HUH...
THERE'S NOTHING PARTICU-LARLY SPECIAL TO SAY...
FWUD
ROLL
HEY, BE-HIND YOU!
HUH? WHAT?
THE RABBIT FLOPPED OVER!
Did it die?
OH, RAB-BITS FLOP OVER...
...LIKE THAT WHEN THEY GO TO SLEEP.
Arm straight out.
Like this.
Sometimes they sprawl out like this.
THEY'RE REALLY CUTE.
I'll email a photo!
KLIK
KLIK
KLIK
KLIK
Sound of the shutter
SMA
CK
THANK YOU!

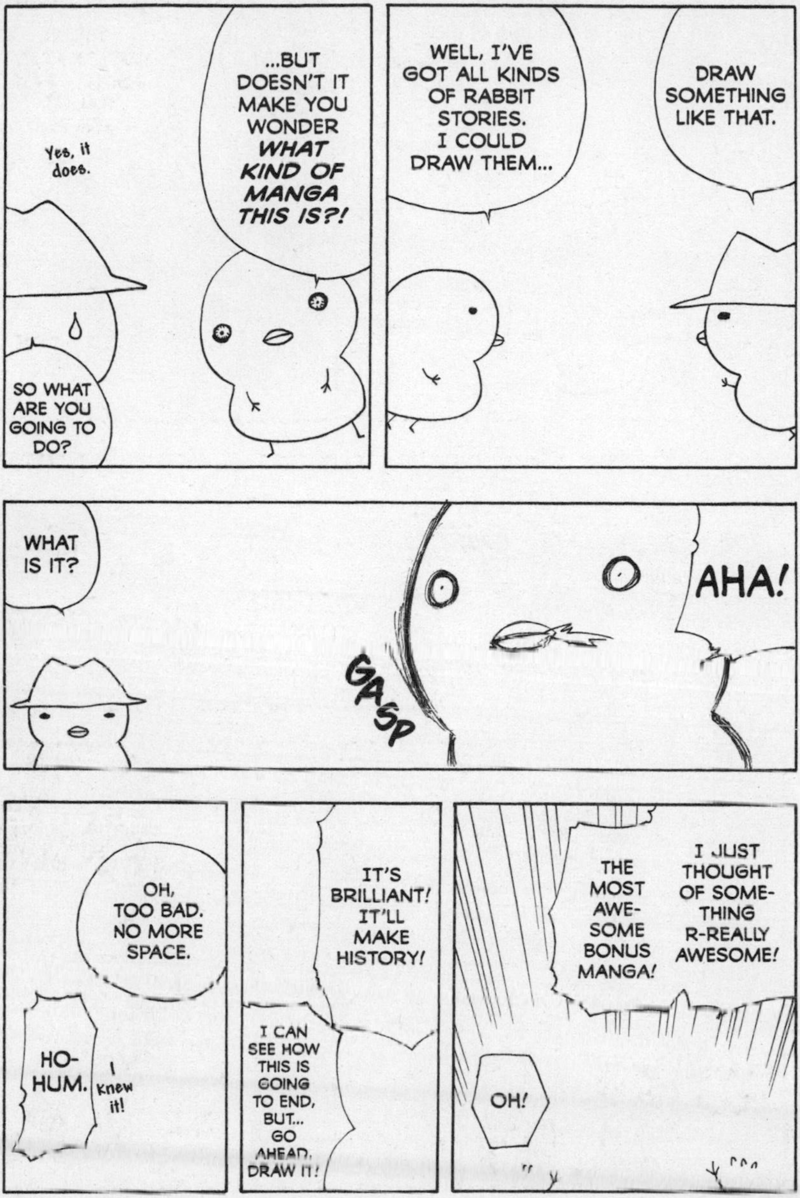
DRAW SOMETHING LIKE THAT.
WELL, I'VE GOT ALL KINDS OF RABBIT STORIES. I COULD DRAW THEM...
...BUT DOESN'T IT MAKE YOU WONDER *WHAT KIND OF MANGA THIS IS?!*
Yes, it does.
SO WHAT ARE YOU GOING TO DO?
AHA!
GASP
WHAT IS IT?
I JUST THOUGHT OF SOME-THING R-REALLY AWESOME!
THE MOST AWE-SOME BONUS MANGA!
OH!
IT'S BRILLIANT! IT'LL MAKE HISTORY!
I CAN SEE HOW THIS IS GOING TO END, BUT... GO AHEAD, DRAW IT!
OH, TOO BAD. NO MORE SPACE.
HO-HUM.
I knew it!

ITSUWARIBITO

Volume 4
Shonen Sunday Edition

Story and Art by
YUUKI IINUMA

© 2009 Yuuki IINUMA/Shogakukan
All rights reserved.
Original Japanese edition "ITSUWARIBITO UTSUHO"
published by SHOGAKUKAN Inc.

Original Japanese cover design by Shu Anzai & Bay Bridge Studio

Translation/John Werry
Touch-up Art & Lettering/Susan Daigle-Leach
Design/Matt Hinrichs
Editor/Carrie Shepherd

Printed in the U.S.A.

Published by VIZ Media, LLC
P.O. Box 77010
San Francisco, CA 94107

10 9 8 7 6 5 4 3 2 1
First printing, December 2011

THEY SAY THAT MONEY CAN BUY ANYTHING.
BUT THERE ARE SOME THINGS MONEY CAN'T BUY.
LIKE WHAT?
LOVE, OF COURSE!
LIFE.
MONEY?

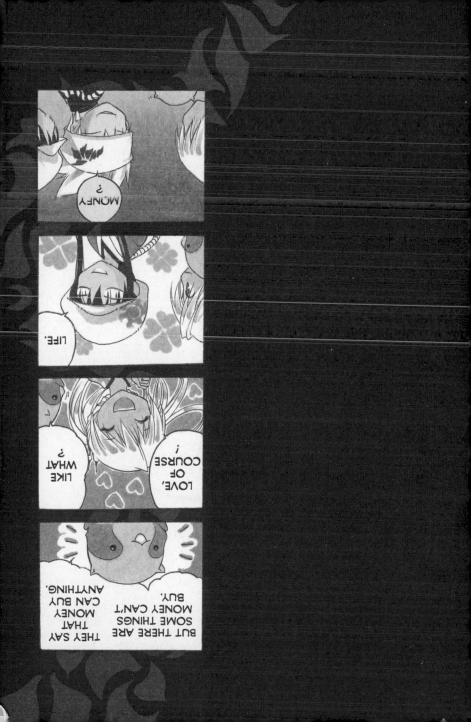

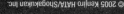